Self-Determination and Secession

Natalija Shikova

Self-Determination and Secession

In Between the Law, Theory and Practice

Springer

Natalija Shikova
Faculty of Law
International Balkan University
Skopje, North Macedonia

ISBN 978-3-031-34321-6 ISBN 978-3-031-34322-3 (eBook)
https://doi.org/10.1007/978-3-031-34322-3

This work was supported by Fulbright Association

This Springer imprint is published by the registered company Springer Nature Switzerland AG
The registered company address is: Gewerbestrasse 11, 6330 Cham, Switzerland

Contents

Part I
Self-Determination of the Peoples

Chapter 1
Phases and Developments of the Right to Self-Determination of the Peoples

1.1 Historical Sketch

> When in the Course of human events, it becomes necessary for one people to dissolve the political bands which have connected them with another, and to assume among the powers of the earth, the separate and equal station to which the Laws of Nature and of Nature's God entitle them, a decent respect to the opinions of mankind requires that they should declare the causes which impel them to the separation.
>
> We hold these truths to be self-evident, that all men are created equal, that they are endowed by their Creator with certain unalienable Rights, that among these are Life, Liberty and the pursuit of Happiness … That to secure these rights, Governments are instituted among Men, deriving their just powers from the consent of the governed … That whenever any Form of Government becomes destructive of these ends, it is the Right of the People to alter or to abolish it, and to institute new Government, laying its foundation on such principles and organizing its powers in such form, as to them shall seem most likely to effect their Safety and Happiness.[1]

When history would be a chronicle of voluntary association and dissociation of human groupings, then there would be no need for the doctrine of self-determination. Without conquest, forced annexations, dynasty unions, and colonial subjugations, the peoples of the world would presumably be organized into freely selected political units. But there is no peaceful evolution of the social organization of humanity, and thus the principle of self-determination, which emerged in the twentieth century, can be regarded as a primary expression of disagreement against all forms of non-free political association.[2] Consequently, self-determination is one of the most frequently demanded and at the same time the least understood concepts of international law.

---

[1] Declaration of Independence (1776).

[2] Buchheit (1978).

N. Shikova, *Self-Determination and Secession*,
https://doi.org/10.1007/978-3-031-34322-3_1

The general idea of self-determination is rooted in liberal democratic principles proclaimed during the French bourgeois revolution.[3] It is further developed within the American Declaration of Independence (1776) and French Declaration (1789), which are stressing the consent of the governed as the only tool for the legitimization of the government. These documents are underlining (1) that the government draws its power from the consent of the governed and (2) that the government, through accountability and responsiveness, gets its unique and equal position within the community of nations.[4] Throughout the nineteenth century, the principle of self-determination related to the principle of nationality (clarified by the renowned Italian jurist Pasquale Stanislao Mancini, 1817–1889),[5] understood as giving mode and a right to each nation to shape its destiny by itself, to decide alone, and, respectively, to self-determinate.[6] But the modern understanding of self-determination is directly linked to the Versailles Peace Conference (1919),[7] the end of World War I and disintegration of empires. US President Woodrow Wilson (alongside other relevant political authorities of this period)[8] is considered that in his "14 points," had established the modern concept of self-determination. The self-determination was proclaimed as a tool for governing in accordance with the governed.[9] For the realization of the principle of national self-determination, an international organization was needed that should ensure the integrity of small states (which could occur under the frame of this principle) and secure them against the threat of external aggression.[10]

[3] Although the roots of "legitimacy" can be found even in the ancient empires, see Watson (1992).

[4] According to some scholars, the right to self-determination in the American Declaration of Independence has an internal dimension (as a form of legitimate government) and an external dimension (the legitimacy of the government in the society of sovereign states). The first one requires a democratic entitlement, making self-determination the root of democracy; see Franck (1992).

[5] See more in Kelly (1992).

[6] In the same line was Giuseppe Mazzini, the Italian political agitator and founder of the Italian nationalist movement "Young Italy," who argued for the reshaping of the European political order on the basis of two seminal principles: *democracy* and *national self-determination*, Gerbet et al. (1973).

[7] There are several stages in the development of the self-determination of peoples: the first phase—the Westphalian system (1648–1815), the second phase—a European concern (1915–1914), the third stage—the League of Nations (1914–1939), the fourth stage—the UN system, and a substage after the fall of communism in the '90s of the last century; see more in Shehadi (1993).

[8] For many, President Wilson introduced a doctrine that has no sense, though it has been widely accepted as a reasonable proposal. "Let the people decide," according to President Wilson, but in fact, this is a dubious proposal as the people cannot decide until somebody decides what the term "people" consists of, Jennings (1956).

[9] Whelan analyzes Wilson's idea and believes that there are three historical roots for its development, namely, (1) the idea of legitimacy, (2) the idea of state sovereignty, and (3) ethnic nationalism, which is often exclusive and irredentist, Whelan (1994).

[10] Buchheit (1978).

Thus, self-determination as a political principle had become a driving force for the transformation of Europe.[11] Self-determination became connected to the Marxist theory as well. Lenin and Stalin viewed self-determination through the context of the "national question"[12] and through such a form in which self-determination should be supporting class struggle. According to the Bolsheviks, secession (as the primary form of self-determination in this period) should be promoted as a tactic of a fight for the oppressed nations, not as a tool to support the bourgeois nationalists.[13] In that sense, secession was considered an ultimate remedy.[14]

Nevertheless, over the ashes of the Austro-Hungarian, Ottoman, and German empires, a gust of nationalism, combined with the belief in the power of the principle of self-determination, betrayed the expectations of newly liberated populations and ruined their efforts for the establishment of a peaceful postwar settlement. The proposal for postwar peace, based on Wilsons' 14 points and adopted as part of the Treaty of Versailles (1919),[15] did not give the expected results, and the frequently quoted statement "No people must be forced under sovereignty under which it does not want to leave. No territory mast change hands except to secure those who inhabit it a fair chance of life and liberty"[16] became an empty phrase. Despite efforts for the ideal of creating a world of cooperation by law, universal justice, and self-determination for all peoples, the big ideas and plans ran into insurmountable obstacles. Europe was not a *tabula rasa*, and boundaries could not be drawn merely under the principle of self-determination of peoples. They were generally reflecting the interests of the great powers and the success of some national groups in lobbying for their states. Hence, after the proclamation of the self-determination of peoples as a political principle, its application received a realistic dimension, according to which

---

[11] According to Hurst Hannum, self-determination was primarily meant for the "nations" within the territories of the defeated empires, Hannum (1990).

[12] In his book "The right of nations to self-determination," Vladimir Ilic Lenin replies to Rosa Luxemburg's critics, saying there is no sufficient space for self-determination in the documents of the Russian Marxists. For Lenin, the national state is the rule and norm of capitalism, and according to that view, the heterogeneous nation-state means a setback. The self-determination of peoples could not have a different meaning than political self-determination, political independence, and the formation of a nation-state, Lenin (1951).

[13] For Hurst Hannum, the communist support for national self-determination and decolonization was more tactical than a philosophical decision. In the Russian context, the practice of the theoretical right to the secession of the border areas would be rejected because it fundamentally opposes the interests of the masses and the center and the border regions, Hannum (1990).

[14] Therefore, at least briefly, according to Lea Brilmayer, it seems that Lenin and Wilson had a common theme, namely, the right of the peoples to determine their own countries as they wish, Brilmayer (1991).

[15] The peace settlement was influenced by the United States and by the principle that Americans particularly promoted the principle of national self-determination; see more in Kelly (1992).

[16] Papers relating to the foreign relations of the United States, 1917, supplement 2, World War, Volume I.

all members of a nation could not always live in a so-called country of origin within the Versailles system or the established regime of the League of Nations.[17]

The period between the two world wars discredited the League of Nations and the principle of national self-determination in general. The principle of self-determination was not included in the Convention of the League of Nations, which as an organization not only failed to ensure the integrity of the principle but was as well blamed for creating small, weak states unable to defend themselves from Nazi aggression. Although there was philosophical support for Wilson's ideas, the states created after 1919 did not commit themselves to establishing a democratic form of government. The League of Nations brought two instruments as subsidies: (a) the holding of internationally monitored referendums for drawing new boundaries (plebiscites) or the determination of sovereignty and (b) establishing international protection for minority rights. Thus, minority rights became an alternative to self-determination. Among the rights protected in minority contracts within the League of Nations were rights to freedom from discrimination regardless of race, language, or religion; the right to use own language in private and public forums; and the right to citizenship, as well as the rights of minorities to establish and control their own humanitarian, religious, and educational institutions.

1.2 From the Principle of Self-Determination to the Right to Self-Determination of the Peoples

1.2.1 Theoretical Debates

The international law literature considers the self-determination of peoples as a norm of international law, i.e., as a principle for the right to self-determination of the peoples. But lawyers' attitudes in this respect are divided, especially toward the existence of a legal rule concerning self-determination. Regarding this issue, there are several theoretical views—for some authors, self-determination is a right and for others a principle; also, there are those for whom self-determination is both—a legal rule and a principle of international law.[18] One of those authors is Antonio Cassese,[19] who, in his attempt to redefine self-determination, believes that self-determination is both a general principle and a definite rule. According to him, at the level of general international law, there is a formulation of a general principle of self-determination. This principle has a very weak standard since it neither determines where it should be applied nor indicates its implementation methods nor specifies what dimension it should have (internal or external) nor what its purpose is

[17] The Fourteen Points Woodrow Wilson and the U.S. Rejection of the Treaty of Versailles; Senate Rejects the Treaty of Versailles (1919).

[18] Knop (2002).

[19] Cassese (1995).

(independent state, integration into another state, etc.), but it simply sets general guidelines for the behavior of states and has the role of a general standard for international relations. The principle of self-determination is an expression of ideological and political conflicts between states, which have prevented it from gaining the necessary precision. Principles differ from treaties or customary law not because they are more general and less precise but because they are the result of conflicting states' views on crucial issues. Principles are a typical expression of the current world community, which differs from the old community (which is relatively more homogeneous and less conflicting) and in which specific and precise rules prevailed.[20]

The dogma of state sovereignty made a strong obstacle to the full acceptance of the principle of self-determination within the norms of international law. This should come as no surprise, Cassese says, given that the transformation of this political principle into a set of international norms represents a radical undermining of state sovereignty and a dramatic reformation of the existing framework of the world community. Therefore, the acceptance of the principle is selective and limited in many respects, and this is mostly because most of the members of the international community are multinational or multicultural countries, so it is difficult to expect that these actors who are also world legislators will enact a legal rule to encourage domestic segregation or secession or fuel ethnic or racial conflicts. Moreover, many member states of the international community are authoritarian states that do not largely respect the will of their people. And, finally, the distribution of economic, political, and military power in the hands of a few international actors makes states dependent on them, so independent statehood is almost a myth. Hence, it is clear why self-determination is accepted in a limited and selective way in international law.[21]

The creation of self-sufficient norm of self-determination is *nonsense*, considers as well James Crawford. The principle is the basis for the interpretation of the law, i.e., the ground for action, in cases that are not covered by the law.[22] James Crawford generally distinguishes a political principle, a legal principle, and a legal norm and argues that the principle of self-determination of the peoples covers all three of them. The difference between the legal principle and the legal rule of self-determination is not in the content. The difference between the principle and the right to self-determination in international law is in the specificity of the subject, i.e., in the definition of "peoples." Thus, the subjects of the right to self-determination, unlike the subjects of the principle of self-determination, are fully defined, which are the entrusted and mandated territories and the territories treated as non-self-governing, covered under Chapter XI of the UN Charter.[23] The principle of self-determination is applied in cases when the subject does not fall under this classification. Therefore, for Crawford, the legal principle of self-determination

---

[20] Cassese (1995), p. 128.

[21] Cassese (1995).

[22] Crawford (1996).

[23] Charter of the United Nations (1945).

plays a secondary role and is applied in the absence of certain criteria for the application of the right to self-determination.[24]

Similarly, Arangio-Ruiz believes that if the self-determination of peoples is categorized as a principle and as an international law norm, then there is more room for evolution in its interpretation than if it is categorized only as a norm.[25] According to Lee C. Buchheit, the authors who deny the position of self-determination as a legal rule generally deny the right to secession.[26] Still, there are authors for whom the self-determination of peoples is only a right, and not a principle, because the principle plays no role other than an additional one, and the traditional international law is rule based. Michel Virally considers that international law is primarily the law of lawyers, which privileges countries with a strong diplomatic tradition and experienced diplomatic bodies, as opposed to international law, which is built on principles.[27]

Although it is very difficult to see the operational difference between characterizing self-determination as a legal rule and as a political principle, even by an opening address of a conference delegate, one can distinguish between those who consider self-determination as a right and those who consider it as a principle. As a middle ground, there are authors who combine the terms "political principle" and "legal rule," like Ian Brownlie, to express his view that self-determination is currently a "legal principle."[28]

The most prominent opponents of the right to self-determination emphasize that the concept not only has no legal status but it also will never have one. For Verzijl, the right to self-determination is "a sport of national or international politics" and has never been recognized as a general political right of nations that has universal and impartial application and will never be recognized as such in the near future.[29] For others, the right to self-determination is a political right, not a right of peoples and so on.[30] Many debates have been developed in this regard, according to which the principle of the self-determination of the peoples has strong moral power, but it is very complex to be pinned down in juridical terms. In many cases and under various conditions, the principle of the self-determination of the peoples has heterogeneous interpretations, and it is driving serious problems related to minority rights and possibly the "right for secession."

In the opposite camp, a growing number of lawyers have accepted the status of self-determination as a right under UN law (1) because they believe that it has acquired that status in customary law under the UN Charter, (2) because they consider that this was the intent of paragraph 1 (2) of the Charter, or because of (3) the

---

24 Charter of the United Nations (1945).

25 Arangio-Ruiz (1977).

26 Buchheit (1978).

27 Virally (1968).

28 Brownlie (1973).

29 Verzijl (1974).

30 Buchheit (1978).

consequential practice that indicated that it would be an appropriate interpretation of that provision. These lawyers support the existence of such a right, finding its legal ground within international instruments such as *Resolution 1514* (XV), the Declaration on the Granting of Independence to Colonial Countries and Peoples, which in time got the status of customary law. Even further, Hans Kelsen interprets the phrase "self-determination of peoples" in the UN Charter as the same as "sovereignty of states." The self-determination of peoples, Kelsen writes, usually means the principle of domestic politics and the principle of democratic government. However, Article 1 section 2 of the UN Charter refers to the relations among states. Hence, according to Kelsen, the term peoples, in connection with "equal rights," refers to states since only states have "equal rights" under general international law.[31]

However, although there is no more doubt about the existence of the right to self-determination, there are different opinions related to its implementation. For some, the right to self-determination is an outcome of conflict between—nationalism and international law—and hence any position toward the right of self-determination of the peoples is an issue of at least two kinds of critiques. From one side, as much as the law narrowed it to certain categories, the arguments are that the right weakens, i.e., that it deviates from the notion of the so-called "right of the peoples." On the other hand,—as much as the right is spreading to encompass a broader definition of—"the peoples," its juridical certainty becomes weaker. No wonder, because of this, international bodies do not always have the goodwill to execute the right based on the principle of self-determination. For example, the Committee of Human Rights, which takes into consideration individual petitions concerning violations of human rights according to the Optional Protocol of the International Covenant for Civic and Political Rights,[32] has, according to Article 1, consistently rejected a series of cases concerning petitions for self-determination.[33]

1.2.2 *Self-Determination Within the UN System*

It can be said that there is a much larger number of those who, within the UN, consider self-determination as a right and that, today, when we speak about self-determination, we speak about the right to self-determination of the peoples.[34] Since the founding of the United Nations, the principle of self-determination of peoples has evolved in two directions. One is its transformation from a principle to a right,

[31] Kelsen (1951), pp. 51–52.

[32] See more at Optional Protocol of the International Covenant for Civic and Political rights (1966).

[33] That is the opposite of what the Optional protocol is expressing, namely that—the Committee is competent to except correspondence about: "*(...) any right established in the Convention*," Summers (2007); in the early days of the self-determination doctrine, it was considered that no group should be excluded and no questions of its self-determinations should be left unreviewed by the Court. Today this looks too optimistic, see more at Wambaugh (1920).

[34] Buchheit (1978).

and the other one is its qualitative change—a transition from the context of decolonization to a wider international application, with emphasis on its internal dimension. The right to self-determination has ceased to be a principle of exclusion (secession) and has become a principle of inclusion: the right to participate.[35]

Apart from the international legal literature, there was a long debate within UN bodies about the legal nature of the principle of self-determination of peoples. Although the UN Charter refers to the principle of self-determination of peoples, in international relations, the view dominates that every UN member state, by signing the Charter, has committed itself to respect the right deriving from this principle. Various international instruments, including the UN Charter, have established the principle as a legal rule. Some UN member states preferred the term "principle" used in the Charter, stressing doubts related to the application of the right to self-determination. However, by reaffirming this right in the International Covenants on Human Rights, the UN has created the necessary conditions for the establishment of peaceful relations between nations and the strengthening of international cooperation. It is widely accepted that the right to self-determination is a necessary condition for practicing all other human rights, i.e., that it is a necessary *bastion* for the defense of other human rights. Thus, in contemporary international relations, the prevailing view is that the right of peoples to self-determination is a collective right that differs from other individual rights contained in international human rights conventions. ***The principle of equal rights and self-determination of peoples*** - is the formulation through which the self-determination of people reflects in several international instruments, and through which it has found its application.

Particular importance have the Declaration on the Granting of Independence to Colonial Countries and Peoples and the Declaration on Principles of International Law concerning Friendly Relations and Co-operation among States in accordance with the Charter of the United Nations. It should be noted that in both cases where the principle of equal rights and self-determination of peoples is mentioned, the Charter speaks about principle and, through the use of the singular, emphasizes that it is a single principle. Additionally, the Charter creates direct obligations for member states regarding the implementation of Article 1 and Article 55. The Statute of the International Court of Justice, in Article 38 (1) (a), determines the sources of international law. The documents that refer to the right to self-determination and that create binding obligations for states are the UN Charter and the two International Covenants on Human Rights, which have the status of treaties and are, therefore, sources of law, although neither of these documents explicitly sufficiently defines the term in order to be able to create specific obligations for states. However, the principle is part of international treaty law as well.

Under the UN Charter, the principle of equal rights and self-determination of peoples combines law and justice and is based on the right to collective free expression. It stimulates the fundamental rights of states, such as the right to sovereignty

---

[35] Franck (1992).

or independence. The principle is the basis for other principles of international law, such as the equality of states, nonintervention, and the nonuse of force, which complement and reinforce each other. The principle of equal rights and self-determination of peoples is incorporated in the UN system into customary international and international treaty laws.

1.3 Content of the Right to Self-Determination of Peoples

An attempt was made within the UN system to define the right of peoples to self-determination. The main dilemmas were what it represents and what it contains. Various interpretations were considered:[36]

- For some, the self-determination of peoples was synonymous with self-government. This was disputed in reference to the UN Charter, which establishes a distinction between the concepts of self-government and self-determination. It has been suggested that the right to self-determination means the right of peoples to decide on their international status (direct access to independence, association, secession, etc.), while self-government means autonomy within a state.
- For others, the right to self-determination only referred to the peoples fighting for independence. The UN Commission on Human Rights should have defined the right to self-determination and decided to what extent separatist movements or vague aspirations for self-government should be included in the concept.
- Some members of the UN Commission on Human Rights have expressed the opinion that the right to self-determination not only should be observed from a political point of view but should also be considered from an economic point of view because political independence is based on economic independence. The realization of the right of peoples to self-determination should enable each state to establish full control over its national resources and apply the national laws over any private industry.[37]

A particular problem occurred in defining the term "status." It was proposed that the term "political status" should be based on the International Covenant for Civil and Political Rights (1966) and the relationship between political, economic, social, and cultural status. Efforts were made to define the right of peoples to self-determination through specific terms, such as "the right of all states and nations to create an independent state," the right of "secession or association with other peoples or nations," etc. Such suggestions were not accepted because of the general fear that any enumeration of the constitutive elements of the right to self-determination

[36] See more at Cristescu (1981).

[37] See more at United Nations General Assembly official records (1955).

would be incomplete. It was considered that it is better if the right is affirmed in an abstract form.[38]

A final definition of the term was not accepted, but UN practice clarified and developed the content of the principle of equal rights and self-determination of peoples. The right deriving from this principle has been constantly expanded to include the political, economic, social, and cultural aspects of the life of the peoples. Today, peoples (regardless of whether they construct an independent state) enjoy all the benefits of the right to self-determination. Individuals participate in the exercise of the right to self-determination directly or through the exercise of other human rights. The right of peoples to self-determination is seen no longer from a political point of view but also from an economic, social, and cultural standing. Although there is still controversy about what is and what is not the norm, there is a general understanding of what the right to self-determination encompasses, including the following.

- ***The Right of Peoples to Freely Define Their Political Status***

  Political status, which all nations have the right to freely define, under the auspices of the principle of equal rights and self-determination of peoples, encompasses the international and domestic political status. Thus, the application of the principle of equal rights and self-determination of peoples has two equally important aspects. The first one is the right of the people to decide their destiny in the international system. The second is the right of the people to freely choose and develop their internal political system in a way that corresponds to their political aspirations and goals. According to the Declaration on Principles of International Law concerning Friendly Relations and Co-operation among States in accordance with the Charter of the United Nations (1970), the models for exercising the right of peoples to self-determination in relation to political status can be "(...) The establishment of a sovereign and independent State, the free association or integration with an independent State or the emergence into any other political status freely determined by a people constitute modes of implementing the right of self-determination by that people."[39]

  When it comes to establishing a sovereign and independent state, the right has two modes. One is negative: the right of peoples not to be subject to exchange or be expelled (from their territory, from each other, etc.), and the other is positive: the right of peoples to become part of a state or to form an independent state. According to Resolution 1541 (1960),[40] free associations should be the result of the free and voluntary choice of the peoples in a given territory, determined through a public, democratic process that respects the individual and cultural characteristics of the people. As for integration into an independent state, it should be based on full equality between the people of the non-self-governing territory and the people of the

[38] United Nations General Assembly official records (1955), pp. 14–15.

[39] UNGA Res. 2625 (1970).

[40] UNGA Res 1541, Principles which should guide members in determining whether or not an obligation exists to transmit the information called for under Article 73e of the Charter (1960).

independent state into which the respective (non-self-governing) territory is integrated. The UN can, when necessary, monitor this process.

- ***Civil and Political Rights***
  The Universal Declaration of Human Rights[41] and the International Covenant on Civil and Political Rights,[42] among other things, place particular emphasis on the prohibition of discrimination. These international instruments not only prohibit discrimination but also provide obligations for the state to establish a remedy against possible discrimination. Another right that is particularly important for the exercise of the right to self-determination is the right of every individual to participate in the government of his country, directly or through freely elected representatives. No less important is the right to freedom of conscience, right to religion, and freedom of thought and expression, as well as the rights proclaimed by the Universal Declaration of Human Rights and the International Covenant on Civil and Political Rights, which allow members of ethnic, religious, and/or linguistic minorities, in community with other members of the group, to practice their culture and religion and use their language.

- ***The Right of Peoples to Freely Pursue Their Economic Development***
  Development, in its various aspects, is of particular importance to all peoples, whether they are dependent nations or peoples constructing a sovereign and independent state. As for the political aspect of development, it is obvious that the independence and sovereignty of the states, the realization of the political aspirations of peoples, the progressive development of their political institutions, and respect for basic human rights are the basic factors for economic, social, and cultural development, which in turn create the conditions for political progress. The strengthening of national independence, the democratization of society, the advancement of social and economic structures, and the establishment of social justice depend on economic and social progress. From an economic point of view, insufficient development and imbalance in the world system give rise to crises and confrontations in all countries.

  Hence, at the sixth special session of the UN General Assembly in 1974 was adopted Resolution 3201,[43] entitled the Declaration on the Establishment of a New International Economic Order (1974). According to this Resolution, the new economic order should be established on the following principles:

– Sovereign equality of states
– Self-determination for all peoples
– Inadmissibility of acquiring territories by force
– Territorial integrity, and
– Nonintervention in the internal affairs of other countries

---

[41] UNGA Res. 217 A (III) Universal Declaration on Human Rights (1948).

[42] UNGA Res. 2200 A (XXI) ICCPR (1966).

[43] UNGA Res. 3201 (S-VI) Declaration on the Establishment of a New International Order (1974).

Also, the Charter of Economic Rights and Duties of States,[44] adopted by the General Assembly on 12 December 1974, proclaims, *inter alia*, that the principle of equal rights and self-determination of peoples is fundamental to international economic relations.

- ***Permanent Sovereignty over Natural Resources***

  Permanent sovereignty over natural resources means that national resources, based on the right to self-determination, belong to the people of the territory in which they are situated. Hence, whether nations constitute a sovereign state or not, the resources concerned must be used for their good. The legal regime governing such exploitation must be established or modified by the will of the people.

- ***The Right of Peoples to Freely Practice Their Social Development***

  The importance of economic development as a material basis for social development must not be neglected. Economic development is only a means to achieve certain social goals, but economic and social development are interdependent. When it comes to developing countries, it should be noted that their modern social problems are the result of a completely unsatisfactory economic situation and the ever-increasing inequality between developed and developing countries, which is a legacy of the colonial past. National independence, based on the right of peoples to self-determination and the principle of noninterference in internal affairs, is an important precondition for social, economic, and cultural progress, but on the other hand, peace and security are preconditions for economic and social development.

- ***The Right of People to Freely Determine Their Cultural Development***

  National and cultural self-determination are determined by each other. Namely, whenever a significant majority of the people are excluded from the control of social goods, many cannot find conditions for the full development of their personality. The right of peoples to self-determination appears as a guarantor and protector of the cultural development of the people. On the other hand, culture encourages individual development and plays an important role in creating a modern structure of life in a community.

- ***The Right to Self-Determination of the Peoples—A Fundamental Human Right***

  The UN Commission on Human Rights tried to answer the question of whether the right to self-determination is a fundamental human right, considering the need for this right to be included in international pacts for human rights.[45] According to the Commission, the execution of the right for self-determination is a—*sine qua non*—both a source and the basis for the practice of other human rights. The right to self-determination belongs to individuals, i.e., to groups of associated individuals, so the exercise of this right as a collective right of a determined group would also

---

44 UNGA Res. 3281 (XXIX) Charter of Economic Rights and Duties of States (1974).

45 See more at Cristescu (1981), pp. 1–36.

lead to the fulfillment of the individual freedom of its members. The opposite dilemmas were that the right to self-determination of the peoples is collective, and as such, it is inadequate to be encompassed within the individual rights instrument. According to Aureliu Cristescu, the principle of equal rights and the self-determination of the peoples cannot be separated from other human rights. Without political freedom, human rights cannot be respected, and the equality of all human beings before the law cannot be secured until the nations – to which those human beings belong, are not recognized as equal. Consequently, the right of self-determination of the peoples has the same universal validity as all other human rights.[46]

Following the opinion of the Commission, the UN General Assembly decided to include an article for the right of all peoples and for self-determination in the International Covenants for Human Rights,[47] which reaffirm the principle included in the UN Charter. Additionally, the UN Security Council, in its Resolutions 183 (1963) and 218 (1965), has recognized the right of self-determination.

- ***The Relation of Self-Determination to Other Principles of International Law***

  When it comes to the relation of the principle of self-determination to other principles of international law, it can be noted that some of them are easier and others are more difficult to harmonize, even though they also express values that are in line with self-determination. First of all, the principle of self-determination is more difficult to harmonize with the principles of sovereignty and noninterference in the internal or external affairs of a state, which belong to the old world order, the so-called Westphalian model, which aims to maintain the *status quo*. The next set of principles includes prohibiting threats or the use of force, the peaceful resolution of disputes, respect for human rights, international cooperation, and goodwill, which are the product of the new world order and the birth of the UN, so they are easier to be harmonized. The principles of peaceful resolution of disputes, international cooperation, and goodwill provide guidance for the proper implementation of self-determination, but the principle of respect for human rights is closest to it as self-determination is the sum or synthesis of individual human rights. People can truly benefit from self-determination only if human rights are respected; on the other hand, the benefit from human rights presupposes the realization of self-determination. These two principles therefore complement and reinforce each other.[48]

---

[46] Cristescu (1981), p. 31.

[47] UNGA Res. 2200 A (XXI) International Covenant on Economic, Social and Cultural Rights (ICESCR) (1966); UNGA Res. 2200 A (XXI) International Covenant on Civil and Political Rights (ICCPR) (1966).

[48] See more at Cassese (1995), pp. 333–337.

1.4 Legal Basis for the Realization of the Right to Self-Determination of the Peoples

The Charter of the UN is the most important UN document since it affirms the right of all people to choose the form of government under which they will live. Still, self-determination is not among the principles of the UN stipulated under Article 2 of the Charter but is within Article 1 (paragraph 2), which sets out the purposes of this organization, namely, "(…) To develop friendly relations among nations based on respect for the principle of equal rights and self-determination of peoples, and to take other appropriate measures to strengthen universal peace."[49] Hence, in practice, the equality of sovereign states, the settlement of disputes amicably, the prohibition of the use of force against territorial integrity, and noninterference in internal affairs are principles that took precedence over the principle of self-determination of peoples.[50] Article 1 of the Charter proclaims that the UN will strive "(…) To achieve international co-operation in solving international problems of an economic, social, cultural, or humanitarian character, and in promoting and encouraging respect for human rights and fundamental freedoms for all without distinction as to race, sex, language, or religion."[51] Article 55 of the UN Charter also states that one of the purposes of the UN is to develop friendly relations between nations based on the principle of equal rights and self-determination of peoples. Article 55 of the UN Charter defines the areas of special interest in achieving the goals of the UN. In that sense, the UN will promote "(…) a. higher standards of living, full employment, and conditions of economic and social progress and development; b. solutions of international economic, social, health, and related problems; and international cultural and educational cooperation; and c. universal respect for, and observance of, human rights and fundamental freedoms for all without distinction as to race, sex, language, or religion."[52]

Regarding the issue of self-determination, the following instruments carry key importance:

1) ***Resolution 1514 (XV)—Declaration on the Granting of Independence to Colonial Countries and Peoples***—to guarantee the independence of the colonial countries and peoples was adopted by the UN General Assembly on December 14, 1960, and focuses mainly on decolonization. It declared that "(…) all people have the right to self-determination; by virtue of this right they freely determine their

---

[49] Article 1§2 UN Charter (1945).

[50] This situation may lead to a misunderstanding of the principle of equal rights and self-determination of peoples due to the possibility of the principle to be observed in isolation without taking into account its relation to other provisions of the Charter. Such an interpretation would be inconsistent with neither the spirit nor the intent of the UN Charter as the rights, duties, privileges, and obligations of the organization and its member states are linked and complementary to each other to form a whole, Cristescu (1981).

[51] UN Charter (1945), article 1.

[52] UN Charter (1945).

political status and freely pursue their economic, social and cultural development."[53] With this act, the right of peoples to self-determination began to be seen as the absolute norm (*jus cogens*) and as a right—the basis of all other rights. But although, according to paragraph 2 of this Resolution, the right to self-determination applies to all peoples, the Preamble specifies that the principle of self-determination of peoples applies only to peoples who are under colonial domination. Resolution 1514 undoubtedly initiated the dynamics of colonization, but it also had an unfortunate consequence because the right to self-determination proclaimed in it was equated exclusively with the achievement of sovereign independence, i.e., the formation of a separate state.[54]

2) ***Resolution 1541***[55] ***titled Principles which should guide members in determining whether or not an obligation exists to transmit the information called for under Article 73e of the Charter*** was adopted by the UN General Assembly in 1960 (just one day before Resolution 1514). Similar to Resolution 1514, Resolution 1541 focuses on decolonization. Resolution 1541 relies on the idea that the implementation of the right to self-determination is not just about achieving sovereign independence. In Principle VI, the Resolution identifies three alternative ways of exercising self-government, namely:

- Emergence as a sovereign independent state
- Free association with an independent state, or
- Integration with an independent state

These three modalities of exercising the right to self-determination exclusively refer to the realization of the external dimension of the right to self-determination.

3) ***Resolution 2625, known as the Declaration on Principles of International Law concerning Friendly Relations and Co-operation among States in accordance with the Charter of the United Nations,*** extended this right to people living under foreign occupation. This resolution was adopted by the UN General Assembly in 1970. Resolution 2625 is usually considered from two aspects, namely, in formulating an additional method for implementing the right to self-determination and the possible implications of the request for the government to represent the entire nation in a certain territory in question. With this, the Resolution opened the door for the internal dimension of the right to self-determination and for the selection of appropriate institutional and state structures. The resolution begins the section on the principle of equal rights and self-determination of peoples with an affirmation that all nations have the right to self-determination and, hence, have the right to determine their political status without external influences and to achieve economic, social, and cultural development. The Resolution further states: "(...) Nothing in the foregoing paragraphs shall be construed as authorizing or encouraging any action

[53] UNGA Res. 1514 (1960).

[54] Henrard (2000).

[55] UNGA Res. 1541, Annex, Principles which should guide members in determining wetter or not an obligation exist to transmit the information called for in Article 73 (e) of the Charter of the United Nations, (1960).

which would dismember or impair, totally or in part, the territorial integrity or political unity of sovereign and independent States conducting themselves in compliance with the principle of equal rights and self-determination of peoples as described above and thus possessed of a government representing the whole people belonging to the territory without distinction as to race, creed or colour."[56]

4) Joint Article 1 of the International Covenant on Civil and Political Rights (ICCPR)[57] ***and the International Covenant on Economic, Social and Cultural Rights (ICESCR)***[58] is also very relevant in terms of the exercise of the right to self-determination: "All peoples have the right of self-determination. By virtue of that right they freely determine their political status and freely pursue their economic, social and cultural development," which guarantees the right to self-determination of all peoples and uses the wording used in Resolution 1514. The General Comment of the Human Rights Committee on Article 1 of the ICCPR does not give any other instructions on the interpretation of the concept of peoples. However, its paragraph 7 refers to Resolution 2625 and takes into account the requirements for a representative government and other remarks made in this context.[59] Therefore, it can be concluded that Article 1 mainly refers to the right to internal self-determination, in terms of broad political, economic, sociocultural autonomy, and political participation. Secession, in any case, can only be accepted as a final solution.[60] Nonetheless, by incorporating the principle of self-determination of peoples into the International Covenants on Human Rights, that principle has undoubtedly acquired international legal status.

5) Other international instruments that guarantee the right to self-determinationapart from the well-known and established international instruments that guarantee the right of peoples to self-determination, in colonial and noncolonial situations, this right is also guaranteed by other international instruments, such as the following:

a) African Charter on Human and Peoples' Rights—in 1981, the Assembly of Leaders of the Organization of African Unity adopted the African Charter on Human and Peoples' Rights (African Charter). Articles 19 and 20 of the African Charter guarantee the right of all peoples to self-determination. Article 20 recognizes it as an inalienable right.[61] The broad interpretation of the African Charter suggests that it applies not only to the colonial peoples but also to the peoples

[56] UNGA Res 2625, Annex, Declaration on Principles of international law concerning friendly relations and cooperation among the states in accordance with the Charter of the United Nations (1970).

[57] UNGA Res. 2200 A (XXI) ICCPR (1966), article 1.

[58] UNGA Res. 2200 A (XXI) ICESCR (1966), article 1.

[59] Human Rights Committee, CCPR General Comment No. 12: article 1 (Right to Self-determination) (1984).

[60] This can happen when the majority of the state does not guarantee autonomy to the people in question; see Henrard (2000).

[61] Banjul Charter on Human and Peoples' Rights, 21 ILM (1982).

living in repressive African republics under repressive governments. In a situation where there are attempts at the physical extermination of a particular group, in the exercise of the right to self-determination, nations may secede, especially if it is the only practical method for ensuring their survival. A state that denies peoples' access to the government violates the principle of equality set out in Article 19 of the African Charter, and in these circumstances, the right to self-determination can be exercised through secession. In that case, the state cannot legitimately invoke the principle of sovereignty and territorial integrity to ban secession because the state has lost the power to govern those peoples.[62]

b) Vienna Declaration and Program of Action[63]—in 1993, the World Conference on Human Rights adopted the Vienna Declaration and Program of Action (Vienna Declaration). It reaffirms Article 1 of the International Covenant on Human Rights, sets self-determination as a collective human right, and stipulates that the denial of the right to self-determination constitutes a violation of human rights.
c) UN Fiftieth Anniversary Declaration[64]—In 1995, the UN adopted the UN Fiftieth Anniversary Declaration (Anniversary Declaration). This Declaration continues to reaffirm the right of all peoples to self-determination, taking into account the special circumstances of peoples under colonial or other forms of foreign domination or occupation, and recognizes the right of peoples to take legitimate action in accordance with the UN Charter to realize the inalienable right to self-determination, which cannot be derogated.

1.4.1 The Case of Katanga vs. Zaire—The African Commission's Decision on Human Rights and Peoples' Rights About Violations of the Right to Self-Determination—An Effort to Balance the Principles of International Law

Katanga was a rich region of Zaire (now the Democratic Republic of Congo), which in 1960 attempted to break away from Zaire. The organization, Katanga People's Congress, in 1992 appealed to the African Commission on Human Rights and Peoples' Rights for Violation of the Right to Self-Determination under Article 20 (I) of the African or Banjul Charter of Human Rights and Rights of the People (1981).[65]

---

[62] Okoronkwo (2002).

[63] The Vienna Declaration and Programme of Action, U.N. Doc. A/CONF.157/24 (1993).

[64] Declaration on the Occasion of the Fiftieth Anniversary of the United Nations, G.A. Res. 50/6, U.N. GAOR, 50th Sess., at 1, U.N. Doc. A/Res/50/6 (1995).

[65] According to this Charter, "1. All peoples shall have the right to existence. They shall have the unquestionable and inalienable right to self-determination. They shall freely determine their political status and shall pursue their economic and social development according to the policy they have freely chosen; 2. Colonized or oppressed peoples shall have the right to free themselves from

The purpose of the complaint was first to recognize the organization as a liberation movement for achieving independence (the organization claimed to represent the Katanga population) and, subsequently, to obtain support for an independent Katanga. The African Commission sought to strike a balance between the principle of self-determination and the principle of state sovereignty and territorial integrity and found that self-determination can be realized in several ways that do not call into question Zaire's territorial sovereignty and integrity. Moreover, the Commission has determined that it should protect Zaire as a member of the Organization of African Unity (OAU, now AU) and as a signatory to the Charter.[66] However, the Commission sought to make this decision as less arbitrary as possible and pursued facts such as concrete evidence of human rights abuses or evidence that the people of Katanga were denied the right to participate in the government. As such evidence in the case was not present, the organization's claim was rejected.[67]

1.5 The Right to Self-Determination of the Peoples in the Jurisprudence of the International Court of Justice

The resolutions of the General Assembly and the opinions of the International Court of Justice (ICJ) are not obligatory; i.e., they have moral power but do not create law obligations. However, along with the UN Charter and the International Covenants for Human Rights, after many years of state practice, a set of norms for self-determination has been developed that has reached the status of customary international law, defined under Article 38 (1) (b) of the Statute of the ICJ as *a general practice accepted by the law.*[68] For a principle to become customary law, state practice is needed (according to the ICJ, the inception of custom needs practice and *opinio juris*), and actually, the right of self-determination is supported by state practice, having particularly in mind that upon it, over 70 territories and former colonies were decolonized (starting from 1946 onward), and a great number of them have become sovereign states and members of the UN.

The process that takes into consideration the freely expressed will of the people under the UN Charter, the resolutions of the UN General Assembly, the opinions of the ICJ, and state practice collectively defined the right of self-determination as a right of decolonization and a right to establish self-government for the peoples who

the bonds of domination by resorting to any means recognized by the international community; 3. All peoples shall have the right to the assistance of the States parties to the present Charter in their liberation struggle against foreign domination, be it political, economic or cultural," Banjul Charter on Human and Peoples' Rights, 21 ILM (1982), article 20.

[66] Katangese Peoples' Congress v. Zaire, African Commission on Human and Peoples' Rights, Comm. No. 75/92 (1995).

[67] The Commission did not determine whether the Catangans were a people and left a series of unanswered questions, see more at Summers (2007); Heraclides (1991); Evans and Murray (2001).

[68] I.C.J. Statute, article 38(1)(b).

inhabit non-self-government colonial territories. But although the ICJ has in many cases recognized the principle of self-determination of the peoples, mainly connected to the process of decolonization, it has shown a great dose of caution in its interpretation. Regardless of the prominent position of the principle in the UN Charter, the ICJ did not make any reference to it until the Opinion for Namibia from 1971,[69] although the principle was previously mentioned in separate opinions of some of the ICJ judges. However, even in the Opinion for Namibia, although the Court accepts that self-determination is one of the essential principles of contemporary international law, it did not go too far from some general vague statements.[70]

In its Advisory opinion for Western Sahara (1975), the Court perseveres to broaden the existing interpretation and the influence of the right of self-determination of the peoples. Referring to Resolution 1514 (XV),[71] it is clear that, according to further formulations, the Court found that self-determination always includes "(...) a need to focus the attention on the freely expressed will of the peoples, but this requirement may be excluded in two cases: when there is no case of – the peoples – in the right sense of the notion, and when the 'certain circumstances,' make the plebiscite or the referendum unnecessary."[72] However, the Court did not elaborate and did not specify what it means by the notion "the peoples" nor by the term "certain circumstances." But while the Court's authoritative opinion is lacking and its decisions focus solely on the legal aspects of self-determination, in the East Timor case (1995),[73] the Court reiterates that self-determination of peoples is one of the fundamental principles of modern international law.

As a general conclusion, concerning the Court's views on the right to self-determination, it can be said at the outset that its application is not easy. There seem to be two approaches that influence the formation of opinion: the first is focusing very narrowly on certain legal aspects of the right while ignoring the broader issues surrounding it, and the second is balancing the principle of self-determination with the other principles of international law, such as the principles of territorial integrity, state sovereignty, and *uti possidetis juris*. The establishment of this balance is often influenced by general political circumstances; the need for peace, stability, and development; as well as the national practice of constructing and shaping peoples' ideas.[74]

---

[69] ICJ Reports (1971), 31, par. 52.

[70] ICJ Advisory Opinion Legal consequences for states of the continued presence of South Africa in Namibia (South West Africa) notwithstanding Security Council Resolution 276 (1970), ICJ Report (1971), 16, par. 31–32.

[71] UNGA Res. 1514 (1960).

[72] ICJ Reports (1975), 32, par. 55.

[73] ICJ Reports (1995), case 84.

[74] This is a departure from the idea of justice and an impartial examination of the facts. These ideas involve subjective interpretations based on selective examination of the facts, see more at Summers (2007), p. 316.

1.5.1 The Case of Israel and Palestine, the Opinion of the ICJ about the Wall of the Occupied Palestinian Territory

The method of creating Israel is difficult to classify. In 1914, Palestine was part of the Ottoman Empire, without a special status, and was occupied by the British troops in 1917, which was followed by a peace treaty. By exchanging notes between France and Britain in 1916, it was agreed that France and Britain would recognize an independent Arab republic on the territory of Palestine and divide the spheres of influence. But in the meantime, the Crown had said that it will support the creation of a Jewish state on the territory of Palestine. Following the revolution in Turkey, the Treaty of Sèvres (1920) signed between the Allies of World War I and the Ottoman Empire was never ratified, and contrary to Article 22 of the League of Nations Convention, according to which territories seized from Turkey could be recognized as independent states, Britain was given a mandate over Palestine. As an occupying force, Britain administered Palestine and, during its rule, allowed the Jews to form their own state on its territory. The Palestinians/Arabs believed that this violated the right to self-determination, so the British government established a Royal Commission to settle the dispute between the Jews and Arabs. The panel proposed that Palestine be divided into Arab and Jewish states.[75] The Zionists expressed reservations about this, and the Arabs strongly opposed it.[76]

But in 1947, the UK gave up its mandate in favor of the UN, or to a special committee of the General Assembly, to resolve the issue.[77] The members of the committee were divided—some were for the division of Palestine into Arab and Jewish states with an international zone in Jerusalem, while others (less) were in favor of a federation of Arab and Jewish autonomous regions.[78] The UN adopted a resolution implementing the plan of the first group because after the British left the mandate, the territory remained *terra nullius*. The Arabs living in border areas opposed it.[79]

Following the declaration of the Israeli state in 1948, it faced a military attack from Egypt, Syria, Lebanon, and Jordan, and at the end of the war, Jordan invaded the West Bank, Egypt took the Gaza Strip, and Israel expanded its territory over significant portions of Palestine, i.e., beyond what was initially determined. In 1967, a new war and a new redrawing of the borders began, by which Israel occupied the West Bank, the Gaza Strip, East Jerusalem, the Sinai Mountains, and the Golan Heights. Later, as part of the 1978 Camp David agreement, which guaranteed Palestinian autonomy in the Gaza Strip and West Bank, Israel returned the Sinai Mountain to Egypt.[80] After 21 years of Israeli occupation, in November 1998, the Palestinian Liberation Organization (PLO) proclaimed the Palestinian state based

[75] League of Nations (1937).

[76] See more at Israeli missions around the world (Internet source).

[77] United Nations Special Committee on Palestine (1947)

[78] Origins and Evolution of the Palestine Problem: 1917–1947.

[79] See more in Summers (2007) and Crawford (2006).

[80] The Camp David Accords, the Framework for Peace in the Middle East (1978).

on the Declaration of Independence, which, again, finds its foundations upon the right of the people to self-determination.[81] The Peace Process Declaration concluded between Israel and the PLO in 1993 provides the right of self-determination for Palestinians living in the Gaza Strip and the West Bank,[82] but as internal self-determination, although the withdrawal of the Israeli military forces, the establishment of peace, solving the problem of refugees, and respecting the sovereignty of any country in the environment were already negotiated.

In the UN case of Palestine, UN documents state that Palestinians have a right to self-determination, but the territorial integrity of the State of Israel must also be respected.[83] This was also the view of the ICJ with regard to the construction of a wall by Israel on the occupied Palestinian territory (2003),[84] namely, Israel built a wall to allegedly protect itself from Palestinian terrorists and claimed that it was a temporary measure. But there was an opinion that the wall was built to bolster Israel's position vis-à-vis the country it had previously occupied illegally. As the wall was built, numerous Arab families remained on the "wrong" side of the border; some were expelled, and Jewish families were brought in their place. The UN Assembly adopted A/RES/ES-10/14 (2003),[85] asking the ICJ to give an advisory opinion on the legal consequences of Israel building a wall along the occupied Palestinian territory of the West Bank. The US voted against the General Assembly resolution, while Russia and the EU countries abstained.

The ICJ found that this vote did not impede its opinion, but it was also particularly cautious in its wording. The Court was aware that the wall issue was only a small issue that was part of a larger issue, and it was unclear what effect the judicial opinion would have on the course of the political negotiations.[86] Finally, the Court decided that the opinion will focus solely on the legal consequences of the construction of the wall and will examine the other questions to the extent necessary to clarify them. For many, this was a narrow focus, so the Palestinians' right to self-determination remained insufficiently clarified. The Court found that the existence of the Palestinian people is not disputed and that they have the right to self-determination. However, the Court examined this right only with the respect of other legal practices and principles, such as a ban on the incorporation of territory by force, and with the respect of the other set of obligations that had Israel, in particular with regard to infringement of international humanitarian law under the Geneva Conventions, as well as the ban of the occupying force for transfer of civilians to the occupied territory. The Court therefore noted that building the wall violates these obligations and impeded the Palestinian people from exercising their

[81] Declaration of State of Palestine (1988).

[82] Israel-Palestine Liberation Organization Agreement (1993).

[83] Crawford (2006) and Cassese (1995).

[84] Legal Consequences of the Construction of a Wall in the Occupied Palestinian Territory, ICJ Advisory opinion (2003).

[85] For more info see the Official document system of the United Nations (Internet source).

[86] Legal Consequences of the Construction of a Wall in the Occupied Palestinian Territory, ICJ Advisory opinion (2003), par. 10.

right to self-determination.[87] However, the Court did not initially establish why the Israeli barrier directly impeded the right to self-determination but found that there was a breach of law only because of a breach of the previous two sets of obligations. The ICJ's view of the wall, therefore, showed that the Court focused very narrowly and put legal rules out of the broader and more complicated political issues surrounding them.[88]

References

Arangio-Ruiz G (1977) Human rights and non-intervention in the Helsinki Final Act (1977- IV). Hague Recueil 157:195–332

Background to the International Covenant on Civil and Political Rights and Optional Protocols. https://www.ohchr.org/en/treaty-bodies/ccpr/background-international-covenant-civil-and-political-rights-and-optional-protocols#:~:text=Background%20to%20the%20Optional%20Protocols&text=The%20first%20Optional%20Protocol%20came,human%20rights%20have%20been%20violated. Accessed 6 Aug 2022

Banjul Charter on Human and Peoples' Rights, 21 ILM (1982)

Brilmayer L (1991) Secession and self-determination: a territorial interpretation. Yale J Int Law 16:177–202

Brownlie I (1973) Principles of public international Law. Oxford University Press

Buchheit LC (1978) Secession, the legitimacy of self-determination. Yale University Press, New Haven and London

Cassese A (1995) Self- determination of the peoples, a legal reappraisal. Cambridge University Press

Crawford J (1996) Book review of determination of the peoples, a legal reappraisal, by A. Cassese. Am J Int Law 90:331–333

Crawford J (2006) The creation of states in international law. Oxford university press

Cristescu A (1981) The right to self-determination, historical and current development on the basis of United Nations instruments. UN

Declaration of Independence (1776). https://www.archives.gov/founding-docs/declaration-transcript. Accessed 6 Aug 2022

Declaration of State of Palestine, Palestine National Council (1988). https://www.un.org/unispal/document/auto-insert-178680/. Accessed 20 Mar 2023

Declaration on the Occasion of the Fiftieth Anniversary of the United Nations, G.A. Res. 50/6, U.N. GAOR, 50th Sess., at 1, U.N. Doc. A/Res/50/6 (1995)

Evans M, Murray R (eds) (2001) Documents of the African Commission on Human and Peoples' rights. Hart Publishing, Oxford

Franck TM (1992) Emerging right to democratic governance. Am J Int Law 86(1):46–91

General Assembly resolution 2200A (XXI), Optional Protocol of the International Covenant for Civic and Political Rights (1966). https://www.ohchr.org/en/instruments-mechanisms/instruments/optional-protocol-international-covenant-civil-and-political. Accessed 6 Aug 2022

Gerbet P, Ghebali VY, Mouton MR (1973) Societe des nations et organisation des Nations- Unies. Richelieu, Paris

Hannum H (1990) Autonomy, sovereignty, and self-determination, the accommodation of conflict rights. University of Pennsylvania Press

[87] Legal Consequences of the Construction of a Wall in the Occupied Palestinian Territory, ICJ Advisory opinion (2003), par. 8&9.

[88] Summers (2007).

Henrard K (2000) Devising an adequate system of minority protection. Kluwer Law International, Hague
Heraclides A (1991) The self-determination of the minorities in the international politics. Frank Cass and Company Limited
Human Rights Committee (1984) CCPR General Comment No. 12: Article 1 (Right to Self-determination) The Right to Self-determination of Peoples. https://www.refworld.org/docid/453883f822.html. Accessed 6 Aug 2022
ICJ Reports (1970) Legal consequences for states of the continued presence of South Africa in Namibia (South West Africa) notwithstanding security council resolution 276 (1970). https://www.icj-cij.org/en/case/53. Accessed 6 Aug 2022
ICJ Reports (1975) International court of justice reports of judgments, advisory opinions and orders Western Sahara. https://www.icj-cij.org/public/files/case-related/61/061-19751016-ADV-01-00-EN.pdf. Accessed 6 Aug 2022
ICJ Reports (1995) East Timor (Portugal v. Australia). https://www.icj-cij.org/en/case/84. Accessed 6 Aug 2022
International Court of Justice, advisory opinion Legal Consequences of the Construction of a Wall in the Occupied Palestinian Territory (2003). https://www.icj-cij.org/en/case/131. Accessed 19 Oct 2022
Israeli missions around the world (Internet source). https://embassies.gov.il/MFA/AboutIsrael/Maps/Pages/The-Peel-Commission-Plan-1937.aspx#:~:text=The%20Peel%20partition%20plan%20was,British%20declared%20the%20plan%20unimplementable. Accessed 20 Mar 2023
Israel-Palestine Liberation Organization Agreement (1993). https://avalon.law.yale.edu/20th_century/isrplo.asp. Accessed 20 Mar 2023
Jennings I (1956) The approach to self-government. Cambridge University Press
Katangese Peoples' Congress v. Zaire, African Commission on Human and Peoples' Rights, Comm. No. 75/92 (1995). http://hrlibrary.umn.edu/africa/comcases/75-92.html. Accessed 5 Jan 2023
Kelly JM (1992) A short history of Western legal theory. Oxford University Press
Kelsen H (1951) The law of the United Nations: a critical analysis of its fundamental problems. (Collected Writings of Rousseau). The Lawbook Exchange, Ltd
Knop K (2002) Diversity and self-determination in the international law. Cambridge University Press
Lenin IV (1951) The right of nations to self-determination. Foreign Languages Publishing House, Moscow
Ligue of Nations, Plan of partition (1937) Summary of the UK Palestine Royal Commission (Peel Commission) report, C.495.M.336.1937.VI. https://www.un.org/unispal/document/auto-insert-197740/. Accessed 20 Mar 2023
Official document system of the United Nations. https://documents-dds-ny.un.org/doc/UNDOC/GEN/N03/646/93/PDF/N0364693.pdf?OpenElement. Accessed 6 Aug 2022
Okoronkwo PL (2002) Self-determination and the legality of Biafra's secession under international law. Loy L A Int Comp Law Rev 25(1):63–115
Origins and Evolution of the Palestine Problem: 1917-1947 (part I). The question of Palestine, United Nations. https://www.un.org/unispal/history2/origins-and-evolution-of-the-palestine-problem/part-i-1917-1947/#Origins_and_Evolution_of_the_Palestine_Problem_1917-1947_Part_I. Accessed 5 Jan 2023
Papers relating to the foreign relations of the United States, 1917, supplement 2, the World War, volume I. https://history.state.gov/historicaldocuments/frus1917Supp02v01/d97#:~:text=No%20people%20must%20be%20forced,payment%20for%20manifest%20wrongs%20done. Accessed 6 Aug 2022
Senate Rejects the Treaty of Versailles (1919). https://www.senate.gov/about/powers-procedures/treaties/senate-rejects-treaty-of-versailles.htm. Accessed 6 Aug 2022
Shehadi KS (1993) Ethnic self-determination and the break-up of states. The Adelphi Papers
Statute of the International Court of Justice, 1945

Summers J (2007) Peoples and international law, how nationalism and self-determination shape a contemporary law of nations. Leiden, Boston
The Camp David Accords, the Framework for Peace in the Middle East (1978). https://www.peaceau.org/uploads/camp-david-accords-egypt-1978.pdf. Accessed 20 Mar 2023
The Fourteen Points Woodrow Wilson and the U.S. Rejection of the Treaty of Versailles. https://www.theworldwar.org/learn/peace/fourteen-points. Accessed 6 Aug 2022
The Vienna Declaration and Programme of Action, U.N. Doc. A/CONF.157/24 (1993)
UN Charter (1945)
UNGA Res 1541, Principles which should guide members in determining whether or not an obligation exists to transmit the information called for under Article 73e of the Charter (1960)
UNGA Res 2625, Annex, Declaration on Principles of international law concerning friendly relations and cooperation among the states in accordance with the Charter of the United Nations (1970)
UNGA Res. 1514, Declaration on the Granting of Independence to Colonial Countries and Peoples (1960)
UNGA Res. 217 A (III) Universal Declaration on Human Rights (1948)
UNGA Res. 2200 A (XXI) International Covenant on Civil and Political Rights (ICCPR) (1966)
UNGA Res. 2200 A (XXI) International Covenant on Economic, Social and Cultural Rights (ICESCR) (1966)
UNGA Res. 3201 (S-VI) Declaration on the Establishment of a New International Order (1974)
UNGA Res. 3281 (XXIX) Charter of Economic Rights and Duties of States (1974)
United Nations General Assembly official records, Agenda item 28 (Part II) Tenth session (1955) Document A/29291. Annotations on the text of the draft International Covenants on Human Rights. https://www2.ohchr.org/english/issues/opinion/articles1920_iccpr/docs/a-2929.pdf. Accessed 20 Mar 2023
United Nations Special Committee on Palestine, Report of the General Secretary (1947). https://digitallibrary.un.org/record/703295?ln=en. Accessed 20 Mar 2023
Verzijl JHW (1974) International law in historical perspective. Martinus Nijhoff Publishers
Virally M (1968) Le rôle des a principes dans le développement du droit international. Recueil d'études de droit international en hommage à Paul Guggenheim, Faculté de droit de l'université de Genève - Institut universitaire de hautes études internationales. Imprimerie de la Tribune de Genève, Genève, pp 531–554
Wambaugh S (1920) A monograph on plebiscites with a collection of official documents. Carnegie Endowment for International Peace, New York
Watson A (1992) The evolution of international society: a comparative and historical analysis. Routledge
Whelan A (1994) Wilsonian self- determination and Versailles settlement. Int Comp Law Q (ICLQ) 43:99–115

Chapter 2
The Right Holders of Self-Determination

2.1 Introduction

The right to self-determination is often a part of nationalist rhetoric and can be subject to two different standards of legitimacy: those of nationalism and those of positive international law.[1] The right to self-determination has developed its own terminology that is different from its everyday use, that is, because the sovereign state is the central subject of international law and states not only incorporate nationalist principles but also provide forums for their expression.[2] States and their institutions are understood as instruments through which national groups exercise their sovereignty. However, in international law, self-determination cannot simply be understood through the attainment of statehood, though all secessions and attempts at secessions in the twentieth and twenty-first centuries are justified on the basis of a nationalist view or nationalist ideology.[3] Nowadays, more than a century after the Versailles Peace Conference (1919), it is generally accepted that the right to self-determination is a collective human right that is part of customary law. Although some of the legal international instruments regulating it do not have binding legal force (UN General Assembly declarations and resolutions are not among the sources of international law), irrespective of their nonbinding nature, one cannot avoid the fact that they protect the rights of peoples and that the UN, as a political organization created based on them, took practical steps to protect them by identifying the ones who possess those rights. Therefore, the identification of the right

[1] Summers (2007).

[2] Nationalism is a political doctrine that presupposes a political argument for how states and other institutions should be structured. Nationalism can be a positive set of demands, but it can also work in the opposite direction. Nationalism is based on the idea of the people, as a single homogeneous group, see more at Moore (2003), Smith (1998) and Summers (2007).

[3] Pavkovic and Radan (2007).

N. Shikova, *Self-Determination and Secession*,
https://doi.org/10.1007/978-3-031-34322-3_2

holders of self-determination is an important legal and political issue and, in many ways, determines the position of the right/principle of self-determination.[4]

2.2 The Peoples

The holders of the right to self-determination are *the peoples*. The right to self-determination is recognized in them, even though it is not defined what constitutes this legal category. Thus, the main question is: *What composes the peoples?* The idea of *the people* necessarily presupposes a certain political one used to legitimize the existence and action of political and legal institutions. Although it is argued whether treating *the people* as a political idea is the most productive way to consider self-determination in international law, for some scholars, that is more useful than understanding *the people* as a social entity. In this respect, there is a significant difference between *the people* having rights under international law and "people" as a sociological construct.[5]

Historically, Johann Gottfried von Herder, one of the founders of the European Enlightenment, a political philosopher, and the founder of the German Romantic movement (as a theologian, historian, literary critic, and, among others, Goethe's teacher), first used the term *Volk* or *the people* to define a community that carries a specific culture through which it identifies itself. He used this term liberally to describe communities of different sizes and characteristics, indicating that each *Volk* has its own qualities and virtues that should be understood and respected more than the measure in the balance of the modern values.[6]

John Stuart Mill considered that "(…) the 'people that exercise power are not always the same people with those over whom that power is exercised. (…) The will of the people practically means the will of the most numerous or the most active *part* of the people; the majority, or those who have succeeded in making themselves being accepted as the majority (…)."[7]

The general definitions of *the people* that exist in the international law literature tend to combine objective elements, such as language, religion, or ethnicity, with subjective elements, like the will to live together. Additionally, some theorists are attempting to establish new categories of *peoples* that are independent from the old colonial categories, rejecting the fact that there is a single definition that encompasses all categories of *peoples*.

---

[4] Hannum (1990).

[5] If the peoples or a nation is treated as a sociological entity, then we will quickly hit a dead end. The peoples have almost no role in the creation of international law, Summers (2007).

[6] Patten (2010) and Herder and Payne (2016).

[7] Mill (1952), p. 269.

Karen Knop considers that *the people* represent the fateful community of inhabitants of a particular territory, defined by attributes that are beyond their control.[8] Yael Tamir believes that the term *people* belongs to the same social category as the term *family* or *tribe*, meaning that *the people* constitute one of those social unities whose existence is independent of the consciousness of their members. Therefore, for Tamir, it is necessary to have some objective element, such as blood line, race, certain territory, and so on, which will allow the outside observer to determine *the people*.[9] On the other hand, Daniel Turp considers that *the people* are a democratically constructed community, a group of individuals who have chosen to determine their destiny.[10] Antonio Cassese meanwhile refers to *the people* as a conglomerate of individuals whose desires and aspirations should not only be taken into account but should also be given as much legal power as possible.[11] Furthermore, Karl Doehring adds, to the generally accepted category of colonial people as a right holder of self-determination, second and third categories: the population of sovereign states and ethnic minorities, respectively.[12] Finally, Aureliu Cristescu finds that it is difficult to come up with a precise definition of the term *peoples*, so various possibilities for interpretation and current uncertainties in many cases turned the right of self-determination into a weapon, easily usable against the territorial integrity and political unity of states.[13]

It is important to note that the vast majority of state constitutions use the term *people* rather than *peoples*. Although several states recognize that different peoples exist within their territories, only a few constitutions of the states are referring to *the peoples,* or to the right to self-determination of those constituent groups.[14]

---

[8] Knop (2002), p. 57.

[9] Tamir (2002).

[10] Turp (1996), pp. 277–283.

[11] Cassese (1995).

[12] Doehring (1994). Dohering is taking into account the Advisory opinion of the Ligue of Nations, Permanent Court of International Justice (1930), about the Interpretation of the Convention Between Greece and Bulgaria Respecting Reciprocal Emigration (1919) considering that communities are "(…) a group of persons of the same religion and race, must be of a character both religious and national and must be designed to serve the common interests of its members in regard to religion, education and charity; and that the question whether such a community still exists or has existed in the past is a question of fact to be decided in each case in accordance with the relevant historical data (…)," PCIJ Greco- Bulgarian Communities, Advisory Opinion (1930).

[13] No state, old or new, can consider itself immune from wrong interpretations of the right to self-determination, which can trigger secessionist movements on the territory of the independent state. The peoples can be manipulated contrary to their interest and support the aggressive or subversive planes, Cristescu (1981).

[14] Russia's 1993 Constitution, the 1995 Ethiopian Constitution, and the 1995 Bosnia and Hercegovina Constitution recognized that right in at least three constitutional peoples. The 1996 Constitution of the Republic of South Africa recognizes self-determination as a right of all but does not presuppose self-determination for communities in the country. Other treaties also recognize more than one people in the country, such as the 2005 Memorandum of Understanding between the Indonesian Government and the Free Movement of the Achaeans, which repeatedly refers to the Achaeans as a people. The Machakos Protocol from 2002, signed by the Government of the People

As for UN practice, it should be noted that although the UN Charter and other UN instruments use the term *peoples*, there is no accepted and certain definition of this term. The UN Charter provides little help in this regard as it does not provide any detail or explanation regarding the concept of *the peoples*. Various UN bodies have been examining the issue of the definition of the term *the peoples*.[15] The opinions varied, opposing the idea that no distinction can be made of the exercise of the right to self-determination, either based on the fact that some peoples are under foreign sovereignty or because they live on a certain continent or they own independent territories and reside on the territory of a sovereign state. However, for some of them, the term *peoples* should refer exclusively to peoples under colonial or foreign domination, and this is the basis for establishing "the real" right to self-determination. Some UN bodies considered that *the peoples* are those who occupy a geographical area and who, in the absence of foreign domination, have formed an independent state (colonial territories, territories under guardianship, etc.) or have occupied a territory that has become independent but can be subject to new forms of domination, more specifically to neo-colonialism.[16]

There are different criteria regarding the characteristics that a group has to possess to be considered *the people*, and one of the most controversial ones is the size of the group.[17] In the middle of the last century, a quite number of debates took place within UN bodies, addressing this issue.[18] Despite the conceptual scope of the debate, no consensus has been reached on the question "What are the peoples?" But it is considered that the term *people* should be understood in the most general sense.[19] Therefore, all the relevant instruments adopted within the UN indicate that *all peoples should enjoy the right to self-determination*. The UN Charter has used the term *peoples* many times, especially in the Preamble, as a synonym for "nations" or "states." It is clear, from reading other UN legal documents and from the practice of the organization, that all *peoples* have this right, whether they have gained independence or the status of a state. Therefore, the Charter should not be interpreted as

---

of Sudan and Sudan People's Liberation Movement/Sudan People's Liberation Army, recognizes such a right for the people of South Sudan and even allowed a referendum six years later.

[15] See more Cristescu (1981).

[16] According to UNESCO, people are a set of individuals connected to each other not only at the level of individual connection but also at the level of mutual awareness and potentially through institutions that express their identity. UNESCO takes into account the following indicative features when defining "people": (a) mutual historical tradition, (b) racial or ethnic identity, (c) cultural homogeneity, (d) linguistic uniqueness, (e) religious or ideological affinities, (f) territorial connection, and (g) mutual economic life, UNESCO (1992).

[17] Kymlicka (1996), Tamir (2002) and Waterbury (2002).

[18] UN Doc. A/AC.125/ SR.70, Special Committee on Principles of International Law Concerning Friendly Relations and Cooperation among the States, Summary record on the seventieth meeting (1967).

[19] UN Doc. A/2929, Annotations on the text of the draft International Covenants on Human Rights A-C.3-SR.447 (1955).

indicating that this right applies only to a particular category of people (colonial nations and peoples under foreign occupation).[20]

But in practice, due to objective factors, it is not always possible or easy to identify who *the people* are.[21] In the attempts to eliminate the colonialism, this was very simple to resolve it by accepting a principle that guaranteed independence to colonial countries and peoples, while for other nations and peoples—the noncolonial, the dilemma remained about the possibility of accepting a universally applicable and generally acceptable rule. Nevertheless, the elements that emerged from the discussions that took place within the UN bodies on this subject matter must not and cannot be ignored. These elements should be taken into account in different situations, especially when it is necessary to decide whether an entity forms a *people with the right to self-determination*. The elements are the following:

(a) The term *people* means a social entity that has a clear identity and its own social characteristics.
(b) The term *people* implies a connection to a particular territory, even if the *people* in question were expelled and artificially replaced by another population.
(c) The term *people* shall not be replaced by ethnic, religious, or linguistic minorities whose existence and rights are recognized in Article 27 of the International Covenant for Civil and Political Rights.

In that sense, the applicability of the principle of self-determination should not be construed as encouraging secessionist or irredentist movements or as justifying actions aimed at forcibly changing the state or the government system. Or in the spirit of international instruments, nothing in their paragraphs is constructed in a way that implies, authorizes, or encourages any action aimed at disintegrating or dividing, in whole or in part, the territorial integrity of a political entity—a sovereign and independent state, which behaves in accordance with the principle of equal rights and self-determination of peoples.[22]

Therefore, although the UN generally avoided defining the term *people*, in practice it sanctioned criteria based on territoriality, in particular, concerning the identification of dependent peoples, whose rights are mentioned in Articles 73 and 76 of the Charter. From then until now, the question that is often asked is: *Did the end of the colonial era seal the number of peoples that could emerge in the future by practicing the right to self-determination?* For former UN Secretary-General U Thant, the emergence of new nations within existing nations is unacceptable, but another former Secretary-General, Boutros Boutros-Galli, was more cautious in that regard:

[20] Cristescu (1981).

[21] Although peoples have a clear identity, historical circumstances may closely link two or more separate communities. In such circumstances, the exercise of the right to self-determination for one of those communities, whether constructing a minority or a majority, cannot be easily applied without prejudice to the rights of other communities, Cristescu (1981).

[22] UNGA Res 2625, Annex, Declaration on Principles of international law concerning friendly relations and cooperation among the states in accordance with the Charter of the United Nations (1970).

"(…) The United Nations has not closed its door. Yet if every ethnic, religious or linguistic group claimed statehood, there would be no limit to fragmentation, and peace, security and economic well-being for all would become ever more difficult to achieve (…)."[23]

For some theorists, the post-Cold War era abandoned the territorial criteria for the *people*, and they support their claims based on the examples of the emergence of many independent states in the past decades, such as Eritrea, East Timor, Monaco, Andorra, San Marino, as well as the states that were established after the disintegration of the USSR: Yugoslavia and Czechoslovakia.[24]

2.2.1 Colonial Peoples

Within international law, in the context of colonialism, *the peoples* were considered to be colonial countries and peoples and, later, those who were subject to foreign domination or occupation. The Declaration on the Granting of Independence to Colonial Countries and Peoples[25] provides an opportunity for the exercise of the right to self-determination but at the same time prohibits a violation of state integrity. Self-determination of the colonies does not violate the territorial integrity of the states, and international law gives the colonies a status that is separate and distinct from that of the state. UN General Assembly Resolution 2625 defines non-self-governing territories as territories that are geographically separate and have a different ethnicity or culture from the administrator country.[26] Geographically separated, in practice, means separated by the ocean, a condition that was called—"a saltwater thesis." According to these international instruments, the principle of territorial integrity prohibits secession but not decolonization. For theorists, the colonial population became a "people" by developing collective awareness of its subordination and exploitation by the imperial powers, as well as through its common struggle for liberation.[27] Hence, the identification marker is whether the territory is under strife or not, that it has an identity other than an administrative one, and that its population

[23] Report of the Secretary-General on an Agenda for Peace – Preventive Diplomacy, Peacemaking and Peace Keeping, June 17, 1992, 31, ILM 953 (1992).

[24] For Eyassu Gayim it is difficult to consider these cases as evidence for the application of socially-based criteria in identifying what constitutes a people and the reasons for the emergence of new states should be sought by identifying other factors, such are at first place, the dissolution of states. Only Eritrea and East Timor can be considered as secessionist and special cases. While in other cases of the creation of small states—cities, this was achieved after the states recognized the situation that already existed. In addition, Bangladesh is a special case because of the separation of the two wings of Pakistan and the role of India in the conflict, Gayim (2006).

[25] UNGA Res. 1514, Declaration on the granting independence of colonial countries and peoples (1960).

[26] UNGA Res 2625, Declaration on Principles of international law concerning friendly relations and cooperation among the states in accordance with the Charter of the United Nations (1970).

[27] Chaumont (1973), pp. 380–385.

is normatively united as a "people" by the fact that it collectively suffers from the injury inflicted on it by colonialism.[28] Because of historical suffering, self-determination ensures corrective justice.[29] According to some theorists, the self-determination of peoples within the UN Charter and Resolution 1514 is defined exclusively on a territorial basis—only the inhabitants of non-self-governing territories have the right to self-determination. Thus, from a legal point of view, ethnicity, culture, and other social characteristics have nothing to do with the right to self-determination, i.e., only the connection with the territory in the context of decolonization can contribute to guaranteeing the right to self-determination.[30]

2.2.2 *Western Sahara Case—Can Tribes Be the People?*

Nations and peoples are usually defined as groups that share certain common characteristics, such as language, culture, and a sense of mutual identity. But they are not the only groups that have such characteristics. Similar connections can be found among tribes, although they are not seen as nations. How then does a nation differ from a tribe? Generally, tribes are smaller than nations, but there are also large tribes and small nations. Are the people part of the tribe? Can the people be made up of different tribes? The following questions were addressed to the International Court of Justice (ICJ) in 1975 to bring an advisory opinion on the Western Sahara case: (1) Was the Western Sahara (Rio de Oro and Sakiet el Hamra) *res nullius* at the time of colonization by Spain? If the answer to the first question is in the negative, 2) what legal ties existed between this territory and both the Kingdom of Morocco and Mauritania as a whole?[31]

Western Sahara was part of Mauritania and Morocco, which in 1884 was colonized by Spain. In 1966, the process of decolonization began, and two of its neighbors—Morocco in 1956 and Mauritania in 1970—placed claims over Western Sahara. The General Assembly has shown interest in Western Sahara and has called on Spain to decolonize and organize a referendum that would have determinate the status of Western Sahara. Although Spain agreed to hold a referendum in 1975. Morocco and Mauritania prevailed in the UN the referendum to be postponed until ICJ considers Moroccan and Mauritanian territorial claims over Western Sahara. The General Assembly passed a resolution (GA res. 3292 (XXXIX)), and the referendum was postponed until UN General Assembly decides on the policy to be followed i.e. until the ICJ gave an advisory opinion—whether the people of Western Sahara had the right to self-determination, namely: Was Western Sahara

[28] Knop (2002), p. 56.

[29] Bhalla (1991); Brilmayer (1991); Duursma (1997), pp. 579–586.

[30] Hanauer (1995).

[31] Western Sahara, Request for Advisory Opinion, Written Statements and Documents (1979).

terra nullius before the Spanish occupation, and were there legal links between Western Sahara with the Kingdom of Morocco and the Mauritanian entity?

Spain, Morocco, and Mauritania had their demands. The Kingdom of Morocco held that Western Sahara was a Moroccan land, separated due to colonization, and the basis for that claim was the argument that the sultan's law was already enforced on Western Sahara, so the tribes paid taxes and were under Morocco's jurisdiction. Mauritania did not dispute Morocco's jurisdiction over the tribes of Western Sahara but pointed out that although the Mauritanian state was created after Spanish colonization, the tribes of Western Sahara had links to the people of Mauritania, namely, they had a common origin, religion, language, and customs.

Spain stated that at the time of colonization, the territory was inhabited by peoples who had an organization and a certain way of life and created a sense of self-awareness and mutual solidarity and that the people of those tribes differed from those of Morocco and Mauritania. Spain opposed Morocco for a lack of solid evidence of jurisdiction and legal links to the tribes of Western Sahara (nomadic tribes) and argued that the sultan's power extended only to some tribes of Western Sahara but not to all. As for the links to Mauritania, Spain has confirmed that some of the tribes have links to the Mauritanian people but not to all of them.

The ICJ tried to strike a balance between the three positions. It concluded that there were links between Western Sahara, Morocco, and Mauritania but that they were cultural and social links that were not as important as the principle of territorial sovereignty and could not affect the application of Resolution 1514 (whose applicability was challenged by Morocco, putting the Treaty from Madrid in 1975, which divided Western Sahara between Morocco and Mauritania, over international law) and that a referendum should be conducted to give the tribes of Western Sahara maximum space for their own further determination.[32] But the Court referred not to "the people" but to "the peoples" and limited the legal consequences of their opinion by saying that this opinion did not affect Western Sahara's right to self-determination. Therefore, the Court set Western Sahara's self-determination as an empty concept, leaving its case, the procedures, and the outcome open to the parties.[33] But apart from this, in its opinion, the ICJ stressed the concept of terra nullius as land that no one ever claimed and is open for grabs. But in this case, the Court found that the land is being populated, that it belongs to that population living on it, and that it is not open for grabs—i.e., the Court found that the Saharans were distant people who historically populated that land[34] and that their territories were not terra nullius.[35]

The Court only found that there are nomadic tribes that have common characteristics and are often in conflict. Because of this nomadic character, it cannot be said that they had established the power of the Sultan of Morocco and that there is some

[32] ICJ Reports, Advisory opinions and orders Western Sahara (1975).

[33] See more at Cassese (1995), Epstein (2009) and Knop (2002).

[34] Knop (2002).

[35] Shaw (2008).

territorial sovereignty. As to the claim of Mauritania, which was not a state, the Court should have rejected its claim on that basis, but the Court did not do so but examined other legal links and concluded that there were racial, linguistic, religious, cultural, and economic links between the emirates of Mauritania and the Sahara tribes, but they lacked joint activities, and mutual institutions or bodies were at a minimum. Therefore, they do not form an entity. The Court found that there was a Mauritanian nation, but it lacked a binding force. It concluded that despite Western Sahara's historic links with Mauritania and Morocco, the people of Western Sahara have a right to self-determination.[36] Consequently, Mauritania, Morocco, and Spain agreed to a tripartite administration agreement and set a date for Spain to withdraw from Western Sahara in 1976. But in 1975, the UN adopted two contradictory resolutions for a referendum,[37] so the troops from Mauritania and Morocco entered Western Sahara. Two and a half months later, the Assembly of Western Sahara expressed satisfaction at the unification with Morocco and Mauritania. It was opposed by the Western Sahara independence movement, after which a conflict broke out. In 1979, Mauritania withdrew its demands, but Morocco's demands remained. Spain disagreed. The UN adopted numerous resolutions to resolve the dispute peacefully, including a peace plan calling for a ceasefire, prisoner exchanges, and a referendum to determine whether the people of Western Sahara are for independence or favor remaining under Morocco's power.[38]

Since 1991, the UN has implemented a ceasefire. Today, most of the territory of Western Sahara is controlled by Morocco and a small part by the National Liberation Movement of Western Sahara, Polisario, which receives assistance from Algeria.[39] For many, the current situation in Western Sahara begins with the question: How useful is it to have UN backing when powerful nations like the United States, France, and Spain are either abstaining on the issue or directly denying the people of Western Sahara the right to self-determination?[40]

2.2.3 Indigenous Peoples

Indigenous peoples are the third and most recent category of right holders of self-determination recognized in international law, that is, despite reservations of states to affirm indigenous self-determination, questioning the extension of the right to self-determination outside the colonial context. However, it becomes prominent that indigenous peoples are a separate legal category that should not be subjugated to

[36] ICJ Reports, Advisory opinions and orders Western Sahara (1975), par. 162.

[37] The question of Western Sahara in the United Nations (1980).

[38] See more at Cassese (1995) and Epstein (2009).

[39] Statement by the F. Polisario (2009).

[40] Although in 2020, US President Donald Tramp, recognized Moroccan sovereignty over disputed territory, although that decision under the Biden administration is under the consideration to be reversed, see Bolton (2020).

minorities or be guaranteed minority rights. They do not perceive themselves as minorities, and according to them (and to many theorists of international law), they are the "original peoples," the first ones occupying the territory, previously self-governed nations, and their rights are undoubtedly linked to the memories of the displacement from the land to which they belonged and with which they have a strong connection.[41] UN Special Rapporteur Jose Martinez Cobo defined indigenous peoples as "(…) those who have a historical continuity with pre-colonial and pre-invasion societies that have developed in their territories and are regarded as distinct from other sectors of society that now dominate those territories, or from parts of them. They form non-dominant sectors of society and are determined to protect, develop and pass on to the future generations their ancestral territories and their ethnic identity as a basis for their continued existence as a people, in accordance with their own culture models, social institutions and legal systems."[42] In his attempt to find common ground, Special Rapporteur S. James Anaya proposed an approach by which he distinguishes between the essential aspects of the principle of self-determination and the principle as a remedy. Substantial self-determination includes the right to participate in the creation or changing of institutions or governments, as well as the right to make choices, while self-determination as a remedy can follow after a violation of rights and can be applied in the case of indigenous peoples. Anaya suggested the foundations for indigenous self-determination, such as nondiscrimination, respect for cultural integrity, control over land and resources, social justice and development, and self-government.[43]

The UN General Working Group on Indigenous Peoples, established in 1982 by the Subcommittee on Prevention of Discrimination and the Protection of Minorities, provided the general impetus for determining the character of indigenous peoples. In 1994, it submitted to the UN Commission on Human Rights a Draft Declaration of the Rights of Indigenous Peoples, which placed the indigenous peoples in the category of peoples entitled to self-determination in accordance with international law, subject to the same criteria and restrictions as applied to other peoples in compliance with the UN Charter.[44] In this regard, the 2007 UN Declaration on the Rights of Indigenous Peoples contains several articles that affirm the principle of internal self-determination for indigenous peoples through the establishment and control of educational institutions in their mother tongue, territorial autonomy, control over natural resources, and promoting and maintaining institutional structures, customs, procedures, and practices in accordance with internationally recognized human rights standards.[45] Hence, the rights of indigenous peoples illustrate the broad doctrine of the rights of the peoples but in another sense represent a dramatic expansion of this doctrine. For the first time since decolonization, the right to self-determination

[41] See more at Moore (2003).

[42] Martínez Cobo (1981).

[43] Anaya (1996) and Anaya and Puig (2017).

[44] Wilson (1996).

[45] United Nations Declaration on the Rights of Indigenous Peoples (2007).

was granted to a subnational group within an existing state and, for many, extended the boundaries of international law.[46]

Indigenous peoples are subject to thorough analysis, but in terms of the range of rights to be enjoyed and the basis for them, they are undoubtedly holders of the right to self-determination. They have this right for several reasons, including the systematic repression (still) exercised by the central government because of the conquest and the complete marginalization they had experienced or are still experiencing, and therefore, they are in an inferior position.[47] Their original culture has been degraded and destroyed, mainly through the policies of the white settler societies within which they live, so they need enormous lifestyle transformations and hence separate governance.[48] In terms of the way indigenous peoples should achieve self-determination, opinions vary in theory—ranging from independence through secession to territorial or nonterritorial autonomy within the unitary, federal, or confederate state structure.[49]

2.2.4 *Gibraltar Case, Difficulties in Defining the Category of People Who Are Right Holders of Self-Determination*

Gibraltar was a Spanish island that Spain ceded to Britain through the Treaty of Utrecht in 1713. This agreement restricts the UK from owning the island, i.e., if the UK decides to sell it or alienate Gibraltar in any way, Spain has the right to preempt it.[50] From the beginning, the Treaty of Utrecht has caused much controversy, and Spain has occasionally alleged British violations of the Treaty of Utrecht. Subsequent treaties periodically confirmed it (such as the Treaty of Madrid, 1721; Treaty of Sevilla, 1729; Treaty of Aix-la-Chapelle, 1748; Treaty of Paris, 1763; and Treaty of Versailles, 1783), although none shed additional light on its interpretation.[51] The United Kingdom ruled Gibraltar, and during the decolonization period, Gibraltar was granted the status of a UN non-self-governing territory, administered by the United Kingdom. After becoming a member of the UN, Spain immediately opposed this UK mandate. Based on the consensus in 1964, the two countries were obliged to begin negotiations, but no solution was reached.[52] In 1967, the British authorities conducted a referendum calling on the people of Gibraltar to decide between two options—to be ruled by Spain or to be governed by the UK. The people voted for UK administration, but according to the UN, the referendum was not in line with

[46] Wilson (1996).

[47] Moore (2003).

[48] Kymlicka (1998), p. 31.

[49] Moore (2003) and Leviat (2003).

[50] Treaty of Peace and Friendship between Great Britain and Spain, signed at Utrecht, 13 July 1713.

[51] Waibel (2013).

[52] UNGA Res. 2070 (1965).

previous negotiating resolutions, and the people were offered no other option except those two.[53] Spain believes that Gibraltar has no right to self-determination because the people of Gibraltar are not indigenous peoples but consist of English settlers.[54] Today, Gibraltar is a British overseas territory and was part of the EU as Great Britain's dependent territory. The UN Decolonization Committee places Gibraltar on the list of non-self-governing territories.[55] Since 1963, numerous resolutions have been adopted calling on the two countries to find a solution. The General Assembly, on an annual basis, adopts decisions concerning Gibraltar.[56]

2.3 Nation

Nations are the bearers of the principle of equal rights and self-determination. Although not explicitly mentioned in the formulation of this principle, in the Universal Declaration on Human Rights,[57] nations are indirectly covered by the term *people*. In Resolution 637, "The right of peoples and nations to self-determination,"[58] the UN General Assembly stated that "(…) the right of peoples and nations to self-determination is a prerequisite to the full enjoyment of all fundamental human rights," and it recommended that "(…) The States Members of the United Nations shall uphold the principle of self-determination of all peoples and nations."[59]

But neither nations nor states have always existed under all circumstances. In its contemporary political relations, the concept of a *nation* historically is a very young one. Although systematically used from 1830 onward, by 1884, the word *nation* meant a population of a province, country, or kingdom. The height of the French Revolution in 1789 is considered to be "the birthday of the nation," but at that time, the nation was perceived as one and indivisible, representing a group of citizens whose collective sovereignty was constructed in a state that was their political expression. The equation nation = state = people, and especially sovereign people, undoubtedly linked the nation to a particular territory, but the nation had nothing to do with ethnicity, language, or anything similar. Ethnic differences, according to this revolutionary view, were of secondary importance. In the early nineteenth century, the number of nation-states was very small. With the collapse of the Ottoman and Austro-Hungarian empires, the basic question was: Which of the many European populations, which can be classified as nations, will seek a state, and to which of the

[53] Waibel (2013).

[54] Trinidad (2021) and Cassese (1995).

[55] Gibraltar, The United Nations and Decolonization.

[56] GA Res. on Gibraltar (since 2008).

[57] UNGA Res. 217 A (III), Universal Declaration on Human Rights (1948).

[58] UNG/RES/637 The right of peoples and nations to self-determination (1952).

[59] UNG/RES/637 The right of peoples and nations to self-determination (1952).

existing states will be attached the character of a nation?[60] Friedrich List, the inspirer of the later Historical School of German Economists, clearly formulated the characteristics of a nation—it had to be of sufficient size to form a viable entity capable of development. If it falls below this threshold, the nation has no historical justification. So a large population and a rather large territory rich in diverse national resources were the basic conditions for functional nationality.[61]

According to Eric Hobsbawm, in this period, there were three criteria according to which a people could be firmly classified as a nation—always proving it was large enough to cross the threshold. The first one was the existence of a historical relationship with an existing state or with a state that had existed for a long time in the recent past. The second was the existence of a long-established cultural elite, with written national literature and administrative jargon. The third criterion was the proven ability to withstand a war. The nation, as a large community capable of surviving, was achieved only in the twentieth century and meant progress and the logical assimilation of smaller communities into larger ones. Elements on which (in this view) the nation was based were as follows:

- *Language*: the official language or the language of the culture of the rulers and the elite, which usually became the current language of the modern state through public education and other administrative mechanisms
- *Ethnicity*: a term in common use, almost always associated with a common origin, blood, kinship, and awareness of belonging to a permanent political community[62]

In the classical liberal era, after abandoning the threshold principle, every group that considered itself a nation claimed and demanded the right to self-determination, which ultimately meant the right to a separate sovereign independent state. The motto was "For every nation—a state," and ethnicity and language became central, decisive, and even the sole criterion for potential nationality.[63]

For Benedict Anderson, the possibility of the emergence, or of the imagination, of a nation arose historically only then and only where these three fundamental cultural concepts occurred: (1) the idea that only one written language offered access to ontological truth; (2) the belief that society, like monks, is organized around high centers of value; (3) the conception of temporality, according to which the roots of the world and man were identical—they lost their axiomatic grip on the

[60] The first, etymological meaning of the word nation initiates—origin, or origin (*nassance*—in French—birth), and is equal to "*nation*" and *state*, i.e. in the context of the American and French revolutions, equal to what would be called today a nation-state, Hobsbawm (1993).

[61] It was considered that small, and especially small and backward nationalities, can be self-realized only by merging with larger nations. Only in this way would they be able to make their contribution to humanity. Thus, some nations or nationalities were condemned to never become complete nations, Hobsbawm (1993).

[62] These are the concepts of the nation in the era of bourgeois liberalism from 1830–1880, Hobsbawm (1993).

[63] Hobsbawm (1993).

human mind. Then a new way of connecting was sought, and nothing made this quest more successful than the so-called print capitalism, which made people think more about themselves and compare themselves with others in completely new ways.[64] For Anderson, the printing languages are the ones that laid the foundations for national consciousness and invented nationalism. "(…) Neither economic interest nor liberalism or enlightenment created or could have created the kind and form of the imagined community (…)."[65] The nation became imagined, and once imagined, it was modeled, adapted, and transformed.[66]

But since its inception, theorists have tried to define the notion of the nation, namely, what exactly is a nation? The different attempts represent combinations of objective and subjective elements that a nation or its members must have in order to be characterized as a nation, but all attempts to fully think of the term have failed.

For Ernest Gellner, two people belong to the same nation if and only if they share the same culture and recognize each other as belonging to the same nation. In other words, nations are an artifact of human convictions, loyalty, and solidarity. These are cultural and voluntary aspects of what constitutes a nation, but for Gellner, none of them is appropriate to define a nation.[67]

Yael Tamir considers that a nation is a community that shares a set of objective characteristics, grouped under the guise of culture and national consciousness.[68] According to her, "(…) a group is defined as a nation if it simultaneously fulfills a sufficient number of common objective characteristics, such as language, history or territory and self-awareness of one's own diversity."[69]

Alfred Koban considers that a nation is "(…) every territorial community whose members are conscious of themselves as members of the community and who wish to maintain the identity of their community."

For Murray N. Rothbard, a nation is a complex of subjective feelings of nationality based on objective reality. People are born into one or several overlapping communities, and the community usually includes an ethnic group with specific values,

---

[64] Anderson (1998).

[65] Anderson (1998), p. 100.

[66] The Creoles (Spanish colonizers of the Americas), pilgrims, and provincial Creole printers played a key role in carrying out this task, instilling in the newly conquered American territories an awareness of themselves as different from others. Regarding this issue see more at Anderson (1998).

[67] A group of people (for example, the inhabitants of a certain territory or a group that speaks a certain language) becomes a nation if, and when, the members of that group will clearly recognize each other's certain rights and duties based on their common membership in it. Their mutual recognition transforms them into a nation, and not some other common features, which, whatever they may be, separate them from the category of non-members of the nation, Gellner (2001).

[68] "I do not intend to idealize the community or to rely on unrealistic assumptions about the supposedly harmonious nature of social relations. The truth is that we may dislike or disagree with other members of our community. What then forms the basis of our relationship? It is neither love nor sympathy, but the connection, the belief that we all belong to the group whose existence we value. Feelings of shame or anger reflect this feeling of connection, as well as feelings of pride and love," Tamir (2002), p. 172.

[69] Tamir (2002), p. 131.

culture, religious beliefs, and traditions. In general, the individual is born in "one country," with its own specific and historical context—time and place, with its own specific neighbor.[70]

Collective self-awareness and self-confidence are the dominant notions on which Benedict Anderson tries to construct the notion of a nation: "(…) The nation is an imagined political community—imagined both as inherently limited, and sovereign."[71] It is conceived—"imagined"—because members of even the smallest nation will never meet most of their compatriots, never face them, or at least never hear about them, even though each of them lives in the consciousness of their own picture—*imago*. A nation is imagined as limited because even the largest, the one that may encompass billions of human beings, has ultimate boundaries behind which another nation lies. Also, a nation is imagined as *sovereign*, and finally, it is imagined as a *community* because whatever current inequalities and exploitations may prevail in it, a nation is always perceived as a deep, horizontal fellowship. It is a historical fatality and represents a community conceived through language.

Hugh Sutton-Watson thinks that no scientifically accurate definition of a nation can be imagined, even though the phenomenon existed and still exists. The most that can be said about a nation is that it exists when a significant number of people within a community consider themselves to be a nation or behave as if they are a nation, considers Sutton-Watson.[72]

The lecture by the ethnologist Ernest Renan, *Qu'est-ce qu'une nation?* (What Is a Nation?),[73] held at Sorbonne in 1862, is certainly one of the most cited attempts to clarify the nation question. For Renan, the formation of a nation is primarily a spiritual principle, meaning a category of spirit that transcends the localizing aspects of race, language, interests, religious affinity, geography, military, and the like. "No, not even the country, more than race, makes up the nation. The earth provides a foundation, a field to fight, and a field to work on, but man is the one who gives the heart. In the formulation of that—'something collective,' which somebody calls—'the people,' the position of the man is essential. In this process, nothing material is never enough. The nation is a spiritual principle, derived from the crucial complexes in history, it is a spiritual family, not a group determined by the configuration of the terrain."[74]

Finally, what does a nation really represent? For Renan, the answer directly aims at patriotism: "The nation is the heart," Renan says, and that heart consists of two things: "One is the past and the other the present. One is the shared wealth of memories; the other is the current agreement, the desire to live together, the desire to continue the transfer of the common legacy, which has been obtained in its entirety, indivisible."[75]

---

[70] Rothbard (2017).

[71] Anderson (1998), p. 100.

[72] Seton-Watson (2020).

[73] Renan (1882) (n.b. the translation of the essay is done by the author).

[74] Renan (1882).

[75] Renan (1882).

According to Max Weber, what defines a "nation" is the common high culture, and it cannot normally survive without its own political shell—the state.[76] Same as Hobsbawm's view, a nation is closely linked to a modern state, which does not grow naturally but develops through social engineering—nationalism, which is able to transform old cultures, rediscover them, or erase them.[77]

Apart from the many definitions of what constitutes a nation, we generally distinguish two views that accordingly classify nations into Western and Eastern models, each with its own characteristics. The Eastern model of a nation, which appeared in Eastern Europe and Asia, is based on the "ethnic" understanding of a nation. Its primary focus is the emphasis on a community by birth and culture. Whether a member leaves his community or emigrates to another, he inevitably—organically—remains a member of the community after his birth and carries its seal forever. In other words, a nation is, above all, a community of people of the same lineage.[78] According to the Western world view, a nation is a political community that implies at least some common institutions and a code of rights and duties for all members of the community.[79] A nation also points to a certain social space, a fairly precisely marked and restricted territory with which the members of the nation identify and which they consider they belong. Anthony D. Smith believes that the Western experience has had a powerful and in fact a major influence on the notion of a unit called the nation. It is predominantly a spatial or territorial understanding that nations must possess compact and determined territories. The people and the territories must belong to each other. The country must be a "historical" country, a "homeland," and a "cradle" of the people, although that country is sometimes not a country of true origin. Additional elements of this model of a nation are legal-political communities, communities of laws, and institutions that are governed by a single political idea. All members of the nation are legally equal, enjoying legal and political rights. Nations have a certain measure of common culture and certain civic ideology, which is a set of common notions and aspirations, sentiments, and ideas that connect the inhabitants to a single homeland.[80]

Therefore, it can be concluded that today, the closest version of what constitutes a nation would be the democratic version of the definition of a nation, which finds justification in democratic ideals. According to this aspect, nation is a synonym for subjects, i.e., a group of individuals living under the same laws. This stems directly from the principle explicitly formulated in the Universal Declaration of Human Rights of 1948, according to which everyone has the right to participate in the management of their country, directly or through freely elected representatives.[81]

---

[76] Weber (1976).

[77] Hobsbawm (1993).

[78] Smith (1998).

[79] Smith (1998).

[80] Smith (1998), p. 23.

[81] UNGA Res. 217 A (III) Universal Declaration on Human Rights (1948).

2.3.1 *Scotland's Right to Self-Determination*

Scotland has a population of about five million inhabitants and occupies the northern third of the island of the United Kingdom. English, Scottish, and Scottish Gaelic are the three official languages of Scotland. Scotland has its own national symbols and anthem. The Scottish educational system differs from the educational system in the rest of the UK, and its healthcare system is self-financed by the Scottish and their government directorates. Scotland is represented in the British Parliament and in the European Parliament. Although it is located within the UK, Scotland has limited self-government, and the constitutional status of Scotland has been the subject of a lasting debate. The Kingdom of Scotland grew as an independent sovereign state in the early Middle Ages and existed until 1707. Scotland first entered into a personal union with the Kingdom of England and then, in 1707, into a political union as well, creating the Kingdom of Great Britain. The union was formalized in both the Treaty of Union 1706 and the Acts of Union adopted by the parliaments of both countries, despite the resistance of the anti-unionists.[82] In 1801, the Kingdom of Great Britain entered into a political union with the Kingdom of Ireland, and together, they created the United Kingdom of Great Britain and Ireland (hereinafter referred to as Great Britain).

Despite the fact that Scotland was part of the United Kingdom for more than 400 years, the Scottish legal system has remained separate from those of England, Wales, and Northern Ireland. Scotland has always been a distinct jurisdiction with regard to public and private laws. Throughout the centuries, the existence of separate legal, educational, and religious institutions—other than those in the UK—contributed to extending the Scottish culture and creating a separate identity. This independence was also reflected in relation to public services. Furthermore, for many decades, the Scottish legal system was unique because it was a legal system without a parliament. Additionally, Scotland has always had a separate currency. Scotland developed the desire for greater autonomy as a result of a cultural and economic renaissance. A proposal for the devolution of the British jurisdiction was included in the referendum in 1997, and in 1998, the UK Parliament adopted the Scotland Act[83] (the Act), which restored the Scottish Parliament. In 1999, elections were held, and the Scottish Parliament and Government came into power. But even when the Scottish Parliament acts in accordance with its jurisdiction under the Act, it is restricted by the European Convention of Human Rights and EU law.

The Scottish Parliament has jurisdiction in many areas relating to Scotland as well as over most Scotland-specific laws. The Act specifically established provisions for the election of Members of Parliament (MPs) and the internal procedures for the work of the Parliament. The Act granted the UK Parliament jurisdiction to

---

[82] Based on this agreement, the Scottish and English Parliaments were united and together formed the Parliament of the United Kingdom in Westminster Palace London. *See* Act of Union, 1707, 6 Ann., c. 11 (U.K.).

[83] See Scotland Act (1998), c. 46.

adopt legislation that applied to Scotland and reiterated the concept of Westminster parliamentary sovereignty. The Act also provided for the creation of the Scottish executive order, transferring executive power away from the UK. The Act set out the legislative competences of the Scottish Parliament, but rather than outlining which issues the Scottish Parliament controlled, the Act listed the issues that are not part of the Parliament's competences. Thus, the Parliament of the United Kingdom, according to the Act, retains the power to determine fiscal matters—including taxes, social security, defense, international relations, and TV broadcasting.[84] The Act established mechanisms for resolving disputes regarding jurisdiction between the Scottish Parliament and executive power, but final decisions regarding these issues are made by the Supreme Court of the United Kingdom. The Act also provided for the adoption and modification of the powers of the Scottish Parliament and Scottish Government with an agreement between both parliaments.[85]

The Scotland Act of 2012[86] (the 2012 Act) transmitted additional powers to the Scottish Parliament, among them particular fiscal powers. Unsatisfied, the Scottish National Party attempted to block the 2012 Act. While the Scottish National Party agreed to certain parts of the 2012 Act, it ultimately opposed it, especially the tax legislation proposals. Through negotiation, an agreement was reached, jurisdiction remained intact, and compliance was achieved.[87] In 2012, the UK Government and the Scottish Government also executed an agreement—the Edinburg Agreement—where they agreed that both governments would accept referendum results and continue to work together regardless of the outcome.[88] The Scottish National Party subsequently announced its plan for a referendum on Scotland's independence, which took place in September 2014. After a huge campaign, the number of votes for no independence for Scotland won by a very small margin.[89] After the Brexit referendum in 2016 and the UK leaving the EU in 2020, the Scottish Government, led by the Scottish National Party, drafted a referendum bill proposing that the vote for independence should take place on October 19, 2023.[90] In the case, that was heard in November 2022, the UK Supreme Court decided if the First Minister of Scotland has the legal powers to press ahead with the vote, and in a unanimous judgment ruled

---

[84] BBC Scotland is a constituent part of the British Broadcasting Corporation, a publicly financed medium of Great Britain. Scotland has its own printed media and radio.

[85] See Act of Union, 1707, 6 Ann., c. 11 (U.K.).

[86] Scotland Act (2012), c. 11.

[87] The Parliament of the United Kingdom did not agree to pass this Act without the prior consent of the Scottish Parliament. Before the Scotland Act of 2012, the Scottish Parliament (Constituencies) Act from 2004, the Constitutional Reform Act from 2005, and the Scotland Act from 1998 were amended, and the institutions of Scotland underwent procedural reforms.

[88] See Agreement between the United Kingdom Government and the Scottish Government on a referendum on independence for Scotland, Scottish Gov't (Oct. 15, 2012).

[89] See more at Shikova (2016).

[90] See more at Scottish government, Next steps in independence referendum set out (2022).

out that the Scottish Parliament does not have the power to legislate for a referendum on Scottish independence,[91]

2.4 Minorities and the Right to Self-Determination

Although there is no generally accepted definition of *minorities*, certain proposals for the definition of such a term have objective and subjective elements. Objective elements are pointing toward the group's ethnic, religious, and linguistic characteristics that differ from the rest of the population of the state in which they live, the smaller size of the group than the rest of the population, and the group's nondominant position within the state. Some of the definitions also include citizenship, though some theorists say this element should not be taken into account since it excludes immigrant groups. Subjective elements, on the other hand, are related to the group's desire to maintain a separate identity, as well as a subjective belief in a common origin.[92]

One of the most quoted definitions of minorities is Francesco Capotorti's definition. Francesco Capotorti was a special rapporteur of the United Nations Sub-Commission on Prevention of Discrimination and Protection of Minorities, and according to him, a minority is (…) A group numerically inferior to the rest of the population of a State, in a non-dominant position, whose members—being nationals of the State—possess ethnic, religious or linguistic characteristics differing from those of the rest of the population and show, if only implicitly, a sense of solidarity, directed toward preserving their culture, traditions, religion or language (…)."[93]

An additional question that brings dilemmas about minorities is the size of the group, i.e., how big the group should be to be considered a minority. When setting the criterion for the minimum number needed for recognizing a group as a minority, several problems arise because the threshold can be too small for some countries and at the same time too big for others. Within the UN system, the predominant notion is that although even the smallest group that meets different qualifications should be considered a minority, from a practical purpose, only those groups that constitute a significant part of the population of the country are usually referred to as minorities.[94] Although that is a condition that takes majority as a point of

---

[91] See more at Scottish independence: Will there be a second referendum, BBC News (2022). https://commonslibrary.parliament.uk/supreme-court-judgment-on-scottish-independence-referendum/#:~:text=In%20a%20unanimous%20judgment%2C%20the%20Supreme%20Court%20has,to%20legislate%20for%20a%20referendum%20on%20Scottish%20independence., accessed 19 Jun 2023

[92] See more at Renan (1882); Henrard (2000); Weber (1976); Poutignat and Streiff-Fenart (2009), pp. 37–38.

[93] Capotorti (1979).

[94] Definition and Classification of Minorities (1949), Memorandum submitted by the Secretary General, United Nations Economic and Social Council, E-CN.4- Sub.2-85.

reference and leaves the smallest minorities unprotected or under the capacity of the state to protect them, [95] still it remains an existing reality.

There has been relatively little substantial development in international law concerning minorities since 1945. Namely, minority rights are more seen as individual rather than collective rights (they refer more to the individual members of the minority group than *per se* to the minority group as a collective) and are granted with legal instruments that do not always envisage the existence of dynamic rights.[96] Nevertheless, it is generally accepted that minorities do not have a right to self-determination, especially in the form of acquiring independent statehood. However, there are a multitude of attempts to expand the scope of self-determination in a way that will involve the minorities and subgroups within the state. The most acceptable one is the stance that minorities have a right to self-determination but in its internal form, i.e., as a right to internal self-determination. In that respect, opinions vary among theoreticians, as well as among practicians.

Judge Rosalyn Higgins considers that in the postcolonial world, it is a mistake to link the rights of minorities with the right to self-determination.[97] There is no legal basis that provides a linguistic minority a right to secession, and minorities can be entitled to the right to self-determination only in extreme cases—if they are treated unbearably.[98] To give an equivalent legal position of *the people* (as a legitimate holder of the right to self-determination) with the minorities conceals a potential danger for the exercise of the right to self-determination through its external way—the secession. In that respect, minorities can have the right to self-determination, but only in its internal form.[99]

Kamal Shehadi finds ethnic self-determination a generator of problems and conflicts.[100] Ethnic nationalism defines a nation as a political community that shares certain genealogical roots, often mythical compared to a real one. As a result, ethnic self-determination can (1) maximize demands for self-determination—demands for an independent state, even when demands have the potential to destabilize the entire region and lead to war; (2) exclude citizens who also live in the territory and are of a different ethnic background from the majority, causing the forced removal of other ethnic groups from the common territory, even at the cost of massacres; (3) include all members of the group, even those who do not want to be a part of the ethnic national community. Finally, the ethnic

[95] Cardenas and Canas (2002) and Gayim (2006).

[96] Cassese (1995).

[97] Higgins (2003).

[98] Franck et al. (2002), p. 377.

[99] On the UN level, this restriction is reflected in several documents. One of them is the 1993 Declaration on the Protection of the Rights of Persons Belonging to National, Ethnic, Religious or Linguistic Minorities, which guarantees minorities only weak forms of internal self-determination such as the participation of minority representatives in the central government, UNGA Declaration on the Rights of Persons Belonging to National, Ethnic, Religious and Linguistic Minorities (1993).

[100] Shehadi (1993), pp. 3–10.

approach reduces the importance of a representative government as an integral part of self-determination.

Pandemonium, Satan's Capital in Milton's "Lost Paradise," is the title of a study by UN Ambassador Daniel Patrick Moynihan, which emerged after the Cold War, exploring the ethnicity of international politics and the state of hopelessness and chaos that followed. In the study, Moynihan links *demos* to the right to democratic government and *ethnicity* to Pandemonium or "postmodern tribalism"—endless fragmentations and secessions. In the "Lost Paradise," Pandemonium is a place of darkness and demagogy, and Moynihan compares that with the chaos caused by the breakup of the Roman Empire and Habsburg's monarchy after World War I. During the processes of disintegration, according to Moynihan, the modest village structures of tolerance and coexistence among many ethnic groups were lost, and that led to the transition from paradise to chaos.[101]

Thomas Franck holds the same line of thinking. For Franck, postmodern tribalism is the promotion of a political and legal environment that helps dissolve multinational and multicultural states to form a new state composed of one nationality or from one culture. The use of the term "tribalism" indicates the primitivism of such decisions. If a democratic government creates a bright universe of *demos* that will persuade us to accept that the right of democratic government has its roots in self-determination, then postmodern tribalism implies the dark underworld of ethnicity and interprets self-determination through the right to secession, considers Franck.[102]

The link between internal self-determination and the adequate system of protection of minorities is indisputable, in particular, the link between the right to internal self-determination and the right to minority identity. Not only does the internal self-determination of minorities improve the system for their protection, but also its acceptance leads to the further promotion of the substance and achievement of these rights.[103] While subnational minority groups are not right holders of external self-determination, they have autonomy as an expression of their internal self-determination. Through such autonomy, they can establish and influence their own political order and control all issues that matter most in their lives, thereby protecting their cultural, ethnic, and historical identity.[104] Still, as the concept of minority rights became generalized, the doctrine of minority rights continued to be driven by political concerns and considerations rather than concerns and considerations regarding jurisprudential consistency.[105] But despite the lack of legal clarity of the concept, in legal theory, there is at least a consensus on the minimum content of international rights relating to minorities, in which the principles of equality before

---

[101] Moynihan (1993).

[102] Franck (1992), pp. 46–91.

[103] Henrard (2000).

[104] Cardenas and Canas (2002).

[105] Wilson (1996).

the law and nondiscrimination (which acquired the status of customary law) are fundamental. Apart from applying the principle of nondiscrimination, minority rights are best realized through special measures for (members) of the minorities. In addition to these measures, minorities can also be guaranteed various forms of internal self-determination, such as territorial autonomy, nonterritorial autonomy, decentralization, federalism, and different measures that enable their adequate protection.[106]

References

Act of Union (1707). https://www.parliament.uk/about/living-heritage/evolutionofparliament/legislativescrutiny/act-of-union-1707/. Accessed 07 Aug 2022

Agreement between the United Kingdom Government and the Scottish Government on a referendum on independence for Scotland, (Oct. 15, 2012). https://www.webarchive.org.uk/wayback/archive/20150218122536/http://www.gov.scot/About/Government/concordats/Referendum-on-independence. Accessed 07 Aug 2022

Anaya J (1996) Indigenous people in international law. Oxford University Press

Anaya J, Puig S (2017) Mitigating state sovereignty: the duty to consult with indigenous peoples. Arizona Legal Studies Discussion Paper: 16–42

Anderson B (1998) Замислени заедници (Imagined communities). Kultura, Skopje

Bhalla RS (1991) The right of self-determination in international law. In: Twining W (ed) Issues of self-determination. Aberdeen University Press, Aberdeen

Bolton J (2020) Biden Must Reverse Course on Western Sahara. https://foreignpolicy.com/2020/12/15/biden-reverse-course-western-sahara/. Accessed 7 Aug 2022

Brilmayer L (1991) Secession and self-determination: a territorial interpretation. Yale J Int Law 16:177–202

Capotorti F (1979) Study on the right of persons belonging to ethnic, religious and linguistic minorities, united nations. UN. https://undocs.org/en/E/CN.4/Sub.2/384/Rev.1. Accessed 07 Aug 2022

Cardenas EJ, Canas MF (2002) The limits of self-determination at self –determination of peoples. In: Danspeckgruber W (ed) Self-determination of peoples, community, nation and state in interdependent world. Lynne Rienner Publishers, pp 101–119

Cassese A (1995) Self-determination of the peoples, a legal reappraisal. Cambridge University Press

Chaumont C (1973) Cours général de droit international. Politique étrangère:380–385

Cobo MJ (1981) Study of the problem of discrimination against indigenous populations: final report submitted by the special rapporteur. 1981E/CN.4/Sub.2/476, https://www.un.org/development/desa/indigenouspeoples/publications/2014/09/martinez-cobo-study/. Accessed 7 Aug 2022

Cristescu A (1981) The right to self-determination, historical and current development on the basis of United Nations instruments. UN

Definition and Classification of Minorities, 1949, Memorandum submitted by the Secretary General, United Nations Economic and Social Council, E-CN.4- Sub.2-85. https://digitallibrary.un.org/record/701713?ln=en. Accessed 07 Aug 2022

Doehring K (1994) Self-determination. In: Simma B (ed) The Charter of the United Nations: a commentary. C H Beck, Munich, pp 56–72

[106] Henrard (2000).

Duursma JS (1997) Fragmentation and the international relations of micro-states: self-determination and statehood. Leiden J Int Law 10:579–586
Epstein P (2009) Behind closed doors: "Autonomous colonization" in post United Nations era-the case of Western Sahara. Annu Surv Int Comp Law 15:107–143
Franck TM (1992) The emerging right of democratic governance. Am J Int Law 86:46–91
Franck TM et al (2002) L'integrite Teritoriale du Quebec dans l' Hypotehese de L'accession a la Souverainete. 1 Exposés et études. Bibliothèque nationale, Québec
Gayim E (2006) Minority and indigenous: interpretation and application of concepts in the politics of human rights, 20 The Erik Castrén institute reports. Erik Castrén Institute of International Law and Human Rights
Gellner E (2001) Нациите и национализмот (Nations and nationalism). Kultura, Skopje
General Assembly Resolutions on Gibraltar. https://www.un.org/dppa/decolonization/en/documents?key=decision%20gibraltar. Accessed 5 Jan 2023
Gibraltar, The United Nations and Decolonization. https://www.un.org/dppa/decolonization/en/nsgt/gibraltar#:~:text=Gibraltar%20has%20been%20on%20the,Charter%20of%20the%20United%20Nations. Accessed 5 Jan 2023
Hanauer LS (1995) The irrelevance of self-determination law to ethno- national conflict: a new look at Western Sahara case. Emory Int Law Rev 9:133
Hannum H (1990) Autonomy, sovereignty, and self-determination, the accommodation of conflict rights. University of Pennsylvania Press
Henrard K (2000) Devising an adequate system of minority protection. Kluwer Law International, Hague
Herder JG, Payne DG (eds) (2016) Outlines of a philosophy of the history of man. Create Space Independent Publishing Platform
Higgins R (2003) Self-determination and secession at secession and international law. In: Dahliz J (ed) Conflict avoidance and - regional appraisals. Asser Press
Hobsbawm E (1993) Нациите и национализмот по 1780 (Nations and nationalism since 1780). Kultura, Skopje
Hutchins RM et al (eds) (1952) John Stuart Mill, On liberty representative government & utilitarianism in Great Books of the Western World, vol 43. Encyclopedia Britannica, Chicago
ICJ Reports (1975) International court of justice reports of judgments, advisory opinions and orders Western Sahara. https://www.icj-cij.org/public/files/case-related/61/061-19751016-ADV-01-00-EN.pdf. Accessed 6 Aug 2022
Knop K (2002) Diversity and self-determination in the international law. Cambridge University Press
Kymlicka W (1996) Multicultural citizenship: a liberal theory of minority rights. Clarendon Press
Kymlicka W (1998) Finding our way: rethinking ethnocultural relations in Canada. Oxford University Press
Leviat JT (2003) Indigenous self-government. In: Macedo S, Buchanan (eds) Secession and self-determination. New York University Press
Ligue of Nations, Permanent Court of International Justice (1930). PCIJ Greco- Bulgarian Communities, Advisory Opinion. http://www.worldcourts.com/pcij/eng/decisions/1930.07.31_greco-bulgarian.htm. Accessed 07 Aug 2022
Moore M (2003) An historical argument for indigenous self-determination. In: Macedo S, Buchanan (eds) Secession and self-determination. New York University Press
Moynihan DP (1993) Pandemonium: ethnicity in international politics. Oxford University Press, New York
Next steps in independence referendum set out, 28 June 2022. https://www.gov.scot/news/next-steps-in-independence-referendum-set-out/. Accessed 07 Aug 2022
Patten A (2010) The most natural state: Herder and nationalism. Hist Polit Thought 34(4):657–689
Pavkovic A, Radan P (2007) Creating new states, theory and practice of secession. Ashgate Publishing Limited
Poutignat P, Streiff-Fenart J (2009) Teorije o etnicitetu (Theories of ethnicity). Biblioteka XX vek, Beograd

Renan E (1882) Qu'est –ce qu'une nation? Conférence en Sorbonne. http://www.iheal.univ-paris3.fr/sites/www.iheal.univ-paris3.fr/files/Renan_-_Qu_est-ce_qu_une_Nation.pdf. Accessed 07 Aug 2022

Report of the Secretary General on an Agenda for Peace – Preventive Diplomacy, Peace- making and Peace- Keeping, June 17, 1992, 31, ILM 953 (1992). https://www.un.org/ruleoflaw/files/A_47_277.pdf. Accessed 07 Aug 2022

Rothbard MN (2017) Nations by consent: decomposing the nation- state. J Libert Stud. http://mises.org/journals/jls/11_1/11_1_1.pdf. Accessed 07 Aug 2022

Scotland Act (1998). https://www.legislation.gov.uk/ukpga/1998/46/contents. Accessed 07 Aug 2022

Scotland Act (2012) The question of Western Sahara in the United Nations. Decolonization, United Nations Department of Political Affairs, Trusteeship and Decolonization (1980). https://www.un.org/dppa/decolonization/sites/www.un.org.dppa.decolonization/files/decon_num_17-1.pdf. Accessed 5 Jan 2023

Scottish independence: Will there be a second referendum? BBC News 21 July 2022. https://www.bbc.com/news/uk-scotland-scotland-politics-50813510. Accessed 07 Aug 2022

Seton-Watson H (2020) Nations and states an enquiry into the origins of nations and the politics of nationalism. Routledge

Shaw M (2008) International law. Cambridge University Press

Shehadi KS (1993) Ethnic self-determination and the break-up of states. The Adelphi Papers

Shikova N (2016) Practicing internal self-determination vis-a-vis vital quests for secession. German Law J 17(2):237–364

Smith AD (1998) Nationalni identitet (National identity). Biblioteka XX vek, Beograd

Statement by the F. Polisario. Caribbean regional seminar on the implementation of the Second international decade for eradication of colonialism, United Nations (2009). https://www.un.org/dppa/decolonization/sites/www.un.org.dppa.decolonization/files/2009_5_nsgt_western_sahara.pdf. Accessed 5 Jan 2023

Summers J (2007) Peoples and international law, how nationalism and self-determination shape a contemporary law of nations. Leiden, Boston

Tamir T (2002) Liberalni nacionalizam (Liberal nationalism). Filip Visnjic, Beograd

The Scotland Act, The Scottish Parliament. http://www.scottish.parliament.uk/visitandlearn/Education/21139.aspx. Accessed 07 Aug 2022

Treaty of Peace and Friendship between Great Britain and Spain, signed at Utrecht, 13 July 1713

Trinidad J (2021) Self-determination and contested peoplehood in Gibraltar: separating the law from the rhetoric. The Round Table. Commonwealth J Int Aff Gibraltar 3(110):347–356

Turp D (1996) The recognition of Québec's right of self-determination and its exercise within a novel body politic in self-determination. In: Clark D, Williamson R (eds) International perspectives. Palgrave Macmillan, London

UN Doc. A/2929, Annotations on the text of the draft International Covenants on Human Rights, 1955, A-C.3-SR.447, https://digitallibrary.un.org/record/748971?ln=en. Accessed 07 Aug 2022

UN Doc. A/AC.125/ SR.70, Special Committee on Principles of International Law Concerning Friendly Relations and Cooperation among the States, Summary record on the seventieth meeting, 1967. https://undocs.org/en/A/AC.125/SR.70. Accessed 07 Aug 2022

UNESCO, Meeting People's rights (Budapest), 1992., https://atom.archives.unesco.org/meeting-peoples-rights-budapest. Accessed 07 Aug 2022

UNG/RES/637 The right of peoples and nations to self-determination (1952). https://www.refworld.org/docid/3b00f0791c.html. Accessed 07 Aug 2022

UNGA Res 2625, Annex, Declaration on Principles of international law concerning friendly relations and cooperation among the states in accordance with the Charter of the United Nations, (1970)

UNGA Res. 1514, Declaration on the Granting of Independence to Colonial Countries and Peoples, (1960)

UNGA Res. 217 A (III), Universal Declaration on Human Rights (1948)

United Nations Declaration on the Rights of Indigenous Peoples (2007). https://www.un.org/development/desa/indigenouspeoples/declaration-on-the-rights-of-indigenous-peoples.html. Accessed 07 Aug 2022

United Nations General Assembly Resolution 2070 on the Question of Gibraltar (1965). file:///C:/Users/Dell/Downloads/A_RES_2070(XX)-EN.pdf. Accessed 5 Jan 2023

Waibel M (2013) Gibraltar, Max Planck Encyclopedias of International Law [MPIL]. https://opil.ouplaw.com/display/10.1093/law:epil/9780199231690/law-9780199231690-e1287?prd=EPIL&q=gibraltar. Accessed 5 Jan 2023

Waterbury J (2002) Avoiding the iron cage of legislated communal identity. In: Danspeckgruber W (ed) Self-determination of peoples, community, nation and state in interdependent world. Lynne Rienner Publishers, pp 119–145

Weber M (1976) The protestant ethic and the spirit of capitalism. Scribner

Western Sahara, Request for Advisory opinion, Written statements and documents (1979). https://www.icj-cij.org/public/files/case-related/61/9467.pdf. Accessed 5 Jan 2023

Wilson J (1996) Ethnic groups and the right to self-determination. Conn J Int Law 11(3):433–486

Chapter 3
Practicing the (External) Right to Self-Determination

3.1 Introduction

According to the traditional general division of the principle of self-determination, it has two aspects: an external and an internal one, depending on whether an entity that pledges the right to self-determination claims to exercise it "within" or "outside" of the existing state.

The right to self-determination in its narrower version means the right of the people to determine the political status of the state in which they would live, that is, to free themselves from foreign domination or colonial rule and to form their own independent state. In the UN setting, the right to self-determination of peoples in their external form is applicable in (a) a colonial context and (b) in the case of any foreign domination or occupation. According to this position, the right to self-determination is in line with the country's territorial integrity.

(a) Colonial Context

The principles proclaimed in Resolution 1514, entitled "Declaration on the Granting of Independence to Colonial Countries and Peoples," are stressing the need for the immediate termination of any domination over any peoples committed by foreign peoples—in any form or manifestation. The resolution declares: "(…) The subjection of peoples to alien subjugation, domination and exploitation constitute a denial of fundamental human rights, is contrary to the Charter of the United Nations and is an impediment to the promotion of world peace and co-operation (…)."[1] According to this resolution, the end of domination and the guarantee of independence should be complete, and any intention to undo any influence on the peoples who had gained independence on this basis should be prevented.[2]

[1] UNGA Res. 1514 (1960).

[2] UNGA Res. 1514 (1960).

N. Shikova, *Self-Determination and Secession*,
https://doi.org/10.1007/978-3-031-34322-3_3

Independence does not only mean political but also signifies cultural and economic independence. The principles of the Resolution are universally applicable—to all peoples in the world, without any restrictions (temporal, geographical, racial, etc.). They are valid not only for attaining but also for maintaining complete and absolute independence.[3] While the external right to self-determination under the colonial context was extremely popular in the 1960s and 1970s, today, demands for external self-determination on this basis are virtually nonexistent.

(b) Foreign Domination

As demands for external self-determination based on the traditional colonial context decline today, so do demands for external self-determination based on foreign domination of one state over another. However, this is primarily about nontraditional forms of foreign domination, such as military domination—when the troops of one country are stationed in another; economic dominance—when one country or group of countries is economically dominant over another; and cultural domination—when one country's culture is violently infiltrated into another. Except in very rare cases, the international community does not, in practice, take any concrete action on the requirements for the exercise of the right to external self-determination due to foreign domination but only affirms the view that nations should be free from foreign domination.[4]

Because of the outdated concept of colonialism, and the rare cases of foreign domination in the traditional sense, in the literature on modern self-determination, when referring to external self-determination, among other things, it is referred to as a process by which secessionist groups from the state seek to gain entry into the international society of states by breaking away from the state structure that does not represent them. However, there are authors who find that the division between internal and external self-determination is highly controversial, and they argue that the traditional internal-external self-determination division is not satisfactory and that multiple expressions of self-determination (which can differ among right holders) should be accepted.[5] However, there are authors for whom the right to self-determination of peoples has two aspects, and it is undoubtedly trapped in its external variant. Many of the authors distinguish different components of the principle of self-determination, apart from colonialism and foreign domination, such as the right of the people of an existing state to freely determine their status without external interference or to determine their own constitution or to achieve an autonomous status, self-government, or to establish a democratic system of government.[6] For some authors, the application of self-determination is based on the title (the right holder) and differs when the title is a colonial entity or an entity under foreign domination, in comparison with the self-determination of a particular segment of a

[3] Cristescu (1981).

[4] Moris (1997).

[5] Tomaselli (2016) and Xanthaki (2007).

[6] Rosas (1993), pp. 225–252.

population living within a state.[7] Therefore, there can be many different ways in exercising the right to self-determination, such as 1) *political self-determination*, which includes territorial solutions; 2) *nonpolitical self-determination*, which includes a set of rights but not territoriality (this way of exercising the right to self-determination can be offered to indigenous peoples who are not territorially concentrated, thus guaranteeing access to human rights and addressing issues through personal autonomy; 3) *nonpolitical self-determination* for minorities, which grants access to human rights and special measures but does not include territorial rights; and 4) *right to self-determination* as a remedy when the denial of rights is repeated and occurs most often in the form of crimes against humanity upon vulnerable groups, indigenous peoples, or minorities. This includes territorial rights, as well as the right to self-determination.[8] In that respect, it is considered that the right to national self-determination can be realized through a multitude of political engagements, such as the establishment of national institutions, the creation of autonomous communities, the formation of federations or confederations, minority rights, etc. The choice and applicability of any of these solutions depend on the circumstances of each individual case and also on the costs of implementing them, which should always be compared with the potential benefits.[9] There are different types of self-determination movements, and many of them fit it in more than one category. They can be *anticolonial self-determination, substate self-determination, trans-state self-determination, self-determination of dispersed people, indigenous self-determination, representative self-determination, etc.*[10]

Certainly, the right to self-determination of peoples includes a whole continuum of options and encompasses more than sovereign independence. In a general view, self-determination has aspects related to both the internal organization of the state and the achievement of a certain international status for a given territory. Different solutions reflect both dimensions of the right to self-determination. Some forms of self-determination, such as the protection of minority rights and the formation of internal state structures, or federalism and models of democratic regimes, are clearly confined to the internal organization of a state, whereas others, such as liberation from foreign domination, are strictly tied to the external way of exercising the right to self-determination of peoples. Therefore, although some authors are contesting the internal aspect of the right to self-determination or find it difficult to accept that self-determination has two equally important aspects, the practice points toward both ways for exercising the right and refers to a range of measures and activities undertaken by the states to address the needs of the various groups that coexist within them.[11]

---

[7] Van Der Vyver (2000).

[8] Castellino (2000).

[9] Tamir (2002).

[10] Halperin et al. (1992).

[11] Weller (2009), pp. 111–165.

3.1.1 The Case of East Timor

Timor is an island located west of Australia. East Timor became part of the international agenda in 1960 when the UN declared it a non-self-governed territory. Previously, its eastern part was colonized by Portugal, while its western part was colonized first by the Netherlands and then by Indonesia. In 1974, Portugal recognized the right of the people of East Timor to self-determination and the right to elect their own assembly. East Timor has begun a democratic process of building an educational system, institutions, and health policies, and hence aspirations for independence have emerged. But soon, conflict broke out between supporters of independence and supporters of integration with Indonesia. In 1975, Indonesia (an archipelago inhabited by various ethnic groups whose idea of a nation was strengthened by the Dutch as they ruled under colonial rule) occupied East Timor as its 26th province. East Timor was an economically underdeveloped area, but Indonesia, with the help of the United States and Australia, was able to convince other countries that East Timor was a danger to it, especially because of the possible expansion of communism, first in East Timor and then to overflow into Indonesia. Portugal protested at the UN, which condemned Indonesia but without taking a firm stand on the matter. After the annexation, Indonesians ruled East Timor brutally, with numerous human rights abuses and military repressive measures.[12] But after 24 years of occupation and the fall of the Eastern bloc, the Indonesian authorities could no longer justify annexation, so in 1999, after nearly a quarter-century of occupation, under international and domestic pressure, they agreed to a referendum on autonomy or again for the independence of East Timor. In the referendum, more than 78% of the population voted for independence.[13] In response, the pro-Indonesian militia, encouraged by the Indonesian military, applied violence against civilians. When the violence went out of control, the UN Security Council decided to establish a multinational force (UNAMET), which was to restore peace and stability in East Timor and assist in humanitarian intervention.[14] The UN restored peace, Indonesia withdrew, and with a 1999 agreement,[15] the UN took control over East Timor through the establishment of an international administration.[16] After three years of United Nations administration, East Timor became independent in 2002 and was admitted to UN membership.[17]

There has been much debate over the previous annexation and its effectiveness. Although illegal, many countries, including Australia, have argued that regardless of the act, the international community cannot ignore the reality and should

[12] United Nations General Assembly (1999).

[13] East Timor - UNMISET - Background.

[14] Press Release SC/6745 (1999).

[15] Agreement between the Republic of Indonesia and the Portuguese Republic on the question of East Timor (1999).

[16] Security Council resolution 1410 (2002).

[17] Press Releases, GA/10069, 2002.

recognize annexation as effective. Of course, this was not taken into account, and the UN acted in accordance with its principles and forced Indonesia to liberate the territory that had been illegally appropriated. But the case of East Timor is special and different from many others as it is not only a clear case of self-determination or protection of human rights but also a way of ending the illegal occupation.[18]

3.2 External Self-Determination Vis-a-Vis the Respect of Territorial Integrity

Many of the authors that regard the right to self-determination solely as external self-determination equate it to secession. However, the external form of the right to self-determination does not necessarily imply secession. A legitimate exercise of the right to external self-determination, for example, can result when a nation enters into a federation with another independent state, conducts its own domestic affairs but hands over the control of its foreign affairs to another state, or entirely, under its own will, merges with an existing state.[19] According to international documents, and according to most authors working in the field of international law, respect for the territorial integrity of a state is primary.[20]

Joshua Castellino belongs to a group of authors who believe that according to the UN Charter, the concept of self-determination and territorial integrity are opposite phenomena. The principle of self-determination proclaims that any people who are repressed, dominated, or exploited within a particular state have the right to seek self-determination. This was easy to accomplish during colonialism, considers Castellino, but in contemporary political relations, the issue is far more complex.[21] Antonio Cassese believes that the principle of territorial sovereignty was, and still is, sacred.[22] The Montevideo Convention on the Rights and Duties of States (1933)[23] defines the elements that constitute statehood. One of those elements is *territory* and is primarily expressed through the *principle of territorial integrity*, which at the same time protects both state territory and its

[18] For the case of East Timor, see more in Tan (2006), Mullerson (2003), and Cassese (1995).

[19] Kolodner (1994).

[20] Montevideo Convention on Rights and Duties of States, Dec. 26, 1933, 165 L.N.T.S. 19, art. 1; UN Charter (1945); UNGA Res 2625, Annex, Declaration on Principles of international law concerning friendly relations and cooperation among the states in accordance with the Charter of the United Nations, (1970); World Conference on Human Rights, Vienna Declaration and Programme of Action, U.N. doc. A/Conf. 157/24 art. I.2 (June 25, 1993) reprinted in 32 I.L.M.1661, at 1665 (1993); Cassese (1995); Crawford (2012); Shaw (2008); Arangio-Ruiz (1979); Domingo (2009).

[21] Castellino (2000).

[22] Cassese (1995) and Arangio-Ruiz (1979).

[23] Montevideo Convention on Rights and Duties of States, Dec. 26, 1933, 165 L.N.T.S. 19, art. 1.

authority—the government.[24] The territory is not only a physical thing or land but also an ideological concept—the idea of a homeland.[25] Since the Peace of Westphalia in 1648, states and sovereignty have been the fruits of imagination or have been at the center of the international system. The symbols of cartography, thick lines, and dotted lines are meant to represent borders and jurisdictions and to portray the image of sovereignty so that we can imagine the existence of a sovereign state and the area it controls.[26]

The *principle of territorial integrity* is closely linked to other principles of international law, such as noninterference in the internal or external affairs of other states, the prohibition of force by threat, the peaceful settlement of disputes, respect for human rights, and the self-determination of peoples. Their application is connected. Under positive international law, *the principle of the territorial integrity* of an existing state is a superior principle and involves the rejection of secession. This practice is neither new nor unknown. Arranged chronologically, the following international instruments guarantee the principle of territorial integrity: the League of Nations Convention (Article 10), the Stimson Note of 1932, the Covenant of Rights and Duties of the State (1933), the UN Charter, the Charter of the Organization of American States (1948), the Charter of the Organization of the African Union (1963), the Helsinki Final Act (1975), and others.

This *principle of territorial integrity* is highly valued by the international community and is a traditional or classical principle of international law, although the new principles that are being developed are pressuring it on various grounds. The development of supranational communities and trends of globalization are just some of the pressures whose full impact remains to be felt.[27] The principle of territorial integrity serves the interests of states, but also protects two morally important goals: (1) protection of individual physical security, rights and stability of expectations and (2) provides a structure that is reasonable for individuals and groups to invest yourself in the political process. Individual rights depend on the effective functioning of the legal order, and for individuals to invest and participate in themselves requires the stability of states and the effective implementation of the law.[28] With the development of *postmodern tribalism*, the major problem becomes the distinction between the original movement for national liberation and the separatist groups seeking to seize political power by using the argument of self-determination. If a particular national liberation movement cannot prove itself to be genuine, then it calls for the right to self-determination because particular people are not represented in the existing state structure. Complaints can be addressed with the compromise of internal self-determination, which can take the form of autonomy or

[24] The same aspects are protected through the *principle of non-interference in the state internal affairs*.

[25] Borgen (2007).

[26] Domingo (2009).

[27] Butler (2003).

[28] Buchanan (1997).

federalism. But it is still difficult to support a national liberation movement because, in the contemporary context, the new statehood can endanger international peace and order, considers Castellino.[29]

As early as 1921, the International Commission of Rapporteurs within the League of Nations had reviewed the request for the secession of the Aaland Islands from Finland and rejected it on the following grounds:

> (...) To concede to minorities, either of language or religion, or to any fractions of a population the right of withdrawing from the community to which they belong, because it is their wish or their good pleasure, would be to destroy order and stability within States and to inaugurate anarchy in international life; it would be to uphold a theory incompatible with the very idea of the State as a territorial and political unity.[30]

The Declaration on Principles of International Law concerning Friendly Relations and Cooperation among States in accordance with the Charter of the United Nations (1970) underlines *the principle of territorial integrity* as inviolable under international law, and if a state has a representative government, it is considered to act within the principle of self-determination. The Declaration points out: (...) Nothing in the foregoing paragraphs shall be construed as authorizing or encouraging any action which would dismember or impair, totally or in part, the territorial integrity or political unity of sovereign and independent States conducting themselves in compliance with the principle of equal rights and self-determination of peoples as described above and thus possessed of a government representing the whole people belonging to the territory without distinction as to race, creed or colour (...)."[31] Restrictively interpreted, according to Cassese, the Declaration on Principles of International Law does not require states to guarantee racial and religious-based rights, nor does it prohibit the imposition of unfair measures but only requires access to government institutions.[32]

Concerning documents dating from recent history, the UN World Conference on Human Rights held in 1993, on behalf of the postulate that the people have the right to freely determine their political status and to exercise their economic freedom and social and cultural development (established by Resolution 2625 of 1970),[33] expressed the view that the right to self-determination does not authorize or encourage any action that could lead to the impairment or division of the territorial

---

[29] Castellino (2000).

[30] A Report presented to the Council of the League of Nations by the Commission of Rapporteurs (1921).

[31] UNGA Res 2625, Annex, Declaration on Principles of international law concerning friendly relations and cooperation among the states in accordance with the Charter of the United Nations, (1970).

[32] Cassese (1995).

[33] UNGA Res 2625, Annex, Declaration on Principles of international law concerning friendly relations and cooperation among the states in accordance with the Charter of the United Nations, (1970).

integrity of states under the principle of equal rights and the self-determination of peoples.[34] The Vienna Declaration and Programme of Action reaffirms, in its relevant parts, Article 1 of the UN International Covenant on Human Rights. Like other international acts enabling the right to self-determination, the Vienna Declaration, after affirming the right of peoples to determine political, economic, social, and cultural issues, states that such rights will not be constructed "(…) as an authorization or as an encouragement to any action which disintegrates or divides, in whole or in part, the territorial integrity or political unity of sovereign and independent States (…)." In the Vienna Declaration, the emphasis is again on a government that represents all the people belonging to a territory—without any distinction. The World Conference on Human Rights considers the denial of the right to self-determination to be a violation of human rights and underlines the importance of the effective realization of this right. Territorial integrity serves as a guarantor for the maintenance of the *status quo*. It protects the unchanged components of the international system, ideological and religious blocs, alliances, and international groupings that have existed for a long time, and therefore the international community sees secession as a *per se* negative phenomenon.

3.2.1 Aaland Islands Case

The Aaland Islands are an archipelago between Finland and Sweden, which became a subject of dispute between the two countries during the Finnish independence in 1917. The islands were neither rich nor very populated (their population was about 25,000 people mainly engaged in fishing and shipbuilding), but the islands were of great strategic importance. Namely, if the sea froze in winter, the ice becomes a passage to Sweden, so the islands could be a route for a possible invasion. The Islanders have a Swedish language and culture, and since 1809, the islands have been a part of the Grand Duchy of Finland. In 1917, Finland declared independence from Russia, and shortly thereafter, a civil war erupted between the Communists and those opposed to them, and a representative of the Aaland Islands proclaimed that the islanders wanted their land to be returned to Sweden. The islanders held a referendum in which they overwhelmingly voted for a union with Sweden, with Finnish troops intervening and the case facing the League of Nations. In the League of Nations, the case was examined by two committees—the Committee on Lawyers and the Committee of Reporters. In this case, the report of the Committee of Reporters was taken into account, and their solution was to suggest autonomy, not independence for the Aaland Islands.[35]

---

34 World Conference on Human Rights, Vienna Declaration and Programme of Action, U.N. doc. A/Conf. 157/24 art. I.2 (June 25, 1993) reprinted in 32 I.L.M.1661, at 1665 (1993).

35 Summers (2007).

Part One: The Committee of Jurists

The Committee was composed of three law professors. Its mandate was very limited, i.e., it had to determine whether the case should be dealt with under international law or be left to settle under domestic jurisdiction. Although the Committee did not directly address the question of whether the Aaland Islands have a right to self-determination, it was certainly at the center of the dispute. The Committee balanced the two principles—the principle of self-determination and the principle of state sovereignty—and, of course, the principle of self-determination was weaker in that respect. The lawyers held that under normal circumstances, the matter would fall under domestic jurisdiction, but in this case, when the State of Finland was not fully formed and was undergoing a transformation process, they, therefore, considered the matter to be an issue of international law. Lawyers also examined another balancing of things, namely, that of self-determination and minority rights, and found that both had the same goal, albeit different methods of achieving it, that is, to provide a particular national group with the maintenance and free development of its social, ethnic, or religious character. They found that during the Russian domination of Finland, Finland was a province and hence could not be considered a state and that it never controlled its foreign affairs. Hence, Finland was not a historical political entity for them but a new political phenomenon; they considered that Finland was not in a position to oppose the future of the Aaland Islands simply because they were a part of the Finnish political organization but within the Russian Empire; therefore, Finnish sovereignty could not be applied retroactively. The lawyers emphasized the uniqueness of the identity of the Aaland people and the level of tendency to continue their relationship with Sweden, which they undoubtedly expressed in a referendum.[36]

Part Two: Committee of Reporters

Following the report of the lawyers, the League Council created a Reporters' Commission in 1920 to investigate the Aaland question and propose a solution. The Committee of Reporters was composed of former politicians, and their report again took into account the two abovementioned balances, but they had a much broader mandate than the previous Committee, allowing them to freely investigate. Their findings were different from those of the lawyers. The question of sovereignty was divided into two questions—whether Finland was sovereign after the separation from Russia and whether Finnish sovereignty extended to the Aaland Islands. Both Sweden and Finland have presented historical documents, maps, etc., but the reporters have focused only on one historical fact, namely, that since 1634, the Aaland Islands have been continually united with the center of Finland, or its administration, with which they supported the historical uniqueness of Finland and the Aaland Islands.[37] Analyzing the establishment of the Grand Duchy in 1809, what the jurisprudents found regarding Finnish sovereignty "half-empty," the reporters found it "almost complete" and found that Finland enjoyed the attributes of sovereignty

[36] Report of the International Committee of Jurists (1920).

[37] Report of the Commission of Rapporteurs (1921).

other than foreign policy and the defense. The result was that the Grand Duchy was an autonomous and constitutional state that existed for 108 years within the same geographical boundaries under the sovereignty of the Emperor. Finland may have been dependent, but it was a state that always had authority over the Aaland Islands. Investigating the self-determination of minority rights, the reporters found that a minority could not be allowed to secede simply because it expressed a desire. The analogy that Finland has determined its status cannot be applied, so the Aaland Islands can do so unilaterally as they are only a small part of the Finnish territory and a small fraction of the Finnish nation, and a minority, in general, cannot be treated as a nation. The reporters were asked what motivated the Aaland people to vote in a referendum and felt that their need to protect their language, culture, and uniqueness was not a sufficient reason for separation as they were only a part of the Swedish minority in Finland at that time, numbering around 350,000 people who were not repressed and were not endangered by their cultural identity, that is, they were not a separate ethnic group but a group within that minority. This also raised the question of the stability of the Finnish state, which could have major implications, so the states that were under the Emperor needed to be allowed to prosper. Finally, according to this Committee, the question of the Aaland Islands had to be resolved with autonomy.[38]

3.3 The Doctrine of *Uti Possidetis Juris*

The doctrine of *uti possidetis juris*, according to which colonial states gained independence within their administrative boundaries, is based on several assumptions that must be further examined. The doctrine equates the people with the state according to the principle of territoriality and assumes that the colonial states began their history with the arrival of colonial powers in their region and the establishment of their borders. Yet self-determination is a very difficult and multifaceted process under international law. In the sphere of diverse international politics in which we live, it is dangerous to adopt an automated and uniform model of action without regard to the circumstances of each individual situation. The doctrine of *uti possidetis juris* essentially preserves artificiality—formalized self-determination, which allows new states to be formed within the administrative lines of the old territorial unit but neglects territorial issues beneath the surface that first promote dissatisfaction and perhaps posture a new round of interstate conflicts and apparent secession. Therefore, the simple extension of the principle of *uti possidetis juris* to modern conflicts does not always address the problems of postmodern tribalism.[39]

Historically, the principle of *uti possidetis juris* derives from Roman law, where it is a procedural principle according to which the burden of proof relies on the

---

38 Summers (2007) and Cassese (1995).

39 Ratner (1996).

party, or on the procedural side that does not own or posses the thing. The principle gained great importance with its acceptance by the International Court of Justice in the case of Burkina Faso *vs*. the Republic of Mali (1986),[40] a border dispute when, ICJ balanced this principle with other legal principles and caused legal inconsistencies. Consequently, the Court underlined the importance of *uti possidetis juris* and stood in the defense of the existing polity. It was evident that there was an entity that could be identified and could not be seen to correspond to colonial borders, but the Court took this into account only superficially and gave priority to nation building and the stability of borders and states. Namely, in order to protect the borders, achieve stability, and avoid further struggles, the Court gave priority to this principle over the right to self-determination.[41]

It is interesting to analyze the extend of the use of the principle *uti possidetis juris* to the modern decay of states. In the case of the disintegration of SFR Yugoslavia and the recognition of the entities that emerged from it, the Arbitration Commission for SFR Yugoslavia, in Opinion no. 3, called for the application of the principle of *uti possidetis juris* and Article 5 of the Constitution of SFRY[42] but ignored other articles where it is stated that the territory of the Federation is indivisible, considering that they are not relevant since the Federation was in process of dissolution, stated in Opinion No. 1. To argue the position taken, the Commission used the case "Burkina Faso vs Mali" and gave the principle a universal character.[43]

For many, this interpretation led to general uncertainty and instability due to the creation of artificial identities that are difficult to accommodate in new countries. Ratner considers that the rule of international law must be reviewed because, according to him, its application today ignores not only the critical distinction between inward lines and international boundaries based on historical and other characteristics but also the assumption that all such boundaries must be transformed is unjustified.

The principle of *uti possidetis juris* relies on several assumptions that need to be reconsidered: first, that the creation of small ethnic states is undesirable because, according to Ratner, it is unsustainable unless we will not take into account the fact that we live in a time of close interaction and that the surge in the creation of such states can develop a sense of xenophobia that would destroy international order. The second assumption is based on the need to maintain international order i.e. the international community must sanction a secession—or can only allow it under extremely limited conditions. If secession is readily available, it can compromise states and encourage secessionist movements. The third assumption is related to the statehood and the demand for the statehood of secessionist movements because at the international level, the state is a generally accepted, recognized form of political public administration on the territory concerned. But that is true if states are made up of

40 ICJ Frontier Dispute (Burkina Faso/Republic of Mali) (1986).

41 Burkina Faso/Mali Frontier Dispute Case (judgment) ICJ Reports (1986) p. 567, para 25.

42 Conference on Yugoslavia, Arbitration Commission, Opinion No. 3 (1992) 31 ILM 1500.

43 See more at Summers (2007) and Frckoski (2005).

governments that gained their legitimacy from the consent of the governed, while in the case of decolonization, it was not, and self-determination was simply the way the colonizers transferred their power over the forces that emerged without taking into account the will of the people who were governed and without creating the necessary democratic institutions. Therefore, that assumption does not hold. The fourth assumption that takes territoriality as the sole objective factor that determines the identity of the people seems to be based on the opinion that the history of colonial nations began with the giving of colonial powers and suggests that territory is more important than other factors—race, tribe, and language—and forgets to take into account that the territory was first artificially established, and that turns to be problematic since it seems to regard the history of colonial countries as irrelevant.[44]

3.4 The Right to Self-Determination and its Polysemic Meaning

In the literature, there are generally two concepts of self-determination.[45] The former is restrictive, gives preference to the territorial unity of states, protects them, and opposes the extension of the principle, while the latter recognizes and justifies, to a certain extent, the practice of disintegrating states and advocates for the reform of the existing approach. Certainly, the principle of self-determination is firmly established in international law, and in particular the self-determination of the colonial territories. It has also been established that peoples have the right to self-determination. But despite attempts to extend the scope of self-determination to categories other than peoples, and to establish other forms of practicing it, those who oppose it are not rare.

James Crawford[46] who, in his attempt to identify the bearers of self-determination, thinks that the definition of the people, broadly defined, is problematic. "In its root, the question of defining 'people' is about identifying categories of territories to which the principle of self-determination is applied as a right,"[47] argues Crawford, and for him, the legitimate categories (territories) are the following:

1) Entities whose right to self-determination has already been established on the basis of international agreements (in particular mandate territories, custody territories, and non-self-governing territories) and
2) Existing states – in this case, the principle of self-determination takes the form of a rule that prevents interference in the internal affairs of the state, and its central element is the right of the people of the state to choose the form of government.

---

[44] Ratner (1996).

[45] Halperin et al. (1992), Cassese (1995), Weller (2009), Castellino (2000), and Sterio (2013).

[46] Crawford (2006).

[47] Crawford (2006), p. 126.

Thus, for Crawford, the principle of self-determination does not derive a right that applies to any group of people who wish for political independence or self-government, and like sovereignty, it applies only after the self-determination unit has already been determined. But for Crawford, other than states, mandate territories, guardian territories, and nongoverned territories, the units to which this principle applies are also other territories that form separate political and geographical areas and whose inhabitants are excluded from participation in the government, as well as any other territories or situations where self-determination is applied by parties as an appropriate solution. When a self-determining unit is not yet a state, according to Crawford, it has the right to choose its own political organization without coercion and on the basis of equality. In this way, self-determination can result in the independence of the self-determination unit, that is, the creation of an independent state or its affiliation or association with another state.[48]

On the same line is Dana Shelton.[49] She is a proponent for a restrictive interpretation of the right to self-determination, and according to her, peoples and minorities are a different category, so whenever possible, the international community should consider the group to be a minority, not a people with the right to self-determination. For her, self-determination should be limited to the colonial context. Similarly, John Dugard[50] considers that self-determination applies to peoples but not to cultures, religions, or linguistic groups, which have no right to secede from an existing state and form a new one. According to him, the exercise of the right to self-determination has three limitations: 1) the right to self-determination relates to the principle of territorial integrity upheld by the practice of the application of *uti possidetis juris*; 2) the term people, according to UN terminology, does not mean different ethnic groups but signifies the people in one state in terms of its population; therefore, minorities do not qualify as holders of the right to self-determination of peoples;[51] and, finally, 3) commitment to the territorial integrity of a sovereign independent state should be about the self-determination of peoples and means that the government of the state concerned should represent all the people belonging to that territory without any discrimination.

On the other hand, there is an argument that the outlines of the right to self-determination have never been and are not a fixed, rigid term in the legal doctrine. Law is fundamentally unstable and continually evolves conceptually and empirically in response to the pressure of events, reflecting changing geopolitical priorities. This combination of factors has created a confusing pattern of precedents, leaving room for disparate interpretations that undoubtedly affect the legal doctrine of the right to self-determination and its application, says Richard Falk. What the Soviet experience suggests, and Yugoslavia has acknowledged, is that demands for

---

[48] Crawford (2006), p. 128.

[49] Shelton (2003).

[50] Dugard (2003).

[51] Rosalyn Higgins considers that "people" are all the inhabitants of a certain territory, Higgins (2003).

self-determination, in situations where there is ethnic, religious, and national diversity, can easily provoke war, an expression of an attempt to form a (new) sovereign state. In the event of a breakup of a state (often by separation) that has a heterogeneous population, the minorities in the new composition, will again be trapped. Chechnya, Kashmir, Tibet, and the large Kurdish population are examples of trapped nations whose legal and political ideals of territorial unity has caused moral chaos; cruel suffering; social, economic, and cultural injustice; as well as endless conflicts. This seems to be legally justified under the strict international law that rests on the doctrine of the limited exercise of the right to self-determination, points Falk. Falk considers that it is unreasonable to make a decision about the claims in advance and only on the basis of international law, doctrine, or practice. It will be controversial to decide and make an assessment without considering the benefits and reasonableness of such a request in a particular context, especially if the group is exposed to decades of suffering and repression.[52] Although there are proponents who consider that it is time to eliminate self-determination as a collective, legal, political, and moral right and limit its relevance to the postcolonial setting, only by adding its role in the field of human rights, and in particular with regard to equal treatment of individuals and minorities within the structures of the authority of the existing state, for Falk, it is too late to put the spirit of self-determination into the colonial bottle again, especially when too much is invested in the language of self-determination and too many additional requirements (outside the colonial context) are validated.[53] In summary, from 1995 onward, it is evident that the scope of the right to self-determination has expanded. In that sense, it is necessary to rethink the right to self-determination since previous doctrinal concepts are no longer eloquent in practice, and yet it is not proper to equate every movement for self-determination with secessionist ambitions, points Falk.[54]

There is no doubt that the legislation about self-determination faces many impurities, loopholes, and legal gaps. Although the balance of the right to self-determination with territorial integrity excludes secession and reflects the general position of states, the practice also shows that there are exceptions to this, considers as well James Summers.[55]

Halperin, Scheffer, and Patricia Small[56] refer to contemporary trends in self-determination and point out the weaknesses of the current approach, such as a *time limit for a reply* (for example, although there were signs of disintegration of the USSR and Yugoslavia, the criteria for recognizing new states were established after the breakup became inevitable); *Eurocentric standards* (the latest established standards were meant for the successor states of the USSR or Yugoslavia, and no effort has been made to develop universal standards); *inconsistent application of the*

[52] Falk (2002).

[53] Falk (2002), p. 38.

[54] Falk (2002).

[55] Summers (2007).

[56] Halperin et al. (1992).

standards (there are situations where the application of one standard is balanced against other standards as well as with the national interest, making self-determination a hostage to selective application; and *lack of realization* (there is no mechanism to enforce standards and criteria for self-determination and encourage their application).[57]

Antonio Cassese[58] has similar conclusions. Cassese believes that the right to self-determination needs to be reconsidered so as to be more acceptable to the existing world community. According to him,

(1) Today's international law is blind to the demands of the ethnic groups and demands of national, religious, cultural, or linguistic minorities.[59]
(2) Self-determination lacks universality because it is guaranteed only for colonial peoples, those under foreign domination, and racial groups that are denied equal access to government.
(3) International rules on self-determination are imperfect, such as internal self-determination for racial groups, because they do not specify what characteristics the government should have in order to be considered representative and fully respect the right to self-determination.
(4) The application of the right to self-determination is impeded by other existing norms of international law, such as the principle *uti possidetis juris.*
(5) The right to self-determination is not supported by effective machinery that would put it into force, or at least the remedies; hence, international law that guarantees a right to some groups or peoples is largely theoretical. Although the general legal standards for self-determination have the status of absolute norms, so far, at the international level, no specific action has been taken to address self-determination as *jus cogens.*[60]

No one disputes that the political or current "popular" concept of self-determination has troubling effects on the traditional proportion of the world community and that it has the potential to act as an earthquake. But ethnic groups are currently suffering from what might be termed a "territorial obsession," says George Scelle.[61] According to Scelle, the personification of a sovereign state completely embroiled the conception of the common good and transformed common resources into the exclusive ownership of the state. Therefore, ethnic groups struggling for independent statehood today, mistakenly believe that having exclusive authority over the territory

[57] Halperin et al. (1992).

[58] Cassese (1995).

[59] For example, Article 27 of the Covenant on Civil and Political Rights protects individual members of the minority, but not the minority as a whole, as a collective. The Convention only protects the preservation of the group's cultural, linguistic, or religious identity but does not grant it the right to expand and develop. In other words, it does not guarantee a dynamic right. The groups that live in the state are protected only from the most extreme form—genocide, Cassese (1995).

[60] Cassese (1995), pp. 327–333.

[61] Scelle (1958), pp. 347–361.

will solve all their problems and not even consider the possibility of fulfilling their aspirations within existing state structures.[62]

Relating to this conceptual fog, Cassese proposes measures such as the right to self-determination to move from *de lege lata* to *de lege ferenda*. The aim is to change the concept of the right so that minorities can enjoy its benefits through the concept of internal self-determination. Cassese believes that existing norms should be crystallized and new ones need to be created. There is a need for mechanisms for implementation as well as for the monitoring of the implementation of this right. Cassese considers that the right needs to gain an *erga omnes* power and should be seen as a right whose purpose is not only to gain independent statehood but also to provide a basis for the development of alternative constitutional frameworks, protect the rights of subordinate groups, envisage a positive action to overcome past injustice through financial and other means, ensure participatory rights and the development of identity, as well as a guaranty, on the one hand, broad measures of territorial autonomy and, on the other, measures of personal autonomy for nonterritorially concentrated minorities. Therefore, the states and the international community need to manifest vision, imagination, and flexibility, so the content of such a reconsidered right can be conceptualized on two basic standards that inspire action: first, pragmatic case-by-case approach, or solutions that need to be adapted to the specific conditions of each country; and secondly establish authority of the international organizations to oversee the implementation of the constitutional schemes agreed upon by the parties.[63]

3.4.1 The Case of Puerto Rico

After Columbus' discoveries, the island of Puerto Rico came under the rule of Spain, which began in 1492 and lasted until 1898 following the conclusion of the Spanish-American Peace Agreement in Paris, when the United States assumed its sovereignty but only as an unincorporated territory (appurtenant territory).[64] In other words, Congress was tasked with determining the political rights and political status of the island. Hence, Puerto Ricans were granted the status of "citizens of Puerto Rico"; a restricted civil government was controlled by US citizens (residents), who at the same time were appointed to the executive, legislative, and judicial branches.[65] However, neither the island was represented in Congress, nor were Puerto Ricans guaranteed US citizenship. Significant political changes in this regard increased autonomy and guaranteed North American citizenship for a certain number of Puerto Ricans, which first occurred in 1917 through the so-called

[62] Cassese (1995), pp. 340–360.

[63] Cassese (1995).

[64] Treaty of Paris (1898).

[65] Foraker Act (Organic Act) (1900).

Jones-Shafroth Act (which established a Senate and Bill of Rights, yet the US President and Congress remained vested with the power to veto Puerto Rican laws)[66] and then between 1950 and 1952 with the adoption of the "Federal Relations Act."[67] Under the Federal Relations Act, the US allowed Puerto Rico to draft a constitution as long as it did not alter its territorial status, establish a republican form of government, and enact a bill of rights. The following draft constitution created the Commonwealth of Puerto Rico and was approved by the President and US Congress in 1952.[68] Under the US Constitution (1787), the US Congress is responsible for enacting or repealing regulations pertaining to Puerto Rico, that is, all legislative power is in its power, and the President of the United States has the right to conclude treaties relating to Puerto Rico with the consent and opinion of the Senate.[69] As for secession, the US Constitution remains silent on the matter.

The states that have colonies were required to report to the General Assembly, and that was United States obligation until more autonomy was established for Puerto Rico. The US submitted such reports, but the with UN Resolution 748 this obligation for transmission of the information under Article 73 of the Charter in respect of Puerto Rico was terminated.[70] The General Assembly noted that Puerto Rico has a new status[71] but did not conclude that Puerto Rico is no longer a US colony.

According to UN Resolution 1514, metropolitan states should respect the right to self-determination and independence, as required by colonial peoples.[72] Resolution 1541 provides for colonial states to have the right to independence, free association with another state, or the right to fusion in another state.[73] Resolution 2625 provides three prototypes of self-determination, and among them is free association or integration within an independent state.[74] However, Puerto Rico's political status as appurtenant to or an unincorporated US territory remains unchanged today. Puerto Rico has no state status because its internal and external sovereignty rests with Congress, not with the people of Puerto Rico, and the territory is not freely affiliated with the United States because it is an unincorporated territory. Everything is in the hands of the US Congress, and the island has no jurisdiction to completely or partially unilaterally withdraw from US sovereignty (which would mean, for example, that if the Congress decides that the English language is the only official language in Puerto Rico, then the island has no right to oppose that rule). On the other hand, in order for Puerto Rico to withdraw from the association, it must

[66] Jones-Shafroth Act (1917).

[67] Puerto Rico Federal Relations Act (1950).

[68] Foreign relations of The United States (1952–1954).

[69] Foreign relations of The United States (1952–1954).

[70] UNGA Res. 748 (1953).

[71] UNGA Res. 748 (1953), p. 2.

[72] UNGA Res. 1514 (1960).

[73] UNGA Res. 1541 (1960).

[74] UNGA. Res. 2625 (1970).

first be a member, and so far, this is not the case.[75] However, the Special Committee on Decolonization, in 2014, urged the United States to again expedite the process that would allow the people of Puerto Rico to fully exercise their inalienable right to self-determination and independence, as well as take decisions, in a sovereign manner, to address their economic and social needs. According to it, the self-determination process did not require United States congressional approval and that the country should cooperate with Puerto Ricans to design a decolonization mechanism.[76]

Considering the recent outcomes, in November 2020, Puerto Ricans voted in a nonbinding referendum on statehood. About 53% of Puerto Ricans favored statehood, while 47% rejected it. However, only 55% of Puerto Ricans voted in the referendum. Statehood proponents viewed the results as proof that most Puerto Ricans want independent statehood, but opponents questioned the validity of the votes as the referendum was nonbinding.[77]

References

Agreement between the Republic of Indonesia and the Portuguese Republic on the question of East Timor (1999). https://peaceaccords.nd.edu/wp-content/accords/East_Timor_Peace_Agreement-1999.pdf. Accessed 8 Jan 2023

Arangio-Ruiz G (1979) The normative role of the General Assembly of the United Nations and the Declaration of principles of friendly relations with an Appendix on the concept of international law and the theory of international organisation. Collected Courses of the Hague Academy of International Law 137

Borgen CJ (2007) Imagining sovereignty, managing secession: the legal geography of Euroasia's "frozen conflicts". Oregon Rev Int Law 9(2):477–536

Buchanan A (1997) Theories of secession. Philos Public Aff 26(1):31–61

Butler WE (2003) Territorial integrity and secession: the dialectics of international order. In: Dahliz J (ed) Conflict avoidance and - regional appraisals. Asser Press, pp 111–125

Cassese A (1995) Self-determination of the peoples, a legal reappraisal. Cambridge University Press

Castellino J (2000) International law and self-determination. The interplay of the politics of territorial possession with formulations of post-colonial 'national' identity. Kluwer Law International

Conference on Yugoslavia, Arbitration Commission, Opinion No. 3 (1992)

Convention on Rights and Duties of States, Montevideo Dec. 26, 1933. https://treaties.un.org/doc/Publication/UNTS/LON/Volume%20165/v165.pdf. Accessed 11 Aug 2022

Crawford J (2006) The creation of states in international law. Oxford University Press

Crawford J (2012) Brownlie's principles of public international law. Oxford University Press

Cristescu A (1981) The right to self-determination, historical and current development on the basis of United Nations instruments. UN

de Passalaqua JLA (2003) Secession in North America: The United States & Puerto Rico. In: Dahliz J (ed) Conflict avoidance and - regional appraisals. Asser Press, pp 207–227

Domingo R (2009) The crisis of international law. Vand J Transnatl Law 42:1543–1593

[75] For the Puerto Rico case see more at de Passalaqua (2003).

[76] General Assembly, Special Committee on Decolonization (2014).

[77] Reichard (2021).

Dugard J (2003) A legal basis for secession - relevantly principles and rules. In: Dahliz J (ed) Conflict avoidance and - regional appraisals. Asser Press, pp 89–97

East Timor - UNMISET - Background. https://peacekeeping.un.org/mission/past/unmiset/background.html. Accessed 8 Jan 2023

Falk R (2002) Self-determination under international law: the coherence of doctrine versus the incoherence of experience. In: Danspeckgruber W (ed) Self-determination of peoples, community, nation and state in interdependent world. Lynne Rienner Publishers, pp 31–67

Foraker Act (Organic Act) (1900). https://www.loc.gov/rr/hispanic/1898/foraker.html. Accessed 8 Jan 2023

Foreign relations of the United States, 1952–1954. United Nations Affairs, Vol III. The Acting Secretary of the Interior (Northrop) to the Secretary of State. 711C.02/10–952. https://history.state.gov/historicaldocuments/frus1952-54v03/d902. Accessed 8 Jan 2023

Frckoski LD (2005) Trends in the recognition of states in international law and the case of Macedonia. Proceedings of the international conference "Macedonian-French days of law - 200 Years of Code Civil", Prosvetno delo, Skopje

General Assembly, Special Committee on Decolonization. Special Committee on Decolonization Approves Text Supporting Puerto Rico's 'Inalienable Right to Self-Determination. Meetings Coverage GA/COL/3269 (2014). https://press.un.org/en/2014/gacol3269.doc.htm. Accessed 7 Jan 2023

Halperin MH et al (1992) Self-determination in the new world order. Carnegie Endowment for International Peace, Washington DC

Higgins R (2003) Self-determination and secession at secession and international law. In: Dahliz J (ed) Conflict avoidance and - regional appraisals. Asser Press, pp 21–39

ICJ Reports (1986) Judgment Burkina Faso/Mali Frontier Dispute Case. https://www.icj-cij.org/en/case/69. Accessed 11 Aug 2022

Jones-Shafroth Act (1917). https://guides.loc.gov/latinx-civil-rights/jones-shafroth-act. Accessed 8 Jan 2023

Kolodner E (1994) The future of the right to self-determination. Conn J Int Law 10(1):153–168

Moris H (1997) Self-determination: an affirmative right or mere rhetoric? ILSA J Int Comp Law 4(1–8):201–219

Mullerson R (2003) Sovereignty and secession: then and now, here and there. In: Dahliz J (ed) Secession and international law, conflict avoidance and - regional appraisals. Asser Press, pp 125–167

Press Release SC/6745 (1999). Security Council Establishes Un Transitional Administration In East Timor For Initial Period Until 31 January 2002. https://press.un.org/en/1999/19991025.sc6745.doc.html. Accessed 8 Jan 2023

Press Releases, GA/10069, 2002. Unanimous Assembly Decision Makes Timor-Leste 191st United Nations Member State. https://press.un.org/en/2002/ga10069.doc.htm. Accessed 8 Jan 2023

Puerto Rico Federal Relations Act (1950). file:///C:/Users/Dell/Downloads/con00157.pdf. Accessed 8 Jan 2023

Ratner S (1996) Drawing a better line: uti possidetis and the borders of new states. Am J Int Law 90(4):590–624

Reichard R (2021) Why Isn't Puerto Rico a State? (Internet source). https://www.history.com/news/puerto-rico-statehood. Accessed 8 Jan 2023

Report of the International Committee (sic) of Jurists entrusted by the Council of the League of Nations with the task of giving an advisory opinion upon the legal aspects of the Aaland Islands question, League of Nations O.J. Spec. Suppl. No. 3 (1920)

Report submitted to the Council of the League of Nations by the Commission of Rapporteurs, League of Nations, Doc. 8.7. 21/68/106 (1921)

Rosas A (1993) Internal self-determination. In: Tomuschat C (ed) Modern law of self-determination. Martinus Nijhoff, Dordrecht, pp 225–252

Scelle G (1958) Obsession du territoire. Symbolae Verzijl. Den Haag, Nijhoff, pp 347–361

Security Council resolution 1410 (2002). http://unscr.com/en/resolutions/1410. Accessed 8 Jan 2023
Shaw MN (2008) International law. Cambridge University Press
Shelton D (2003) Self-determination and secession: the jurisprudence of the international human rights tribunals. In: Dahliz J (ed) Conflict avoidance and - regional appraisals. Asser Press, pp 47–75
Sterio M (2013) The right to self-determination under international law, secession, and the rule of the great powers. Routledge
Summers S (2007) Peoples and international law, how nationalism and self-determination shape a contemporary law of nations. Leiden, Boston
Tamir Y (2002) Liberalni nacionalizam (Liberal nationalism). Filip Visnjic, Beograd
Tan L (2006) From incorporation to disengagement: East Timor and Indonesian identities, 1975-1999. In: Rothbart D, Korostelina KV (eds) Identity, morality and threat, studies in violent conflict. Lexington Books, pp 177–211
Tomaselli A (2016) Indigenous people and their right to political participation. Nomos, Baden Baden
Treaty of Paris of 1898. https://loc.gov/rr/hispanic/1898/treaty.html. Accessed 8 Jan 2023
UNGA Res 1541, Principles which should guide members in determining whether or not an obligation exists to transmit the information called for under Article 73e of the Charter (1960)
UNGA Res 2625, Annex, Declaration on Principles of international law concerning relations and cooperation among the states in accordance with the Charter of the United Nations (1970)
UNGA Res. 1514, Declaration on the Granting of Independence to Colonial Countries and Peoples (1960)
UNGA Res. 748 Cessation of the transmission of information under Article 73 e of the Charter in respect of Puerto Rico (1953)
United Nations General Assembly (1999) Situation of human rights in East Timor, Note by the Secretary-General A/54/660. https://digitallibrary.un.org/record/404721?ln=en. Accessed 26 Mar 2023
Van Der Vyver JD (2000) Self-determination of the peoples of Quebec under international law. J Transnatl Law Policy 10:1–27
Vienna Declaration and Programme of Action (1993), Un World Conference on Human Rights. https://www.ohchr.org/en/instruments-mechanisms/instruments/vienna-declaration-and-programme-action. Accessed 11 Aug 2022
Weller M (2009) Settling self-determination conflicts: recent developments. Eur J Int Law 20(1):111–165
Xanthaki A (2007) Indigenous rights and United Nations standards: self-determination, culture and land. Cambridge University Press, Cambridge

Chapter 4
Statehood and Recognition of Statehood

4.1 Introduction

There are two ways in which new states are formed: the first one is the guarantee of independence by the former sovereign, and the second one is the secession of the territory in question. The former is referred to as devolution, and the latter is secession. The main distinguishing feature is the existence or nonexistence of consent by the metropolitan (parent) state,[1] although, in certain circumstances, this distinction is formal and even arbitrary. In particular, the relevance of the consent of the metropolitan state varies in different situations, especially where the principle of self-determination is at stake.[2]

Despite its incomplete definition, "statehood" is one of the main concepts of international law. According to the International Court of Justice (ICJ), the term "state" is interpreted according to the objectives of international law. Despite the theoretical challenges, however, we must have in our mind that international law takes into account the traditional criteria for statehood, and statehood depends on fulfilling those criteria. Apart from the traditional ones, there are also additional criteria that are applied in the event in which the traditional ones are not sufficient to determine presumed statehood. On the other hand, questions of statehood are reopened with the emergence of a new entity that is a case in itself and has some, but not all, elements of statehood. From that point, the legal dilemmas surrounding the entity's status also arise, i.e., can the entity be considered an independent state

[1] Crawford uses the term "metropolitan" to refer to a state in whose territory a new state is created, and in relation to the term "manifestation of consent," it refers to the consent of the government of that state and points out that from 1945 onward, most of the new states were created through a clear guarantee of independence by the former sovereign; see more at Crawford (2006) and Brownlie (1961).

[2] Crawford (2006), p. 330.

N. Shikova, *Self-Determination and Secession*,
https://doi.org/10.1007/978-3-031-34322-3_4

after the act of declaring independence? Although the question of statehood is a general one, the answer to the question about statehood or statelessness varies by context.[3]

For a long time, there was no universally accepted definition of what constitutes "statehood." Attempts to explicate *statehood* were unsuccessful, so, for example, the International Court of Justice (ICJ) in several of its documents indicates that the term "state" is used as it is intended in the UN Charter (1954) in the Statute of the Court, in the Geneva Convention on the Law of the Sea (1958) and in the Vienna Convention on Diplomatic Relations (1961), which in other words would mean "state"—according to the goals of international law. However, despite the established principles, in addition, the topic of recognition of states and governments remained on the agenda of the International Court of Justice from 1949 onward, but in terms of defining this issue, very little interest was shown and minimal progress was achieved.[4] It is indisputable that statehood is a central concept of international public law, but attempts to define the concept of statehood are based on certain premises: (1) there is full competence to undertake acts and conclude agreements in the international sphere; (2) there is exclusive jurisdiction over internal matters beyond the control of other states; (3) states (in principle) are not subject to a mandatory international process, jurisdiction, or agreement without their consent; (4) in international law, states are recognized as equal.[5] In legal theory, these principles through legal terms constitute the essence of the concept of statehood, that is, the essence of the special position of states according to general international law.[6] When it comes to forming states, there are several legal ways to do so, but secession is not one of them. Namely, creating a new independent unit, especially through unilateral secession, is considered a legally unacceptable way. However, although secession is not permitted under international law nor is it generally accepted, there are no rules that expressly prohibit it, so there is a practice of realized secession in this sphere. When a certain socioeconomic group practices secession, a conflict usually arises between the entity that prefers an independent status of a state and the parent state. Almost always the act of declaring independence is followed by state violence and the connected dilemmas about the legal status of the entity, which can be resolved exclusively according to the principles of international law, i.e., according to traditional and additional criteria for determining the existence of statehood.

[3] Crawford (2006).

[4] International Court of Justice, basic documents (2017–2022).

[5] Charter of the United Nations (1945) article 2 (1)... "The Organization is based on the principle of the sovereign equality of all its Members."

[6] Crawford (2006).

4.2 Criteria for the Existence of Statehood According to International Law

The criteria for statehood are set in Article 1 of the Montevideo Convention on the Rights and Duties of States (1933).[7] These are classic criteria for statehood (*ex factis jus oritur*) and refer to the following:

(1) A defined territory—a state should possess a certain effectively managed coherent territory.[8] A state can exist despite claims against its territory.[9]
(2) A permanent population—states, apart from territorial entities, represent aggregates of individuals; therefore, a permanent population is necessary for statehood, although there is no prescribed minimum for the required number of population.[10]
(3) A government—the establishment of an effective government is a particularly important condition for statehood because of the dependence of other components on the central state authority. The existence of a governmental authority is the basis for normal relations between states. Although the law distinguishes between the terms states and governments, normally it is only the government of the state that can bind the state (for example, through a treaty).
(4) Capacity to enter into relations with other states—this is not an exclusive prerogative of the state but is related to the requirement for the existence of a government and independence.
(5) Independence—it is a central criterion for statehood. The lack of independence can lead to the conclusion that a certain entity is not a state but a part of another dominant state or a puppet state.[11]

Apart from the traditional criteria according to which the existence or nonexistence of statehood is determined, sometimes the use of other alternative criteria is also suggested, such as the following:

1) *Persistence*—especially when some of the criteria for statehood are not fulfilled, the entity's continuity over time gains importance. Persistence therefore is not a criterion for statehood in the sense of an attribute of statehood but can be important evidence of the possession of other attributes.

---

[7] Montevideo Convention on Rights and Duties of States, Dec. 26, 1933, 165 L.N.T.S. 19, art.1.

[8] nb. There is no prescribed rule for the minimum required territory, nor is there a rule that requires the uniqueness of the territory of the state.

[9] Two issues are distinguished here—when the demands refer to the entire territory of the new state, and secondly—issues related to the borders of the state, although for some authors, such as Rosalin Higgins, when doubts arise regarding the future borders, and they are of a serious nature, statehood is called into question, Higgins (1963).

[10] Neither the territory nor the population has to be clearly defined; it is enough that they are definable, Alland (2014).

[11] The entity may even be independent in a general sense, but for specific issues can act as if under the control of another state, Crawford (2006).

2) *Willingness and ability to respect international law*—this is not a criterion that indicates the existence of statehood; however, the nonrespect of or the refusal to respect the obligations arising from the UN Charter may lead to nonrecognition by, or nonadmission to, the UN.
3) *A certain level of civilization*—this is a subjective standard, often applied in a discriminatory way because international law does not assume any general religion or culture but only minimum order and stability.
4) *Recognition*—an entity that is not recognized as a state but fulfills the requirements for statehood can have rights even in relation to a state that does not recognize it, so recognition is not a classic condition for statehood.
5) *Legal order*—since the modern state is a territorial base for legal order, it can be considered that the existence of a legal order,[12] or at least the existence of basic rules (although many authors are disputing this), is a useful criterion for determining the existence of a state.[13]

4.2.1 Territorial Integrity

In the Montevideo Convention on the Rights and Duties of States (1933), which defines the constituents of statehood, territory is one of the elements of statehood and is primarily expressed through the principle of territorial integrity, which simultaneously protects both state territory and its authority, i.e., the government.[14] The relationship between statehood and territorial sovereignty is of a special kind and is not analogous to the possession of the land. Moreover, international law defines territory not by adopting private law analogies applicable to immovable property but by reference to the scope of governmental power that is exercised or has the capacity to be exercised in relation to the territory and population.[15] Territory is not only a physical thing, a land, but also an ideological concept—the idea of a homeland—and the states and sovereignty are figments of that imagination.[16] Since the Peace of Westphalia (1648), states have been the center of the international system. The symbols of cartography and the thick and dashed lines are intended to represent borders and jurisdictions to portray the image of sovereignty in order to imagine the existence of a sovereign state and the area it controls.[17]

---

[12] For Kelsen, a state is a legal order, and the three elements of a state (people, territory, and government) can only be determined jurisdictionally, that is, they can be understood as valid only within the spheres of the validity of the legal order; see more in Kelsen (1967).

[13] About the recognition criteria, see more at Crawford (2006).

[14] The same aspects are protected through the principle of non-interference in the internal affairs of the state.

[15] Crawford (2006).

[16] Borgen (2007).

[17] Domingo (2009).

The principle of territorial integrity is guaranteed through numerous documents, and the principle is closely related to other principles of international law, such as nonintervention in the internal or external affairs of other states, the prohibition of threats of force, the peaceful settlement of disputes, respect for human rights, and self-determination of peoples. Their application is related, and they do not exist without each other. Territorial integrity serves as a guarantor for maintaining the *status quo*. It protects the unchanged components of the international system, the ideological and religious blocs, the alliances, and the international groupings that have existed for a long time, and therefore the international community sees secession *per se* as a negative phenomenon. Hence, the principle of territorial integrity is highly valued by the international community and is a traditional or classical principle of international law, although the new principles that are developing are pushing for secession on various grounds.[18]

4.2.2 Independence

A special prerequisite for the existence of a state as a legal order is its independence, or at least its legal independence, that is, the absence of real subordination and the existence of an internal self-sufficient legal order.[19] Independence is the capacity to enter into relations with other states.[20] Independence as an attribute of statehood can be formal or real, i.e., true independence. Formal independence exists when the state exercises power over a specific territory.[21] This element corresponds to Rousseau's *plentitude de la competence*. Current independence is relative or, according to Rousseau, quantitative, that is, it is a matter of conditionality. An analysis of the current practice shows that the degree of actual independence required for the entity to be defined as a state can be minimal, but in the event of a conflict of legal rules, this element takes on special significance. Conceptions of sovereignty assume power over the territory, power aspirations, and the application of legal norms on that territory. Ideas about sovereignty were born out of a desire to

---

[18] This principle is tied to what G.I. Tunkin calls—old international law. It is challenged by the development of supranational communities and trends in globalization, and their impact remains to be felt, see more at Butler (2003).

[19] For Denis Alland, independence and sovereignty are synonyms, and this is confirmed by Opinion no. 1 of the Arbitration Commission for Yugoslavia, according to which the state characterizes sovereignty, i.e. that it is an independent legal order, Alland (2014).

[20] A state is not subject to other sovereign, although according to Malcolm N. Shaw, it is debatable whether a certain degree of actual or formal independence is necessary; see more in Shaw (2003, 2008).

[21] This power may derive from the state's constitution or may result from a grant of full power by a past sovereign, or even be established, recognized by an international or bilateral treaty. Formal independence in Rousseau's terminology includes *l'exclusivite de la competence* (exclusivity). Even where formal independence exists, it may be necessary to examine the actual or effective independence of a given state, Crawford (2006).

understand and explain power, as well as to claim, legitimize, and challenge it. The idea of independence is related to the no less ambiguous concept of sovereignty. The idea of independence assumes that entities similar in kind can act without any permission or authorization from outside. Independence implies equality among sovereigns—at least in the formal sense.[22]

It is important to distinguish between independence as an initial qualification for statehood and independence as a condition for the continued existence of the state. A new state attempting to secede must demonstrate substantial independence (formal and real) from the state from which it was a part to be considered definitively created. Certain situations can derogate the current real independence of a state, and one of them is the illegality of its origin, that is, when the entity is created by violating the basic rules of international law. In that case, the question is whether the entity can be called a "state." Regarding the issue of statehood, traditional international law generally adheres to the principle of effectiveness, but the illegality of origin can lead to the nonrecognition of the entity by other states.[23]

4.3 Sovereignty

4.3.1 The Concept of Sovereignty

If sovereignty is considered a freedom of action for the state, then its historical traces lead to the *sovereign* in whom all power was concentrated. Many authors equate sovereignty with independence as an authorization of the state to exercise its power without being subordinated to any other external authority.[24] Sovereignty is the political and legal rule to control or govern the inhabitants of a certain territory and includes other rights that enable the exercise of that power of control.[25] A state

[22] MacCormick (2010).

[23] Crawford (2006), p. 72.

[24] The concept of sovereignty first appeared in Jean Bodin's "Six Books on the Republic" as an absolute and permanent power exercised by the Republic. Thomas Hobbes, in "Leviathan," finds sovereignty in the indivisible power of the monarch. And for Jean-Jacques Rousseau, sovereignty is indivisible, but the bearer of that sovereignty is a general will, the people. The concept of sovereignty has always been a part of the thinking of most theorists whose object of interest is the state, namely, Kant, Hegel, Locke, Bentham, Austin, Montesquieu, and Tocqueville. It is part of the political action of the founders of the United States as the sovereign of the people. With the birth of the new German state, the concept of sovereignty is modernized and is a quality of the modern constitutional state. In the twentieth century, Hans Kelsen made an attempt to establish sovereignty as a technical legal concept, and according to him, sovereignty is a quality of normative order. For Kelsen, without sovereignty, there is no state, and without a state, there is no law. Hence, sovereignty is superior, independent, and capable of limiting itself through the legal order. In contemporary theory, according to Crawford, sovereignty appears in all shapes and sizes. More on the development of the concept of sovereignty in Domingo (2009).

[25] Pavkovic and Radan (2007).

is legally independent, that is, sovereign when the domestic legal order itself determines what its competencies are and how they are exercised.[26] For certain authors, sovereignty is a phenomenon or consequence of statehood, that is, it indicates full competencies that the state *prima facie* possesses,[27] that is, it indicates the full authority of the state in relation to internal or external affairs. [28]

Concerning theories, there are three core elements of sovereignty that are analytically distant. The elements are not logically related, i.e., political entities can have all the elements of sovereignty or only some of them. They can be elaborated as follows:

1. International legal sovereignty—meaning international recognition of the state in relation to the right to conclude treaties with other states, state membership in international organizations, and judicial equality with other states
2. Westphalian sovereignty—meaning the entity is not subject to other external authority or structure
3. Domestic sovereignty—related to the establishment and maintenance of effective control over the territory[29]

Despite the proposed elements that constitute sovereignty, sovereignty is not an objective characteristic but a concept—part of the language of positive law and an element of complex theories that, in their attempts to explain it, are neither true nor false.[30] It is very difficult to articulate a coherent doctrine concerning sovereignty and its barrier. In essence, ideas are split between the ones that have a legal approach and the ones that have a factual approach to the understanding of sovereignty. However, the question of sovereignty cannot be separated from the question of where sovereignty resides .[31] Additionally, the question of sovereignty cannot be analyzed, apart from the many contexts in which it has been invoked to support a variety of positions, starting from initiatives for independence, arguments for integration into the system, and the basis for the claiming and denying of rights, powers, and privileges.[32] This means the relationship between sovereignty and its reality is always open and unstable,[33] and the concept often serves as a smoke screen to cover the reality of political ambition. In most of the cases in which we are arguing about sovereignty, we argue about the allocation of power. The ambiguity of sovereignty has historical depth, and it is not a result of conceptual confusion, especially the notion of popular sovereignty and its relation to the ambiguity of the term "people,"

[26] Alland (2014).

[27] Rousseau (1948).

[28] Hinsley thinks similarly, and according to him, this principle presupposes nothing more than the existence of a supreme authority within the political community; see more in Hinsley (1966) and Hannum (1990).

[29] Krasner (2010).

[30] Troper (2010).

[31] Kalmo and Skinner (2010).

[32] Koskenniemi (2010).

[33] Kalmo and Skinner (2010).

though sovereignty is a legal notion and not always a purely factual matter that constantly passes through transformation.[34] The legal perspective brings sovereignty under international law, where it is regarded as a higher normative code.[35]

4.3.2 Phases and Developments of the Concept

In the sixteenth century, ideas about sovereignty include supporting tendencies for unity, ideas for overcoming fragmentations, and the need to put various municipal powers under the same political realm. The term *state began* to be used to refer to a specific type of union or association of a community of people living together under the sovereign monarch or the ruling group. Jean Bodin (1530–1596) claimed that neither the walls nor the people make the *citie (state)* but the union of people under the same sovereign government. There is nothing higher than the sovereign except God. The sovereign community is complete in itself, it is not a part of another state, and it has its own laws, council, and magistrates, considered Francisco de Vitoria (1483–1546). According to Thomas Hobbes (1588–1679), the sovereign is representative and represents others. Sovereignty is the glue that holds political society together and enables living under shared rules. The sovereign creates the conditions for civil peace and establishes rights to maintain a regime of justice. The essence of this social contract is subjection to the sovereign where an individual who is weak and isolated seeks protection from the ruler. Samuel von Pufendorf (1632–1694) considered that this social contract establishes not only the people's submission to a ruler but also the state's promise for their protection. Similarly, John Locke (1632–1704) considered that once a community government is created that represents the will of the majority, it has only one function, and that is to protect the community members' property. In the frames of sovereignty, the government is supposed to deliver social order and protection against internal and external enemies, and if it loses those protective characteristics, it loses its legitimacy. Sovereignty is a supreme and indivisible authority within a given territory, considered Hugo Grotius (1583–1654), but the sources of its legitimacy—except the need for own persistence—remain unclear.[36]

Different theories attempted to give an explanation. For example, according to the absolutist theory, actions are legitimate as long as they are performed by the recognized sovereign as the head of state. According to the populist theory, actions are only legitimate if they are performed in accordance with the will (or the represented will) of the sovereign body of people. According to the fictional theory, the actions of the sovereign should aim to preserve the life and health of persons, and

[34] Krasner (1993).

[35] Koskenniemi (2010).

[36] Bartelson (2010).

the common good is reflected through the perpetuity of those actions.[37] Rousseau (1712–1778), in his social contract theory, considered that the only legitimate power is the one that is connected with the general will and that assumes the unity of power. He presented a social contract theory that went beyond the explanation of the state and offered its justification.[38] Common to all of those theories is that they consider that the legitimacy of any political authority is driven by an implicit social contract between the ruler and the ruled, where the ruler is accepted because it possesses the ability to provide peace and social order.[39]

In its original sense, sovereignty refers to the supreme character of state power; additionally, it refers to the whole range of powers that are part of state authority. For Immanuel Kant (1724–1804), state sovereign power belongs to the "united will of people," and this power is unlimited since the individual will is submitted to the general will.[40] The state has the highest state authority reflected through the sovereign power of its highest organ and the norms it enacts.[41] The sovereign can be identified by the hierarchy of norms. In countries in which a written constitution exists, the highest norm and the sovereign are the bodies that have the power to enact and amend the constitution. If the constitution does not exist in written form, then the highest norms are statutes and the body that enacts them.[42] In a modern state, the concept of sovereignty is related to democracy; it is driven by and belongs to the people of the state.[43]

4.3.3 Modern Understanding of Sovereignty

The Peace of Westphalia (1648) ended the Thirty-Year War and set the state as a distinct legal personality in the theory of public and international law. The state became visible through signs and symbols and gained the right to territorial integrity and political sovereignty. Its sovereignty became inherent, and its rights became rooted in the law that confirms its internal and external sovereignty.[44] Jeremy Bentham (1748–1832) wrote about the law on nations and stressed the idea of *international*. In these contexts, nations should imply the general principle of utility in their conduct, and that in the end should result in reaching the greatest possible welfare for all the nations of the world. For John Austin (1790–1859), the existence of a sovereign is a condition for the existence of a political society. The sovereign is

[37] Skinner (2010).

[38] Kelly (1992).

[39] Bartelson (2010).

[40] Kelly (1992).

[41] Carre de Malberg (1920–1922).

[42] Vedel (1992).

[43] Troper (2010).

[44] Piirimäe (2010).

not necessarily an individual but a group or assembly of individuals.[45] State sovereignty meant supremacy over all other authorities on a certain territory and independence from any other authorities. States drove their rights from the rights of individuals, which became a basis for state rights.[46] The sources of state legitimacy ranged from democratic constructs, such as the will of the people through the desire for the self-preservation of a political community—if it is needed with violent means. The territorial state claims to be the barrier of sovereignty, while sovereignty emerged as an essential element of the state.[47] Modern state constitutions have provisions about "national" or "popular sovereignty, where they locate the essence of sovereignty not in a state but in the people of the state.[48] H. L. A. Hart points that the sovereign is in the people, or in the electorate—i.e., the citizens through parament are becoming an effective lawmaking agent.[49] In contemporary times, the attributes of sovereignty are changed, but the states whose locus of legitimate authority stayed relatively uncontested[50] remained to be the most significant political actors within their territories.[51] Still, in comparison to the conventional notion of sovereignty, in the contemporary world, there are two deviations from it: one is the example of failed or weak states, which enjoy international recognition but are not able to exercise domestic sovereignty and secure the legal order, and another is the European Union (EU) as a construct in which sovereignty (despite the traditional notion of indivisibility) is shared among the EU and its member states (or in other situations, among states and other regional and international organizations).[52] With those transformations and, considering the limitations—perhaps no state today is not fully sovereign in the traditional sense, but sovereign in a new modern sense, from the international perspective, sovereignty remains the key concept of international law.[53] The question of sovereignty is decided and redecided again and again, but some aspects of sovereign states (in the wording of the Permanent Court of Justice) are solely within the jurisdiction of the state.[54] Additionally, the United Nations is based on sovereign equality, the independence of all states, and noninterference in the domestic affairs of states.[55] The same is restated in the Vienna Convention of the Law on Treaties (1969).

Sovereignty persists due to the notions associated with self-determination, nationhood, and independence. For Martti Koskenniemi, the concept of sovereignty

[45] Kelly (1992).

[46] Walzer (2006).

[47] Lipping (2010).

[48] Troper (2010).

[49] Hart (1994).

[50] Bartelson (2010).

[51] Piirimäe (2010).

[52] Krasner (2010).

[53] Kalmo (2010).

[54] Kalmo (2010).

[55] UN Charter (1945).

still attracts many critics. It has been analyzed by lawyers, political theorists, and sociologists, but it is still difficult to establish solid authority to speak about. Despite its polysemic meaning, which is contextually dependable, sovereignty continues to be a "fundamental" aspect of the world we live in without being able to describe it with our vocabularies or to catch its full meaning. Sovereignty represents a life of a collective within the set of institutions and practices, which are constantly imagined, debated, criticized, and reformed. In its initials, it was used as a tool for the ones that were suffering under the theocratic rulers in the birth of the Enlightenment; later, in the twentieth century, it was invoked to support decolonization; and now it holds the possibility, although perhaps an idealistic one, that the peoples are masters of their own fate and not pawns in others' games.[56]

Currently, sovereignty is regarded as an attribute of the state. A state is sovereign if it is fully self-governed and independent from external control. Sovereignty is an aggregate of state powers, which can be within an individual or a collective power holder or an entity or an agency, such as a king, dictator, or parliament. That entity is the "sovereign" of the state. Regarded as popular sovereignty, sovereignty belongs to the people of the territory, who are self-governing. The people establish the state with government bodies that have constitutionally limited powers. In that way, the people exercise their sovereignty, and in that way, the popular sovereignty transforms itself into limited constitutional sovereignty.[57] Although the concept of sovereignty and all those theories surrounding it arguably work imperfectly, still they prove to be more functional than any other decision-making structure.[58] Therefore, although the concept of sovereignty is currently being relativized, international law still protects sovereignty.[59]

4.4 Recognition of States

Recognition is not a classic condition for the existence of statehood and is not a part of the traditional determining criteria contained in the Montevideo Convention on the Rights and Duties of States (1933).[60] For a long time, international lawyers have been interested in whether the formation of a state is a fact or legal acceptance, stressing the ideas under the rival doctrine of state recognition. Without much success within the limits of law and philosophy, lawyers try to solve the puzzle and the most fundamental problem of law concerning the birth and death of a legal order. The question of recognition is related to the question of sovereignty—if sovereignty is the original power, how can its emergence be subjected to a rule that comes from

[56] Koskenniemi (2010).

[57] MacCormick (2010).

[58] Krasner (2010).

[59] Reisman (2000).

[60] Montevideo Convention on Rights and Duties of States, Dec. 26, 1933.

another legal system? For some theoreticians, such as Georg Jellinek,[61] the creation of states is an event that is outside the realm of law—meaning the emergence of a state is a matter of fact, not of law. An opposite group of lawyers claims that states are a creation of law. Hans Kelsen considered that a state comes into existence as a legal consequence of relevant rules. The creation of a state is a question not *de facto* but *de jure*.[62]

These two theoretical groups continue to have proponents among international lawyers.[63] Regarding the meaning of the recognition of states as a condition for statehood, similarities can be generally distinguished between two lines of thought and two theoretical ways. According to the first group, the act of recognition is only declarative and the existence of statehood does not depend on it, while according to others, recognition is constitutive, that is, it is fundamental for the existence of statehood even though it is not a part of the traditional criteria for statehood. For proponents of the declarative theory of state recognition, an entity is not a state because it is recognized, but it is recognized because it is a state.[64] According to the opposite point of view, which is supported by the advocates of the constitutive theory of state recognition, recognition is constitutive, that is, it forms statehood. International organizations can establish extremely influential criteria that require the fulfillment of legal and political conditions before making individual decisions on recognition or nonrecognition, as practice recognition by the state is a matter of policy, even when it depends on legal factors.[65] Hence, the constitutive theory of state recognition currently dominates the international sphere.[66] Additionally, the three-element theory bundles sovereignty with population and territory as necessary conditions for the existence of a state. Within, an important element is the government and its capacity to enter into relations with other states. All of that supports the image of the state as a venture that encompasses facts and legal institutions—the state as an association of the land and sovereignty.[67]

4.4.1 Additional Principles for Creating an Independent State Through Self-Determination

Authors from the Carnegie Endowment for International Peace consider the standards and criteria needed to be established that will serve to better inform analysts and policymakers and adequately respond to the growing number of

[61] Jellinek (2008).

[62] Kelsen (1967).

[63] Kalmo (2010) and Troper (2010).

[64] Crawford (2006), p. 93.

[65] Shaw (2003).

[66] Worster (2008).

[67] Hall (1924).

self-determination movements seeking to form a new state. In this respect, they propose principles that need to be observed in creating an independent state through self-determination. They are proposed to be the following:

1. UN Standards (established in the UN Charter, Article 4 (1)).

2. Respect for international law.

3. Inviolability of borders—international borders of other countries should remain unchanged. The new state can, by agreement with its neighbors, adjust its borders. When the international community supports the emergence of a new state, it does not necessarily accept the boundaries that the self-determination movement seeks to establish. In many cases, there will be areas where there is no generally accepted border between the region that seeks independence and the rest of the original state. In other cases, the traditional boundary may no longer reflect the current distribution of the population. The new state may have an area that is largely inhabited by the majority group of the original state. In such situations, the international community should support political arrangements that distinguish between "citizenship" and "territory." These agreements will allow people living in a particular area to choose which country's citizenship they will accept. Such areas must have substantial local autonomy, and the functions that will be implemented centrally may be placed under the joint control of both governments. Where necessary, an international force may be stationed on the territory to ensure that the rights of the people are respected.

4. Nonuse of force—new states must commit to accepting and respecting agreements that limit the use of force and the size and structure of military services. States should commit and not use force to resolve any border issues; use peaceful means, such as mediation, consolidation, and arbitration; accept nuclear nonproliferation agreements; accept limits on the size of a conventional military force; and use force only in the case of self-defense or a collective security action.

5. Peaceful settlement of disputes—the state must commit itself to a peaceful settlement of internal and international disputes. The new government will best demonstrate its commitment to a peaceful resolution of disputes by adhering to relevant arbitration conventions and accepting the jurisdiction of the ICJ.

6. Constituent democracy—the new state should stand for democracy clearly and firmly. It generally means that the government withdraws its legitimacy from the people through free elections. In order for elections to be considered free, all citizens must have the right to vote. Any group of citizens should be able to form a political party and compete on an equal footing in elections. There must be a secret ballot. The winning party must have the right to form a government. The timely conduct of elections must be stipulated in the constitution. So it is necessary to have a "limited" constituent democracy, not just democracy.

7. Right to political opposition—the people must have the right to freely, and without fear of arrest, express their disagreement with the government and its policies and actions. The opposition must be able to communicate those views to others through the tools of freedom of the press and association. The state must not prohibit the expression of opposing views through the media. Independent political organizations and parties must have the right to function freely and to communicate with their supporters and support groups.

8. Protection of individual and minority rights—the state must provide evidence that it protects rights. Individual rights include the right to opposition, the right to be free from arbitrary police power, and other internationally recognized rights, such as the formation of trade unions, the right to strike, the right to cultural freedom, the right to travel, and the right to exchange ideas through state borders. Minority rights do not have to be expressed as a right to veto state decisions or the right to political autonomy, but they must go beyond the limits of guaranteeing the individual freedom of each minority member and must ensure that the group shares ethnic, religious, linguistic, or cultural practices and receives respect despite its different status. This includes guarantees of freedom of religion, the ability of minorities to educate their children in special schools, and the freedom to form political parties. If a minority lives in a particular geographical area, then local political autonomy or a federal structure may be appropriate.

9. Restriction of arbitrary political power—the constitution must prohibit torture and establish limits on the right of the police to arrest people and detain them without charge and public trial. Both domestic and international human rights should be reasonably guaranteed to prisoners.

10. Market-oriented economy—an established market-oriented economy and free and fair trade are needed, inter alia, for the new entity to receive international economic support from international financial institutions such as the World Bank and International Monetary Fund (IMF).

11. Implementation mechanisms—Examples of this are accepting the authority of the Security Council and establishing a new mechanism. Some states may not be happy with this, especially since practically only new states will be subject to such a mechanism. But the mechanism must guarantee the rights and interests of the people in the new states, though it can be expected that it will be followed by ambiguities and political powerlessness. Certainly, it is necessary to strengthen links between governments and the people that underline the peaceful resolution of conflicting aspirations, to a more responsive and more representative government.[68]

However, in guaranteeing independence, the right to self-determination can be deliberately violated, and in practice, two different situations arise. The first one is when the metropolitan state guarantees the independence of a nonrepresentative fraction of the people on the territory, and the second one is when the metropolitan state makes an attempt to divide the territory in order to avoid the obligation to guarantee independence for the territory as a whole.

James Crawford puts in place several principles that must be observed for the achievement of independent statehood. Namely, he considers that (1) the self-determination unit must first be guaranteed the right to self-determination as a whole unless the unity of territory is clearly contrary to the wishes of the people or

[68] About the conditions that need to be met in order to obtain and maintain independent statehood see more at Halperin et al. (1992), pp. 84–93.

is not aimed at achieving international peace and stability and the division schemes are approved by UN bodies; (2) it is necessary to exclude any attempt to divide the territory in order to avoid the obligation to guarantee independence for the territory as a whole; (3) the territory must not be alienated without local consent, i.e. without the consent of the local population; (4) it is important to resolve issues concerning the cession of the territory of the self-determination unit and, in particular, the establishment of military bases; and (5) the colonial enclaves should be considered not an aspect of the right to self-determination but an exception of the rule.[69]

It can be undeniably concluded that self-determination is not a self-regulating process, nor is it merely a peaceful act. The demand for self-determination can cause violence, repressive dictatorships, humanitarian crises, and wars. Internal military conflicts can very quickly become a threat to international peace and security and cause mass migration, systematic human rights abuses, arms transfers, cross-border fighting, and economic disruption. Additional principles need to be established, except traditional ones. In any way, it would be irresponsible for the world community to stand aside, indolently, and watch how primitive bloodshed engulfs both old and new states.[70]

References

Alland D (2014) International public law. Ars lamina

Bartelson J (2010) Double blinds: sovereignty and the just war tradition. In: Kalmo K, Skinner Q (eds) Sovereignty in fragments. Cambridge University Press, pp 81–96

Borgen CJ (2007) Imagining sovereignty, managing secession: the legal geography of Euroasia's "frozen conflicts". Oregon Rev Int Law 9(2):477–536

Brownlie I (1961) Transition of Independence: the legal aspects. Review of Contemporary law 1: 381

Butler WE (2003) Territorial integrity and secession: the dialectics of international order. In: Dahliz J (ed) Conflict avoidance and - regional appraisals. Asser Press, pp 111–125

Carre de Malberg R (1920–1922) Contribution à la théorie générale de l'Etat: spécialement d'après les données fournies par le droit constitutionnel français. Dalloz (2003)

Charter of UN (1945)

Crawford J (2006) The creation of states in international law. Oxford University Press

Domingo R (2009) The crisis of international law. Vand J Transnatl Law 42:1543–1593

Fundación para la Libertad., https://paralalibertad.org/wp-content/uploads/InformeCompleto_Ingles.pdf. Accessed 21 Oct 2022

Hall WE (1924) A treatise on international law. Clarendon Press

Halperin MH et al (1992) Self-determination in the new world order. Carnegie Endowment for International Peace, Washington DC

Hannum H (1990) Autonomy, sovereignty, and self-determination, the accommodation of conflict rights. University of Pennsylvania Press

Hart HLA (1994) The concept of law. Oxford University Press

[69] Crawford (2006), pp. 336–337.

[70] Halperin et al. (1992), p. 95.

Higgins R (1963) The development of international law through the political organs of the UN. Oxford University Press, London
Hinsley HF (1966) Sovereignty. Basic Books, New York
International Court of Justice, basic documents (2017–2022). http://www.icj-cij.org/en/basic-documents. Accessed 3 Sep 2022
Jellinek G (2008) The declaration of the rights of man and of citizens. Lulu Press
Kalmo H (2010) A matter of fact? The many faces of sovereignty. In: Kalmo K, Skinner Q (eds) Sovereignty in fragments. Cambridge University Press, pp 114–132
Kalmo H, Skinner Q (2010) Introduction: a concept in fragments. In: Kalmo K, Skinner Q (eds) Sovereignty in fragments. Cambridge University Press, pp 1–26
Kelly JM (1992) A short history of Western legal theory. Oxford University Press
Kelsen H (1967) The pure theory of law. California University Press
Koskenniemi M (2010) Conclusion: vocabularies of sovereignty – powers. In: Kalmo K, Skinner Q (eds) Sovereignty in fragments. Cambridge University Press, pp 222–243
Krasner S (1993) Economic interdependence and independence statehood. In: Jackson RH, James A (eds) States in a changing world: a contemporary analysis. Oxford University Press, pp 301–321
Krasner SD (2010) The durability of organized hypocrisy (2010). In: Kalmo K, Skinner Q (eds) Sovereignty in fragments. Cambridge University Press, pp 96–114
Lipping J (2010) Sovereignty beyond the state. In: Kalmo K, Skinner Q (eds) Sovereignty in fragments. Cambridge University Press, pp 186–205
MacCormick N (2010) Sovereignty and after. In: Kalmo K, Skinner Q (eds) Sovereignty in fragments. Cambridge University Press, pp 151–169
Montevideo Convention on Rights and Duties of States, Dec. 26, (1933)
Pavkovic A, Radan P (2007) Creating new states, theory and practice of secession. Ashgate Publishing Limited
Piirimäe P (2010) The Westphalian myth and the idea of external sovereignty. In: Kalmo K, Skinner Q (eds) Sovereignty in fragments. Cambridge University Press, pp 64–81
Presentation of the political reality in the Basque Country: from defamation to tragedy
Reisman MW (2000) Sovereignty and human rights in contemporary international law. In: Fox GH, Roth BR (eds) Democratic governance and international law. Cambridge University Press, pp 239–259
Rousseau C (1948) L' independence de l'etat dans orde international. Collected Courses Hague Acad Int Law 73:17. https://doi.org/10.1163/1875-8096_pplrdc_A9789028611023_03. Accessed 2 Sep 2022
Shaw MN (2003) The role of recognition and non-recognition with respect to secession: notes on some relevant issues. In: Dahliz J (ed) Conflict avoidance and - regional appraisals. Asser Press, pp 243–259
Shaw MN (2008) International law. Cambridge University Press
Skinner Q (2010) The sovereign state: a genealogy. In: Kalmo K, Skinner Q (eds) Sovereignty in fragments. Cambridge University Press, pp 26–47
Troper M (2010) The survival of sovereignty (2010). In: Kalmo K, Skinner Q (eds) Sovereignty in fragments. Cambridge University Press, pp 132–151
Vedel G (1992) Schengen et Maastricht (à propos de la décision n° 91-294 DC du Conseil constitutionnel du 25 juillet 1991. Dalloz
Vienna Convention on the Law of Treaties (1969). https://legal.un.org/ilc/texts/instruments/english/conventions/1_1_1969.pdf. Accessed 7 Sept 2022
Walzer (2006) Just and unjust wars. Basic books, 4th edn
Worster WT (2008) Law, politics and the conception of state in state recognition. Boston Univ Int Law J 27:115–171

Part II
Secession

Chapter 5
The Phenomenon of Secession

5.1 Introduction

The term secession is based on the Latin words *secede*, meaning *separation*, and *cedere*, meaning *departure*, which indicates a departure or withdrawal from somewhere or something. During the Roman Republic (510 BC–27 BC), this act was used as an expression of plebian discontent since the plebian assemblies lack political power and because of the plebeians' low economic welfare in comparison to the patricians (nobles). During the *secessio plebis*, it was the practice of the plebeians to abandon the city and encamp on the surrounding hills, threatening the wealthy upper class—the patricians—that they will establish a rival city unless their demands are met.[1] Despite the centuries-long practice and the general meaning of interruption of certain continuity, still it is difficult to understand this political phenomenon and find an acceptable definition of secession. Various authors use numerous suggestions, but in most of the cases, the definitions of secession do not contain sufficiently comprehensive elements (or at least sufficiently clear elements), thus lacking the potential to become a commonly accepted one.

Nevertheless, in theory, it is accepted that the question of secession arises when a significant number of the population in a particular territory, part of a particular state, expresses words or deeds toward becoming an independent state or joining another sovereign state and becoming a part of it.[2] Different authors envisage particular elements of secession. Aleksandar Pavković and Peter Radan consider that secession is the creation of a new state through the withdrawal of the territory and population that are previously a part of an existing state.[3] For Alexis Heraclides, secession is a special kind of territorial separatism that affects states. For him,

[1] Borkowski and Plessis (2005).

[2] Dahliz (2003), p. 6.

[3] Pavkovic and Radan (2007), p. 5.

N. Shikova, *Self-Determination and Secession*,
https://doi.org/10.1007/978-3-031-34322-3_5

secession is an unexpected move toward the independence of a part of the region that is a territory of a sovereign and independent state (metropolitan state). The secession movement is opposed by the "center," the central government of the multiethnic state or the state that has centrifugal tendencies.[4] Lea Brilmayer finds secessionist demands as, first and foremost, territorial. In that sense, the question about secession is a question that envisages not the relationship among peoples and states but the relationship among peoples, states, and territory.[5]

In addition to attempts to legally formulate the term, the meaning of secession in public discourse is often a negative one and is often associated with the idea of some kind of violence. At the global level, states oppose the act of secession, as well as everything related to it, but the scope of such opposition frequently varies according to circumstances. The support or opposition of other states to secession that transcends national boundaries is usually determined through the internal assessment of those states and depends on their strategic and other interests. On the other hand, when it comes to secession or an attempt to segregate a part of their own state territory, states see it as a betrayal of their homeland, and therefore secessionist aims in many countries are considered harmful to the interests of the majority. They are considered illegal, unconstitutional, unpatriotic, and even treacherous. Not only are they politically unacceptable, but they are also legally banned in many states, whereas secessionist organizations are often suppressed and exposed to state violence.[6] Despite a theoretical lack of clarity, secession demands exist almost everywhere around the world. Some of them had bloody outcomes or are still ongoing (such as in the former Socialist Federal Republic of Yugoslavia (SFRY) and the recent case of Ukraine), some of them are trying to post the quests for separation within the democratic frames and with democratic means (for example, Scotland), and some of them are in a loophole, without any possibility of legally achieving separation (for example, Catalonia).

Secession is not prohibited by international law, but it is not allowed either. However, international law is clear on one point—that the principle of territorial integrity of an existing state is a superior one and thus implicitly means the rejection of secession. There are no legally established standards for secession, but there are different opinions that tend to justify secession in some cases or at least put it in a legal frame. Those opinions range from finding the political phenomenon as utterly inadmissible, unacceptable, and illegal to ideas that are advocating for the permission of secession in predefined circumstances. According to the proponents of the notion, international law should accept and codify a certain limited or qualified right for secession. Nonetheless, most of them agree that a possible "right to secession" should not be set as a general rule, but its acceptance and practice should depend on factual conditions following a case-by-case approach.[7]

---

[4] Heraclides (1991).

[5] Brilmayer (1991).

[6] Pavkovic and Radan (2007).

[7] Beran (1991), Buchanan (1991), and Cassese (1995).

5.2 Theories of Secession

There are many attempts to explain secession and, as an outcome, the vast theory in that regard. For scholarly reasons, theories explaining the phenomenon of secession can be grouped into several categories, covering explanatory theories, economic theories, normative theories, and moral theories of secession.

5.2.1 Explanatory Theories of Secession

Explanatory theories of secession are generally sociological theories that refer to the beliefs and wishes of the leaders and supporters of secessionist movements. These sociological theories attempt to explain why and how different social phenomena emerge into secessionist tendencies. Some of the theoreticians in that group are Aleksandar Pavkovic, John R. Wood, Anthony D. Smith, Donald L. Horowitz, Michael Hechter, etc. Aleksandar Pavkovic believes that under certain circumstances, sociological theories can help us predict when and where a case of secession will occur.[8] Wood establishes a theoretical framework for examining secession as a social and political phenomenon in order to determine the process that potentially leads to secession—regardless of the outcome. However, despite such foreknowledge, in many cases, according to Wood, it is difficult to predict how the secessionist process will develop.[9] Smith studies the ethnic movements of secessionists who have a defined historical community based on shared memories and community culture upon which secessionism is grounded. In his explanations, Smith takes into account the secession attempts motivated by nationalist or ethnically based ideologies.[10] Horowitz, like Smith, thinks that the agents of secession attempts are ethnic groups, which are groups defined by a shared culture and faith with a common origin. He believes that if the economic interests, preferences, and attitudes of the group are followed, secession can be predicted since the ethnic conflict is the result of the group's anxiety over its position in relation to other groups. Still, Horowitz considers that it is a difficult task to foresee when and how ethnic groups will attempt secession.[11] Unlike Horowitz and Smith, Hechter argues that secession cannot be predicted, but he considers that the group's views and calculations are the primary motivations for secession attempts. Unlike Horowitz, he finds that the basis for those calculations is not the social positions of the ethnic groups but individual or private interests.[12]

---

[8] Pavkovic and Radan (2007).

[9] Wood (1981), pp. 109–135.

[10] Smith (1981, 1997).

[11] Horowitz (2003).

[12] Hechter (1992).

5.2.2 Economic Theories of Secession

Representatives of economic theories of secession consider economic movements as primary indicators of attempts for secession. Milica Zarkovic Bookman takes the following five economic variables as the most important factors shaping secessionist aspirations: (1) the income of the parent state, (2) the level of development, (3) the region's trade dependence on the parent state, (4) the region's networking, and (5) the level of decentralization of the parent economy.[13] According to her, secessionist claims occur in regions that have a relatively high income or in regions with lower development than the average of the country. On the other hand, Collier and Hoeffler believe that secession occurs when a part of the population sees secession as an opportunity for economic progress and support Zarkovic Bookman's thesis, but unlike it, they consider that there are also secessions that are not affected by economic considerations of any kind.[14]

5.2.3 Normative Theories of Secession

Normative theories of secession are based on an explicit or implicit assumption of the *right to secession*. However, despite the usual assumption that the right to secession exists as such, each theory sets a different basis and the conditions under which that right can be exercised. Normative theories of secession are usually grounded on two types of norms and principles: (a) freedom to choose a preferred state (*theories of choice or theories of fundamental law*) and [15] (b) the right to live and function in a state that protects (*theories of secession as a cure or remedial secession*).[16]

According to the *theories of choice*, the group that is territorially concentrated within an existing state, and not the group that is dispersed, has the right to own the state. Within these considerations, some theories justify unilateral secession under certain conditions. For these theories, the state is a voluntary association in which citizens and groups of citizens can access and exit from it at their own discretion. Such theories are *the anarcho-capitalist theory,* according to which individuals can choose their own state by means of a free agreement with other individuals, meaning the state borders, state membership, and the number of states are open for constant change.[17] In contrast, *democratic theories* hold that the process of group decision-making is the only valid procedure by which secession is permissible.[18]

[13] Bookman (1992).

[14] Collier and Hoeffler (2005).

[15] Buchanan (1991).

[16] Pavkovic and Radan (2007).

[17] For Murray N. Rothbard, the creator of this theory, boundaries are often unjust and need not be maintained at all costs. Every group and every nationality should be allowed to secede and join another nation-state. That would increase the number of new nations, but the larger their number and the smaller their size, the better. Rothbard (1994).

[18] Beran (1984, 1998).

In contrast to the *anarcho-capitalist theory* that justify the right to unlimited choice, some theories limit the population categories that possess this "right" as well as the ways in which that "right" can be exercised. The basis for such restraints lies in the democratic or ethnic factors or in the size of the group. According to them, the "right to secession" can be allowed to certain groups, i.e., it is denied to groups that do not possess certain characteristics.[19] Allen Buchanan refers to theories of choice as *theories of fundamental law*, and according to him, they include the "right to secession" regardless of whether the element of injustice is present or not.[20] According to this classification, the *theories of fundamental law* can be divided into the following:

- *Ascriptive group theories*: according to these, group membership is defined by ascriptive characteristics. Those characteristics exist independently, and based on them, the group has the right to its own political association, regardless of whether or not it suffers injustice. In that regard, being a nation or a people is an ascriptive characteristic.[21]
- *Associative group theories*: the group does not need to share any common characteristics other than the desire to have its own independent state. The simplest version of these theories is *the pure plebiscite theory*, or according to them, the right to secession exists when a substantial part of the population of the state wishes to secede.[22] According to some variants of this theory, there is a primary right to a political association or political self-determination.[23]

All *theories of choice* agree that certain (but not all) depraved consequences of secession should be avoided. Those consequences can be the creation of minority problems in the new state, infringement of the interests of the residents of other states, and the like, albeit the *theories of choice* do not propose ways how to do it.

Unlike the theories of choice, the *remedial theories of secession* focus on the possible ways of treating the violation of the rights exercised by the parent state and thus lay the groundwork for the demands posed by secessionist groups. According to them, the right to secession is similar to the right to revolution, except that this right applies to certain citizens who are concentrated in the territory of the state and who suffer injustice. As a basis for acquiring this right, different theories of secession identify different injustices upon which a group has the right to secede, but in general, they consider that secession as an ultimate remedy is acceptable (1) if the

---

[19] Avishai and Raz (1990) and Miller (1995).

[20] Buchanan (1991).

[21] Avishai and Raz (1990).

[22] Such a variant proposes Harry Beran, according to which, the group has the right to secede if (1) it represents a significant majority in the state that wants to secede and (2) if it can manage resources in order to achieve sustainability of the new state, Beran (1991).

[23] According to Christopher Willman, this right belongs to any group that (1) is a majority in a certain territory (2) the state that will be formed will have the capacity to perform state functions (3) if this will not prevent the parent state from continuing to perform its state functions, Wellman (1995).

actions of the state endanger the physical survival of its members or (2) if the previously sovereign territory was unjustly confiscated by an existing state.[24] According to these theories, secession is permissible if the state fails to protect the interests of the citizens, groups, and their human rights and to perform certain functions.[25] These theories do not require a democratic decision-making procedure that would legally precede the secession, but if the injury exists and certain criteria and conditions are met, even a unilateral secession can be justified.

It is not expected that *the theories of choice* will be incorporated into international law as they authorize the disintegration of states even when they perform their state functions well.[26] In contrast, *the remedial theories of secession* can be in line with the territorial integrity of states, and it is more likely that in the prospective future, in some form, they can supplement the corpus of international law. In codifying the "right" to secession, which can possibly exist under the normative theories, some of the authors are proposing a David Miller theory, which suggests a simple criterion, namely, if the secessionist movements are seriously threatening to violate the ethnic or national identity of the groups within or outside the secessionist state, such secession or secession attempts should not be recognized or accepted by other states.[27] Additionally, as an alternative norm of assessment, the principle of *no irreparable harm* is proposed. This principle, proclaimed by Harry Beran, [28] has the potential to determine not only whether the group can have a "right to secession" but also whether a particular secession attempt is morally permissible or not. Other than that, other conditions may need to be met for certain secession attempts to be morally justified. The primary advantage of this principle is that it seeks to systematically address the problems of violence in achieving secessionist goals. Thus, this principle suggests that it is permissible for a group or its political leaders to seek a separate state in the territory of an existing state, as well as the recognition as a new state, unless this requirement is harmful or involves a denial or restriction of political and civil rights for individuals in or outside the new state. For Aleksandar Pavkovic, there is no reason, in principle, for such a request to be banned, and the new state should create an institutional framework for accommodating or meeting such requirements. This principle reinforces the understanding of secession as an ultimate cure, and it is assumed that, as such, it is implicitly acknowledged in the

[24] According to these theories, there may be a special right of secession if: (1) the state guarantees the right to secession (as in the case of Norway from Sweden in 1905) or (2) if the country's constitution includes the right to secession (such as the Ethiopian Constitution from 1993) or perhaps (3) the agreement that the state was created by previously independent political entities included an implicit or explicit assumption that secession would later be allowed (as some US states have argued).

[25] Birch (1984), Buchanan (1998), and Tamir (2002).

[26] For Buchanan, these theories do not distinguish between legitimate and illegitimate states. According to the guidelines of international law, states are illegitimate if they commit ethnic or religious discrimination, physical harassment, and institutional racism and deny access to economic and political rights, Buchanan (1991).

[27] Miller (1995).

[28] Beran (1984).

Declaration on Principles of International Law Concerning Friendly Relations and Co-operation Among States.[29]

5.2.4 *Moral Theories of Secession*

Moral secession theories are very close to normative theories of secession since they tend to legitimize secession if certain conditions are met. Overall, these are the following theories: (1) *nationalist secession theory*—which considers that a territorially concentrated group can secede only if the majority of the population is for that solution, (2) *theory of secession as a choice*—if the majority of those who want to secede are for that solution, and (3) *causal theory of secession*—according to which a case of secession can exist only if there is a strong justifiable reason (for example, the group has been a victim of systematic discrimination or exploitation).

It seems that the best moral basis for the right to secession provides the "just-cause" theory of secession. Proponents of this theory recommend procedural mechanisms that would allow repressed groups to secede if they have a reason but would also discourage the so-called "vanity secessions," or the secessions of groups that simply do not have a reason to do so. Thus, if there are justified reasons, the "right" to secession can be exercised through various procedural mechanisms, such as the requirement for a super-majority of voters that support the secession, or by conducting a referendum.[30]

5.3 Causes of Secession (Theoretical Considerations)

According to secession theories that consider that it is possible to predict a secessionist tendency, the circumstances and causes are often associated with long-standing injustices and systematic discrimination of the group seeking to secede from a state. The secessionist group generally expresses a strong identity that perceives itself as distinct from others and the majority of the population in the state, as well as a need to protect it.

The approaches that elaborate on the causes of secession can be divided into three groups. According to the first, so-called *human rights approach*, the reasons for secession stem from discrimination, repression, and subordination. For the second, so-called *historical-territorial approach*, the basis for secession tendencies lies in the demands for the territory, i.e., the territorial claims, while according to the third approach, claims of secession arise from discriminatory distribution by the

[29] Pavkovic and Radan (2007).

[30] Many theorists oppose this because there may be reasons for secession without the ability to animate as many percentages as necessary for secession to be considered successful, Norman (2003).

state and *the need to protect the particular culture*, though it is not subject to any other discrimination or injustice.[31]

It is undisputed that discrimination and isolation help reinforce the feeling of group uniqueness. Hurst Hannum says that many minorities have retained their identity due to relative geographic isolation from the central government and mainstream culture, and usually peripheral regions are far less developed than those in the center and are therefore neglected. This so-called *internal colonialism* or the exploitation of politically and economically weaker regions by very strong urban elites is a matter of political marginalization and economic subordination (though both evidently go hand in hand) and gives a good explanation for the rise of ethnic or regional conflicts. If there were no obvious economic and political discrimination but the minority's position in society is still weak, then the question related to the protection of purely cultural attributes might not even be raised. When political power is concentrated in a large, centralized state government, even regular democratic elections may not be particularly relevant for individual voters, who see their single vote as an empty gesture among millions. Returning the power locally or regionally is one of the ways to really increase perceived participation in the political process, considers Hannum.[32]

One reason for secession claims is the dissatisfaction or economic subordination of the group making the request. The group believes that secession will bring more chances and benefits; thereby, it will boost its standard of living as well as its power to control the policies that concern it. But secession is not the only way to resolve injustices or gain benefits, argue Aleksandar Pavkovic and Peter Radan. Unequal distribution of power and economic resources within the home state can be resolved by the secession of one of its parts, but they can also be resolved by the redistribution of power and economic resources within the existing (parent, home) state. The existing state can establish institutions that will implement various policies to address injustices. For example, it may establish participatory/democratic institutions in federal units that would give minority groups control over their affairs or implement economic policies whose primary beneficiaries will be residents of federal units or members of national minorities. Moreover, there are not many benefits that the secessionist population can achieve in a small country, and some regions may lose the economic benefits they already enjoyed in their home country, so secession for the secession population can be costly as well.[33]

Nationalist agitation needs mass, and it only becomes meaningful when minority members find that the cultural repression they suffer is accompanied by much more damaging discriminatory treatment in terms of economic opportunities, educational attainment, and social progress, considers Jack Rees. He refers to the group's need to emphasize and protect its particular identity, and that is the ground on which

[31] Basic (2008).

[32] Hannum (1990).

[33] Pavkovic and Radan (2007).

(among other things) it bases its claim for secession.[34] But in addition to economic subordination and geographic isolation, for Hannum, the groups can suffer from discrimination simply because they are different. Racial prejudice and religious intolerance remain common in many regions around the world. Even when individual members of minority groups may prefer to assimilate or participate in a larger society, they can still be forced to define their interests as part of the group if discrimination is sufficiently powerful or is established as a practice.[35] But even when the state has no systematic intentions to discriminate against the group concerned, as the influence of transnational economic actors grows, the individuals are yet increasingly alienated from political and economic decision-making centers.[36]

Anthony Alcock also considers that the will for secession is crucial in determining the secession movement.[37] For Geertz Clifford, social or economic discrepancies *per se* can create dissatisfaction and may initiate a revolution, but only dissatisfaction based on ethnic symbols, such as language, religion, culture, origin, or race, can lead to separatism.[38] Anthony D. Smith believes that discrimination and special identity are not in themselves sufficient reasons for the initiation of a secession movement, but also there is a need for a level of awareness of such circumstances. He believes that the secessionist movement emerges as a model based on a historical process and encompasses three phases: (1) the existence of a centralized bureaucracy and the development of a bureaucracy composed of professionals; (2) ethnic awakening as a result of the uneven distribution of resources and the rise of state regulation, with the past being reinterpreted by the intelligentsia; and (3) government denial of ethnic movements, discrimination, and lack of job opportunities. Smith links the demands for secession with the failure of the government to accommodate the demands of minorities based on various injustices.[39] Although not entirely in the same line, Pavkovic and Radan also consider that many of the secession cases are the usual outcome of continually denied political claims.[40]

International law is based on the idea of statehood, but events from the current and last centuries have shown that statehood (whether colonial or modern) that is most dependent on force is still not stable, and if it is forcibly imposed upon the people in the state concerned, that is, if it does not reflect the wishes of its members, it is even less justifiable, opines Judge Rosalyn Higgins. Such a situation combined with discrimination and the endangerment of its particular identity can become a catalyst for secession. In international relations, secession, as an option, is *a long stop* or *a bolt hole*, the ultimate opportunity for the group caught in total failure and

---

[34] Reece (1977).

[35] Hannum (1990).

[36] Reece (1977).

[37] Alcock (1979).

[38] Geertz (1967).

[39] Smith (1981); Smith (1997), pp. 21–35.

[40] Pavkovic and Radan (2007).

the unfulfilled balance between self-determination for all peoples and minority rights for some of the people.[41]

For Lea Brilmayer, when it comes to secession requests, it is surprising that the existing norms of international law focus on whether the group is considered to be a separate *people* and does not refer to the territoriality of its requirements. According to this *historical-territorial approach*, secessionist demands depend primarily not on the considerations of whether or not the concerned group represents a separate people but on the arguments based on the right to territory. Secession is typically a cure for past injustice, and the fact that the secessionist group is made up of people who are different does not in itself give any reason or "right" to secede. The secessionists claim that they have a right to a particular piece of land on which they seek to establish a new state and the relevance of their explicit territorial claim should be recognized under international law. The secessionists establish territorial claims upon a historical background, historical injustice, or some historical event when the territory was taken away by the dominant group in the country (or by a third party), and it was included within the borders of the existing state from which they want to secede. The secessionists firmly believe in the moral imperative of their territorial claims; they prefer to stay in the territory they aspire to keep and fight for it rather than simply leave the state. According to this territorial interpretation of the demands for secession, ethnic identity is not irrelevant, but it serves to explain the existence of these territorial claims. Individuals involved in secessionist movements generally identify with those who have been ill-treated in the past. Ethnic identification keeps historic injustice alive by passing the story from one generation to another as part of the legacy, considers Brilmayer.[42]

Ivo D. Duchacek reasons that there are stages in the development of the causes for secession. The group that seeks to secede is territorial-ideological, so at the beginning, the territorial alienation of the region from the center leads to the creation of a separatist ideology. Apart from injustice, the negligence of the center also plays a role, but when the independence movement begins, the further impetus is based on emotions and nationalism.[43]

Crawford Young distinguishes the primary factors for secessionism (ethnicity, religion, injustice, neglect, etc.) and the catalysts (such as a series of events that can trigger secession).[44]

For Donald L. Horowitz, the causes of secession are related and conditioned by the structure of the group. According to him, there are potentially four secessionist groups that outline different causes of secession: (1) regressive groups in a regressive region, (2) advanced groups in a backward region, (3) advanced groups in an advanced region, and (4) regressive groups in an advanced region. The first group secedes early, regardless of economic costs; the second group secedes only if

[41] Higgins (2003).

[42] Brilmayer (1991).

[43] Duchacek (1970), pp. 67–68; Duchacek (1977), pp. 8–9.

[44] Young (1975).

economic costs are low; the third group rarely secedes and only if the economic costs are low; and the fourth group rarely secedes, and if it does, then it does so regardless of economic costs. The first group would find a reason in, for example, disproportionate representation in public service and symbolic issues, such as language and religion; the third and fourth ground their reasons on cruel discrimination and violence, while for the second group, separatism is linked to the denial of proportionality and the political demands of foreigners or immigrants in the region.[45]

Alexis Heraclides [46] systematizes theories that explain the causes of separatism and the claim for independence, arguing that all of them point toward several descriptors:

1. *Internal colonialism* (a theory initiated by Lenin and later developed by Michael Hechter) [47]—according to this theory, states that are not integrated tend to be divided into two cultural groups: the core as the dominant group and the periphery. For this group of theorists, because of economic inequalities, the deprived cultural group opposes integration and aims at separatism (*these theories can hardly explain situations where a rich region wants to secede even though it is neither deprived nor put in an unequal position, e.g., the Flemish in Belgium*).
2. *Ethnicity or primordialism*—these are theories with a larger group of followers, such as Walker Conor, Cynthia Enloe, Nathan Glazer, Daniel Moynihan, Donald L. Horowitz, Harold Isaacs, Antony D. Smith, as well as the proponents of consociationalism, such as Arend Lijphart and Leo Cooper, who see ethnicity as a moving force, an independent variable regardless of inequality or dominance (*the disadvantage of these theories is that they cannot explain the secessionist movements of groups that can hardly be called ethnic, such as militant movements against inequality and the like*).
3. *Communalism*—the theory of communalism provides a much more general approach. The focus of this approach is on modernization as well as on the rise of the aspirations and interests of the elites who may disagree about resource allocation or directions for change, as well as when the privileged group fears losing them. Modern states, and especially those with medium levels of economic development, are unable to cope with social mobilization and are unable to meet the aspirations generalized by different groups. The followers of this theory are Samuel Huntington, Milton Esman, Rabuska and Shepsle, Orlando Patterson, Melson/Wlope, and Michael Banton (*these theories exaggerate the elements of greedy elites and manipulative leaders craving for power and diminish the importance of inequality and ethnic elements as an impetus for separatism*).[48]

[45] Horowitz (2000).

[46] Heraclides (1991).

[47] Hechter (1992).

[48] Hechter (1992).

Heraclides summarizes all these theories as (a) negative theories of cohesion, given by advocates of consensual democracy; (b) negative integration theories, according to which primordialism is a cause for disintegration; (c) indirect theories of disintegration or separatism, which include different interpretations of the phenomena of revolution, intergroup conflicts, and aggression; and (d) theories that provide social and psychological explanations and present the concept of deprivation or rapid growth of aspirations, which frustrates individuals and groups and causes even greater discord between expectations and opportunities.[49]

5.4 Secession Movements

5.4.1 Types of Session

There are multiple divisions of secessionist activities, which depend on their complexity, the consequences they cause, the acts on which they are based, the degree of violence that occurs in conflict, and the like. In any case, secession should be distinguished from other similar activities like irredentism [50] and revolutionary activities aimed at achieving a certain social change.[51] The closest to the secessionist movements are the secessionist-irredentist movements as well as the secessionist-adjoining movements. Some of them have historical requirements but no solid territorial basis or a separate territory on which they form a clear majority (such as Jews, Armenians, etc.), and for some, independence is a step toward integration or eventual union with an existing independent state. Based on the existing scholarship evolving around the types of secession, the following are the distinctions among secession movements:

(A) ***Sequential and recursive secessions*** [52]—the first type of secession appears as successive acts that lead to state decay, and the latter refers to additional sequences of secession from a state that has already parted. Unlike secession from the parent state, which is a single act, sequential secessions seek to destroy the parent state by withdrawing a greater territory that was under its jurisdiction (as in the case of the USSR and SFRY). Recursive secessions, on the other hand, are an attempt to separate the disaffected minority from the secessionist state and to join either their parent state or form their own state (Serbian Krajina in Croatia, Republika Srpska in Bosnia and Herzegovina, etc.).

[49] Heraclides (1991).

[50] N.b. Irredentism means the breaking away of a part of a state and its annexation to another neighboring state, while secession means the formation of a new independent state.

[51] See more at Connor (1972), p. 320; Wiberg (1983).

[52] Pavkovic and Radan (2007).

(B) ***Secession stricto sensu or simple secession (simpliciter) and progressive secession or secession in the broadest sense (incremental)*** [53]—in the first case, there is some formal act, such as a declaration of independence for the concerned region, adopted by the secessionist movement, while the latter case is a broader political activity that takes place in a violent or nonviolent manner and aims toward independence or some form of self-government, different from independence, and ranges from autonomy to a binational or multifederal system. In such a movement for secession, there is no formal act of independence, but secession is an ongoing process.[54]

(C) ***Nonviolent and violent secessions***—typically, secessions are divided into nonviolent and violent, depending on whether violence is used as a tool to achieve independence. Almost all authors try to determine why some secessions and secession attempts are extremely violent and some not. What is it that determines and what causes violence, and finally, what strategies do the parties apply in trying to avoid violent conflicts? The existence or nonexistence of violence during secession depends solely on the political environment. The political environment that contributes to a lack of violence in secession has several characteristics: there is a constitutional framework that has the capacity to channel secessionist demands; the secessionist units often form a different political entity of a federal or administrative type, with its own parliament or representative body; and the existing, parent state does not use force or threat of force against the secessionist movement.[55] In these cases, the use of violent methods would be counterproductive for the purposes of the secessionists. Pavkovic and Radan analyze cases of nonviolent secession in Iceland and Czechoslovakia and the attempted secession of Quebec and try to draw general conclusions. According to them, although violence and force are neither necessary nor preferred instruments for achieving secessionist goals, some of the organized groups use violence most often because they believe there is no other way to achieve their desire.[56] Secessionist movements often provoke the authorities, believing (and often rightly) that they will use force over time (e.g., Kosovo, Chechnya, and North Macedonia), not only against the militants but also against the civilians. This, they hope, will bring them international recognition and support.[57] In contrast to nonviolent secession, other factors

---

[53] Research by Heraclides (1991).

[54] According to Heraclides after the Second World War, almost all the secessionist movements are from this type, Heraclides (1991).

[55] See more at Pavkovic and Radan (2007), p. 65.

[56] Aleksandar Pavkovic examines why the demand for secession arose in these political environments. According to him, the probable reason is that in all these cases, the secessionist group differs from the majority population in terms of language and cultural characteristics, or the group has already been recognized as separate from the parent state. In all of these cases, the political and intellectual leaders of the group believe that their group is economically and socially downgraded; see more in Pavkovic and Radan (2007).

[57] Ormond (1993), p. 128.

that, according to Pavkovic and Radan, contribute to the outbreak of violence in the event of secession are the readiness and capacity of the existing, parent state to use force to prevent secession and suppress the secessionist movement; the readiness of the secessionist movement to use force to achieve its secessionist goals (which may include not only secession and international recognition but also an attempt to secure the desired boundaries of the secessionist territory); opposition to secession from the existing, parent state, led by a territorially concentrated group within the secessionist state; the existence of armed groups beyond the control of the main secessionist authorities and the control of the parent state.[58] In addition to these features of the political environment, there is always a trigger (drive) that leads to an escalation of violence (declaration of independence, referendum, rejection of secessionist demands, breach of contract, violence against the secessionist population, etc.).

Successful secessions (successful in terms of gaining independent statehood) add fuel to other secessionist movements. At the same time, governments have become increasingly restricted in response to secessionist attempts due to changes in international law and policy. The use of violence can often have an effect and can be used as an instrument to attract international attention. But if secessionist movements have at their disposal other effective instruments for achieving their goals, such as elections and negotiations within their parent state, the attractiveness of violence as a political instrument can be reduced though will not completely disappear.[59]

5.4.1.1 Examples of Violent Secessions: Biafra, Bangladesh, and Chechnya

In examining the violent secessions in Biafra, Bangladesh, and Chechnya, it is difficult to find common ground, so peaceful secessions seem to be similar, but in violent secessions, each case is separate, and it is very difficult to put them under a common denominator, although the circumstances and actions of the parties leading to violence are almost always the same. In all of this cases, violence and its threat were extensively used to achieve political ends, so the proclamation of secession was either followed or instantly escalated into political violence. The use of force followed unsuccessful negotiations or—due to non-compliance. Negotiations in the above examples concerned a division of power and competences between the secessionists and the central government, which was prepared to transfer power and guarantee a degree of autonomy but refused as in Confederate arrangements and the recognition of the legitimacy of the secessionist government. The leaders of both the secessionists and the parent state were prepared to use force but not be held accountable, that is, the elected body did not verify the use of force. And finally, it

[58] See more in Pavkovic and Radan (2007).

[59] see more at Pavkovic and Radan (2007).

turned out that during the negotiation process, the leaders of both the secessionist movement and the parent state publicly displayed personal animosity toward each other.[60]

5.4.2 Elements of Secession Movements

How can one recognize a secession movement? What are the elements that differentiate it from other social changes? The scholars are pointing toward the following basic elements of secession movements:

1. *Bordered territory* (the boundaries need to be determined and also have to be marked in due time).
2. *Population in that territory* (sometimes there is a minority that opposes secession and wants to stay within the existing state, but most often, this minority is not a major obstacle in the secessionists' paths. This minority is referred to as a "trapped minority").
3. *A political movement that addresses a targeted population in a particular territory* and (a) proclaimed independence for the new state in the form of a public statement by the new political authorities, sent to the population of the secessionist state and to other states. This statement/proclamation has at least two elements: naming the new state and publicly announcing that it has been established in order to dissociate it from the previous state. The word *secession* is often avoided because (in the sense of unilateral secession), it is seen as a violation of the territorial integrity of the existing state, so the secessionists rather use the term independence, which has a more positive connotation. Next, it (b) has made an effort to gain recognition from other states and international organizations.[61]

In the process, sociological elements are quite important. An important element also is negotiations between the secessionists and their parent state done during the whole process of secession. For the prospect of the success of secession, first of all, the secessionists must formulate the injustices in a way that shows that they personally affect each member of the target group, that the target group as a whole is a victim of gross injustices without their own guilt, and that the only remedy for those injustices should be the creation of a state that is controlled by the target group. A successful secession also includes the proclamation of independence and its international recognition, while in a failed secession, independence is declared without international recognition, i.e., it is considered merely an attempt at secession.[62]

[60] Pavkovic and Radan (2007) and Andrews (2020).

[61] Pavkovic and Radan (2007).

[62] Pavkovic and Radan (2007).

5.4.3 The Case of Catalonia: Attempt of Secession

The case of Catalonia is ongoing, and its trajectories are not clear. The latest developments—the referendum on the independence of Catalonia from Spain, the declaration of independence, and its suspension—are just a part of a series of events related to the tendencies of political movements for independence in this administrative unit. The trends stem from a modern wave of nationalism that has grown in Spain due to internal legal disagreements over the degree of autonomy. The internal mechanisms through which independence was sought (a series of referendums with disputed status, transitional laws, etc.) have a disputable legal basis. Legal and political theories know several examples that have the capacity to give effectiveness to the secessionist movement, that is, to initiate the act of secession, and one of them is the declaration of independence, but this is not the same as acquiring statehood. In the case of Catalonia, independence was declared but immediately suspended. The case of Catalonia is legally and politically complex. However, if the declaration of independence was effective or if it becomes effective in the future, the new entity—according to the traditional criteria and principles of international law—will face legal obstacles.

Catalonia is an autonomous community in the parliamentary monarchy of Spain. Its relations with Spain are governed by the Statute of Autonomy [63] and the Constitution of Spain.[64] The Statute of Autonomy defines the rights and obligations of the citizens of Catalonia, the political institutions in the Catalan region, their competencies and relations with the rest of Spain, as well as the financing of the Government of Catalonia. The enjoyed autonomy is limited in its scope and political in its content. The Constitution lists the competencies that the autonomous communities can have and at the same time provides a list of competencies that is reserved only for the state. The Statute is subordinated to the Constitution, and it is subject to the Constitutional Court's control.[65]

Catalan nationalism is an ideology according to which Catalans are a nation, and the Movement for the Independence of Catalonia is a political movement that historically stems from Catalan nationalism and advocates the independence of Catalonia from Spain. Despite the large degree of autonomy, the region, with 7.5 million people, has a strong separatist movement that was not always peaceful.[66] Although historically the initial idea of the nationalist movements was to restore or preserve self-government, to gain recognition for the Catalan language, etc., after a series of disagreements with the Spanish State regarding the degree of autonomy, the idea developed toward creating an independent state. The government and the

[63] Text of the Statute approved in 2006 (Internet source).

[64] Constitution of Spain (1978).

[65] Flores Juberías (1998).

[66] Andrews (2020).

Constitutional Court of Spain declared it illegal and banned [67] the last referendum on October 1, 2017, for the independence of Catalonia, but it still took place under heavy police pressure, accompanied by violence. The result of the referendum was in favor of independence, [68] and on that basis, on October 27, 2017, the Parliament of Catalonia approved the Resolution declaring independence from Spain by a secret ballot but immediately suspended it.[69] After several weeks of struggle, and under ultimate pressure to define Catalonia's status, the leaders of the political independence movement did not proclaim a clear declaration of independence. As a result, Article 155 of the Spanish Constitution was triggered, the Catalan Government was dismissed, and the central government from Madrid imposed direct rule. New elections were held in Catalonia under direct rule, and the three pro-independence parties again retained control of Parliament, but with a reduced majority. The Spanish Government arrested the Catalan officials involved in the organization of the referendum. Some of them are in exile and are calling for negotiations to find a common political solution to the independence crisis.

References

Alcock AE (1979) The development of governmental attitudes to cultural minorities in western industrial states. In: Alcock AE, Taylor BK, Welton JM (eds) The future of cultural minorities. Macmillan, London, pp 102–119

Andrews J (2020) The world in conflict. The Economist

Avishai M, Raz J (1990) National self-determination. J Philos (87):439–461

Basic NZ (2008) International law and security dilemmas in multiethnic states. Annu Surv Int Comp Law 8(1):1–32

Beran H (1984) A liberal theory of secession. Polit Stud 32(1):21–31

Beran H (1991) The consent theory of political obligation. Routledge Kegan & Paul

Beran H (1998) A democratic theory of political self-determination for a new world order. In: Lehning PB (ed) Theories of secession. Routledge, pp 33–61

Birch AH (1984) Another liberal theory of secession. Polit Stud 32:596–602

Bookman M (1992) The economics of secession. St. Martin Press, New York

Borkowski A, Plessis P (2005) Roman law. Oxford University Press

---

[67] The law for the creation of an independent republic was approved by the Catalan parliament in a session on September 6, 2017. Opposition parties protested the law, calling it "a blow to democracy and a violation of opposition rights." On September 7, the Catalan parliament passed a "transition law" to provide a legal framework pending the adoption of the new constitution. The same day, Spain's Constitutional Court suspended it and ruled that the referendum could not legally go ahead.

[68] The referendum was disputed, and irregularities in the voting were noted, where anti-independence groups claimed that the same people voted more than once. The result was an overwhelming vote for independence, but because of the boycott of the opponents of secession, the turnout was only 43% for secession, Andrews (2020), p. 8.

[69] The decision was made by a vote of 70-10 in the absence of the deputies, who refused to participate in the vote because they considered it illegal, that is, contrary to the decisions of the Constitutional Court of Spain.

Brilmayer L (1991) Secession and self-determination: a territorial interpretation. Yale J Int Law 16:177–202
Buchanan A (1991) Secession: the morality of political divorce from Fort Sumter to Lithuania and Quebec. Westview Press
Buchanan A (1998) The international institutional dimension of secession. In: Lehning PB (ed) Theories of secession. Routledge, pp 225–255
Cassese A (1995) Self-determination of the peoples, a legal reappraisal. Cambridge University Press
Collier P, Hoeffler A (2005) The political economy of secession. In: Hannum H, Babbitt EF (eds) Negotiating self-determination. Lexington Books, pp 37–61
Connor W (1972) Nation building or nation destroying? World Polit 24(3):319–355
Constitution of Spain (1978)
Dahliz J (ed) (2003) Conflict avoidance and - regional appraisals. Asser Press
Duchacek ID (1970) Comparative federalism, the territorial dimension of politics. Holt, Rinehart and Winston, New York
Duchacek ID (1977) Antagonistic cooperation: territorial and ethnic communities. Publius 7(4):3–29
Flores Juberías C (1998) Regionalization and autonomy in Spain: the making of the "Estado de las Autonomías". In: Suksi M (ed) Autonomy: applications and implications. Kluwer Law International, pp 195–223
Geertz C (1967) The integrative relations: primordial sentiments and civic politics in the new states. In: Welch CE (ed) Political modernization, Belmont, pp 167–188
Hannum H (1990) Autonomy, sovereignty, and self-determination, the accommodation of conflict rights. University of Pennsylvania Press
Hechter M (1992) The dynamics of secession. Acta Sociol (35):267–283
Heraclides A (1991) The self-determination of the minorities in the international politics. Frank Cass and Company Limited
Higgins R (2003) Self-determination and secession at secession and international law. In: Dahliz J (ed) Conflict avoidance and - regional appraisals. Asser Press, pp 21–39
Horowitz DL (2000) Ethnic groups in conflict. University of California Press
Horowitz DL (2003) The cracked foundations of the right to secede. J Democr 14(2):5–17
Miller D (1995) On nationality. Clarendon Press, Oxford
Norman W (2003) Domesticating secession. In: Macedo S, Buchanan A (eds) Secession and self-determination. New York University Press, pp 193–237
Ormond J (1993) The North Caucasus: fragmentation of federation? In: Bremmer I, Taras R (eds) Nations and politics in the Soviet successor states. Cambridge University Press, pp 448–477
Pavkovic A, Radan P (2007) Creating new states, theory and practice of secession. Ashgate Publishing Limited
Reece JE (1977) The Bretons against France. University of North Carolina Press
Rothbard MN (1994) Nations by consent: decomposing the nation-state. J Libertarian Stud 11(1):1–10
Smith AD (1981) The ethnic revival. Cambridge University Press
Smith AD (1997) Towards a theory of ethnic separatism. Ethn Racial Stud 2(1):21–37
Tamir Y (2002) Liberalni nacionalizam (Liberal nationalism). Filip Visnjic, Beograd
Text of the Statute approved in 2006. https://web.gencat.cat/en/generalitat/estatut/estatut2006/. Accessed 3 Sept 2022
Wellman C (1995) A defense of secession and self-determination. Philos Public Aff 24(2):142–171
Wiberg H (1983) Self-determination as an international issue. In: Lewis IM (ed) Nationalism and self determination in the Horn of Africa, pp 43–65
Wood JR (1981) Secession: a comparative analytical framework. Can J Polit Sci 14:109–135
Young C (1975) Nationalism and separatism in Africa. In: Kilson M (ed) New states in the modern world. Cambridge, pp 166–175

Chapter 6
The Dynamics of Secession

6.1 Introduction

Once the secession demands are put in place, the secessionists will strive to convince the target group that the state they inhabit is foreign and that they will have better protection from injustice, more political power, and more economic resources in their own state. [1] But besides this, the population needs to be mobilized to act in that direction. Mobilization is done in different ways, and the message is transmitted through different channels, but most often through educational institutions and educational texts, whereas the simplicity and actuality of the message play a great role. Additionally, the message can be disseminated through posters as well as propaganda in print and electronic media. [2]

In the event of an attempted secession (proclaimed independence, an outbreak of violence), the parent (existing) state may not be ready to negotiate a full transfer of power and jurisdiction but may be prepared to negotiate with the secessionist leaders to transfer a part of the power to the secessionist groups. But sometimes negotiations do not result in an agreement. In that case, the secessionists proclaim secession unilaterally without prior agreement with the parent (existing) state, and the parent states only accept such a unilateral declaration of independence when it is weakened by internal fragmentation and is no longer in a position to impose control over the secessionist territory. The secessionists usually proclaim unilateral secession at a time when they believe that such a proclamation will have a maximum effect on both the parent state and other states seeking to gain recognition. This is called an opportunistic moment, a moment when it has the best chance of pushing the political withdrawal of the targeted territory and of gaining international recognition of its independence. The secessionist leaders decide when "that

[1] Hechter (1992), pp. 267–283.

[2] Pavkovic and Radan (2007).

N. Shikova, *Self-Determination and Secession*,
https://doi.org/10.1007/978-3-031-34322-3_6

moment" is, and if that moment does not exist, then they create conditions where such a chance would appear by itself. [3]

In all cases of secession, there is a group that is culturally and linguistically different from the majority group. But national diversity in itself is not a factor in the group's secession (though for many theorists, it is a necessary condition for secession), but the triggers are the ones that encourage the secession (such as an independence declaration, a referendum, a rejection of secessionist demands, breach of contracts, violence against the secessionist population, or a combination of some or all of them). [4] It is even difficult to single out or identify an event or set of events leading to secession. However, secession has its own dynamics and generally has a certain trajectory in which the secessionist activity moves. The following components determine the dynamics of secession: [5]

i. ***Conditions of secession***—anything that makes people receptive to the proposal for secession (e.g., alienation from the state; geographical conditions—segregation; social prerequisites, such as ethnicity (expressed in language, culture, race, etc.), other than the majority of the population of the state; the way the group fits into the state; economic preconditions and economic injustice; political preconditions, such as a lack of political legitimacy; psychological preconditions, such as the desire for self-protection and self-preservation). [6]
ii. ***The rise of the secessionist movement (mobilization)***—what distinguishes secessionist movements from others types of mobilization is the ideology, such as nationalism, and having a leadership/political entrepreneurship that is able to articulate dissatisfaction and emphasize it in everyday politics, but also the ability to use strategies that will lead to success or the overall organization that aims to gain support from the target group. [7]
iii. ***The response of the central government*** to the secessionist movement and its demands, which can be divided into two categories: violent suppression and accommodation.
iv. ***Direct triggers of secession***—confrontations that lead to unconditional demands for a particular state (actions when leaders openly declare secession or actions aimed at forcing the state to react).
v. ***Resolving the secessionist crisis with armed conflict***, although many of these movements do not escalate to a state of complete war.

[3] Pavkovic and Radan (2007).

[4] Pavkovic and Radan (2007).

[5] The theoretical framework is developed by John. R. Wood; see more in Wood (1981), pp.109–135.

[6] For Wood, neither of these circumstances, nor several of them together, are sufficient for secession, although each past and current secession or attempt for secession contains some of them, Wood (1981).

[7] If the minority/secessionist group does not have a very coherent agenda as a condition for negotiations, the escalating conflict will soon turn into empty political power, and both sides are in a position where absolute positions—separatism or coercive unity, which the majority seeks to impose—are the only options, Hannum (1990).

6.2 Prerequisites (Predictors) for Secession

According to Ernst Haas, political integration is a "(…) process whereby political actors from several separate political systems are persuaded to move their loyalties, expectations, and political activities to a new center and to new institutions that already possess or need to establish a new jurisdiction over the pre-existing system."[8] In contrast, secession decision is a decision of political disintegration and is a process whereby political actors from one or more subsystems withdraw their loyalties from the center of jurisdiction to focus on their own center.

Alexis Heraclides[9] seeks to establish a model through which secession is studied and to explain the circumstances and conditions that lead to the emergence of armed separatism and secession. According to Heraclides, there are three basic and independent variables that interact, which pose a threat to the center, and without them secession is meaningless. They are (1) territory and the territorial basis for collectivity; (2) the existence of a significant part of the population, a collective that defines itself as different; and (3) the type of relationship that exists between the center and the collective.

Heraclides seeks to answer which kind of territory, what collectivity, and what relation is more likely to create separatism, including armed conflict and secession. For him, the territory that was previously independent, especially if it is a land by the sea, is a more appropriate reason for the development of a secessionist movement on it. This is more likely if the population has historical roots in that territory. The more the territory is different and further away from the center, the capital, and the decision-making site, the more it can contribute to inspiring a sense of group identity. Heraclides is particularly interested in groups that have the potential to create a secessionist movement, and according to him, those groups are concentrated and constitute the majority of a given territory within the state. Secessionists are emerging everywhere, says Heraclides, as groups with a different language and culture (such as the Kurds) or groups with the same language and culture (such as the American Confederation). The question is which group is more likely to develop a secessionist movement, whether violent or not?

The demands of groups that have weak or no territorial basis often remain underdeveloped and unrealistic, says Heraclides. A group that is significant by number in the state but spreads across several enclaves or cities also cannot be a basis for serious demands for secession (such as the African American population in the United States), and such groups most often seek different forms of pressure to make a change. Although through migrations the dispersed group can strengthen its territorial base, or even form a base for the very first time. Various terms are used to describe communal or separatist groups, such as tribe, race, minority, ethnic group, nation, and its affiliates. A very interesting question is, why do some groups seeking greater power and control more easily accommodate, while others enter into a

[8] Haas (1968), p. 16.

[9] Heraclides (1991).

military-repressive circle, and their demands escalate in secessionist movements that threaten the territorial integrity of the established state?

Certainly, the most explosive are ethnic conflicts, and they are a subset of the larger set of political conflicts, involving conflicts over classes, castes, or party lines, which mark the political landscape of developing democracies, although many radically underline the diversity of ethnic conflicts and point them out as opposed to other types of political conflicts. Some scholars think that mobilizing ethnic groups is the same as mobilizing other groups to gain greater power and control. Thus, this perspective shows that ethnic conflicts are not irreparable expressions of deep-seated differences and imbalances caused by modernization.[10] However, for Heraclides, of all the separatist groups, the minority group has the greatest potential, regardless of disagreements in legal and political theory about what constitutes a minority. According to him, not just the minority, but all the concepts that apply to different groups are not sufficient to define all groups that are aspiring for secession, so he introduces two concepts: "community" and "society," and under them, he lists all groups seeking some form of separatism—from autonomy to independence. According to this classification, a separate community can be any group in the country that can clearly define itself as different from other groups based on prescribed cultural markers. A separate society is a society whose members believe that self-existence is not associated with such symbols of oneness but is based on territory and perhaps on history and ideology. Members of a separate society are convinced that self-government will result in far greater justice and equality for different ethnic groups than the previous single unified state system. [11]

Separate communities may be based on a sense of nationality where language does not have to be a unifying factor but may be based on ethnonational identity, religious or historical identity, and, in some cases, race or a very broad definition of common culture. A separate society can be an alliance of territories or territories defined by a community that defines itself on the basis of territory or ideology. For a group to become a different community or a different society, it must be able to challenge, to create a boundary between itself and others. Such a boundary can cut across religious, cultural, racial, historical, and even linguistic links and replace other forms of identity, such as class, sex, or ideology, at a given historical moment, considers Heraclides. [12]

Similarly, Viva Ona Bartkus, [13] seeks to analyze secession movements and operates in terms of a "separate community," which represents any territorially concentrated community of people seeking to change their own political situation through demands for either increased autonomy or complete independence, peacefully or

---

[10] Kohli (2002).

[11] Heraclides (1991).

[12] Heraclides (1991), p. 16.

[13] Bartkus (1999).

through the use of force. For Bartkus, this (*rather simplistic*) approach has two benefits—firstly, the term "separate communities" does not cause political associations; secondly, it is inclusive of all communities seeking to change political circumstances, whether they persist within the bounds of an established state and want to stay where they are or push for secession. For the author, a community is "separate" if it has certain objective characteristics, such as religion, language, culture, race, or ethnicity, and more importantly, people in this group perceive these characteristics as separate. It is a community, in the sense of the imagined community that Benedict Anderson is talking about, reasons Bartkus.

For Bartkus, there are four essential elements that are associated with each secession crisis, and they include the following: (1) the existence of a diverse community, (2) territorial requirements, (3) leadership of the diverse community, and (4) dissatisfaction. For the secessionist crisis to occur, these four elements must be present, but they do not have to be in specific or fixed values, levels, or proportions. Secessionist crises are possible when a particular community demands a particular territory and are more or less persistent or when definitions of a particular group are more or less fluid or when sources of dissatisfaction are more or less ignored or when community leadership is more or less inspired. On the other hand, the relatively strong community awareness and sense of injustice require less inspirational leadership to provoke a secessionist crisis. Skilled leaders can act as catalysts, and they can articulate cultural or economic demands in a political debate. The secession crisis presupposes the community's belief in the inherent justice that lies behind its cause. [14]

Heraclides agrees that the boundaries that the group establishes between itself and others do not have to be inflexible, but for separatism to be born, there must be some inferiority to the group (disadvantage, inequality or disparity, discrepancy), present or past, current or suppositional. If such a deficiency does not exist, it must be invented to achieve or provoke territorial separatism. The more the group can be characterized as an ethnic group or nation, the more secondary is the role of inequality or inferiority in triggering separatism. Conversely, the more the group lacks national or ethnic identity, the bigger the importance of inequality is and the greater the degree of inequality should be to develop separatism. However, for Heraclides, economic, class, or intellectual discontent causes a revolution, but discontent based on race, language, or culture causes division, irredentism, merger, or the redrawing of the boundaries of an existing state. [15]

Apart from the previously established variables—territory, group, and interconnections, which can initiate secessionist movements in different environments (from underdeveloped to modern states, even in those that have already gone through a secession process)—for scholars, there are series of factors that can further enhance secessionist movements, such as political, economic, social, psychological,

[14] Bartkus (1999).

[15] See more at Heraclides (1991).

international, and other factors, but the most prominent are colonialism and colonization, increased state intervention in the social and economic field, modernization and communication, alienation, the sinking of the political scene, and the lack of action. [16]

6.2.1 The Moro Region: Preconditions That Determine the Success of a Secession Movement

The Philippines was a Spanish colony from 1523 to 1898, and the United States took over it in 1898, followed by the Japanese occupation, and finally, the independence of the Philippines came in 1946. [17] There are two large groups of the population living in the Philippines—Christians and Muslims, who are poor and deprived and living in the southeastern part of the country, which is rich in natural resources. Over the years, Muslims have been able to resist Spanish attempts at Christianization, but the United States has also managed them in a special way. The Muslim-populated territory is an archipelago of islands, representing 39% of the entire Philippine country and is populated by 13 Islam-related ethnic groups, with a historical region and territory. With the independence of the Philippines, Muslims were able to enjoy cultural rights, but in 1966, Ferdinand Marcos, a Filipino leader who came to power, ruled an authoritarian government and advocated centralization. As a result, hostilities began, and in 1968, a movement of resistance emerged in the Moro region, without a clear vision for independence. The rebels from the Moro region had outside help, especially from Islamic countries, but they were lacking strong leadership and had no clear ideology, which divided them based on ethnic differences and personal ambitions. In 1976, they signed a deal with the center to acquire autonomy in their region, spanning 13 out of the 21 provinces of the Philippines. [18] That divided them, so Marcos took advantage of the situation and raised the issue of independence in a referendum, with the residents of the Moro region having to say whether they wanted to continue with their resistance or agree to their autonomy within the Philippines. The option of autonomy won, which Marcos implemented according to his own vision and form. However, the movement dissolved, disintegrated, and lost its core and orientation. [19] Now, the issue of the Moro region is still unresolved, and guerrilla groups are still active. In 2018, the Philippine President, signed new legislation, the Organic Law for Bangsamoro in the Autonomous Region in Muslim Mindanao, which grants extra autonomy to Muslim communities living in the southern Philippines. [20] The effort was welcomed by the UN and raised hopes

[16] Geertz (1967).

[17] Andrews (2020).

[18] Tripoli Agreement (1976).

[19] Heraclides (1991); Petty (2019); Andrews (2020).

[20] Republic Act No. 11054 (2018).

that it will help end the years of violence among the central government troops and militants from the Moro Islamic Liberation Front. [21]

6.2.2 Calculations Regarding Secession

The secessionist attempt has an express purpose, which is to break up a previously united, independent state. Territories resulting from secession may, at least in the first years of separation, lack state-building economic and military power. Besides that, there is always the danger that secession will push the secessionist entities under international economic mercy to survive economically, and on the other hand, the other danger is that they need to defend themselves from external aggressors. [22] There are three separate benefits associated with self-determination and secession. First, nations can best guarantee their own security if they possess sovereign power. Second, there is the opportunity to organize political life according to the values and culture of the community. Third, nations that aspire statehood on the basis of the first two gains continue to upset world peace if such aspirations are denied. Secession can be logical but not an inevitable outcome of the process of political disintegration. [23]

Viva Ona Bartkus proposes an analytical framework for analyzing the costs-benefits of staying and the costs-benefits of secession from an existing state, arguing that such a framework does not negate or minimize moral issues that are part of the decision to secede. For Bartkus, a secessionist crisis arises when leaders of a territorially concentrated and diverse community within a larger state transform dissatisfaction into secessionist demands and gain power either through sufficiently strong internal mobilization or through the use of force to coerce the central government to respond to those demands. She structures her analytical framework around several variables. [24] Some of these costs and benefits are clearly quantitative, while others are almost impossible to quantify. But these variables cannot be considered static conditions. Secession only occurs when the different community perceives that there is a shift in the balance between these four variables, within each and between them. Only change motivates the dynamics of secession. These changes that shift the balance represent changes at the state level, as well as changes at the international system level, and include rapidly moving events, such as sequences of political or economic initiatives and also a gradual change in attitudes, such as increasing discrimination or changing levels of diversity tolerance. Although the community may want its own country, which will be governed by its members and embody its values and culture, the desire itself does not cause a sectarian crisis.

---

[21] UN News (2018).

[22] Buchheit (1978).

[23] Bartkus (1999).

[24] Bartkus (1999), p. 10.

Some factors related to human nature and motive for secession do, such as the emergence of an opportunistic moment, habits, traditions, or inertia, which according to Bartkus constitute an additional direct cost of secession.

In using the term "cost," the author abstracts it from its normal use, which implies a financial loss, and connects it to the position of a victim, with no economic chances, no political rights, and no autonomy or whose cultural heritage is endangered, which together escalate into political repression and systematic violence. Benefits can be seen as the opposite of costs, and their definition is also abstracted from potential economic benefits and refers to the rights and chances of a decent living without major external threats. For the author, human behavior is not so rational as to use this entirely to explain a current or historical secessionist crisis. [25]

(a) Benefits of Peaceful Cohabitation

The benefits of staying in the existing state are linked to the potential services and advantages that the state provides for a particular community in general, not just for some particular individuals—its members. These are security benefits, economic benefits, and benefits related to social factors. *Security benefits* are reflected in the maintenance of state order and the protection of citizens from violence, as well as the guarantees of protection from external aggressors. *The economic benefits* can be achieved in two ways: by unifying more regional economies with a coherent set of regulations (e.g., placing products on the wider market, access to raw materials, integration into the wider network of transport and communications, etc.), and benefits that the state provides to its citizens through the development of specific policies, assistance, subsidies, use of the technology in education, health, etc. Citizens who perceive these benefits are therefore most opposed to secession. *Social benefits* consist of the social opportunities that the existing state offers to different communities, such as cultural diversity and protection of that diversity, educational opportunities, social programs for adequate development and protection of certain groups or individuals belonging to them, and guarantee of full and equal enjoyment of human rights. In sum, the communities enjoy security and economic and social advantages through the maintenance of their position in the larger, existing state, but the relative importance of each of these constituent benefits is difficult to determine as it depends on every case.

(b) Costs of Secession

The state's opposition to secession and the existence of international hostility to such an act is one of the most common costs of secession. These factors include the attitude toward secession and the inherent conflict between the principle of self-determination and territorial integrity, which are the most effective means for deterring the idea of secession. Even if the secessionist movement wins the battlefield, it is likely to lose the diplomatic battle, mainly because states are usually reluctant to recognize the secessionist entity or accept its membership in a regional or international body. *International hostility to secession* as diplomatic isolation is a high

[25] Bartkus (1999).

expense of secession, though both the state and the secessionist entity may find international support for their causes in international law. In many cases of secession, international organizations have remained silent, and states have sought to keep such crises out of the UN agenda. States believe that secession and the loss of territory will harm interests and, above all, security, wealth, and prestige, and cause fears of a *domino effect*. Therefore, states almost unanimously (except in a few rare cases) oppose secession, but that does not discourage the secessionists in their idea either. This set of factors includes other very complex economic challenges, such as currency creation, trade, the banking system, and the like. However, these economic holdings have low priority in secession calculations as secessionist leaders are much more occupied with the reactions from the state to which they are segregated as well as with the reactions from the international community than with the real calculation of economic challenges.

(c) Membership Costs

The cost of membership can be divided into two groups. The first group is physical suffering, such as hunger, poverty, deportation, death threats, mass murder, genocide (where the true degree of security against these threats is not as important as the perception of the community for its own security). The second group is the threat over the group's culture, such as forced assimilation and destruction of the community's cultural wealth, to completely merge it into the larger community, as well as the political, economic threats as official policies that create political domination or economic exploitation of a particular ethnic group.

(d) Benefits of Secession

The benefits of secession are—above all—the satisfying interests of the ethnic elite, or the community at large, in terms of realized national self-determination, as a way in which the community determines its own political destiny. Other benefits include chances for social gain and the social promotion of ethnic elites, whose historical claim is to dominate in an independent state and maintain power and privileges. [26]

Bartkus proposes a comprehensive perspective on secession, to overcome the defects of the current prominent but segmented theories. Although the proposed analytical framework has obvious inconsistencies, it aims toward a better understanding of the decision to secede. In theory, cost-benefit analysis is most often used as a justification for future action and not to explain past action. The inconsistency of the author is obvious concerning the terms used in the frame because she simplifies them due to greater clarity. About the proposed framework, its value can be emphasized as an experiment or an indicator of something. The strength of the proposed framework lies in its intercultural (cross-cultural) applicability and in its ability to help detect common patterns of secession, to indicate some of the policies that can be effective in preventing and resolving secessionist crises, and to establish conditions that may limit their effectiveness, and, finally, to highlight some factors that may influence future trends in determining the phenomenon of secession. Other

[26] Bartkus (1999).

authors consider the costs and benefits of secession in the general sense, that is, as circumstances rather than as preconditions for secession.

6.3 Economic Justification of Secession

Many of the recent quests for secession are based on economic predictions. [27] The proponents of secession try to convince the inhabitants of the region striving for independence that independence will bring them economic and social welfare. Additionally, they present their secessionist quest to the outside countries as economically justified, hoping that, in that way, they will gain political points and possible international recognition for the new entity. However, this is quite unclear. With the data on disposal and even the complicated economical estimations, it is not quite possible to predict what the future holds and whether it will push forward or bring backward the new "independent" state.

Although the financial market, banks, and insurance companies are increasingly uniting, we live in a global world where cultures are more and more differentiated. Globalization exposed particularities and strengthened nationalistic feelings and increased the wishes for separate statehood. As an opposite trend, seemingly contradictory, political entities that attempt to become independent are guided by the wish to obtain or maintain an EU membership. However, globalization made the social relations of countries less local and opened ways toward new rights of choice which are crossing borders that, until recently, were protected by tradition, nationalism, language, or ideology. The growth of these transnational interdependences changed the continuity of the nations, and it became harder to preserve separate national characteristics. [28] Moreover, the role of the state has changed. The state is permanently changing, and in the contemporary times, there has been a substantive change in its character. Besides the need to serve national bodies, the state faces the need to serve global institutions. The traditional nation-state is also weakened, not only because it transferred to regional organizations the power of decision-making in regard to economic, strategic, and ecological issues but also because it transferred the power to create a cultural policy to the local and national communities. [29]

Despite many economic theories dealing with the aspects of secession, in this complex situation and interdependent world, it is difficult to justify secession on economic grounds. The quests for secession are based on nationalistic sentiments, and the nation is not a ratio but a feeling or, as Ernst Renan pointed out, a heart! [30]

---

[27] (Nb.) That has been a dominant argument for the Scottish referendum for independence, as well as in Catalonia, where several documents about the potential economic benefits of a Catalan independent state were outlined.

[28] Falk (2002); Hannum (1990); Alger (2011); Anderson (1982); Giordano (2001); Baudrillard (1991); De Soza Santos (2003).

[29] Tamir (2002).

[30] Renan (1882).

From a legal point of view, it is clear that international law does not accept secession, although the political phenomenon exists, and with or without the support of the international community, there have been cases of secession realized in several "waves of secession." The last one—done after the fall of the iron curtain in the '90s of the previous century and later under the cover of continuation of the dissolution of the Socialist Federal Republic of Yugoslavia (SFRY) – created many new entities and left many open questions. Some of them are the following: Are the newly created political entities substantially capable of making independent decisions in the period of globalization and regionalization? Did the separation and independence bring them economic benefits and welfare? In that sense, can we prove that their secessions are economically justified? [31]

The economic implications of independence may vary according to the level of development of the countries. Most scholars indicate that achieving independence from any given country is likely to be more beneficial for richer than for poorer countries [32] and that the economic benefits of independence depend on how the process of secession took place. In essence, it is considered that where secession happened without real conflict and without significant alteration of previous socio-economic links to the rest of the world, the secession did not have any noticeable impact on the resulting economic performance. When secession is achieved by conflict and the disruption of preexisting trade patterns, all those factors involved in the process suffer. [33]

Despite the fact that, in the recent quests for secession, economic arguments are dominant, there is relatively little research about the economic implication of secession and how independence affected the economy of new countries. Studies that have been done are confirming that the evidence of a correlation between the economy and secession is still highly imperfect. That is due to the lack of data for analysis and not having sound historical cases for conducting appropriate research. [34] Hence, it is difficult to make these secession cases justified on economic grounds and even make any future predictions that can stand on solid empirical data. For example, in shaping the secession quest, in the case of Kosovo, there were other issues in question concerning the decision for secession irrespectively of economic considerations; on the other hand, the secession of Montenegro was seen as a possibility for economic growth. However, the attempts to make an ex ante evaluation of possible secession, which can confirm and economically justify the decision for separation and independence, are even more questionable. The arguments for secession can be found in some other indicators connected to separate identity, desire for self–rule, oppression, and remedy, but it can hardly be said that empirically

[31] Shikova and Sadiku (2017), pp. 38–60.

[32] Brosio and Revelli (2003), pp. 127–142.

[33] Rodrigues and Stermsek (2014).

[34] Rodrigues and Stermsek (2014).

measurable and objective economical parameters can provide grounds for the justification of secession. [35]

6.3.1 *The Example of Kosovo*

Kosovo is one of the smallest countries in Europe. [36] It declared its independence in 2008 and is still a disputed territory. [37] Kosovo is not a member of the UN, but it is a member of many international and regional organizations. [38] However, many countries do not accept Kosovo's statehood because of the many issues concerning the legality of its creation and since it does not possess all the attributes needed to obtain full statehood. One of them is the Republic of Serbia from which Kosovo declared its independence. [39]

In regard to the legality of its creation, unilateral secession is not acceptable under international law, so scholars who are in favor of its independence consider the case of Kosovo as *sui generis*. For the ones that are supporting Kosovo's independence, the separation of Kosovo is a continuation of the dissolution of SFR Yugoslavia, done by the principle *uti possiedetis juris*, previously applicable during the decolonization. For some theorists, the secession of Kosovo is legitimate since it was done as a last resort— it is remedial secession implicitly recognized in Resolution 1244. [40] However, with the previous governance of the UN administration over the territory, the application of the last resort or remedial secession theory can be questioned as well. [41] In this respect, many scholars do not accept Kosovo as a legitimate state; they even consider that the recognition of Kosovo as a state is against the UN Preamble, which protects the principle of territorial integrity (in this case, the territorial integrity of Republic of Serbia). But the opposite notion is that

---

[35] Shikova and Sadiku (2017).

[36] According to the 2011 census, Kosovo has less than two million inhabitants.

[37] Allcock (2022).

[38] As of September 2020, 97 UN member states recognized the Republic of Kosovo and 22 EU member states.

[39] Historically, the problem of Kosovo is a problem of dominance of two ethnic groups (Serbian and Albanians) that demographically predominated in the territory in different historical periods. The breakup of former Yugoslavia in the 1990s, the denial of rights and the abolition of Kosovo's autonomy, and then the ethnic cleansing left coexistence a fragile concept, add to that the long-time rivalry between groups, which makes mutual acceptance hard to achieve despite all conflict reconciliation efforts. Since the establishment of the UN administration—after the NATO intervention in 1999 done without the UN General Council's decision, Kosovo has set the road toward its independence with clear international help. Resolution 1244 did not set the final status of Kosovo, but for many, it was clear that after the UN administration, Kosovo would not be returned under Serbian sovereignty; see more in Popović et al. (1990); Bekaj (2010); Krasniqi (2010); Baskin and Pickering (2010).

[40] Security Council Resolution 1244 (1999).

[41] Vidmar (2004), pp. 779–849.

with the establishment of UN administration over the territory and setting up Kosovo as a protectorate, the parent state—the Republic of Serbia—already lost its sovereignty.

Nevertheless, Kosovo is a fact, but it can hardly be said that it is an independent entity, it being completely dependent on international support and donors and not having effective control over a part of its territory. Considering its economic situation before and after the secession of Kosovo, in analyzing two transitional periods—the period under UN administration and the period after the declaration of independence in 2008—it is difficult to obtain solid results in those periods as Kosovo's economy depends on the presence of international forces that boost GDP and current international support. In that sense, any analysis can be only indicative. In Kosovo's case, economic growth jumped in 2001 but decreased in 2002, and it had been lower than Serbia's until 2008; at that juncture, the global financial crisis attacked all the economies in the region and Serbia's as well. Moreover, the wave of the public debt crisis that seized a great number of Eurozone members in the second half of 2011 stopped the mild recovery of all Balkan countries. Though the economy of Kosovo was less affected by the global financial crisis than the economy of Serbia and Montenegro, its economy had suffered from the negative effects of the war and long-term conflict. Growth perhaps will depend on further development—if the country will gain full international recognition and will join the UN. [42]

6.3.2 *The Example of Montenegro*

Montenegro is a tiny republic that encompasses an Adriatic coastline, lowlands, and high mountains. [43] The isolation and special military tactics helped the inhabitants keep their separate characteristics and, in the fifteenth century, obtain substantive autonomy from the Ottoman Empire. As an independent principality, Montenegro emerged in 1878, and during that same year, its independence was recognized by international treaties. Before the First World War, Montenegro was free; afterward, although there were opponents to the incorporation, it became a part of the Kingdom of Serbs, Slovenes, and Croats (later renamed the Kingdom of Yugoslavia). The resistance was present even when the Kingdom of Yugoslavia became SFRY and Montenegro a constitutive republic. Following the breakup of Yugoslavia, in the '90s, the pro-independence string was still strong, but the unionist prevailed, so Montenegro became a part of the new federation—first federative Yugoslavia and later the Federation of Serbia and Montenegro. Since one part of the Federation (Republic of Serbia) was facing different challenges—especially in regard to Kosovo—the balance shifted toward independence. [44]

[42] Shikova and Sadiku (2017).

[43] Montenegro's population is around half a million inhabitants.

[44] Montenegro votes to secede from Serbia (2006).

In the beginning, the EU was not in favor of further separation of the Balkan countries and set conditions for obtaining independence—as an agreed threshold that had to be reached in a forthcoming referendum. In this respect, a referendum was held in 2006, and the majority of votes were for independence. Although the Republic of Serbia, at first, objected to the country's independence, soon it accepted it. Montenegro immediately became a member of the UN and, in 2007, took steps toward EU accession. In 2010, Montenegro became a candidate country for EU membership, and in 2012, accession negotiations began. In the meantime, Montenegro was accepted by many international and regional organizations. [45]

Montenegro's secession was not labeled as violent. The people were not suffering from an oppressive or repressive government. Although done as unilateral secession, soon the "parent state," the Republic of Serbia, accepted the referendum results for independence, and there was no violation of international law. The case of Montenegro was seen as a further dissolution of Yugoslavia, and with the Montenegrin secession, this process ended. The secession triggers were not related to national identity, and there were no disputes over Montenegrin recognition. [46]

During the period when the debate over whether to stay or leave the federation was led, the main arguments of the proponents were economically related. The pro-union camp claimed that Montenegro is too small to be viable on its own, whereas the pro-independence camp considered that breaking away will bust the economy and speed up the country's path toward the EU. [47]

Presently, Montenegro has an upper- and middle-income economy. [48] However, the economy of Montenegro is predominately service based and significantly depends on foreign direct investments. But its tourism sector is well developed and contributes highly to the country's economy. Regarding Montenegro's economic growth, it had been lower than Serbia's until 2005 and higher in 2005–2008, but the financial crisis of 2008 had a more negative impact on Montenegro's economy. Thus, the economic benefits of secession for Montenegro might be more expressed after a longer period. [49]

---

[45] Montenegro Country Profile (2018) (Internet source).

[46] *De facto* independence existed, and there are theoretics who think that Montenegrin secession was made *de jure* secession by the EU and the USA mainly as a strategy for undermining the Milosevic regime. As a result, the de facto small state has become the second largest per capita recipient of direct USA financial assistance, Montenegro Country Profile (2018) (Internet source).

[47] Many of them believed that they were a hostage to Serbia on an economic level. The reforms launched in Montenegro were not followed in Serbia, which had been in a long economic crisis; for more, see 'After twenty-four years of union with Serbia Montenegro is independent again' (2006).

[48] The World Bank Country Overview (Internet source).

[49] Shikova and Sadiku (2017).

6.4 Possible Supporters of Secession Movements

It is easy to conclude that half of the countries in the world are involved in some sort of secession movement, usually in more than one. If, according to Alexis Heraclides,[50] the distance from the center of the territory and its exit to the sea are factors that play a major role in developing a secessionist movement and deciding on secession, if weak ethnic links between groups cause a higher level of injustice and inferiority to the group's positions, and then if there is a group seeking to secede after the secession movement begins, the concern of the neighboring states is expected. Although states express lower levels of verbal support and rarely engage in the recognition of secessionist movements, some behaviors are typical for small, medium, and large states. When small states intervene or when they support the secession movement, they usually do so for emotional reasons; the middle states do so out of interest, while the large states for the sake of benefit. When activated, secessionist movements can unite or divide around two or more secessionist fronts. The most commonly united movements are those who formally declare independence and manage to establish effective control over their territory, but most of the supposed secessionists have no single leadership, especially if the armed conflict has been aggravated for years. The most pressing issues are ethnic differences, the rivalry between political leaders and the military, personal conflicts and personal ambitions, the divergence between setting goals and related strategies, ideological differences, and third-party sponsorship. A charismatic and capable leader is an important factor that contributes to the success of the secessionist movement, its endurance, or its ability to survive. The secessionists should be prepared to continue the armed conflict and should not agree to compromise even when a good chance arises. The efforts to attract a third party to support the movement are as well important as they are an overall international activity of the secessionist movement. [51]

6.4.1 *Attracting a Third Party*

The possibility of engaging a third party in a secessionist movement is limited by the environment and the available resources available, as well as a calculation of the possible costs of such a tendency. Participants in secessionist movements are generally aware that a third party, and in particular the involvement of a state, is costly, though they may not be aware of the magnitude of the total costs. The most obvious cost of external involvement is donor dependency. All secessionist movements that rely heavily on a donor can end up as pawns in a game that is played either between states or within them. Another obvious cost is that inclusion can give the conflict a different dimension and thus limit the inclusion of other supporters. In fact, the most

[50] Heraclides (1991).

[51] Heraclides (1991).

important question is to what extent the secessionists are in a position to limit the negative effects of inclusion above the basic danger – donor dependence. Any form of involvement, especially a third-party one, is often paid for by the secessionists, so they tend to include a third party only if it is absolutely necessary. Material support for the success of the secessionist movement usually is sought from as many sources as possible, including assistance from nonstate parties, in most of the cases on reciprocity. Hence, that particular assistance often makes the secessionist ideology diffuse or flexible, although in essence is largely based on the "struggle for liberation" or nationalist myths. Still, without it, the secessionists cannot survive. One of the main persuasion techniques available to the secessionists is ensuring the publicity of the case (propaganda), touching on the emotional and intellectual components of the third actor. [52] Secessionist propaganda is usually expected to be full of misinterpretations, repetitions, and the use of attention-grabbing means intended to exploit the emotions of the target group, presenting its case as a factual one and not as a case that is open for arguments or manipulation. [53]

6.4.2 International Activity Concerning Secessionist Movements

The international system can affect internal conflicts in three different ways: through encouragement, through isolation and suppression, and through reconciliation. Historically, there have been several types of relations between the external parties and the two conflicting parties: international civil war, where both sides receive external assistance from other states; the case of a traditional alliance, where a great power supports the center; *concert,* when third parties try to help find a peaceful solution; and, finally, withdrawal, that is, the refusal to be involved at all. [54] In practice, third parties may be involved in the secessionist conflict as facilitators, supporters of the movement as a whole, or supporters of one of the secession fronts; be hostile or indifferent to others; and, of course, actively support the central government threatened by the secessionist movement.

Some theorists believe that noninvolvement or passive neutrality is almost impossible to achieve, especially because of the universal or regional policy of intergovernmental organizations (IGOs) whose member state is involved in secession conflicts. For them, noninclusion is not fundamentally different from inclusion. The neutrality of the regional policies of IGOs or international nongovernmental organizations (INGO) can only be considered the current policy on countries that are geographically distant or not in their interest.

---

[52] Heraclides (1991), p. 41

[53] Kelman (1958), pp. 51–60; Heraclides (1991).

[54] Modelski (1964); Suhrke and Garner Noble (1977).

For a third party to present itself as a facilitator, it must have the impression of being independent, neutral, virtuous, and respected by both parties involved. These qualities need to be reinforced by the moral qualities of the individuals who take on that role. State mediators know they tread on thin ice and most often begin the process privately and quietly. But publicly or privately, the formula is usually the following: we want to mediate, and both sides need to reach a peaceful solution respecting the territorial integrity of the state concerned, [55]

The third party can be regarded as biased toward the secessionist movement if its activity aims at reinforcing secessionist positions. Such one-sided support may be visible as material and humanitarian aid or nonmilitary or military action, human-potential support, or political-diplomatic or moral assistance that is verbal and involves diplomatic pressure on the center, and it may range from expressing concern for the secessionist entity or support for their recognition. [56]

States may not support secession if the case of self-determination has serious shortcomings, if the secessionist movement is a pure illusion or if it is too ambitious or militarily weak, if there is any doubt about the legitimacy of the movement, if tendencies are directed at creating a state that cannot economically survive, or if support depends on the role or involvement of a third party in the process. Whether the motives for involvement are taking a side or mediation, they include, on the one hand, international policies and strategies, short-term or long-term economic motives, internal motives such as fear of overflow or domino effect, or short-term military benefits and, on the other hand, emotional involvement based on a sense of justice, humanitarian care, ethnic, racial, or ideological affinities, as well as personal relationships and friendships. When it comes to international organizations, they are often indifferent to the secessionist movement or become more involved in the state threatened with secession, whether or not it is their member. They rarely use unconventional measures and rarely assist without clear state consent. But once aid agencies override central authority, they can cooperate with the secessionists directly; popularize their case; supply them with food, medicine, and fuel; and even serve as a shield for weapon delivery and access to the outside world. [57]

6.5 Dealing with the Secessionist Movement (Crisis)

The rise of international humanism and the expansion of democratic principles of government contribute to the success of the prospect of secession globally. Even if the international community continues to tolerate states that inadequately protect citizens' rights, awareness of actions related to human rights abuses is growing. But the practical effect of international humanitarianism is limited by a respect for the

[55] Young (1967).

[56] Heraclides (1991), pp. 46–49.

[57] Heraclides (1991).

principle of nonintervention, the economic dependence of other countries from the West, and the selectivity of the international community in terms of what interests it will protect. If the decision to secede is made within a liberal democracy as the wish of the majority from the individual community and if supported by a referendum or election, then the possible government response will be limited. In this case, if the state opposes secession, it is likely to cause irreparable damage to domestic political institutions. [58]

Of course, it is very difficult to speculate on the trends of secessionist activity, but it is even more difficult to predict how the government will respond to a potential secessionist crisis. When the secessionist movement begins, successful government policies are needed to deal with the crisis, and one of them is the significant transfer of political and economic power from the central government to the institutions of different communities. Devolution policies empower the community to provide its own protection and promote its culture. The specific design of certain government proposals depends on addressing the unique needs of the community and recognizing the capabilities and limitations of the central government. Successful policies are naturally different in that they cover many different community concerns, such as cultural assimilation, land control, religious practice, economic exploitation, political dominance, and educational discrimination. The assessment of the benefits and costs of possible secession and membership extensions may depend hugely on state initiatives. Hence, policies that reinforce benefits and reduce membership costs will help the heterogeneous state gain political loyalty to the various communities under its jurisdiction, thereby reducing the likelihood of suffering a painful and costly secessionist crisis. [59]

A mixture of significant devolution, accommodation of specific ethnic needs, and acceptance of diversity constitutes crisis prevention and, in doing so, can resolve secessionist wars without guaranteeing full independence. Conflicts are often endemic, not because of the structure of relations but because of the specific choices made by the government and by the elites of individual communities. In fact, the structure of such conflicts implies that there are elements to resolve them. But resolving the secessionist crisis largely depends on the willingness and commitment of leaders on both sides. Sometimes it is not in their personal interest to negotiate a solution to the secessionist crisis. [60] When the secessionist movement begins, it can only be prevented if the center redefines its positions and ensures broad autonomy and power sharing with the regional separatist group. This can only happen if the center is ready to meet the demands of the secessionists and transform the political system into one that will give them a chance. As the conflict develops into an armed one, its internationalization grows, which is often on the side of the center. For the secessionists, it is very important to provide great international support and hope for some form of autonomy or federal status, as well as some degree of power sharing

[58] See more at Bartkus (1999).

[59] Bartkus (1999).

[60] Bartkus (1999).

with the center. [61] In times of crisis, it is necessary to make every effort to reach a solution that preserves territorial integrity and also does not assimilate the secessionists and does not suppress the center so that the maximalist demands and both sides will be rejected and their real needs will be met.

In addition to dealing militarily with the violent development of some of the independence movements, some authors propose other answers that need to be applied first, rather than military force. [62] Such as the following:

1. *Monitoring*—many governments, multilateral institutions, and private bodies undertake a wide range of monitoring activities around the world through election and human rights monitoring, weapon delivery, democracy development, and so on.
2. *Diplomatic intervention*—negotiations between the government of the parent state and the leaders of the movement are the first attempt to protect the existing state. When the diplomacy attempt fails, the parties to the dispute may resort to mechanisms that may include third parties to facilitate settlement: mediation, consolidation, arbitration, and adjudication. Mediation is perhaps the most effective means of bridging the gap.
3. *Denial of international legitimacy*—the international community has two ways of denying legitimacy: the denial of recognition and suspension or exclusion from international institutions. Denying recognition includes severing diplomatic relations with the state government, withdrawing its diplomatic staff, and firing diplomats. Revoking recognition can be more symbolic than effective, but in some situations, it can do more harm than good as it can lead to the alienation of a government that can become even more insecure and disruptive as well as disrupt communication channels with the rest of the world. But the denial of recognition can also leave some diplomatic channels open and thus serve as a useful and very symbolic act of disagreeing with government action, without isolating that government. Dismissal, the expulsion of diplomatic personnel, or the suspension of government by international or regional organizations is another delegitimizing and sometimes complementary action, but problems can arise when the procedures for dismissal from the international organization are unclear and inconsistent or when the act is opposed by other member states.
4. *Conditionality and economic sanctions*—it is one of the most effective mechanisms for influencing the old or new government. But it can also lead to great suffering for the people of the country or the region. Economic conditionality and sanction tools can be used when the parent state violates the norms of international law regarding minorities, including those struggling for independence, when it fails to establish a reasonable dialogue with the independence movement, but they may also be applied to the new government when it fails to meet and maintain the necessary criteria for statehood internationally. Economic

[61] Heraclides (1991).

[62] Halperin et al. (1992).

conditions are set to obtain bilateral foreign assistance or to provide multilateral development or financial support. Here, the World Bank and the International Monetary Fund (IMF) are the lenders that set conditions for loans, the most important of which is a market economy. But economic sanctions need to be carefully scrutinized as to their likely impact on government behavior and the civilian population. Also important is the time when sanctions are imposed. If the world community waits too long before imposing sanctions, they can have very little impact. Sanctions can sometimes be an appropriate way to carry out disciplinary action while avoiding difficult decisions that must be made to put an end to aggression, protect minorities, and end the humanitarian crisis. Economic sanctions can prove impractical in harsh circumstances that require timely collective intervention.

5. *Military intervention*—although each conflict is different, in principle, the international community must act very quickly and with great commitment to include military forces when they are needed and also when feasible. Unilateral interventions to oppose or support the movement are not an option. In most cases, a unilateral intervention will violate the principles of international law and establish precedents that can lead to many other injustice misconducts by governments. [63]

The other different, appropriate response to address groups' demands is creating inventive and flexible constitutional engagements. Soft statuses that will allow parties to negotiate to address complaints on the basis of pragmatic creativity, should be sought, not just a simplified federalization or decentralization formulas. It is clear, of course, that group rights need to be recognized. [64] From the other side, even if states pursue flexible policies by promoting diversity and guaranteeing broad autonomy, sometimes this may not be enough to prevent or timely intervene in a secessionist crisis, and that is because the impacts outside the parameters of a certain secessionist confrontation influence the decision to secession and necessarily limit the effectiveness of central government decisions. It may be sufficient to comment that over time and through a greater acceptance of liberal democratic values, many of the states' calculations of their economic, security, and geopolitical interests in a period of secessionist crisis are likely to undergo a gradual change. This change will certainly reduce the likelihood that the political community will be maintained by force. [65]

[63] Halperin et al. (1992).

[64] Hannum (1990).

[65] Bartkus (1999), p. 230.

6.5.1 *Cases and Attempts of Secession Before and After the Formation of the UN*

Successful secessions are those that have resulted in independent statehood. After 1945, i.e., after the end of World War II and the formation of the UN, the list of successful secessions is as follows:

- Senegal, 1960 (Senegal was part of the Mali Federation, composed of Senegal and Sudan. Shortly after its founding, the federation was divided into two. Sudan initially opposed but later agreed. Senegal was admitted to the UN under the name Mali.)
- Singapore, 1965 (shortly after being a part of a federation with Malaysia)
- Bangladesh, 1971 (The UN treated Bangladesh not as a case of self-determination despite a good basis for it but as a *fait accompli* achieved as a result of foreign military intervention in special circumstances.)
- The three Baltic states: Lithuania, Latvia, Estonia (1990)
- 11 USSR successors—Armenia, Azerbaijan, Belarus, Georgia, Kazakhstan, Kyrgyzstan, Moldova, Tajikistan, Turkmenistan, Ukraine, Uzbekistan (1991)
- Five SFRY successors—Slovenia, Croatia, Macedonia, Bosnia and Herzegovina, the Federal Republic of Yugoslavia (created by Serbia and Montenegro) (1991)
- Czech Republic and Slovakia, 1992
- Eritrea, 1993 (Ethiopia's transitional government helped Eritrea apply to the UN.)
- East Timor of Indonesia, 2000
- Montenegro from the Federation of the Republic of Serbia and Montenegro, 2006
- Kosovo, 2008
- South Sudan, 2011

It is important to note that none of these cases is referred to in the UN resolutions and documents as a case of realized self-determination!

Before 1945, that is, before the UN was formed, the successful secessions were as follows:

- Panama from the Republic of Colombia, 1903
- Norway from the United Kingdom of Norway and Sweden, 1905
- Finland from Russia, 1917
- The Irish Free State from the Kingdom of Great Britain and Ireland, 1922
- Iceland from Denmark, 1944

Failed secession attempts, or attempts to gain minor international recognition or no international recognition at all, are as follows:

- Katanga from Congo (1960)
- Biafra of the Federation with Nigeria (1967)
- Turkish Republic of Northern Cyprus from Cyprus (1974)
- Bougainville of Papua New Guinea (1990)
- Transnistria from Moldova (1990)

- Chechnya (Chechnya Republic of Ichkeria) from the Russian Federation (1991)
- Somaliland from the Republic of Somalia (1991)
- Herzeg-Bosnia from Bosnia and Herzegovina (1992)
- Serbian Krajina from Croatia (1992)
- The Serbian Republic from Bosnia and Herzegovina (1992)
- South Ossetia from Georgia (1992)
- Republic of Western Bosnia and Herzegovina (1993)
- Abkhazia from Georgia (1994)
- Puntland (East Somaliland) from Somaliland (1998)
- Tibet (China)
- Kashmir (India)
- East Punjab (India)
- Karen and Jean States (Burma)
- Tamil Elam (Sri Lanka)
- Kurdistan (Iraq, Turkey)
- Anjouan (Islamic Republic of Comoros)
- Gagauzia (Moldova)
- Nagorno Karabakh (Azerbaijan)
- Democratic Republic of Yemen (Yemen)

Attempts to carry out a referendum secession that failed due to an unsecured majority or the lack of consent by the home state include the following:

- Western Australia from Australia, 1932
- Quebec from Canada, 1980 and 1995
- Nevis from St. Keats and Nevis, 1998

Regions and groups with active secessionist movements are as follows:

- Basque Country and Catalonia in Spain
- Province of Cabinda in Angola
- Casamance in Senegal
- Chittagong Hill in Bangladesh
- Corsica in France
- Flanders in Belgium
- Jammu and Kashmir in India
- Karen in Burma
- Kurds in Turkey
- Kurds in Iraq (in Kurdistan)
- Mindanao in the Philippines
- Naga in India (Nagaland state)
- Punjab in India (Sikh population)
- Sanjak in Serbia and Montenegro (Bosniaks Muslim population)
- Scotland in the UK
- South Cameroon in the Republic of Cameroon
- South Moluccas in Indonesia
- Tamil in Sri Lanka
- Taiwan and Tibet in China

- West Papua in Indonesia
- Xinjiang in China [66]

References

After-twenty-four-years-of-union-with-serbia-montenegro-is-independent-again, World Bank. http://www.robert-schuman.eu/en/eem/0522-after-twenty-four-years-of-union-with-serbia-montenegro-is-independent-again. http://www.worldbank.org/en/country/montenegro/overview. Accessed 15 Aug 2022

Alger CF (2011) Searching for democratic potential in emerging global governance: what are the implications of regional and global involvements of local governments? Int J Peace Stud 16(2):1–24

Allcock J B, Lampe J R, Young A (2022) Kosovo, self-declared independent country. Encyclopedia Britannica. https://www.britannica.com/place/Kosovo. Accessed 16 Aug 2022

Anderson M (1982) The political problems of frontier regions. West Eur Polit 5(4):1–17

Andrews J (2020) The world in conflict. The Economist

Bartkus VO (1999) The dynamic of secession. Press Syndicate of the University of Cambridge

Baskin M, Pickering P (2010) Former Yugoslavia and its successors. In: Wolchik S, Curry J (eds) Central and East European politics: from communism to democracy. Rowman & Littlefield Publishers, New York

Baudrillard J (1991) Nasilje globalnog (The violence of the Global). https://journals.uvic.ca/index.php/ctheory/article/view/14558/5403. Accessed 16 Aug 2022

Bekaj R (2010) The KLA and the Kosovo war: from interstate conflict to independent country. Berghof Transitions Series, 8

Brosio G, Revelli F (2003) The political economy of regional opting out: distributive implications of a prospective Europe of regions. Econ Gov:127–142

Buchheit LC (1978) Secession, the legitimacy of self-determination. Yale University Press, New Haven and London

Crawford J (2006) The creation of states in international law. Oxford University Press

De Soza Santos B (2003) The processes of the globalization. Revista Crítica De Ciências Sociais. https://www.eurozine.com/the-processes-of-globalisation/. Accessed Aug 16 2022

European Neighbourhood Policy and Enlargement Negotiations, Montenegro EU. https://ec.europa.eu/neighbourhood-enlargement/countries/detailed-country-information/montenegro_en. Accessed 15 Aug 2022

Falk R (2002) Self-determination under international law: the coherence of doctrine versus the incoherence of experience. In: Danspeckgruber W (ed) Self – determination of peoples, community, nation and state in interdependent world. Lynne Rienner Publishers, pp 31–67

Geertz C (1967) The Integrative relations: primordial sentiments and civic politics in the new states. In: Welch CE (ed) Political modernization. Wadsworth, Belmont, pp 167–188

Giordano C (2001) Ogledi o interkulturnoj komunikacii (Reviews about intercultural communication). Biblioteka XX vek, Beograd

Haas E (1968) The uniting of Europe. Stanford University Press, Stanford

Halperin MH et al (1992) Self – determination in the new world order. Carnegie Endowment for International Peace, Washington DC

Hannum H (1990) Autonomy, sovereignty, and self-determination, the accommodation of conflict rights. University of Pennsylvania Press

[66] Used sources are: Carnegie group official documentation; Unrepresented Peoples and Nations Organizations (UNPO); Crawford (2006).

Hechter M (1992) The dynamics of secession. Acta Sociologica 35:267–283
Heraclides A (1991) The self - determination of the minorities in the international politics. Frank Cass and Company Limited
Kelman HC (1958) Compliance, identification and internationalization: three processes of attitude change. J Confl Resol ii:51–60
Kohli A (2002) Can democracies accommodate ethnic nationalism? The rise and decline of self – determination movements in India. In: Danspeckgruber W (ed) Self – determination of peoples, community, nation and state in interdependent world. Lynne Rienner Publishers, pp 287–315
Krasniqi G (2010) Citizenship as a tool of state-building in Kosovo: status, rights, and identity in the new state. CITSEE Working Paper Series, 10
Modelski G (1964) International settlement of internal war. In: Rosenau JN (ed) International aspects of civil strife. Princeton University Press, Princeton, pp 14–44
Montenegro Country Profile, BBC News (2018). http://www.bbc.com/news/world-europe-17667132. Accessed 15 Aug 2022
Montenegro votes to secede from Serbia (2006) Internet source. https://www.nytimes.com/2006/05/21/world/europe/21iht-montenegro.html
Montenegro Votes to Secede from Serbia, Washington Post (2006). http://www.washingtonpost.com/wp-dyn/content/article/2006/05/22/AR2006052200154_2.html. Accessed 15 Aug 2022
Pavkovic A, Radan P (2007) Creating new states, theory and practice of secession. Ashgate Publishing limited
Petty (2019) Explainer: What's behind autonomy vote in the Philippines' Muslim Mindanao?. Reuters. (Internet source). https://www.reuters.com/article/uk-philippines-politics-autonomy-idAFKCN1PF0VJ. Accessed 9 Jan 2023
Popović S, Janča D, Petovar T (1990) Kosovski čvor, drešii ili seći (The Kosovo knot, untying or cut). Izveštaj nezavisne komisije (Report of the independent commission). Shronos, Titograd
Renan E (1882) Qu'est –ce qu'une nation? Conférence en Sorbonne. http://www.iheal.univ-paris3.fr/sites/www.iheal.univ-paris3.fr/files/Renan_-_Qu_est-ce_qu_une_Nation.pdf. Accessed 7 Aug 2022
Republic Act No. 11054 (2018) Act Providing for the Organic Law for the Bangsamoro Autonomous Region in Muslim Mindanao. https://lawphil.net/statutes/repacts/ra2018/ra_11054_2018.html. Accessed 9 Jan 2023
Rodrigues PA, Stermsek M (2014) The economic of secession. analyzing the economic impact of the collapse of the former Yugoslavia. GEN - Governance and Economics Research Network
Security Council Resolution 1244 (1999). https://peacemaker.un.org/kosovo-resolution1244#:~:text=This%20resolution%20provides%20a%20framework,refugees%20and%20the%20withdrawal%20of. Accessed 21 Oct 2022
Shikova N, Sadiku L (2017) Economic justification of the secession; case analysis of Kosovo's and Montenegro's separation from Serbia. Polit Sci Forum 6(2):38–60
Suhrke A, Garner Noble LG (1977) Ethnic conflict in international relations. Praeger Publishers, New York
Tamir Y (2002) Liberalni nacionalizam (Liberal nationalism). Filip Visnjic, Beograd
Tripoli Agreement (1976). https://peacemaker.un.org/sites/peacemaker.un.org/files/PH_761223_Tripoli%20Agreement.pdf. Accessed Jan 9 2023
UN News (2018) UN chief welcomes new law giving extra autonomy to Muslims in Southern Philippines (Internet source). https://news.un.org/en/story/2018/07/1015812. Accessed 9 Jan 2023
Unrepresented Peoples and Nations Organizations (UNPO). http://www.unpo.org. Accessed 15 Aug 2022
Vidmar J (2004) International legal responses to Kosovo's declaration of independence. Vanderbilt J Transnatl Law 42:779–849
Wood JR (1981) Secession: a comparative analytical framework. Can J Polit Sci 14:109–135
Young OR (1967) The intermediaries: third parties in international crises. Princeton University Press, Princeton

Chapter 7
"Right to Secession"

7.1 Introduction: Can We Talk About the "Right to Secession?"

There are different opinions on whether or not there is a "right to secession." Some authors consider that in international law, there is a tacit right to secession recognized in certain documents, while for others, such a right does not exist and should not exist at all. Although there is a group of theorists advocating for the introduction of a specific, limited right to secession, by defining the conditions under which secession can be realized, the current situation in the international community is not at a stage where it would conditionally accept a qualified right to secession. The debates about the real need for international regulation in this area are in a similar direction.

The basis for the existence of a right of separatist self-determination in international law (as Lee C. Buchheit calls the phenomenon of *secession*) is theoretically possible to be sought in (1) the principles of natural law and (2) the principles of positive international law.[1] If we seek the basis for the existence of the right to secession in natural law or if we want to establish whether the "right" of secession is a natural right, we need to go into the doctrine of natural law that emerged in the Middle Ages. An analysis of this doctrine shows that it does not take into account secession, having in mind that at the time of the appearance of this legal doctrine, the concept of the state as we know it today was not existing. Proponents of secession as a natural right often base their arguments on an existing social contract, and under such doctrines, political associations are reduced to a basic functional agreement in which individuals surrender their natural rights in exchange for the positive benefits of living in the social group, while the right of secession is restitution, the retrieval of such conferred rights. Although studies of the most influential theories

[1] Buchheit (1978).

N. Shikova, *Self-Determination and Secession*,
https://doi.org/10.1007/978-3-031-34322-3_7

of natural law demonstrate the importance of individualistic and necessary elements of resistance, theorists who have investigated natural law, such as Locke (1632–1704)[2] or Pufendorf (1632–1694),[3] did not consider the basis for such resistance, that is, for secession, although at no point in the evolution of the doctrine of natural law has the right of resistance been affirmed in an unqualified manner, nor had the inherent right of resistance included the right to the secession of the group, except in isolated cases, as in the jurisprudence of the German jurist Johannes Althusius (1563–1638). Hugo Grotius (1583–1645) considered that there may be a right to minority secession, but only under extreme circumstances. The state has no right to secede a part of its territory without the consent of the inhabitants, just as a segment of the population of that state cannot unilaterally withdraw from it unless it is evident that there is no other way to save and maintain itself.[4] In that respect, under the theories of natural law, there is no basis in supporting modern secessionist movements, which means that they do not provide a ground for the legitimacy of the secessionist movements.[5]

Concerning the principles of positive international law, some theoretics reason that the right to secession exists only under certain conditions. For example, Georges Scelle (1878–1961, active in the period of the League of Nations)[6] believed that the right of peoples to collective self-determination implies not only a condemnation of the classical principle of forced annexation or cession but also a freedom for secession. At the same time, Robert Redslob (1881–1962)[7] considered that it is necessary to limit the right of secession to those groups that have a separate nationality and a strong will for separation, and evidence of this particularity can be found in the group's history and potentially in the differences existing in their religion or language. If we seek the basis for secessionist self-determination in contemporary international law, we cannot avoid considering the Declaration on Principles of International Law concerning Friendly Relations and Co-operation among States (1970). Although the Declaration does not give unlimited recognition of separatism, on the contrary, the open lines of paragraph 7 reaffirm the territorial integrity and political unity of an independent and sovereign state, which suggests that the authors of the text have chosen to start from a conservative position of giving *prima facie* respect to the existing state-centered order. The inventiveness of the Declaration rests on its implicit restriction on the territorial integrity of states, which in turn stems from the state's obligation to provide democratic government and the protection of fundamental human rights.[8]

[2] Locke (1690).

[3] Pufendorf (1934).

[4] Grotius and Kelsey (1925).

[5] Buchheit (1978).

[6] Scelle (1932).

[7] Redslob (1931).

[8] Buchheit (1978).

There are scholars, for example, Horowitz,[9] for whom the right to secession does not exist nor needs to exist because the existence of such a right will not solve things but make them worse. He is among the ones who strongly criticize those who advocate such a venture, even those who abstain from it or demand that certain conditions for secession can be considered "legitimate." According to him, secession does not create a homogeneous state, nor does it reduce conflicts. Thus, the eventual establishment of a right to secession will only undermine the attempts for coexistence in an undivided state, including autonomy and federalism, which may address some of the minorities' demands. He suggests looking for accommodation models within the state, not to justify or thematize secession. He insists on this tendency, although he admits that in some rare cases, if the partition of antagonists is ultimately the best option, the partition should be achieved very carefully, without recognizing the right to secession. But neither partition nor secession should be seen as a generally desired solution to the problems of the ethnic conflict.[10] The complete rejection of possibility of codifying "right to secession" is justified because it including within international law it does not resolves anything. Secession does not solve the problems of intergroup accommodation, but it only allows the former minority (which will become a new majority) to cleanse the secessionist state from its minorities, something that it could not have done before. Therefore, recognizing the existence of the right to secession will not be an end of old bitterness but the beginning of new ones, concludes Horowitz.[11]

The "right" to secession is seen as a remedy against discrimination and pressure from the central government in addressing minority rights. On the other hand, international law is notoriously ineffective in securing long-term internationally recognized minority rights, and proponents of secession are not offering new ideas that address this issue. If the failure to respect minority rights in an undivided state has prompted a regional group to consider secession, then there is little space to consider that the situation would be different when the minority group within the undivided state will constitute a majority in the new state.[12] However, there is no incompatibility between territorial integrity and putting forward opposing arguments.[13] The case about the possible right to secession has almost never been presented as an absolute right for anyone to claim it. It is more a call for the articulation of adequate criteria or standards of legitimacy, where only legitimate secession requirements fall within the scope of the principle of self-determination.[14] In general, current international legal theories still doubt the possible status of secession as a "right."[15] Rarely are commentators who completely deny its legitimacy, but

[9] Horowitz (2003).

[10] Horowitz (2003), p. 51.

[11] Horowitz (2003), p. 55.

[12] Horowitz (2003), p. 54.

[13] Brilmayer (1991).

[14] Heraclides (1991), p. 28.

[15] Buchheit (1978).

there are many theorists who believe that such a "right" (if any) should be subject to enormous restrictions.

7.2 Secession and the Right to Self-Determination

Balancing the right to self-determination of the peoples (which could involve secession) with the maintenance of territorial integrity is a major challenge in the twenty-first century. The issue of secession is most often seen through the prism of the rules concerning self-determination and territorial integrity, the prohibition on the use of force, as well as the rules on recognition and nonrecognition. Theoretical dilemmas regarding the relationship between secession and self-determination are an old topic in international legal thought. Perceptions of acceptance of secession as one of the possible expressions of the right to self-determination of peoples include (a) a total denial of any link between the right to self-determination of peoples and secession, (b) acceptance of secession as a legitimate right, and c) acceptance and realization of the right to secession under certain conditions, or the so-called "legitimate secession."

A primary legal dilemma is, does the right to self-determination include a "right to secession?" Because of the fear of a possible secessionist interpretation of the principle, some lawyers argue not only to exclude secession from the scope of self-determination but also to deny any legal content on the concept of secession. Even among those willing to give some legitimacy to the concept of secessionist self-determination, there is a disagreement in attitudes, although there is a tendency to establish certain criteria for its application.[16] For some scholars, within international law, the right to self-determination and the eventual "right to secession" must be considered two distinct segments, each with its privileges, constituent elements, conditions for legitimate application, and consequences.[17] For the other group of theorists, if there is a "right of secession," then its origin should be sought in the principle of national self-determination. The principle of self-determination applied during the decolonization remained stable until the end of the Cold War, when there were only a few cases of secession, exceptions to the principle of non-violation of territorial integrity, and ever on, the international community and the jurists of international law trying to set conditions to limit and discourage secession.

Horowitz found the roots of the phenomenon of secession in national self-determination.[18] Similarly, Heraclides finds it ironic to oppose secessionist movements through the principle of self-determination since it is precisely that principle that causes secession.[19] Horowitz and Heraclides oppose any right to secession or

[16] Buchheit (1978).

[17] Van der Vyver (2000).

[18] Horowitz (2003).

[19] Heraclides (1991).

formulating the phenomenon in legal terms. However, there are scholars, such as Charles Rousseau, who believe that the right to self-determination in international law has two aspects: one negative, the other positive. The negative contains the right of the population not to be exchanged or subject to cession against their will, while the positive aspect is the right to secession. However, Rousseau considers that the exercise of this right must be limited, that is to say, applied only if the concerned state recognizes that right or refuses the exercise of the right of its population to determine its own political status through a plebiscite or otherwise.[20]

For James Summers, if internal self-determination is a means for underscoring the liberal aspects of self-determination (which through the liberal theory of government helps the state become more representative of the various national groups living in it), then this emphasis on the liberal aspect opens the door to another form of external self-determination—secession as a cure. Therefore, support for liberalism implies support for secession. If the state is unrepresentative and excludes or harasses a part of its population, then the population can legitimately break away and establish a more representative government.[21]

Chernichenko and Kotlyar[22] justify secession under precisely defined circumstances and regard it as part of the right to self-determination within the established UN practice. According to them, secession is supported by the 1970 Declaration on Principles of International Law concerning Friendly Relations and Co-operation among States[23] and the 1993 Vienna Declaration and Program of Action.[24] In these legal frameworks, secession can be accepted as a legitimate element of the right to self-determination in the following cases:

- In the process of decolonization
- If it is mentioned in the constitution of the state
- If the territory with all its people was annexed after 1945
- If the people live in the territory of a state that does not respect the principle of equal rights and self-determination of peoples and do not provide representation in government without discrimination to all its peoples.

Within the group that considers that secession and self-determination are two distinct phenomena are Johan D. Van der Vyver, Lea Brilmayer, etc. According to Lea Brilmayer, secession should not be viewed through the principle of self-determination. The principle of self-determination focuses on the right of the people, while secession is related to the right to territory. Self-determination generally or insufficiently focuses on the history of the conflict. Properly understood, the principle of territorial sovereignty accommodates the right to secession and gives a

[20] Rousseau (1953).

[21] Summers (2007).

[22] Chernichenko and Kotlyar (2003).

[23] UNGA Res. Declaration on Principles of International Law concerning Friendly Relations and Co-operation among States (1970).

[24] World Conference on Human Rights, Vienna Declaration and Programme of Action, U.N. doc. A/Conf. 157/24 art. I.2 (June 25, 1993) reprinted in 32 I.L.M.1661, at 1665 (1993).

better basis to secession claims than the principle of self-determination. But if there is a conflict, it is certainly not a conflict of principles but a conflict for the territory.[25] A direct reference to the principles of consent, mutual agreement, and self-government does not justify secession. Traditionally, the norm of self-determination, on the basis of which the secessionists lay their demands, is placed in line with the democratic principles of consent and popular sovereignty. According to this argument, self-determination is a liberal democratic value, and secession is a liberal democratic alternative, whereas the principle of territorial integrity is feudal, undemocratic, and repressive. This idea that the government must come from the consent of the governed seems to lead dissatisfied groups to the possibility of leaving, i.e. breaking away from the existing state, or more generally, those who disagree with the way the government manages the country should have the opportunity to leave it. In this way, the principles of democratic government have been transformed into a right of secession. Such theses are wrong, says Brilmayer, because they place too much emphasis on consent as the basis for state legitimacy. Despite the rhetoric of liberal democracy, genuine consent is not necessary for political legitimacy. Consent is an important part of democratic rhetoric, but in this way, philosophers are to simply justify the power of the state. Therefore, separatists cannot base their arguments on the basis of such a right as it does not exist in democratic theory. Moreover, the separatists will not be satisfied with the rights of democratic participation. They are separatists precisely on the basis of their desire to leave the state and form a new one. The fact that some states deny certain groups the right to participate does not explain why secession, rather than full participation, is the appropriate remedy, reasons Brilmayer.[26]

The self-determination of peoples who are discriminated against in political rights does not include *per se* secession from the state that implements such a policy but merely refers to the abolition of discriminatory rules and practices, considers Van der Vyver.[27] According to classical theory, self-determination applies to colonies and is a principle against domination, and the UN and various international organizations are committed against secessionist self-determination, as is any different interpretation that causes an attack on the unity and integrity of UN member states. The existing UN system does not encourage or justify violations of or threats to the territorial integrity of the member states.[28] In practice, however, support for the "right" to secession is very minor, and the balance in international documents is clearly set on the side of territorial integrity, not of secession.[29]

[25] Brilmayer (1991).

[26] Brilmayer (1991), p. 185.

[27] Van der Vyver (2000).

[28] Van der Vyver (2000), p. 26.

[29] Summers (2007).

7.3 An International Normative Framework for the “Right” of Secession

Contemporary international law considers secession only in two cases:

(1) If the people freely make the decision to secede, which means the entire population of the state, not just the inhabitants of the region, wishes to secede
(2) When national borders are changed after an armed conflict as part of a reached peace agreement[30]

In international practice, secession is often accepted only as an ultimate remedy, whereas its application depends on specific circumstances. Authors who accept the restricted right to secession consider that all basic requirements (e.g., severe forms of discrimination, repression, exclusion, etc.) need to be fulfilled, as well as certain practical conditions, such as territorial concentration of a particular population group, the possible viability of the new state, and the like. Although positive international law (still) does not recognize the right of secession as part of peoples' self-determination, it can be said that Resolution 2625 is a confirmation of an evolution made since the League of Nations, which is aimed at the current, limited acceptance of the legitimacy of secession.[31]

Under positive international law, the principle of the territorial integrity of an existing state is superior and involves the rejection of secession. This practice is not new, nor is it unknown. As early as 1921, the International Commission of Rapporteurs reviewed the request for the secession of the Aaland Islands from Finland and rejected it. Still, the Committee of Rapporteurs concluded that minorities residing under foreign domination may be allowed to secede, but as a last resort—when the state lacks either the will or the power to incite and exercise law, as well as to establish effective guarantees concerning religious, linguistic, or social justice.[32]

But regardless of the superiority of the principle of territorial integrity, today, the prevailing view is that under precisely defined but restrictive conditions, secession is acceptable. Many theorists find this to be precisely included in Resolution 2625, Declaration on Principles of International Law concerning Friendly Relations and Co-operation among States,[33] and according to them, paragraph 7 recognizes, for the first time in an international document of this kind, the legitimacy of secession. In this regard, Resolution 2625 opens the door to the so-called forms of “legitimate secession,” but again, if certain conditions are met—or if a sovereign and the independent state do not respect the rights of self-determination of the people of the

[30] Van der Vyver (2000), p. 26.

[31] Henrard (2000), p. 306.

[32] A Report presented to the Council of the League of Nations by the Commission of Rapporteurs (1921).

[33] UNGA Res. Declaration on Principles of International Law concerning Friendly Relations and Co-operation among States (1970).

colony or non-self-governing territory and do not have a government that is representative and represents all peoples living in the territory without distinction based on race, creed, or color.

For Lee Buchheit,[34] the concluding clause of this Resolution is a direct reflection of John Locke, Jefferson, and Wilson's beliefs that the legitimacy of governors derives from the consent of the governed and, moreover, that consent must be based on the consent of all segments of society. By using this terminology, at the end of the paragraph, in the form of a final clause, the authors of the text have affirmed the concept of "consent of the rulers" by saying that if the state government does not represent the whole nation, then it is illegitimate, which in turn violates the principle of self-determination. This illegitimacy goes in favor of "legitimate action" that seeks to disintegrate, in whole or in part, the territorial integrity and political unity of a sovereign and independent state. Consequently, the compilers of this document did not intend to offer a complete list of conditions and circumstances that would indicate where a state is not acting in accordance with the principle, yet the requirement for a representative government should be understood as an extension of the principle or as a necessary condition for its complete satisfaction.[35]

Antonio Cassese[36] also analyzes the Declaration on Principles of International Law concerning Friendly Relations and Co-operation among States[37] but considers that it has a restrictive scope and applies exclusively to religious and racial groups and raises the question of whether these groups are carriers (under the conditions outlined in the Declaration) only of internal self-determination, or can they demand external self-determination, even the right to secede from a repressive state? That is, does the Declaration's right to self-determination also include the right to dismember the territorial integrity and political unity of a state? Thus, secession is not regulated, but it can be allowed only when very strict conditions are met because when the division of territorial integrity is not completely excluded, then it is logically allowed. Hence, secession is implicitly authorized by the Declaration and thus interpreted, with all exceptions. For Cassese, it can be assumed that secession is permissible when the central authorities of the sovereign state consistently refuse to guarantee the participation rights of religious or racial groups, completely and systematically trampling on their fundamental rights and denying the possibility of reaching a peace agreement within the state structure. In other words, the denial of a fundamental right of representativeness does not in itself challenge the right to secession, but there must be a complete violation of fundamental human rights and—even more so—an exclusion of any potential peaceful solution within the existing state structure. So the Declaration binds external self-determination to internal self-determination under exceptional circumstances, says Cassese, meaning

[34] Buchheit (1978).

[35] Buchheit (1978).

[36] Cassese (1995).

[37] UNGA Res 2625, Annex, Declaration on Principles of international law concerning friendly relations and cooperation among the states in accordance with the Charter of the United Nations (1970).

that racial or religious groups can seek external self-determination and legitimately secede when their internal self-determination is absolutely out of reach and when all attempts to achieve that failed or tend to fail.[38]

The possibility of an extensive interpretation of the Declaration, as a different theoretical option than Cassese's restrictive approach (relating the possibilities to secession only to the certain type of peoples and a certain type of discrimination), is given by Eyassu Gayim,[39] who considers that the Declaration is recognize people's right to independent state, if the benefits of self-determination within the existing state were systematically denied. The gross denial of political rights and the nature and extent of the group's human rights abuses are the only credible test for determining the reasonableness of secession, says Ved Nanda.[40] That is to say, according to Alfred Koban, a state will not be condemned for its diversity in language, religion, or origin nor for its homogeneity, but a state can be condemned and the secession approved only if it does not protect and promote, in reasonable measures, the rights of individual citizens, including their interests as members of national communities.[41]

However, the controversy of secession is likely to remain an open burning issue today, with very little prospect of a solution. There is hardly any author who argues that international law recognizes an unlimited right to secession but many who consider that secession should be put within a restricted legal frame. Considering the the criteria that could give a legitimacy to a case of secession, predominates the criterion related to the violation of the fundamental rights by the parent state, thus to say the secession can be viewed as legitimate if the group within the state is exposed to the vast abuse of the human rights.

7.3.1 Eritrea: An Example of an Exercised "Right" to Secession

From an international point of view, Eritrea's resistance is considered to be the longest-running secessionist resistance against much stronger Ethiopia. Ethiopia was never under colonial rule but only briefly under Italian occupation from 1936 to 1941. The mosaic of ethnic groups and cultures has long been under the authoritarian rule of Emperor Selassie, overthrown by the Marxist junta known as Derg, which in turn established a military dictatorship that resulted in five secessionist movements.[42] Eritrea, from the first to the fifth centuries, was part of the Axum Kingdom, but it was always preferred by Ethiopia, with which could have direct

[38] Cassese (1995), p. 119.

[39] Gayim (2006).

[40] Nanda (1980).

[41] Cobban (1969), p. 140.

[42] Andrews (2020).

access to the sea. In its history, Eritrea went through two colonial periods: from 1881 to 1941 under Italy and from 1941 to 1952 under Britain. In the aftermath of decolonization, the United Nations began discussing its status in the early 1950s by establishing a United Nations Commission for Eritrea to ascertain more fully the wishes of the inhabitants[43] and with a decisive tendency for independence, which was supported by the USSR, Czechoslovakia, and Italy, while the United States and Great Britain stood by the side of Selassie (Ethiopia), that is, against independence. In 1950, the United Nations (UN), under the prompting of the United States, resolved to join Eritrea to Ethiopia within two years.[44] The proposed federation would provide Eritrea with autonomy under its own constitution and elected government.[45] The British, who were asked to leave Eritrea no later than September 15, 1952, organized legislative elections, and in 1952, the National Assembly, with 68 members, was formed. On July 10, 1952, this new body accepted a constitution put forward by the United Nations and later the same year was ratified by Emperor Haile Selassie. From the start of the federation, Emperor Haile Selassie took steps toward undermining Eritrea's autonomy. He suppressed Eritrean political movements and arrested newspaper editors, forced elected community leaders to resign, replaced the Eritrean flag with that of Ethiopia, and imposed the use of Amharic in public services and schools.[46] Newspapers were banned, Eritrean courts were subordinated to their courts, and the Constitution was suspended. This escalated into bloody demonstrations and three decades of war.[47] On November 14, 1962, Ethiopian troops forced the Eritrean Parliament to dissolve, and on that day, Eritrea was officially annexed as the 14th province of Ethiopia.[48] Ethiopia claimed that Eritrea was a part of it before it was colonized. It is an artificial creation of Italy and not a single nation but composed of nine ethnic groups and exercised its right to self-determination when the Eritrean assembly voted to unite with homeland Ethiopia. On the other hand, Eritreans consider that there was never the uniqueness of a nation between Ethiopia and Eritrea. The unification was done by the National Assembly, and there was no referendum that will reflect the will of the people as a whole. Additionally, there was a full denial of the right to self-determination when the federal status of Eritrea was fully abolished by Ethiopia.[49]

In the historical period described, Eritrea was made up of Muslims and Christians, with a population of 30 million, of which 9% were Ethiopians. Following the abolition of its federal status and its annexation to Ethiopia, only Muslims initially were for independence, but later, Christians also joined, primarily due to the extremely

[43] GA Res. 289 A (IV) (1949).

[44] Federation with Ethiopia (Internet source).

[45] GA Res 617 (VII) (1952).

[46] UN Human Rights Council (2015).

[47] Andrews (2020).

[48] UN Human Rights Council (2015).

[49] Cassese (1995).

bad economic situation, worse than even under the colonial rule of Italy or Great Britain. The idea of a separate state came from an independent way of governing.[50]

In 1960, an Eritrean Independence Movement was formed, which began as a guerrilla war against the regime of Derg. Ideologically, the Movement was based on various demands—from independence to autonomy or confederation—yet the Eritreans, who as a result of diplomatic pressure led negotiations with senior Ethiopian officials, were executed as traitors. The Movement lacked solid leadership and unity, perhaps because Eritreans do not have the same language, they are ethnically diverse, and they lack ethnic bonding, so the fight was fought on several fronts and with several wings, and Muslims often got financial and military assistance from different Arabs countries.[51] Seeking to secure international support, the Movement received backup from the United States and succeeded in Ethiopia's Eritrean independence referendum in 1993, which gained an overwhelming vote for independence.[52] The UN approved an Observer Mission to ratify Eritrea's referendum.[53] After the referendum, Eritrea became an independent state and was admitted to UN membership.

7.4 Constitutional "Right for Secession"

Apart from the analysis of the possibility for an international codification of a limited "right to secession" within the scope of international law, there are few opinions regarding the creation of a legal provision related to secession and its incorporation into the national constitutions. The arguments stress the need to avoid unpredictable situations and, with that, to minimize the possibility of the devastation of society. The opinions vary—from the acceptance of such a possibility to a complete denial thereof under the stance that the political phenomenon of secession is quite opposite to the core principles of constitutionalism and cannot generate a legitimate right and, thus, cannot be accommodated within the constitutional frames.

Ideas to integrate the "right" of secession into the constitution are not new and constitute a complex mix of legal arguments relating to justice, democracy, recognition, and the right to self-determination. It goes alongside the reflections on political sociology for multiethnic societies and nationalism, as well as encompasses views on the constitutionality and state building of federal democracies. Nonetheless, the provision that tackles secession, in most cases, does not exist in most constitutions in the world, i.e., the constitutions are silent about this phenomenon. However, only a few constitutions in the world historically envisaged this possibility, but the

[50] Federation with Ethiopia (Internet source).

[51] For the case of Eritrea see more at Heraclides (1991); Cassese (1995); Demissie (1996); Micheau (1996).

[52] Amhazion (2018).

[53] United Nations Observer Mission, A/48/283 (1993).

conditions for this practice were extremely difficult to fulfill. For example, the Burma Constitution, between 1947 and 1974, predicted the right to secession but established almost impossible conditions and procedures for its realization and did not give such a right to the two states that have the greatest aspirations for securing independence – the Karen and Kachin states. Another example is the Constitution of the previous Socialistic Federative Republic of Yugoslavia from 1974, which stipulated the right to self-determination that involves secession, but territorial revisions were only possible through a consensus of the six republics and the two provinces.[54] The Constitution of the USSR from 1977, in Article 72, gave the republics a right to freely secede, but without a modus for practicing that right. Consequently, when Georgia and the other republics claimed the right, its exercise was denied.[55]

When established as a constitutional right, the conditions toward secession are often subject to different interpretations, which regularly do not encourage secession. Thus, for example, the First Russian Constitutional Court, in its decision from 1992, protected the territorial sovereignty of the Russian Federation and denied the Declaration of State Sovereignty of the Republic of Tatarstan, in particular, the referendum regarding the status of the Republic. Although other republics in the USSR had similar referendums for their independence, the Court disputed the Declaration because the referendum polling did not mention the option of Tatarstan being a part of Russia. Although the right to self-determination and the possibility for its practice can be found in domestic law and was guaranteed by the Russian Federation, the Court balanced the right and the principle of respect for territorial integrity and human rights. As a supportive argument, it cited Article 29 of the Universal Declaration of Human Rights, pointing out that the exercise of own rights implies respect for the enjoyment of the rights and freedoms of others and gave an opinion that practicing the rights otherwise represents an abuse of justice. Consequently, according to the Court's opinion, unilateral secession not only violates the territorial integrity of a sovereign state and disturbs the national unity of the people but also violates the constitutional order. On the other hand, secession can only be possible and just if it is reached through a negotiation process that involves all the stakeholders.[56]

Another example is the Constitution of the Federal Democratic Republic of Ethiopia, from 1995, which predicts representative democratic structures and the recognition of the right to self-determination, including the right to secession for every nation, nationality and people in Ethiopia. Still, although the right to secession is recognized in this document, its application in practice is extremely limited.[57]

---

[54] Constitution of Socialistic Federative Republic of Yugoslavia (1974), Preamble and Article 5 para. 3.

[55] Silverstein (1958); Heraclides (1991).

[56] Summers (2007).

[57] Micheau (1996).

7.4.1 Arguments Pro *and* Against *Establishing a Constitutional Provision on Secession*

There are different opinions about whether or not constitutions should have provisions for secession. For some international law scholars, international law, in certain documents, tacitly recognizes the right to secession (such as UNGA Resolution 2625, in cases when the government of the state is not representative), while others explicitly reject such ideas, pointing out that the main concepts of secession are against not only the states but also the international order, whose main subjects are the states. International law is primarily the law of the states, and in that sense, it should not include provisions for their own destruction.[58] For others, a more pragmatic group, secession already exists in practice, and consequently, a specific and limited right to secession needs to be introduced within international law.[59] However, the international community, in the current state of affairs, is far from accepting even a conditionally qualified right to secession.

In a similar manner, there are debates about the possibility of including such provisions in the national constitutions, but the opinions on whether secession is justified in a constitutional sense vary in theory.

7.4.1.1 Arguments "Pro"

Certain theorists advocate for the introduction of the right to secession in the constitutions but in parallel with the conditions for its fulfillment, such as the necessity of a super majority that would limit the secessionist elections and would "protect" and "support" democracy.[60] The opposite block sees this constitutional engineering as pointless if the main idea is to create situations with little or no chance of realization.[61]

Wolfgang Danspeckgruber is one of the theorists who consider that the existence of a constitutional provision will remove secession from daily politics. Consequently, the abovementioned provision will be a mechanism for voluntary agreement, which will contribute to the partnership and its consolidation. This provision will support confidence building among different ethno-social groups that exist within the territorial borders, it will diminish antagonism, and it will increase stability and peaceful realization of the right to self-determination.[62] As an argument, Danspeckgruber cites two constitutions as examples: the Constitution of Ethiopia and the Constitution of South Africa. According to Article 39 (1) of the Constitution of Ethiopia, "(…) every nation, nationality, and people of Ethiopia shall have an unconditional right to

[58] Horowitz (2003).

[59] Beran (1991); Buchanan (1991); Buchanan (1991) a.; Cassese (1995).

[60] Sunstein (1991).

[61] Norman (2003).

[62] Danspeckgruber (2002).

self-determination, including the right to secession,"[63] and Chapter XIV Section 235 of the Constitution of South Africa stipulates that "The right of self-determination of the people of South Africa as a whole, as manifested in this Constitution, does not exclude, within the scope of this right, recognition of the idea of the right to self-determination to any community that shares a common cultural and linguistic wealth within the territorial entity of the Republic, or is otherwise determined jointly by the national law."[64]

Without a doubt, for some theoreticians, secession is inconsistent with the conventional expectations of the constitutional order, and that is to hold the political world together and not allow it to fall apart, but Mark E. Brandon considers the importance of the incorporation of secession norms into national constitutions. According to Brendon, if people who are united together in a political society find themselves divided in what they consider to be significant, this division is long-lasting, and if they do not want to live together anymore, then secession can be a practical option. The existence of a clear provision in the constitution, in cases that are extreme, can prevent full destruction, claims Brandon. Consequently, constitutionalism need not only be concerned with creation and maintenance but should also consider the dissolution of the political order.[65] Brandon establishes his thesis on the ideals of Alexander Hamilton, for whom the US Constitution is an experiment in making it possible to reestablish the government through "reflection and choice" instead of "incidentally, by force."[66] Alongside this opinion, it is a lack of pragmatism to be fixed with contracts that exist more than 400 years.[67]

For Wayne Norman, interestingly, the greatest enthusiasts around the constitutional regulation of the right to secession are the theorists with little or no sympathy for secessionist movements and with a paradoxical tendency for secession to be legally possible but practically impossible, hoping that possible right holders will not use that chance. Until now, the justification for a possible incorporation of a secession provision into the constitution is determined by the existence or nonexistence of a moral right to secession, that is, considering under what conditions a territorially concentrated group has a moral right to secede. If the group has secured its moral grounds, then a question is asked whether this right should be incorporated into the constitution. However, for Norman, this issue should not be treated in isolation and needs to be examined within a broader discussion considering all the aspects of constitutionalism. Nevertheless, Norman is not for a general acceptance of secessionist clauses within constitutions. Considering the fact that 90% of the states in the world have significant minorities, secession clauses need to be put in the constitutions of certain types of states, preferably into the constitutions of advanced democracies (such as Canada, Belgium, France, the UK, etc.). The

[63] Constitution of the Federal Democratic Republic of Ethiopia (1995).

[64] The Constitution of the Republic of South Africa (1996).

[65] Brandon (2003).

[66] Hamilton (1787).

[67] Brandon (2003).

outcomes of those constitutional designs can generate options that can be applied into the divided societies, such as the ones in the Balkans. This secessionist provision should stem from constitutional negotiations and build on a wide range of constitutional provisions that at the same time would protect the interests of minorities (such as provisions promoting autonomy or recognition) and the majority (such as provisions promoting uniqueness and stability). According to Norman, the non-existent constitutional provision for secession can be worse than its existence because (1) the popular secessionist movement, which lacks the legal means to carry out its political agenda, will cause political uncertainty and (2) the legal procedure for practicing such a right can reduce the chances for the raising of a serious secessionist movement.[68]

For Allen Buchanan, it is necessary to identify the different types of secession, as well as the conditions under which secession can be achieved but also to offer a moral framework that will enable substantive (though incomplete) guidance to resolve disagreements surrounding secession. However, the moral framework without proper constitutional embodiment is only a moral vision, and the vision, although it is necessary for action, is far from permissible. Buchanan considers that secession should be embedded in a particularly powerful institution, such as the constitution of the modern state, and such an agreement should be established upon liberal values that support autonomy, liberty, and diversity.[69]

Another set of reasons that advocate why provisions for secessions should be embedded in the constitution of a multinational state is based on the possibility or likelihood that the secessionist movements will increase the territories controlled by the national minorities, regardless of whether there is an explicit recognition of such a right. Therefore, the state should deal with the secessionist quests and bargain within the rule of law and not as a part of political questions. The primary criticism of such an interpretation of the possible right to secession stems from the potential realization of other, morally dubious, activities, such as prostitution, narcotics, and the like. By analogy, it may be arguable that those activities will happen, whether legal or illegal, and thus may be better legalized so they can be removed from the black market.[70]

Secessionist politics may involve a spectrum of activities, ranging from arguable, legally acceptable acts, such as advocacy and propaganda for secession, to legally and morally dubious activities, such as unilateral declarations of independence and armed actions. The identification of these possible "legal activities" can further help the state to give a proper response in order not to reach the ultimate spectrum—unilateral independence and military conflict. Still, Buchanan argues that it is important to determine what behavior should be regulated—whether it is secession advocacy, secession mobilization, attempts for secession, or secession itself. It is possible that some of the abovementioned situations can fall under the freedom of

[68] Norman (2003).

[69] Buchanan (1991); Buchanan (2003).

[70] Buchanan (1991).

speech or the freedom of association, but only if the law and public security are respected. Therefore, although legally possible, it is difficult to determine which behaviors or acts can be eventually legalized by a constitutional theory of secession.[71]

For Diane F. Orentlicher, there is no unique formula for dealing with secessionist quests. She proposes a problem-solving mechanism through mutual agreements and negotiations, rejecting unilateral acts. The commitment to resolve disagreements over separatist movements through mutual agreements underscores two situations: (1) the negotiating partners should accept the possibility of secession as a result of the negotiations, and (2) in principle, the disagreements about secessionist quests should not be solved solely through a referendum. If the separatist's issues are resolved only by voting, the losing party could invoke the political authority and reject the results of the voting. However, voting can play a legitimate role in resolving disagreements within the broader context of the negotiations. The same applies to a referendum, which in turn can only play a role if the negotiating parties agree to hold a referendum and accept its results. For the same reason, a vote that can lead to a political divorce could undoubtedly have legitimacy only if the national constitution provides that possibility – assuming that the constitution was enacted in a democratic, legitimate way.[72]

For Orentlicher, the ideal situation is if negotiations over disagreements related to secessionist demands take place in a framework that (1) is set upon strong prerequisites for mutual accommodation, (2) minimizes the risk of a dead end, and (3) does not encourage secession. The first two objectives aim toward achieving mutually acceptable results and securing that none of the parties prevents the mutually acceptable agreement. On the other hand, the effective institutional design of the negotiations must be able to address situations where a mutually acceptable result cannot be achieved, especially where the survival of the group is seriously compromised. The third objective serves the same interest as the first two and protects potential political divorces.[73]

7.4.1.2 Arguments "Against"

There are several reasons why theorists argue *for* or *against* incorporating secession into the constitutions, and generally, they are geostrategic (envisaging aspects of defense and security), moral reasons, as well as economic reasons. For many American theorists, the existence of a secession provision in the Constitution is unjustified since the union of states existed prior to the Constitution. Therefore, any secession would destroy the union and, according to them, will lead to a complete undoing of the shared American values.[74] Following that line, Cass Sunstein

[71] Buchanan (1991).

[72] Orentlicher (2003).

[73] Orentlicher (2003).

[74] Sunstein (1991).

advocates against the introduction of the constitutional right to secession and claims that such a right does not exist under American constitutional law and argues that secession is prohibited under the principles of constitutionalism.[75]

Those who are against the incorporation of the provision of secession into the constitution point out that incorporating such a "right" will destroy the spirit and ideals of constitutionalism. Additionally, it is impossible to set such a detailed constitutional provision since many situations are uncertain and they are too difficult to be predicted in a constitutional text.

The strongest argument against incorporation of a provision on secession within the constitutions is given by the Venice Commission of the Council of Europe, on the question of the Parliamentary Assembly of the Council of Europe, to give an opinion over the matter if the question of self—determination and secession can be addressed by the constitutional law. The given answer was based not on international law but on national constitutional sources, and it was analyzed through rulings of the constitutional courts and equivalent authorities.

According to the Commission, secession in its inherent nature is contrary to constitutional law since the intention of secession is to dismember and destroy the very foundation of the state. Most constitutions in the world are silent on the issue of secession, and that silence may sometimes be used to outlaw situations. However, each constitution must be interpreted in its context, and therefore, it is difficult to find a general understanding of that silence. Nevertheless, the prohibition of secession is implicitly based upon provisions that protect and proclaim the indivisibility of states, national unity, and, more commonly, territorial integrity.[76]

Within this context, fundamental rights, such as the *freedom of association* and the *freedom of thought and expression*, can be restricted for the goal of protecting territorial integrity, and that can refer to programs or acts of political parties or other organizations that agitate against territorial integrity. Consequently, any contrary actions can be considered unconstitutional. Unlike secession, self-determination is not alien to constitutional law, although provisions for its practice are not clear. Self-determination must be dissociated with secession and can be seen as the right of independence of a state that is already constructed or as internal self-determination, that is, the right of the people to freely determine their political status within state borders.[77]

Referring to the destructiveness of secession, the Commission points out that after many years of total stability, the process of dissolution of the three federations (SFRY, USSR, and Czechoslovakia) was peaceful in the example of Czechoslovakia, extremely bloody in the case of Yugoslavia, and to-a-lesser-extent bloody in the

---

[75] Sunstein (1991), p. 633.

[76] Council of Europe, Venice Commission Report, Self-Determination and Secession in Constitutional Law (2000).

[77] Council of Europe, Venice Commission Report, Self-Determination and Secession in Constitutional Law (2000).

case of the Soviet Union. It is interesting that two of the abovementioned states, in their constitutions, had provisions for the secession of their constitutive republics.[78]

Although for some authors secessionism is inconsistent with constitutionalism and as such it cannot be incorporated, for certain international law theorists, secession can be legitimate if it is constitutionally constituted. By that notion, secession as an option should exist in the constitution, alongside the conditions under which it can be exercised. In contrast, many of the constitutionalists find secession alien to the core ideas of constitutionalism, and they consider that such ideas cannot be incorporated into the major legal act. There are only a few constitutions in the world that historically predicted the possibility of secession, but those provisions were only set in a declarative manner. The possibility for secession demands to be addressed within the constitutional frame, under democratic principles, is presented in the given example of Québec and Canada, whereas the inquiry about the legality of secession was balanced against other fundamental principles. Nonetheless, the question of whether secession can be justified in a constitutional sense remains an open and controversial topic.

7.4.2 The Canada-Quebec Case: Reviewing Secession Demands Within the Constitutional Framework

In 1995, the Canadian Supreme Court argued the case of the secession claim of Quebec from Canada. Namely, the Canadian Minister of Justice formally asked the Court to look at a number of issues regarding the legality of the secession. The subject of the issue was whether Quebec has the right to a unilateral secession from Canada. The Supreme Court of Canada ruled that there is no right for Quebec either under the Constitution or under international law to secede unilaterally.[79] Although the Supreme Court unequivocally rejected the existence of such a right, it sought to deal with the potentially destructive issue of secession through the rule of law, in the absence of explicit constitutional norms regarding secession.[80] The Court concluded that secession causes constitutional change and therefore cannot be exercised simply with the vote of the majority of the secessionist region. Consequently, it must be achieved through a constitutional change that should result from a negotiation process. By stating that secession must be achieved through negotiation, it is clear that secession must be a consensual, not a unilateral, action. The Court concluded that in the Quebec case, the right to secession could not be applied as an ultimate remedy.[81]

[78] Council of Europe, Venice Commission Report, Self-Determination and Secession in Constitutional Law (2000).

[79] Reference re Secession of Quebec, S.C.C. no. 25506, Aug.20, 1998, 2 S.C.R. 217, sec 94-95 of the opinion.

[80] Buchanan (2003); Turp (2003).

[81] Reference re Secession of Quebec, S.C.C. no. 25506, Aug.20, 1998, 2 S.C.R. 217, sec 104.

Under international law, external self-determination can be enjoyed by former colonies, people who are repressed or under military occupation, or groups whose access to the government is denied or in cases where the realization of internal self-determination is impossible. The Court found that the Province of Quebec does not belong to the abovementioned groups.[82] The people of Quebec are not victims of attacks on their existence, or on their physical integrity, therefore it seems it is unrealistic to seek consent from the state for secession, but it only can be understandable in the cases where the secession is seen as a remedy against injustice over oppressed people. The same point can be drawn in terms of legitimacy. A state that respects the rights of all its citizens, both individually and collectively, is legitimate, and in that state, the whole territory belongs to the people as a whole. In other words, the territory belongs to the people, not to the government, and therefore the territory can be alienated only with the consent of all the people, not exclusively with the consent of the people who live in the secessionist territory.[83]

Nevertheless, according to some scholars, the Supreme Court read a modest secessionist clause in the Canadian Constitution, although the Constitution itself does not explicitly regulate secession. Namely, the Court analyzed the question upon the fundamental and organizational principles of the Constitution, that is, federalism, democracy, the rule of law, and minority rights. In those aspects, the Court dismissed the legality of unilateral secession but did not find that the basic idea of secession was contrary to the principles of constitutionality.[84]

In the Quebec-Canada case, the proponents of secession have invoked ordinary democratic arguments, calling upon the moral right that derives from the principle of democracy and underlies the majority procedure at the federal and provincial levels. However, according to the Court, the principle of democracy is not the only fundamental principle and must be balanced against other fundamental principles, such as the protection of minorities, constitutionality, the rule of law, and federalism. The decision to split on the basis of a simple democratic argument, based on an exit procedure, which requires a majority vote in the region ready to break away, actually makes the exit too easy, terribly underestimating the state's commitment to deliberative democracy.[85]

References

Amhazion F (2018) A Look Back on Eritrea's Historic 1993 Referendum (Internet source). https://tesfanews.net/revisiting-eritrea-historic-1993-referendum/. Accessed 9 Jan 2023

Andrews J (2020) The world in conflict. The Economist

Beran H (1991) The consent theory of political obligation. Routledge Kegan & Paul

---

[82] Reference re Secession of Quebec, S.C.C. no. 25506, Aug.20, 1998, 2 S.C.R. 217, sec 138.

[83] Buchanan (2003).

[84] Norman (2003), p. 213.

[85] Buchanan (2003).

Brandon EM (2003) Secession, constitutionalism and American experience In: Macedo S, Buchanan (eds) Secession and self- determination. New York University Press, pp 272–314
Brilmayer L (1991) Secession and self-determination: a territorial interpretation. Yale J Int Law 16:177–202
Buchanan A (1991) Secession: the morality of political divorce from Fort Sumter to Lithuania and Quebec. Westview Press
Buchanan A (2003) The Quebec Secession Issue: Democracy, Minority Rights and the Rule of Law. In: Macedo S, Buchanan A (eds) Secession and Self-Determination. New York: University press, pp 238–271
Buchheit LC (1978) Secession, the legitimacy of self-determination. Yale University Press, New Haven and London
Cassese A (1995) Self- determination of the peoples, a legal reappraisal. Cambridge University Press
Chernichenko SV, Kotlyar VS (2003) Ongoing global legal debate on self-determination and secession main trends. In: Dahliz J (ed) Conflict avoidance and - regional appraisals. Asser Press, pp 75–89
Cobban A (1969) The national state and national self- determination. Thomas Y. Crowell Rev
Constitution of Socialistic Federative Republic of Yugoslavia (1974). https://www.worldstatesmen.org/Yugoslavia-Constitution1974.pdf. Accessed 9 Sept 2022
Constitution of the Federal Democratic Republic of Ethiopia (1995). https://www.wipo.int/edocs/lexdocs/laws/en/et/et007en.pdf. Accessed 9 Sept 2022
Council of Europe, Venice Commission Report (2000) Self-Determination and Secession in Constitutional Law. file:///D:/Local%20Disk%20C/Desktop/default.pdf. Accessed 9 Sept 2022
Danspeckgruber FW (2002) Self-determination and regionalization in contemporary *Europe*. In: Danspeckgruber W (ed) Self – determination of peoples, community, nation and state in interdependent world. Lynne Rienner Publishers, pp 351–352
Demissie D (1996) Self - determination including secession v.s. the territorial integrity of nation – states: a prima facie case for secession. Suffolk Transanatl Law Rev 20:165–192
Federation with Ethiopia (Internet Source). https://www.britannica.com/place/Eritrea/Federation-with-Ethiopia. Accessed 9 Jan 2023
GA Res. 289 A (IV) (1949). http://www.worldlii.org/int/other/UNGA/1949/51.pdf. Accessed 9 Jan 2023
GA Res 617 (VII) Eritrea: Report of the United Nations Commissioner in Eritrea. Resolutions adopted on reports of the Ad Hoc Political Committee (1952). http://www.worldlii.org/int/other/UNGA/1952/127.pdf. Accessed 9 Jan 2023
Gayim E (2006) Minority and indigenous: interpretation and application of concepts in the politics of human rights, 20 The Erik Castrén Institute Reports. Erik Castrén Institute of International Law and Human Rights
Grotius H, Kelsey FW (1925) De jure belli ac pacis libri tres, vol 2. Clarendon Press, Oxford
Hamilton A (1787) The Federalist, No. 1. https://founders.archives.gov/documents/Hamilton/01-04-02-0151-0001. Accessed 9 Sept 2022
Henrard K (2000) Devising an adequate system of minority protection. Kluwer Law International, Hague
Heraclides A (1991) The self - determination of the minorities in the international politics. Frank Cass and Company Limited
Horowitz DL (2003) A right to secede? Secession and self-determination. In: Macedo S, Buchanan A (eds) Secession and self- determination. New York University Press, pp 84–132
Locke J (1690) Two Treatises of Government, A New Edition, Corrected (1824) http://www.rwi.uzh.ch/elt-lst-kley/verfg/grossbritannien/de/pdf/Two_treatises_of_government_orig.pdf. Accessed 9 Sept 2022
Micheau AP (1996) The 1991 Transitional Charter of Ethiopia: a new application of the self –determination principle? Case Western Res J Int Law 28(2):367–394

Nanda VP (1980) Self- determination outside colonial context: the birth of Bangladesh in retrospect. In: Alexander Y, Friedlander RA (eds) Self - determination: national regional and global dimensions. Westview Press, Boulder, CO, pp 193–220
Norman W (2003) Domesticating secession. In: Macedo S, Buchanan A (eds) Secession and self-determination. New York University Press, pp 193–237
Orentlicher FD (2003) International responses to separatist claims: are democratic principles relevant?. In: Macedo S, Buchanan A (eds) Secession and self- determination. New York University Press, pp 19–49
Pufendorf S, Oldfather FCH, Oldfather WA (1934) De jure naturae et gentium libri octo. The Clarendon Press, Oxford
Redslob R (1931) Le principe des nationalités. (Volume 37). In: Collected Courses of the Hague Academy of International Law. https://doi.org/10.1163/1875-8096_pplrdc_A9789028607422_01 First published online: 1931. Accessed 9 Sep 2022
Reference re Secession of Quebec, S.C.C. no. 25506, Aug.20, 1998, 2 S.C.R. 217. https://scc-csc.lexum.com/scc-csc/scc-csc/en/item/1643/index.do. Accessed 9 Sept 2022
Report presented to the Council of the League of Nations by the Commission of Rapporteurs (1921). https://www.ilsa.org/Jessup/Jessup10/basicmats/aaland2.pdf. Accessed 9 Sept 2022
Rousseau C (1953) Droit international public. Sirey, Paris
Scelle G (1932) Précis de droit des gens: principes et systématique: Réimpression de l'édition de 1932, 2008 Daloz
Silverstein J (1958) Politics in the Shan State: the question of secession from the Union of Burma. J Asian Stud 18(1):43–57
Summers J (2007) Peoples and international law, how nationalism and self-determination shape a contemporary law of nations. Leiden, Boston
Sunstein C (1991) Constitutionalism and secession. Univ Chicago Law Rev 58(2):633–670
The Constitution of the Republic of South Africa (1996). https://www.justice.gov.za/legislation/constitution/SAConstitution-web-eng.pdf. Accessed 9 Sept 2022
Turp D (2003) Quebec right to secessionist self-determination: the Colliding Paths of Canada Clarity act and Quebec' s Fundamental Rights Act. In: Dahlitz J (ed) Secession and international law, conflict avoidance and - regional appraisals. Asser Press, pp 167–207
UN Human Rights Council, Report of the detailed findings of the Commission of inquiry on human rights in Eritrea, 5 June 2015, A/HRC/29/CRP.1. https://www.refworld.org/docid/55758bab4.html. Accessed 23 Mar 2023
UNGA Res 2625, Annex, Declaration on Principles of international law concerning friendly relations and cooperation among the states in accordance with the Charter of the United Nations, (1970)
United Nations Observer Mission to Verify the Referendum in Eritrea, Report of the Secretary-General, A/48/283 (1993) file:///C:/Users/Dell/Downloads/A_48_283-EN.pdf. Accessed 9 Jan 2023
Van Der Vyver JD (2000) Self-determination of the peoples of Quebec under international law. J Transnatl Law Policy 10:1–27
World Conference on Human Rights, Vienna Declaration and Programme of Action, U.N. doc. A/Conf. 157/24 art. I.2 (June 25, 1993) reprinted in 32 I.L.M. 1661, at 1665 (1993)

Chapter 8
The Emergence of a Secessionist Entity

8.1 Introduction: What Is Achieved with Secession?

In general terms, successful secessions result in a change of political and legal institutions, as well as in a change of the political and legal status of the secessionist territory.[1] Historically, secession was most often accomplished through full intervention, of course, if the intervening state was militarily stronger than the state threatened with secession and the result was the defeat or neutralization of the center. Although full interventions are rare, for successful secession to be a *fait accompli,* it needs to be followed by numerous diplomatic recognitions of the new entity (a state) that has emerged through secession.[2]

The actors involved in secession occurrences are as follows:

- The state on whose territory the secessionist movement is taking place (the existing state)
- The secessionist movement
- Third countries assisting the existing state
- Third countries that assist the secessionist movement
- International organizations that support the existing state
- International organizations that support the secessionists.[3]

Considering that, the act of secession can be seen as a political instrument that brings political, social, legal, and economic changes to a given territory. The acquisition of a sovereign status leads to a change in the community status—from a

[1] Pavkovic and Radan (2007).

[2] Heraclides (1991).

[3] Nico Schrijver uses the term "the victim state" instead of the term used here – "the existing state;" see more in Schrijver (2003).

N. Shikova, *Self-Determination and Secession*,
https://doi.org/10.1007/978-3-031-34322-3_8

minority to a nation that controls its own state. In those endeavors, presumably, the group members expect that the secession will:

- Resolve the injustices highlighted by the secessionist movement
- End the political crisis or violent conflict that arose over secession issues
- Empower the political leaders of the secessionist population
- Increase the political control of the secessionist population over their government and the policies that affect them
- Bring a multitude of economic benefits, such as increasing job prospects and income for different levels of the segregated population.[4]

It is expected that the new state authorities will establish institutions that will bring the abovementioned benefits. But in some cases, the new state authorities lack the means to significantly improve the standard of living simply because the new state depends on international economic resources and has a weak position in the global economy. Independence gives state-owned officials access to international organizations as equal partners to other states and enables them to receive investments, funds, and assistance. Unless the unit is separated, the parent state could provide it, but still, the group is put in a position of dependence, and therefore, despite the costs of secession, the group usually prefers sovereign statehood rather than staying within the existent state. In that endeavor, secession movement elites suggest that the advantages of sovereign statehood are reserved not only for the elites, but they also create benefits for the general population—though secession may have some economic setbacks, and for sure, a certain segment of society will benefit more from secession than others. However, the role of political elites is to present secession and their actions not only as a mere interest but also as actions justified by universal principles.[5]

8.1.1 The Case of the Republic of Katanga: An Example of Unsuccessful Secession

The Belgian Congo—known as Congo-Leopoldville—gained independence under the name Republic of the Congo on June 30, 1960, and it was recognized by the United States, France, Great Britain, Italy, Netherlands, Spain, Russia, and Portugal. In 1964, the Republic of the Congo was renamed as, what we know today, the Democratic Republic of the Congo (DR Congo). In 1971, the name was changed to the Republic of Zaire, which name remained until 1997, when it was restored to its former name. The Republic of the Congo was almost, in the beginning, immersed in

[4] Pavkovic and Radan (2007).

[5] Pavkovic and Radan (2007).

conflict with the southeastern mineral-rich province of Katanga, which wanted to secede.[6]

Although the total territory of the former Belgian Congo was 70 to 80 times bigger than the size of the colonizer's territory—the Kingdom of Belgium – nevertheless, neither that geographical location nor the demographically, ethnically very diverse population was decisive for the Congolese people gaining independence from the Belgian colonial slavery, which lasted since 1908. It was not until the late 1950s when the National Congolese Movement took a swing on the colonized territory, with the primary political tendency for secession from Belgium and independent Congo. Finally, after the parliamentary elections held in the spring of 1960, the Democratic Republic of the Congo declared its independence on June 30.[7] However, very quickly, the same year, the young politically immature Republic becomes a global infamous example of a puppet state when leader Mobutu Sese Seko, instructed by the United States and powerful Belgian mining and processing companies, waged a military coup and seized power. That same year, just one month after the proclamation of the independent democratic republic, on July 11, 1960, the autonomous province of Katanga, by area the largest and richest in natural and mineral wealth (copper, cobalt, gold, tin, uranium, diamonds) and the most prosperous territory of DR Congo, under the dictatorial rule of Moise Tshombe, fanatically backed by several thousand heavily armed gendarmeries from domestic and European mercenaries (Belgian companies and the Belgian army), successively declared the Independent Republic of Katanga, which lasted for 31 months. The first Prime Minister of DR Congo, Patrice Lumumba, appealed to the UN for the forces to end the secessionist movement. The UN initially refused, considering the rebellion an internal issue. After the Prime Minister was deposed by *Mobutu* Sese Seko in November 1960, and was later killed in early 1961,[8] the UN decided to take action. To prevent civil war in the Congo, the UN passed Resolution 161, which authorized UN forces to take "all appropriate measures" against the Katangan state.[9] The conflict ended in January 1963 after UN and US forces overwhelmed the Katangan military and Moise Tshombe stepped down as President of Katanga.[10]

Katanga passed through three phases of independence. In the first phase, which lasted for several months, Belgium militarily and diplomatically supported Katanga for economic interests and also for the sake of the promotion of independent democratic values, which were not based on race, nation, ethnicity, etc. In the beginning, Katanga gained sympathy from other countries, even verbal support from the United States. In the second phase of independence, the Katangans tried to push away Belgium and its influence and also to attract other supporters. At that time, the country was divided by internal conflicts and clashes and was marked by political

[6] Andrews (2020).

[7] The Congo, Decolonization, and the Cold War, 1960–1965 (Internet source).

[8] Congo in Crisis: The Rise and Fall of Katangan Secession (2015).

[9] UNSC Res. 161 (1961).

[10] Congo in Crisis: The Rise and Fall of Katangan Secession (2015).

executions. In the third phase of independence, the Congo rejected the Declaration of Confederation with Katanga, and in the fourth, the United States stood on the side of the Congo and supported it in its intervention against Katanga.[11] The Katanga secession was not internationally recognized either by the Belgian government that supported it. As a result, the Congolese people became victims of an ambitious clash between two autarchic puppet dictators—the unitarist Sese Seco and the secessionist Tshombe. After a fierce two-and-a-half years of diplomatic and military intervention, this bitterness finally ended in 1963, when the current political status of the Katanga as a province within DR Congo was restored. The brutal, fratricidal civil war, fueled by the political intrigues of DR Congo and Katanga leaders, was a typical tragic occurrence of the higher political and economic interests of the former USSR and the United States. In this Cold War era and in the global ideological clash between communism and capitalism, the interests of Belgian mining companies, as well as the ideological interests of the United States on the African continent, played a catalyst role as well.[12]

8.2 Recognition of the Secessionist Entity

Until 1914, secession was perhaps the most common method of creating new states. Since 1919, new states have more often been created with the consent of the former sovereign, and this was especially emphasized during decolonization. But attempts for secession and the creation of states using or threatening to use force without the consent of the former sovereign have been frequent, and some have even been successful, such as the cases of Indonesia, North Korea, North Vietnam, Bangladesh, Guinea-Bissau, and Eritrea. But many secession attempts have failed, such as the cases of Katanga and Biafra, or are still underway, such as those in Somalia and Chechnya.[13] In addition to gaining control over the secessionist territory, the goal of the secessionist movement is the international recognition of such control over the concerned unit as sovereign. When a state exercises sovereign power, it excludes the establishment of any control by other states over it, and for that exclusion to take effect, other states must recognize that state as sovereign. Hence, the secessionists do not only seek to establish control in the new state, but they need this right of control to be recognized by other states as well as by the existing state from which they are seceding. Sovereignty implies the independence of a state from other states, and the process of recognizing sovereignty is carried out through the establishment of diplomatic relations. So, from a legal point of view, the recognition of the new

[11] See more at Situation in the Republic of Congo (Internet source).

[12] For the case DR Congo – Katanga, see more at Crawford (2006); Cassese (1995); Summers (2007); Dugard (2003); Moris (1998); Andrews (2020).

[13] Crawford (2006).

secessionist entity by other states and international organizations means the completion of its state creation process.[14]

Apart from the formal recognition of the new state through the establishment of diplomatic relations and its admission in international organizations (*de jure* recognition), there is *de facto* recognition, which occurs if the secessionists took and maintain control over the territory and effectively govern it through their established institutions. This *de facto* recognition means that other states or international organizations treat the representatives of the secessionist entity the same as they treat the representatives of a sovereign state, without formally recognizing them. *De facto* recognition, though not always, can be a transition period toward the formal recognition of the new state.[15]

In that respect, we can distinguish between (1) the recognition of the statehood of the newly created entity by the former sovereign and (2) the recognition of the new statehood by third countries.[16] It is clear that if the former sovereign recognizes and accepts the new entity's control over a particular territory, then the entity is a *prima facie* state. But if the entity effectively controls a particular territory and the existing state does not recognize or accept this situation, the answer is not so clear.[17] There are two streams in this regard, one arguing that recognition by the existing (parent) state is crucial and necessary for statehood[18] and the other according to which recognition by the existing (parent) state is not necessary for the establishment of statehood.[19] Although there is a difference between *de jure* recognition and *de facto* recognition, the practice points toward the notion that recognition by the existing (parent) state is not crucial for obtaining statehood, but diplomatic recognition done by third states is seen as constitutive in that process.[20]

Recognition is not a factor of statehood, but it is one of the few indicators of statehood.[21] Significantly, an entity that has elements of statehood but is not a self-determined unit (such as a colony, unmanaged territory, etc.), such as Katanga and Biafra in 1960 and the Republic of Northern Cyprus today, is unlikely to be recognized by other states. On the other hand, if the entity is self-defined but does not meet the strict criteria for statehood, such as Algeria in 1950 or the former Portuguese colonies in Africa, the chances of it being recognized by other states are far greater without the act being seen as interfering in the state's internal affairs.[22]

In general, international recognition is a political process historically marked by arbitrariness. It is the result of a unilateral action by members of the international

---

[14] Pavkovic and Radan (2007).

[15] Pavkovic and Radan (2007); Hannum (1990).

[16] Crawford (2006).

[17] N.b. Crawford uses the term "metropolitan state"; see Crawford (2006).

[18] Pufendorf et al. (1934).

[19] Vattel and Lapradelle (1916).

[20] Crawford (2006).

[21] Moris (1998).

[22] Crawford (2006); Brownlie (1973); Heraclides (1991).

community that determines whether an entity seeking recognition has met the established criteria for statehood.[23] In the postcolonial era, cases of secession are less common (if the cases of SFR Yugoslavia and the USSR are not considered secession but rather disintegrations, though this is highly questionable), and in terms of the recognition of secessionist entities, states are much more relying on political factors.[24] The precedent was established during the process of the dissolution of SFRY and the USSR when the uniqueness of the traditional criteria for statehood (a defined territory, a permanent population, a government, and the capacity to enter into relations with other states)[25] were being bypassed by the Yugoslav Declaration and the Criteria for Recognizing New States from Eastern Europe and the Soviet Union (hereinafter "Criteria").[26] With the introduction of the Criteria, the countries (at that time) of the European Communities considered that the recognition should be more an instrument of international politics rather than a formal declaration of facts. That became a subjective approach for meeting objective criteria, and this amorphous but very important political element made recognition more difficult.[27] Some scholars saw those processes not as a recognition of secessionist movements *per se* but as an international recognition of the entities that emerge from the breakup of states. This qualified international recognition and made it dependable, whether or not the new state arises as a result of the disintegration of the old state or as a result of secessionist movements.[28] In that respect, unilateral secession for an existing state remained void and was not accepted (such as Biafra from Nigeria and Katanga from Congo), but a dissolution, a disintegration of a state that does not continue to exist, can be classified as a special case (such as the Baltic states, the Yugoslav republics, and Kosovo).[29]

However, despite states' free assessment about the recognition of the secessionist entity, the metropolitan state or the existing states clearly oppose and do not recognize nonconsensual secession.[30] State governments' clear disapproval of secession sometimes contains formulations that imply that secession is contrary to international law, although there is no international legal rule that prohibits secession. In that respect, the law against secession is undoubtedly the law of the metropolitan state or the existing state.[31]

As far as the recognition of secessionist movements is concerned, recognition by third states has always been an important issue, especially concerning secession

[23] Shaw (2003).

[24] Rich (1993).

[25] Montevideo Convention on Rights and Duties of States, Dec.26, 1933, 165 L.N.T.S. 19, art.1.

[26] Guidelines on the Recognition of New States in Eastern Europe and in the Soviet Union, 16 December 1991.

[27] Rich (1993); Shaw (2003), p. 246; Worster (2009); Frckoski (2005).

[28] Rich (1993).

[29] Moris (1998).

[30] Shaw (2003); Borgen (2007).

[31] Crawford (2006).

stricto sensu.[32] Traditional international law provides to rebels a different kind of recognition, that is, it grants them rebel status and belligerent status, unlike to the secessionists. The first one is a freer concept and depends on whether the states establish legal relationships with the rebels. The application of the second concept depends on several criteria that need to be met, as well as some factual tests. The rebel status and belligerent status generally mean that the movement can gain a status of a legitimate military, freedom fighters, or anticolonial movement with a recognized right to self-determination (for example, the Palestinians). Some of those movements have a certain status in international organizations and some of them full membership.[33] So when it comes to the recognition of rebel movements, unlike the recognition of a secessionist entity, rebel movements are most often recognized when the secessionist movement has reached a certain level of governance and military organization. The recognition of rebels can especially occur when (a) the existing state government (the government of the parent, metropolitan state) undoubtedly treats the rebels as an organized military force relating to the practice of martial law, or (b) the rebels have an organized authority capable of pursuing hostilities following martial law and bear the consequences of their actions. At times, the recognition of the rebel movement is seen as a substitute for the recognition of the new entity as a state. But even if they are not recognized, if they maintain a certain level of territorial and administrative effectiveness long enough, the rebel movements have certain rights. The recognition of the rebels formalizes their legal status, raises the issue of nonintervention concerning both sides, and authorizes the application of martial law to both parties.[34]

8.2.1 The Case of Biafra (May 1967–January 1970) – An Example of the Nonrecognition of a Secessionist Entity

The Federal Republic of Nigeria is the most populous country in Africa with more than 200 million people. Nigeria gained independence in 1960 from the colonizer Great Britain. With more than 350 ethnic groups and languages, Nigeria is almost always in tribal conflicts and tensions between mainly Christians in the south and Muslims in the north. At the basic division, Muslim North is dominated by the Hausa and Fulani people (most of them are Muslims), and in the mainly Christian southeast, dominant are Yoruba (Christians and Muslims) and Igbo (predominantly Catholic).[35] Among the diversity of ethnic groups in Nigeria, three of them (Hausa–Fulani, the Igbo, and the Yoruba) are the largest and make up 2/3 of the population.

[32] Heraclides (1991).

[33] Falk and Tormented (1964), pp. 194–209; Higgins (2003).

[34] Pavkovic and Radan (2007).

[35] Andrews (2020); Nigeria (02/08) (Internet source).

The colonists divided the region into three administrative units without regard for their specificity, and each of them governed it differently, applying different models of education and modernization. Apart from the relations with the center, the regions had nothing to do with each other, so even after independence, Nigerians did not have the same values upon which to build a society.[36] Nigeria was granted full independence in October 1960 as a federation of three regions (northern, western, and eastern) under a constitution that provided for a parliamentary form of government. Under the Constitution, each of the three regions retained a substantial measure of self-government.[37] The political system was divided into three groups of highly corrupt actors, and the small ethnic groups lacked the opportunity to participate. There was no mechanism for adapting to changes, nor was there any identification of citizens with the new state. The various groups also had separatist aspirations, but the Igbo tribe, which lived in the previously lagging region (in comparison to the other two), by mixing with other ethnic groups, became advanced and aware of the oil wealth on its territory. Besides the nonparticipation in the legislature, lack of participation in the decision-making, and the general boycott on the elections, the secession was preceded as well by an act passed by Nigeria's central government that divided the Igbo region into three parts. This initiated secession aspirations, and after several attempts, they finally succeed in 1967, proclaiming the independent Republic of Biafra, which comprises the three states in the eastern region where the Igbo live.[38]

The Republic of Biafra was recognized by five states (Tanzania, Gabon, Ivory Coast, Zambia, and Haiti—four of them African) and received assistance and some support from France and the United States. But soon, due to weak democracy, poor foreign policy, vague ideology, and co-opting with the communist bloc, they lost their supporters, especially from the Union of African Republics, as well as from the UN, which, in turn, abstained from supporting Biafra's independence. Biafra fell into isolation and did not receive international support. Fearing the spread of communism, the possible escalation of conflicts in Africa, and further fragmentation, the international community diplomatically and militarily supported Nigeria and, in 1970, finally suppressed the Eastern Nigeria movement.[39]

8.3 Principle of Effectiveness

When it comes to the recognition of a new state created by an act of secession, it is important to determine when recognition by third states is internationally acceptable. When, due to exhaustion or for some other reason, the sovereign state has

[36] Heraclides (1991); Moris (1998); Okoronkwo (2002).

[37] The Constitution of the Federation of Nigeria (1960).

[38] See more at: Heraclides (1991); Moris (1998); Okoronkwo (2002); Andrews (2020); Remembering Nigeria's Biafra war that many prefer to forget (2020).

[39] Heraclides (1991); Moris (1998); Okoronkwo (2002); Andrews (2020).

virtually or substantially abandoned the struggle for supremacy, it cannot complain when foreign states treat the independence of its former part(s) as de facto established, nor can it prolong its sovereignty solely by claiming an existing right. On the other hand, if the battle is not absolutely or permanently resolved, then the recognition of the rebel's premature independence can be seen as a hostile act toward the sovereign state.[40]

According to nineteenth-century practice, the secessionist territory can be recognized as a state if the secessionists are managed effectively and with sufficient stability. This is one of the ways to limit states' discretion in respect of the act of recognition. However, according to twentieth-century practice, there is a distinction between secession from an existing state and secession of an entity that has the right to self-determination—that is, a non-self-governing territory. When self-determination is denied to the entity entitled to self-determination, as a prerequisite for recognition, a lower level of effectiveness is required—in comparison to the entity that performed an act of secession from an existing state. Before 1945, it was acceptable for a group other than the majority population of the state to achieve independence by establishing control over a particular territory, even, if necessary, by winning the war of independence. Secession was a process that could take years but did not have to have a successful outcome. However, unilateral secession did not (and does not) give any rights under the international legal system. The state government was empowered by all means, and it was allowed to oppose unilateral secessions. Third parties were expected to remain neutral during the conflict, and international law recognized political reality when the independence of the separating entity was already firmly established and the territory was effectively controlled.[41] But later, effectiveness as a condition for recognition has not been widely accepted, as evidenced by the admission of microstates into UN membership, which are in fact dependent on their larger, more powerful neighbors, which in turn suggests that perhaps effectiveness and independence are no longer central criteria for the recognition of the new statehood.[42]

There is an assertion that the classical criteria for statehood, the so-called "Montevideo Criteria," are generally based on this principle of effectiveness. Additionally, the assumption that statehood is a matter of fact recently has received much support, giving much importance of the effectiveness in acquiring of the statehood. Because effectiveness was perceived as a condition, though not as a self-sufficient fact, it was generally denounced that the criteria for the recognition of statehood, which are not based on effectiveness, cannot exist. However, some entities have effectiveness but are not recognized as states (for example, Rhodesia, Taiwan, and Northern Cyprus). On the other hand, some entities were ineffective but had acquired recognition (for example, Ethiopia, Poland,

40 Harcourt (1863), p. 383.

41 Crawford (2006).

42 Grant (2000).

Czechoslovakia, Croatia, Bosnia and Herzegovina, etc.).[43] Therefore, the assumption that the recognition of statehood must be equated with effectiveness is not supported by practice.[44]

Aside from the problem of having coherent state practice in applying the principle of effectiveness in the recognition of states, there are also theoretical problems connected with the applicability of these criteria. In this respect, it is important to distinguish two probable positions: (1) there are no *a priori* criteria for the recognition of statehood that are not connected to effectiveness, and (2) such criteria cannot be a part of international law. There is no doubt that effectiveness remains the dominant, general principle of recognition, but there are certainly exceptions based on other fundamental principles. Establishing principles for recognition, other than effectiveness, is an attempt to bring facts and law closer together, especially in a situation where they conflict over a long period. However, for some scholars, if the struggle lasts long (for example, in Namibia, East Timor, or Rhodesia), with decades spent before it is resolved, then it is best to keep the issues on the agenda until conditions change and reconciliation becomes possible.[45] In that respect, it may be better to leave things as they are—*quieta non movere*—especially when it is clear that merely effective possession cannot create a rule for legal ownership—meaning not all actual possessions result in sovereignty. On the other hand, there is nothing incoherent if the recognition of statehood is set on other bases, except on effectiveness.[46] However, it must not be forgotten that if the international community denies the legal status of an effective legal entity, the situation can result in a legal vacuum, as a particularly problematic and unwanted legal situation.

8.3.1 Examples of Effectiveness Without Recognized Statehood

The most intriguing cases in international law are those of secessionist entities that have not achieved full statehood or are under the sovereign control of the former state. The Turkish Republic of Northern Cyprus and the Pridnestrovian Moldavian Republic (PMR) are not recognized as states although they are effective, they are not fulfilling the basic standards for legality. In the first example, the entity is not recognized by any other state than the one that supports it in ensuring effective

[43] The recognition of Croatia by the European Commission happened when the entity did not control 2/3 of its territory, contrary to the opinion on the recognition given by the Badinter Commission (Recognition Guidelines of December 16, 1991). The same applies to the recognition of Bosnia and Herzegovina, which was admitted to the UN at a time when there were armed conflicts on its territory; see more in Shaw (2003).

[44] Crawford (2006).

[45] Crawford (2006).

[46] Koskenniemi (2009); Crawford (2006); Borgen (2007).

control (Turkey) and the other represents one of the frozen conflicts in Eurasia,[47] not because there are no other options under domestic and international law (besides the secession) but because the separatists have made the conflict to seem unsolvable and refuse solutions other than independence.

8.3.1.1 The Case of the Turkish Republic of Northern Cyprus

After decolonization from Great Britain, there were (are) two communities in Cyprus seeking to exercise their right to self-determination: one community composed of ethnic Turks inhabiting the north and another one composed of Greek Cypriots inhabiting the south of the island. Turks wanted to join Turkey, and Greeks wanted to join Greece. The 1960 Treaty of Guarantee,[48] signed by the Republic of Cyprus on one side and Greece, Turkey, and the United Kingdom of Great Britain and Northern Ireland on the other side, prohibited any activity likely to promote, directly or indirectly, either union with any other state or the partition of the island. The signatories obliged themselves to respect the Constitution of Cyprus (1960) as a single state comprised of two political communities with a power-sharing system that should provide a framework in which both communities should work together.[49] The Treaty of Guarantee has international guarantors and prohibited their intervention. In 1964, the UN Security Council called the parties to refrain from the threat or use of force against the territorial integrity of Cyprus and established the Peacekeeping Force.[50] However, after numerous failures to establish effective power sharing and after the coup carried out by Greek Cypriots wanting unity with Greece, in 1974, Turkey intervened, attempting to establish a new state of affairs. In 1983, Turkish Cypriots unilaterally declared the Turkish Republic of Northern Cyprus, which, despite its effectiveness, is not recognized by any state other than Turkey.[51]

There is an international commitment to settle the question of Cyprus, but so far, all attempts have failed. The closest step toward resolving the Cyprus problem was the plan put by UN Secretary-General Kofi Annan (known as the Annan plan),[52] which, in 2004, was put to a referendum, but the Greek Cypriots rejected it.[53] Under that plan, Cyprus would survive as a single state consisting of two states, and the rights of each would be guaranteed by a set of internal and external mechanisms. The purpose of the plan was to have one state of Cyprus, which has municipal autonomy and extensive constitutional and international guarantees. The guarantees

[47] Apart from Moldova (Transnistria), these are the secessionist regions of Georgia (Abkhazia and South Ossetia) and Azerbaijan (Nagorno-Karabakh). For all of them see more at Borgen (2007).

[48] Treaty of Guarantee (1960).

[49] Cyprus's Constitution of 1960 with Amendments through 2013.

[50] UN SC Res. 186 (1964).

[51] Andrews (2020).

[52] The Comprehensive Settlement of the Cyprus Problem (2004).

[53] Report of the Secretary-General on his mission of good offices in Cyprus (2004).

would be based on an agreement among the United Kingdom, the United Republic of Cyprus, Greece, and Turkey.[54] The plan also proposed a Monitoring Committee, composed of representatives of the guarantor powers, the federal government, and the constituent states and chaired by the UN.[55] After the rejection, there were no serious attempts for negotiation. In May 2008, the two sides began a new round of negotiations after previously pledging to work for a binational federation, as put forward by Security Council resolutions.[56] The Turkish army still retains effective control over Northern Cyprus, which the Republic of Cyprus considers an illegal occupation force. The Cyprus talks are still ongoing, without any eventual outcome that, in the near future, would bring to end the dispute over the partitioned Island.

8.3.1.2 The Case of Transnistria: Pridnestrovian Moldavian Republic (PMR)

Transnistria is an area located in the belt between the Dniester River and the Moldovan border with Ukraine. Following the unilateral Declaration of Independence in 1990, the territory, known as Pridnestrovian Moldavian Republic (PMR), declared itself as a state and established a new state government,[57] with close relations with Russia. The entity is not recognized as a state by any of the UN member states. It has special relationships with Nagorno-Karabakh, Abkhazia, Artsakh, and South Ossetia. They are part of the Union of Unrecognized States (or a Commonwealth of Unrecognized States), all of them founding members.[58] PMR has two official representations abroad (embassies): in Abkhazia and South Ossetia[59] (both disputed entities). The Republic of Moldova does not recognize PMR and still considers most of Transnistria's territory as its part (as is regarded by regional and international organizations),[60] although it is seen as well as a *de facto regime* or analogous to control by an occupying power.[61] After the proclamation of independence and the collapse of the USSR, the tensions between Moldova and the secessionist republic escalated into a civil war (known as the Moldo-Russian war), which lasted until 1992 and ended with a ceasefire agreement between the Russian Federation and the

[54] See more at Loizides and McGarry (2019); Wippman (2000); Crawford (2006).

[55] The Comprehensive Settlement of the Cyprus Problem (2004).

[56] UN Documents for Cyprus: Security Council Resolutions (Internet source).

[57] Constitution of the Pridnestrovian Moldavian Republic (2016).

[58] Wolfschwenger and Leontiev (2022).

[59] Shelest (2015).

[60] Remler (2022); Popescu (2005); Deen and Zweers (2022); European Parliament Resolution (2022/2651) (2022); Parliamentary Assembly Council of Europe Resolution 2308 (2019); Parliamentary Assembly Council of Europe Resolution 24033 (2022); OSCE (1993).

[61] Borgen (2006).

Republic of Moldova.[62] Under the agreement, security arrangements should have been overseen by a joint Control Committee consisted of the representatives of the three sides that are part of the settlement (n.b., the Russian Federation, the Republic of Moldova, and Transnistria).[63] Despite the ceasefire, the political status of the territory remained unresolved. Transnistria is an independent but unrecognized presidential republic under huge Russian influence. It is a partial subject of international law and an incomplete secession through the establishment of a *de facto regime*. Although there is no longer any armed conflict between PMR and the Moldovan government, the situation is still considered a state of occupation.[64]

8.4 Types of Recognition of a Secessionist Entity

In terms of the recognition of an entity as a state, there is an enormous discrepancy in international law and practice. Not only the established state can be recognized but also the emerging entity. On the international stage today, there is a shift from individual to collective recognition, collective rejection, or simply collective delaying of the recognition of the new entity. In any case, when it comes to creating an entity through secession, recognition can give effect to effective secession even if it is contrary to domestic law and even if it is questionable in relation to international law. Nonetheless, when it comes to decolonization, it is easy to apply the Montevideo Convention (1933), which establishes clear criteria for statehood (territory, government, people, and ability to enter into international relations), meaning it determines when an entity can be considered a state and when it can be recognized, but there are also situations when entities do not meet those criteria but are recognized as states.[65]

There are two theories regarding the recognition of states—declarative and constitutive. According to the declarative theory, the recognition of statehood requires meeting the objective criteria, and recognition is based on fact, not on individual states' discretion. On the other hand, according to the constitutive theory, a state is a state only after other states have recognized it as such. The act of recognition is not automatic; it is a political act that depends on states' discretion.

[62] Agreement on the Principles for a Peaceful Settlement of the Armed Conflict in the Dniester Region of the Republic of Moldova (1992).

[63] Agreement on the Principles for a Peaceful Settlement of the Armed Conflict in the Dniester Region of the Republic of Moldova (1992), art. 2.

[64] Borgen (2007); Crawford (2006).

[65] For example, Congo in 1960 and Angola in 1975–1976, which was recognized although in war and without an effective government; see more in Shaw (2003).

8.4.1 Collective Nonrecognition

When a state is created through an act of secession, then its nonrecognition by third states is usual, but when it comes to collective nonrecognition, then the act itself and its legal effects are subject to controversy. Of course, there is a difference between nonrecognition for legal reasons and nonrecognition for political reasons. Political nonrecognition is discretionary, and its effects can be purely nominal. The recognition of an illegal situation is not prohibited under international law, although sometimes the validity of the act does not have to be acknowledged, only its consequences. Of course, one has to distinguish between what is null and what is illegal. A null act does not have legal consequences; if the creation of an entity violates a mandatory norm of general international law, then that violation is erga omnes, i.e., it affects everyone, but the illegal act is still an act and can have direct legal consequences. When an entity claims to be a state but does not have sufficient elements of statehood, its recognition can have a legal effect but on a bilateral basis.[66]

Collective nonrecognition has arisen in the situation of Southeast Rhodesia, Namibia, Northern Cyprus, Kuwait, and in many other cases, with no formal UN resolution on the matter. Nonrecognition can be abstention from contractual relations with the entity, abstention from diplomatic and consular activities, abstention from establishing economic or other relations, nonrecognition of the legality of the administration of the entity, and the like.[67]

Collective nonrecognition usually occurs in two cases. The first one is when the illegality of the act is substantial and, especially, when it involves a violation of a mandatory norm of international law. In that respect, according to James Crawford, under international customary law, states have an obligation not to recognize the act as legal. But the process of collective nonrecognition is more explicitly seen through the practice of international organizations. For example, international organizations may establish criteria to impede international recognition, such as the Declaration on Yugoslavia[68] and the Guidelines for the Recognition of New States,[69] when states seeking recognition need to meet criteria beyond the traditionally accepted criteria for the recognition of statehood.[70] But, according to Malcolm Shaw,[71] although international organizations may establish extremely influential criteria that require legal and political decisions before making individual decisions on recognition or nonrecognition, state recognition is a matter of policy, even when linked with the assessment of the fulfillment of legal facts.[72]

---

[66] Crawford (2006).

[67] Crawford (2006).

[68] Declaration on Yugoslavia (Extraordinary EPC Ministerial Meeting) Brussels, 16 December 1991.

[69] Guidelines on the Recognition of New States in Eastern Europe and in the Soviet Union, 16 December 1991.

[70] Frckoski (2005).

[71] Shaw (2003).

[72] Worster (2009).

8.4.2 Collective Recognition

Despite collective nonrecognition, there is a situation of collective recognition. The recognition of entities in modern practice may be individual or the result of a collective act. But for those who adopt a constitutive view of statehood recognition, individual recognition has serious disadvantages, and as a result, many authors find it necessary to establish a standard for a collective procedure for recognizing new states.

In practice, the confirmation of the status of statehood is achieved in various ways. Thus, in some situations, the collective recognition of status (or collective denial) has a substantive, probative value. In others, its effect is to legitimize the *de facto* situation or to underline a certain status.[73] Often, collective recognition occurs when an entity is admitted to UN membership. Membership in universal political organizations (such as the UN) is usually restricted to states or entities that, regardless of their formal status, have substantial independence. As accession requires strong support from existing member states, acceptance, thus, is strong evidence of the status of the entity. In order for the applicant to be admitted to UN membership, it must fulfill the following criteria: it must (1) be a country, (2) be peaceful, (3) accept the obligations from the Charter, (4) be able to cope with those responsibilities, and (5) be willing to do so. The organization assesses if the conditions for admission are met. However, it is clear that admission does not create an obligation for recognition by the member states as a whole, not even for those that had voted in favor of admission. Although collective recognition does not play a major or predominant role in respect of the entity's status, in many cases, it has been proven to be extremely important.[74]

8.4.3 Collective Conditional Recognition

Conditional recognition depends on meeting certain conditions other than normal statehood requirements.[75] It is sometimes strongly criticized and may be justified in cases where *quid pro quo* recognition is offered in return for something. However, in some cases where conditions for recognition are a part of mandatory international norms, the failure to comply therewith may not only hinder recognition but may also be treated as a breach of international obligations. Hence, conditional recognition has limited applicability. This conclusion can be tested with regard to the collective recognition of the new states of the USSR and Yugoslavia, where in some of these new states, democratic standards, such as the conduct of free elections, were

[73] Crawford (2006).

[74] Lauterpacht (1947); Jessup (1952).

[75] N.b. For example, post-World War I states were required to sign treaties protecting minorities on their territory.

not respected, which, although being a condition for recognition, did not lead to the suspension of recognition or even the disruption of mutual relations.[76]

8.4.4 Additional Recognition Criteria

In addition to the standard criteria for statehood, there is a tendency to incorporate additional criteria for the recognition of statehood into international law, which presumably will be accepted and generally applied. However, there are many challenges in respect of their establishment, such as the lack of the necessary consensus on them, as well as the legitimacy of applying those criteria if there is no consensus, or applying them for the benefit of certain countries or being selectively applied. In fact, the whole concept dilutes one of the presumed benefits of the declarative model of recognition by clearly stating which entities are states.[77]

One of the possible additional criteria for statehood, which tends to be introduced as a necessary condition for the recognition of new states, is the existence of democracy. Sean D. Murphy[78] relies on what Thomas Frank has termed the birth of a democratic government in international law, that is, the acceptance of the new government by other states should depend on whether or not the government ruled according to the will of its people.[79] According to Murphy, if it can be shown in practice that one of the criteria for the recognition of states is the existence of democracy in the political system, then it can be argued that democracy is on its way to becoming a globally established criterion. But this is not supported by general practice. In the international community, the recognition of a particular entity as a state depends on whether the entity enters into legal relations with other states. Additionally, very few international organizations place democracy as a condition for membership. One of them is the Council of Europe. Even the UN franchise does not depend on whether states are democratic or not, nor the accession to UN of non-democratic states is prohibited by the UN Charter. Consequently, nondemocratic states have been admitted to the UN and other international organizations for decades. So, for Murphy, there is no evidence that states refuse to recognize other states simply because they are undemocratic, that is, whether the state is democratic or not, it is not subject to objective criteria; even if the state changes from democratic to undemocratic, the international community continues to respect the legal status of the state, although certain economic or diplomatic sanctions may apply.[80]

With the dissolution of the USSR and SFR Yugoslavia, apart from the traditional Montevideo criteria, the new recognition criteria were set out in the Guidelines for

---

[76] See more at Crawford (2006).

[77] Worster (2009).

[78] Murphy (2000).

[79] Franck (2000).

[80] Murphy (2000).

the Recognition of New EU States, requiring, inter alia, that the state should be democratically established.[81] However, these clearly set criteria, beyond the traditional ones, did not significantly influence the decisions of states whether or not to recognize emerging states.[82] Consequently, that democratic legitimacy is certainly present in the contemporary practice of recognizing states, but the evidence for that knowledge is not uniform. Though it may be said that there is a tendency to apply these criteria as a condition for the recognition of new states, there is no further tendency (even by democratic states) to apply these conditions to existing states.

As for governments and their recognition, in respect of their democratic features, the first and foremost question related to the recognition of government is whether or not the government has effective control over the territory, and it depends on the degree to which people respect the state and follow the government. But state practice suggests, however, that the decision for recognition is not simply based on this fact, but states are concerned whether the government came to power by force or by aggression. But despite this, the idea of recognizing new governments is problematic in terms of the states that need to recognize them, not only because the general opinion is that the way the government came to power is a domestic matter. For this and various reasons, many countries found it difficult to publicly declare that they recognize a particular government; hence, they prefer to develop diplomatic relations with the new government or to open new diplomatic channels, which essentially means its approval. In short, in deciding whether to recognize the government, states do not find the democratic quality of government decisive, but other factors are taken into account.[83] If an undemocratic government is acknowledged, a possible reason would be that the transition to democracy would be better achieved by establishing links with the undemocratic government than by isolating it. Indeed, the interest in recognizing an undemocratic government is not always driven by the view of what is best for the people, i.e., it is in the interest of the people to have the government recognized, but by respectable arguments that depend on the economic and political interests of the states.[84]

Therefore, it is difficult to see that the international community has taken a step toward creating a legal norm for democracy, and although the international community seems to be advocating democratic governments, the fundamental motivations of the most relevant actors are far from clear. According to Thomas Frank, respect for international rules can be required, but only if those rules are true and coherent.[85] Under the current rules of international law, the state needs to have

[81] Among the EC criteria for statehood were: "(…) compliance with the provisions of the UN Charter and the obligations laid down in the Helsinki Final Act and the Paris Charter, in particular as regards the rule of law, democracy and human rights"; Guidelines on the Recognition of New States in Eastern Europe and in the Soviet Union, 16 December 1991.

[82] Turk (1993).

[83] Murphy (2000).

[84] For Murphy (2000), for some states, a democratic form of government may not be the best option. In the same direction is the opinion of Kaplan (1997), p. 55.

[85] Franck (2000).

effective, not only democratic, control in order to be recognized.[86] No norm in international law prevents a state from recognizing another state that is in the process of creation and is undemocratic.

8.5 Considerations in Respect of the Recognition of a Secessionist Entity

Various international organizations are deliberating on their attempts to take a stand on secession and move the legal status quo. The need is to clarify the nature of problems related to secession, to propose as far as possible universally applicable rules, to provide support from the states, and to bring in harmony many opposed perceptions about secession.[87] In addition, we present several opinions of scholars and practitioners upon which debates are still open.

For the ones that consider that secession is permissible under international law and practice, the reference point is the Declaration on Principles of International Law concerning Friendly Relations and Co-operation among States in accordance with the Charter of the United Nations (1970) and the Vienna Declaration and Program of Action (1993). Under these auspices, secession is permitted

1. If it refers to the territories and peoples to be decolonized
2. If there is a basis in the Constitution or other laws of the state
3. If the territory was annexed after 1945
4. If the people live in the territory of a state that does not act in accordance with the principles of self-determination of the people, if the state does not respect equal rights and does not allow everyone to be represented in the government.

According to this explanation, the state has no right to use force if the question of self-determination is raised without the use of force and without violating the constitutional order, while in all other cases, the state can use adequate force in accordance with human rights norms. States that came into force should not be recognized, and third states should not intervene without the consent of the Security Council.[88]

Scholars and practitioners of international law are considering that at this stage, international law neither grants the right to unilateral secession nor denies it. Self-determination and secession are two different concepts, which are about peoples, not about territory. When secession occurs, existing administrative boundaries should be replaced with the mutual consent of the state and the secessionists and

[86] Ormond (1993).

[87] In that direction are the studies entitled "Peaceful resolution of major international problems", issued by the Vienna-based Consortium of International Dispute Resolution (CIDR), as well as a series of conferences related to them, see more at Dahlitz (2003).

[88] Commonwealth of Independent States (FIS) Conference, Dahlitz (2003).

without coercion, and whatever is done, it should best reflect the wishes of the people concerned. In the light of these opinions, secession is legally possible

1. With the consent of all to whom it refers
2. In accordance with the law or the Constitution of the state
3. When the people are under colonial rule or under foreign domination
4. Provided decolonization is not seen as secession.

Therefore, it is suggested that secession be recognized by international law as a remedy when the population of a particular territory is subject to systematic discrimination and human rights violations and, in particular, where that population is limited or does not participate in the government of the state concerned. In that respect, subsidiarity, a transfer of competencies to the lowest possible unit capable of making decisions, should precede any decision on secession. If it comes to changes, they need to be made peacefully, and the state retains the right to reply, legally and appropriately, to any attempt to subvert force or violence. In order to reduce the prospect of secession, the state should respect the rights of minorities and Indigenous peoples. Peaceful means of resolving conflicts should be used. Regional and international organizations should facilitate the process—either the existing organizations or a newly formed body. Nevertheless, in case of secession, all parties must respect international humanitarian law.[89]

In theory, European scientists and practitioners more or less agree with American ones, except that they believe that a state, in the event of secession, can only use force with the permission of the Security Council. If a problem arises, states should provide a climate for political dialogue and negotiate in good faith to overcome the problem. If there is a need to use force, the parties to the conflict must be delineated from the civilian population, and no means should be used that will cause unnecessary suffering or loss of lives. In the event of secession, the state concerned has the right to seek assistance from another state or an organization. If a new unit emerges as a result of secession, however, its recognition can be achieved, *inter alia*, by admission to international organizations. In the case of secession, international organizations have a special responsibility in establishing a representative government, as well as have a mediator role in reaching a peaceful solution. When necessary, even they should be involved in collective recognition decisions. Similarly, American colleges do agree that borders do not have to be maintained at all costs.[90]

Concerning the question of which theory is the right one regarding the issue of recognition, the states will have to ask themselves whether the act of recognition will contribute to the peaceful resolution of conflicts, and if the answer is yes, then the traditional criteria of statehood should be modified. It is questionable if the recent practice of state recognition relevant for the recognition of new entities resulting from disintegration is geographically limited to Europe and only for federated countries of Eastern Europe? Although this was applied only in the case of the

---

[89] American Regional Conference, Dahlitz (2003).

[90] See more at Dahlitz (2003).

dissolution (for some secession) of the USSR and SFRY, it is difficult to accept such an idea. Thus, it can only be seen as a consequence of the Cold War.[91] It is evident that there is a shift from an individual to a collective recognition of statehood,[92] and therefore there is a need for the conditions to be precisely established, especially in situations where secession is not agreed upon. This may include enacting of guidelines or codes for recognition or nonrecognition, agreed by the international organizations, and even the establishment of a formal body with the authority to determine whether the actual criteria have been met. Although there is not a single test for the validity of secessionist independence, secession can be justified when it is realized as an aspect of the right to self-determination. When a metropolitan or parent state violently impedes the self-determination of the people in the territory concerned, then the right to self-determination is in favor of the statehood of the secessionist territory, assuming that the secessionist government is representative—i.e., it represents the people in that territory. In that respect, although the government of the new unit fails to provide control over the territory, the principle of self-determination has the potential to legitimize the situation. As for the recognition of the secessionist movement, although it is not entirely clear at what stage of the conflict recognition is allowed, especially because of the need to maintain neutrality, the recognition of the rebels replaces the recognition of the new entity's statehood.[93]

References

Agreement on the Principles for a Peaceful Settlement of the Armed Conflict in the Dniester Region of the Republic of Moldova (1992). Accessed 10 Jan 2023 https://www.peaceagreements.org/viewmasterdocument/1024

Andrews J (2020) The world in conflict. The Economist

Borgen CJ (2006) Thawing a frozen conflict: legal aspects of the separatist crisis in Moldova, a report from the association of the bar of the City of New York, St John's University school of law. Legal Studies Research Paper Series, 06-0045. https://gov.md/sites/default/files/thawing_a_frozen_conflict.pdf. Accessed 22 Mar 2023

Borgen CJ (2007) Imagining sovereignty, managing secession: the legal geography of Euroasia's "frozen conflicts". Oregon Rev Int Law 9(2):477–536

Cassese A (1995) Self- determination of the peoples, a legal reappraisal. Cambridge University Parliamentary Assembly Council of Europe, Resolution 2308 (2019). The functioning of democratic institutions in the Republic of Moldova. https://assembly.coe.int/nw/xml/XRef/Xref-XML2HTML-en.asp?fileid=28241. Accessed 22 Mar 2023

Congo in Crisis: The Rise and Fall of Katangan Secession (2015) (Internet source). https://adst.org/2015/09/congo-in-crisis-the-rise-and-fall-of-katangan-secession/. Accessed 10 Jan 2023

Constitution of the Pridnestrovian Moldavian Republic (2016). https://mid.gospmr.org/en/constitution. Accessed 10 Jan 2023

Crawford J (2006) The creation of states in international law. Oxford University Press

---

[91] Rich (1993).

[92] Shaw (2003).

[93] Crawford (2006).

Cyprus's Constitution of 1960 with Amendments Through 2013. https://www.constituteproject.org/constitution/Cyprus_2013.pdf?lang=en. Accessed 10 Jan 2023
Dahlitz J (ed) (2003) Secession and international law, conflict avoidance and - regional appraisals. Asser Press
Declaration on Yugoslavia (Extraordinary EPC Ministerial Meeting) Brussels, 16 December 1991
Deen B, Zweers W (2022) Walking the tightrope towards the EU, Moldova's vulnerabilities amid war in Ukraine. Clingendael Report. https://www.clingendael.org/sites/default/files/2022-10/walking-the-tightrope-towards-the-eu.pdf. Accessed 22 Mar 2023
Dugard J (2003) A legal basis for secession - relevantly principles and rules. In: Dahliz J (ed) Conflict avoidance and - regional appraisals. Asser Press, pp 89–97
European Parliament Resolution on the State of Play of EU-Moldova Cooperation (2022/2651(RSP) B9-0242/2022. https://www.europarl.europa.eu/doceo/document/B-9-2022-0242_EN.pdf. Accessed 22 Mar 2023
Falk R, Tormented J (1964) The international law of internal law. In: Rosenau J (ed) International aspects of civil strife. Princeton University Press, Princeton, pp 194–209
Franck TM (2000) Legitimacy and democratic entitlement. In: Fox GH, Roth BR (eds) Democratic governance and international law. Cambridge University Press, pp 25–47
Frckoski Lj D (2005) Trends in the recognition of states in international law and the case of Macedonia. Proceedings of the international conference "Macedonian-French days of law - 200 Years of Code Civil", Prosvetno delo, Skopje
Grant TD (2000) States newly admitted to the United Nations: some implications. Colum J Transnatl Law 39(1):177–192
Guidelines on the Recognition of New States in Eastern Europe and in the Soviet Union, 16 December 1991
Hannum H (1990) Autonomy, sovereignty, and self-determination, the accommodation of conflict rights. University of Pennsylvania Press
Harcourt WV (1863) Letters by Historicus on some questions of international law. Reprinted from 'The Times' with Considerable Additions
Heraclides A (1991) The self - determination of the minorities in the international politics. Frank Cass and Company Limited
Higgins R (2003) Self-determination and secession at secession and international law. In: Dahliz J (ed) Conflict avoidance and - regional appraisals. Asser Press, pp 21–39
Jessup PC (1952) A modern law of nations: an introduction. Macmillan
Kaplan RD (1997) Was democracy just a movement. The Atlantic Monthly, pp 55–80
Koskenniemi M (2009) From apology to utopia. Cambridge University Press
Lauterpacht H (1947) Recognition in international law. Cambridge University Press
Loizides N, McGarry J (2019) The 2002-04 Annan plan in Cyprus: An attempted UN-mediated constitutional transition. Forum of Federations
Montevideo Convention on Rights and Duties of States, Dec.26, (1933)
Moris H (1998) Self-determination: an affirmative right or mere rhetoric? J Comp Int Law 4(1):201–219
Murphy S (2000) Democratic legitimacy and the recognition of states and governments. In: Fox GH, Roth BR (eds) Democratic governance and international law. Cambridge University Press, pp 123–154
Nigeria (02/08). U.S. Department of State. Diplomacy in action. Internet Source. https://2009-2017.state.gov/outofdate/bgn/nigeria/101189.htm#:~:text=Nigeria%20was%20granted%20full%20independence,substantial%20measure%20of%20self%2Dgovernment. Accessed 10 Jan 2023
Okoronkwo PL (2002) Self-determination and the legality of Biafra's secession under international law. Loy L A Int Comp Law Rev 25(1):63–115
Ormond J (1993) The North Caucasus: fragmentation of federation? In: Bremmer I, Taras E (eds) Nations and politics in the Soviet Successor States. Cambridge University Press, p 451

OSCE (1993) Mandate of the Mission to Moldova. https://www.osce.org/files/f/documents/6/0/41137.pdf. Accessed 26 Mar 2023

Parliamentary Assembly Council of Europe, Resolution 2433 (2022) Consequences of the Russian Federation's continued aggression against Ukraine: role and response of the Council of Europe. https://pace.coe.int/en/files/30017/html. Accessed 22 Mar 2023

Pavkovic A, Radan P (2007) Creating new states, theory and practice of secession. Ashgate Publishing Limited

Popescu N (2005) The EU in Moldova- settling conflicts in the neighborhood. The European Union Institute for Security Studies. Occasional paper n. 60. https://www.iss.europa.eu/sites/default/files/EUISSFiles/occ60.pdf. Accessed 22 Mar 2022

Pufendorf S, Oldfather CH, Oldfather WA (1934) De iure naturae et gentium libri octo. Clarendon Press

Remembering Nigeria's Biafra War That Many Prefer to Forget (2020) Internet source. https://www.bbc.com/news/world-africa-51094093. Accessed 10 Jan 2023

Remler P (2022) Transdniestria, Moldova, and Russia's war in Ukraine. Carnegie Endowment for International Peace. https://carnegieendowment.org/2022/08/02/transdniestria-moldova-and-russia-s-war-in-ukraine-pub-87609. Accessed 10 Jan 2023

Report of the Secretary-General on his Mission of Good Offices in Cyprus (2004) United Nations Security Council, S/2004/437. https://www.securitycouncilreport.org/atf/cf/%7B65BFCF9B-6D27-4E9C-8CD3-CF6E4FF96FF9%7D/Cyprus%20S2004437.pdf. Accessed 10 Jan 2023

Rich R (1993) Recognition of states: the collapse of Yugoslavia and the Soviet Union. Eur J Int Law 4(1):36–65

Schrijver N (2003) Secession and the ban on the use of force: some reflections. In: Dahliz J (ed) Conflict avoidance and - regional appraisals. Asser Press, pp 97–111

Shaw MN (2003) The role of recognition and non-recognition with respect to secession: notes on some relevant issues. In: Dahliz J (ed) Conflict avoidance and - regional appraisals. Asser Press, pp 243–259

Shelest H (2015) Foreign policy particularities of the de facto states in the Black Sea Region. In: Nodia G, Stefes CH (eds) Security, democracy and development. Peter Lang, pp 259–260

Situation In the Republic of Congo (Internet Source). https://www.un.org/securitycouncil/sites/www.un.org.securitycouncil/files/en/sc/repertoire/59-63/Chapter%208/59-63_08-8-Situation%20in%20the%20Republic%20of%20Congo.pdf. Accessed 10 Jan 2023

Summers J (2007) Peoples and international law, how nationalism and self-determination shape a contemporary law of nations. Leiden, Boston

The Comprehensive Settlement of the Cyprus Problem, 31 March 2004. https://www.mfa.gov.tr/un-comprehensive-settlement-plan-of-the-cyprus-question.en.mfa. Accessed 10 Jan 2023

The Congo, Decolonization, and the Cold War, 1960–1965 (Internet Source). https://history.state.gov/milestones/1961-1968/congo-decolonization#:~:text=The%20first%20such%20confrontation%20occurred,independence%20on%20June%2030%2C%201960.&text=In%20the%20months%20leading%20up,in%20the%20Congo's%20numerous%20provinces. Accessed 10 Jan 2023

The Constitution of the Federation of Nigeria (1960). https://www.worldstatesmen.org/nigeria_const1960.pdf. Accessed 10 Jan 2023

Treaty of Guarantee (1960). https://peacemaker.un.org/sites/peacemaker.un.org/files/CY%20GR%20TR_600816_Treaty%20of%20Guarantee.pdf. Accessed 10 Jan 2023

Turk D (1993) Recognition of states: a comment. Eur J Int Law 4:66–71

UN Documents for Cyprus: Security Council Resolutions (Inrernet Source). https://www.securitycouncilreport.org/un_documents_type/security-council-resolutions/?ctype=Cyprus&cbtype=cyprus. Accessed 10 Jan 2023

United Nations Security Council Resolution 161 (1961). file:///C:/Users/Dell/Downloads/S_RES_161(1961)-EN.pdf. Accessed 10 Jan 2023

United Nations Security Council Resolution 186 [S/5575] (1964). https://peacemaker.un.org/sites/peacemaker.un.org/files/CY_640304_SCR186.pdf. Accessed 10 Jan 2023

Vattel E, Lapradelle A (1916) Le droit des gens; ou Principes de la loi naturelle appliques a la conduite et aux affaires des nations et des souverains (Fenwick C G - Translato). Carnegie Institution of Washington

Wippman D (2000) Pro – democratic intervention by invitation. In: Fox GH, Roth BR (eds) Democratic governance and international law. Cambridge University Press, pp 293–327

Wolfschwenger J, Leontiev L (2022) The legal system of Transnistria, international and European considerations. In: Harzl B, Petrov R (eds) Unrecognized entities perspectives in international, European and constitutional law. Brill | Nijhoff, pp 249–269

Worster WT (2009) Law, politics and the conception of state in state recognition. Boston Univ Int 27:115–171

Chapter 9
The Legitimacy of Secession Claims

9.1 Introduction

While there is no objective standard for evaluating the legitimacy of secession claims, there are some theorists who believe that denying the formulation of the right to secession will not solve the problems, nor will it reduce the demands for the independence of particular groups. Therefore, they propose different solutions, including recognizing a qualified right of secession, when secession can be realized when fulfilling specific conditions (such as severe forms of discrimination, the territorial concentration of a particular population group, possible viability of the new state, etc.);[1] and the use of secession as a cure, which application will depend on the specific circumstances and when all other opportunities have been used to eliminate an injustice.

The conditions that can possibly give legitimacy to a secession claim can be the following:

1. A model of systematic discrimination or exploitation against a sizable (self-defined) minority
2. The existence of a different (self-defined) community in the state, densely populated in a region that openly supports separatism
3. Inability to establish a model for conflict resolution and peace building
4. Refusal of the central government to compromise solutions.

Opposite of that, there is a theory according to which the right to secession exists if it is possible to achieve it. In that sense, the legitimacy of the secession is linked to the level of success achieved by the secessionist movement. If the separatist movement in a particular region lacks public support, it is evident proof that the movement, or that region, lacks both the power and the right to secede. On this

[1] Henrard (2000), p. 306.

N. Shikova, *Self-Determination and Secession*,
https://doi.org/10.1007/978-3-031-34322-3_9

basis, some theorists treat secession not as a right but as a feature of history that *ex post* recognizes a particular situation. Of course, there is a clear jurisprudential inconsistency in establishing the legitimacy of such claims.[2]

9.2 Theoretical Standings

For some scholars of international law, there is a clear need for establishing international standards in determining the legitimacy of secession claims. Consequently, it is better to include legitimate secession claims in the scope of self-determination and to place the emphasis of discussion on these standards of legitimacy on secession rather than on the persuasive, inflexible denial of such claims. Establishing rules that would limit the applicability of the phenomenon would remove the potential anarchist effect from the unlimited realization of secession. The doctrine of self-determination has never been interpreted in terms that a particular group with a predominant *self* has the right to political independence. The realization of self-determination always requires a nation, a people, a colonial people, or some other category with a similar ethnological base. The doctrine has never been set up to include a group of people united only by mutual economic interests, and hence, this limitation of principle, though perhaps a little arbitrary, is firm. But in addition to the basic common features of language, history, and the like, a group aspiring to acquire such a right inevitably occupies a separate territory. A group that is mixed with ambient populations, such as the European Jews or African Americans or the Roma, may wish to break away from the ruling population but politically, not territorially, and that desire can most likely result in dual sovereignty, although examples for this kind of relationships are rare. Therefore, when the group lacks a geographical homeland, a country, the solution to the problem may involve minority protection in the existing framework, not political secession.[3]

Typically, the unit seeking to secede is required to be a viable, independent entity that can be empirically verified, but these requirements may not be part of traditional statehood requirements. The criterion for the survival of an estranged entity should be minimal and not significant despite the fact that its people may suffer from a decline in living standards or some discomfort after the secession. The international community may reasonably seek to prevent the group from committing social "suicide," but it cannot forcefully prevent self-sacrifice when it is freely chosen by the people.[4] An extremely important argument against the "right" of secession is the factor of disturbance, i.e., whether and how secession will affect the political environment. Namely, the dilemma is whether secession is vital for the state for economic, political, or geostrategic purposes and whether this activity will

[2] Buchheit (1978).

[3] Buchheit (1978).

[4] Buchheit (1978).

disturb the balance of power in that area. In this case, consideration should be given to the minorities that will remain trapped, then to the will of the new entity's government to commit to respecting human rights and other norms of international law, as well as the effect that such a secession will have on the international arena and, in particular, in encouraging other entities to act in the same way. Concerning the danger of the demonstrative effect of recognizing secession (the domino effect), for some scholars, such as Lee C. Buchheit, it should not be a factor in assessing the legitimacy of a secessionist claim.[5]

Robert Redslob[6] elaborates on a detailed theory of exercising the qualified right to secession. When determining the legitimacy of the proposed secession, the first thing that needs to be taken into account is the geographical conditions of the rest of the country after separation. The argument about separate nationality as a justification for secession cannot be applied when the proposed division severely cuts the organic structure of the state. But this is not absolute. Secession can be justified even when the vital interests of the existing state are violated if the state has committed serious human rights violations and abuses. In that respect, Robert Redslob proposes to limit the possible right to secession to those groups that have a separate nationality, strong will for separation, and suffered from human rights abuses.

Marlies Galenkamp[7] sets the criteria that groups must meet in relation to their secession requirements in order to give legitimacy to possible secession. One of them is the criterion analogous to the claim for secession as a last remedy, and its fulfillment depends on the prior fulfillment of two additional subcriteria: (a) the population group should be seriously threatened with a violation of its right of survival, and hence its identity is under constant attack, and (b) there are no adequate measures that would be less radical.

Although difficult, we may need to be prepared to consider secession as a reality, considers Will Kymlicka. But secession is not always possible, nor desirable, and shared rights over resources and territories would make peaceful secession almost impossible.[8] Alexis Heraclides[9] considers that if secession is accepted as right, then the conditions for its exercise, that most authors propose should be continually set and move from very strict, to lighter, and finally easy requirements posed to the group. For Johan D. Van der Vyver,[10] international law acknowledges the redrawing of state borders, but this practice is applied in some exceptional circumstances: (1) if they had arisen from the general support of political society and (2) if the redrawing of state borders arises as a result of a truce following an armed conflict. But while ethnic-national self-determination must be controlled as it can be destructive to the international system, when relations are extremely bad and there is no

[5] Buchheit (1978).

[6] Redslob (1931).

[7] Galenkamp (1995).

[8] Kymlicka (1996).

[9] Heraclides (1991).

[10] Van der Vyver (2000).

prospect of cessation of hostilities and bloodshed, there is a need to create a framework for negotiating border change, which must include regional organizations, regional forces, and major forces, points Kamal Shehadi. In cases where international security is at stake, international organizations must use their influence to find a political solution that includes a (desirable) new political system and keeps national borders unchanged. But if that is not possible, the international community must create strict conditions for negotiation and the recognition of the entity that will emerge as a result of these negotiations. Those conditions must include measures to protect the rights of national minorities in the new political entity. Democratic forms of government must be promoted, but ethnic and other side demands aimed at further rectifying the changing of the frontiers should also be closed.[11]

Lee C. Buchheit proposes a scheme consisting of the standards that need to be articulated by the international community, upon which the legitimacy of the secessionist claims can be determined, taking into account all the disturbing factors of secession that must be balanced against the benefits of the secessionist claims. In this regard, Buchheit proposes that calculations need to be made after formulating forecasts of the potentially troubling consequences of allowing the potential secession by the international community or by a credible body. The result of this weighing would not be in favor of secession when the future danger of allowing secession outweighs the risk of maintaining the *status quo*. The result would be the same if none of these alternatives were likely to cause a measurable increase in disturbance and would be low when the risk of future disturbance is minimal in relation to the current disturbance. Obviously, *the disruptive factor* used here is necessary to allow flexibility. The second step of the preliminary evaluation takes into account the strength of the group's *self* in relation to the usually accepted dimensions in that category. The final determination of legitimacy will be the result of the relationship between the disturbing factor and the intrinsic benefits of the claim.[12]

To be effective, the eventually established standards must be reasonable. They should allow conservatism, but at the same time, they should not completely ignore the wishes for self-government (when possible, without major disturbances to the global or social order). These standards must be articulated in advance, not *ad hoc*, and should not depend on the political pressure that appears in a particular situation. Although these methods do not imply scientific or mathematical solutions, nor do they allow precise quantification, their use can help in clarifying the arguments. However, it is almost certain that states would not be willing to accept a framework that might one day work against them, considers Buchheit.[13]

---

[11] Shehadi (1993).

[12] See more at Buchheit (1978).

[13] Buchheit (1978).

9.2.1 Secession as a Cure (Remedial Secession) – Theoretical Explications

In the last decade of the twentieth century, the notion that secession may be the last cure has received considerable support. Although international law generally disagrees with secession and views it with disapproval, its instruments and other relevant sources have provided a possible exception (implicitly in the essence of international law's commitment to fundamental human rights and democratic principles), considering secession as a last resort when the right of participation is denied to members of the group concerned.[14] It seems that this theory of secession as an ultimate remedy is aimed at protecting the current state-centered order and implies that each state has the opportunity to neutralize the quests coming from any segment of its population mainly through measures of representative government or through the protection of human rights.

Scholars are divided on this question, presenting two opposing stances. For some authors, remedial secession can be an ultimate form of self-determination, while for others, it has little in common with the positive doctrine of self-determination.[15] Secession can be seen as an ultimate form of self-determination when there is a tradition of independent sovereignty, when there is a combination of historical factors, or when the desire for political independence has reached a point where it can no longer be satisfied even with the removal of all the injustices. In that respect, a "right" to secession can be exercised as the last step, a *panacea* when everything else fails, considers Alfred Cobban.[16] Lea Brilmayer[17] suggests that secession can be a cure but not for the bad treatment of the government toward a particular group. The bad treatment does not permit a new state to be established in the same location. A cure for the bad treatment is a better treatment. If a minority experiences injustice or suffers from human rights abuses, it may seek secession as a remedy, but a claim for territory must be established independently.[18] Diane F. Orentlicher considers that democratic principles should be a part of international law, and there is some practice in that respect (such as the Guidelines for the recognition of the new states applied during the dissolution of SFRY and the USSR).[19] For her, it is very dangerous to oversee this conceptual void, especially when it comes to secession as a last resort.[20] Such options have been the subject of sharp criticism by Donald Horowitz, who holds that international law neither

[14] Orentlicher (2003).

[15] See more at Buchheit (1978).

[16] Cobban (1969).

[17] Brilmayer (1991).

[18] The same for Joshua Castellino, the right to self-determination is in relation to the right to land (territory); see more in Castellino (2000).

[19] Declaration on the Guidelines on the Recognition of New States in Eastern Europe and in the Soviet Union (1991).

[20] Orentlicher (2003).

implicitly nor explicitly recognizes the right of secession as a last resort or as a cure for the repressed group. On the contrary, according to Horowitz, international law implicitly and explicitly prohibits secession. The aspect of democratic participation (related to the practicing of a secession as the last resort), does not exist within the international documents, because during the period of drafting the most important documents concerning self-determination, only a few states were truly democratic.[21] James Summers, similar to Horowitz, believes that secession as a last resort suffers from a lack of state practice and secession as a last resort is possible only with others' state intervention (for example, Indian intervention in support of Bangladesh secession).[22]

Despite the differing attitudes among theorists, secession as an ultimate cure seems to occupy the position of *lex lata*, a scheme through which international law recognizes a continuum of legal remedies, ranging from the protection of individual and minority rights to secession as a final cure.

9.2.2 The Bangladesh Case

East Pakistan's secession from Pakistan in 1971 was the only case of secession within the UN system during the Cold War and before the fall of the Eastern Bloc. East Pakistan was part of Pakistan and was one of the two Muslim wings, which, in 1947, formed an independent state separate from the Hindu people. Geographically, between these two wings of Pakistan was India, and it has been said that they were united by Islam, the fear of India, and the interconnected airlines.[23] East Pakistan-Bengal, was the poorer part, or practically a colony of Western Pakistan. It was poor and overpopulated, with jute as the only product it was selling to Western Pakistan. There was one official language in Pakistan, spoken only by a small part of the population, while Bengali as an official language in East Pakistan was only introduced in the mid-1950s. Eastern Pakistanis, Bengalis, have endured all kinds of discrimination, mirrored in the nonparticipation in political life, in abuse and exploitation, and in the backwardness of the educational system. The end of such a state was quite certain—it became clear that it is inevitable that such a state would come to an end because not only was there not a Pakistani nation, but they could hardly be called a political entity as well. Separatism began to grow in East Pakistan in the 1960s, and this led to its growing exclusion from the Pakistani government. To overcome this, the Bengals have proposed a loose federation with Pakistan on foreign affairs and defense, currency independence, financial and tax policy, and their own police. This was strongly opposed by Western Pakistan, and it resulted in a series of conflicts,

[21] Horowitz (2003).

[22] Summers (2007).

[23] Nanda (1972).

assaults, and bloody clashes, which culminated in elections in East Pakistan in which won a political party that had unified the population around a vision of secession.[24] The Bengalis were militarily organized, and so conflicts broke out. They did not have enough funds, their foreign policy was inexperienced, but India was involved in the situation and began to assist them militarily and diplomatically. India's interest in dismembering Pakistan and promoting itself as an undoubted force in the Asian region was clear, and in that respect, India entered into an agreement with the USSR. Fearing USSR intervention, the United States and China did not engage in the dispute, so India defeated the army of Western Pakistan and granted East Pakistan-Bangladesh independence.[25] At first, the UN stood by Pakistan and opposed secession. The discussions in the Security Council show that most member states were primarily concerned with the restoration of the status quo, an immediate ceasefire, and the mutual withdrawal of forces.[26] Since the Council was paralyzed with mutual member state vetoes and there were apparently no prospects for a consensus among the major powers,[27] the Council adopted a resolution in which it decided to refer the question to the General Assembly[28] within the frame of the General Assembly Resolution "Uniting for Peace" (1950) (the General Assembly to take actions to restore peace in situations when the Security Council's action is blocked).[29] The UN's response to India's intervention, aside from the divided Security Council, was GA Res. 2793 in 1971, which urged India and Pakistan to end the ceasefire and withdraw their forces from the border.[30] None of these documents deal with secession. Outside the Eastern Bloc and India, Bangladesh was not supported and received no international recognition until Pakistan was defeated, and it was not clear that it was incapable of regaining control of the territory. India's intervention was crucial to the success of the secession,[31] and although Bangladesh was economically unsustainable, poor, corrupt, and politically unstable, it was subsequently recognized as an independent state, and in fact, it became the first successful post-WWII secession.[32]

---

[24] Heraclides (1991).

[25] Buchheit (1978).

[26] Situation in the India-Pakistan subcontinent (1970).

[27] Nanda (1972).

[28] UNSC Res. 303 (1971).

[29] UNGA Res. 377 A(V) of 1950.

[30] GA Res. 2793 (XXVI) 7 December 1971.

[31] Summers (2007).

[32] See more at Crawford (2006); Summers (2007); Dugard (2003).

9.2.3 A Parochial Theory for the Legitimacy of Secessionist Claims

The parochial theory has an entirely different focus on the justification of secessionist claims than the doctrine about secession as the ultimate remedy and offers a different framework for assessing the legitimacy of the secessionist demands. The proponents of this theory are advocating for accepting only one basis for assessing the legitimacy of secessionist claims—and that is the existence of a special "self." This "self" is the "self" that wants to control its political destiny, and it can be found in states that are repressive toward their minorities, as well as in democratic, nondiscriminatory societies. Extreme repression of a segment of a population by the state may intensify international concerns, but it will not necessarily create the "self." A legitimate "self" is based on historical, racial, cultural, and religious differences of the peoples and their originality, i.e. the source of the desire for their political independence. To be a separate "self" and to desire the process of "determination," in this view, are all that is needed to use the international principle of self-determination as a basis for acquiring legitimate secession.[33]

The difference between the theory of secession as a cure and the parochial theory stems from a fundamental disagreement. Proponents of the remedial secession are concerned about protecting the integrity of sovereign states and preserving international order and accept the fragmentation of the state only under extreme conditions. On the other hand, the parochial theory does not give value to the international order, or at least when it conflicts with a primordial claim of human inner nature. According to the parochial theory, the satisfaction of this primordial claim is of the utmost importance, even if it means dismantling artificial institutions of states and replacing them with something else.[34]

Although international law does not allow for the articulation of a middle principle between the exceptional affirmation of the supremacy of sovereign states and complete submission to the parochial sentiment (as opposite sides), possibly both principles need to be respected for their importance and usability. For some theorists of international law, it is exactly a middle ground for the formulation of the possible standards for the legitimacy of secession claims.[35]

---

[33] Buchheit (1978).

[34] Buchheit (1978).

[35] Buchheit (1978), p. 228.

9.2.4 The Case of South Sudan – An Example of a Distinct "Self"

Sudan was a British-Egyptian condominium divided into two parts—the North and the South—and was governed differently. The South was populated by Africans and was a backward region, while the North was more advanced and was populated by Arabs. In 1947, at a conference organized by the United Kingdom (the Juba Conference), it was clear that a common future was planned for the two parts of Sudan. Leaders from the South of Sudan, instructed by the English, though they considered themselves different from the North, accepted to be a part of the common independent Sudan state, established in 1956. After independence, the country was ruled by the North. In the South, which is not rich in natural resources (South Sudan oil was discovered only in 1979), live different ethnic groups that speak different languages, have different religions, but share the same Christian roots. Besides, the people of South Sudan suffered persistent discrimination because even after independence, the people of this region were guaranteed only a few seats in the joint assembly, and only six seats out of 400 senior administration officials were occupied by them. In Sudan, the Africans were second-class citizens exposed to racial and cultural discrimination, which escalated into numerous conflicts and casualties.[36]

South Sudanese Africans tried to propose the creation of a binational state and were close to succeeding, but after their hopes were dashed, armed action began in 1960. At the beginning of the independence movement, Africans emphasized their uniqueness based on the same race, the sharing of the same African culture, the same religion, as well as a different, distant geographical position from the centrist administration. Because of ethnic rivalries, personal ambitions, and clashes and, especially, because of the absence of ideology, or at least a coherent one, the independence movement was split into two parts. One part was for confederation with the North, while the other part was for independence, with groups operating in that direction falling into several guerrilla groups. South Sudan had a poor foreign policy, lacked educated people, and had no support from the great powers, only weak support from African countries and Israel, which supplied them with insufficient weapons. Attempts to unite all movements were unsuccessful.[37] Apart from the United Nations High Commissioner for Refugees (UNHCR), South Sudan was not receiving any assistance from international organizations.[38]

This conflict lasted for ten years and ended with the Addis Ababa Agreement (1972), where the South gained significant autonomy.[39] But in 1982–1983, the

[36] For the case of South Sudan, see more at United Nations High Commission for Refugees, Refugees and asylum-seekers from South Sudan (2020); McNamee (2012); Chand (1995); Marzatico (2011); Ylönen (2017); Heraclides (1991); Deng (2002).

[37] Heraclides (1991); Deng (2002).

[38] South Sudan (Internet source).

[39] The Addis Ababa Agreement (1972).

Arabs adopted an Islamic law that was to be applied throughout the territory. The South made peaceful attempts to avoid imposing that right, but to no avail, which led to the emergence of new guerrilla movements and the reactivation of old ambitions.[40] After exhausting conflicts and after long-standing discrimination, the UN-backed South Sudanese people, in 2011, voted in a referendum, in which 98% of the population supported South Sudan's independence.[41] As an independent state, It was admitted in UN membership as the 193rd member.[42]

9.3 Possibilities for the Institutional Settlements of Secession Claims

Under international law, as well as under UN practice, secession is inadmissible. However, the UN has, on several occasions, condemned secession, as in the case of Katanga and Northern Cyprus, but in other circumstances, it remained silent and allowed the events to take their own course without taking any position, such as in the case of Biafra. In principle, the UN has never committed itself to solving this issue, possibly because the question is too complicated to have an absolute answer, so ambivalence and ambiguity remain the preferred option.[43]

That the UN does not oppose secession can be seen from Israel's acceptance as a member state (created by secession from Palestine), then the acceptance of Bangladesh, as well as the entities comprising the former SFR Yugoslavia and the USSR. However, international law has principles that halt secession. However, international law neither grants the possibility for unilateral secession nor explicitly denies the existence of such an option. The general argument against secession is stability and avoiding chaos and instability, especially when it comes to Africa and the Balkans.[44]

Lee Buchheit (1978) suggests a framework for the realization of a limited qualified secession or for the declaration of the legitimacy of secession in certain circumstances. Although it may be too much to expect that this will hinder future secession efforts, in his opinion, it will certainly significantly reduce them. According to him, although an international consensus on secession does not exist, rejecting it from the doctrine of self-determination and limiting the possibility of realizing secession only to the colonies are unrealistic. Either we will establish standards, or we will leave this question for the future, wiser generation. At least, it needs to be

[40] For the case of South Sudan, see more in McNamee (2012); Chand (1995); Marzatico (2011); Ylönen (2017); Heraclides (1991); Deng (2002).

[41] With a strong independence vote turnout in South Sudan, the UN sees no need for an extension (2011).

[42] UN welcomes South Sudan as 193rd Member State (2011).

[43] Dugard (2003), p. 91.

[44] Dugard (2003).

determined which groups are authorized to invoke the principle of self-determination in relation to secession. This will inevitably involve an investigation of the nature of the group, its position within the state, its possibility for survival, and the effect of the separation on the rest of the population and the world community as a whole. According to Buchheit, this approach is valid since it will give the international community an opportunity to adjust its position to certain separatist demands without imposing a single rule. Many of the groups will not be in a position to meet the set requirements, but even if a certain group meets all the criteria required for secession, such a group still has to overcome the biggest obstacle, and that is international recognition since in international law, there are no binding rules for the existing state to recognize the emergence of a new state. Consequently, the secessionists may hesitate in deciding to start a secessionist movement, knowing that it will be unlikely for them to receive external support, and hence, instead of pursuing full territorial separation, they will direct their demands toward greater regional autonomy or minority rights within the existing state. This will also enable governments to adjust their behavior, making both unionists and secessionists more aware of their positions and more prepared to negotiate a resolution for the conflict.[45]

It is unrealistic to avoid questions about secession because of the previously established social or international contracts. It is unrealistic to consider that the group that had made a choice hundreds of years ago must stick to it forever, and on top of that is the question of whether and to what extent this choice was made freely. The conventions reflect the time in which they were adopted, but that does not mean that we should interpret them exclusively through the prism of that time. If we decide on that, we do not go beyond legal paganism, i.e., the norm that exists on its own and does not solve anything. It is evident that international law is the law on states, but there is a change in modern international law since within individuals are also subjects, especially when it comes to human rights violations (not only humans but also transnational corporations, which have some form of international personality). Perhaps the establishment of a "right" to secession is a too rigid and radical approach, but a framework through which secession claims should be viewed should be considered. And that does not mean favoring secession movements.

9.3.1 Standards for Secession (?!)

Theoretical dilemmas—whether there is a connection between secession and self-determination—are not new. Moreover, the inherent tension between the obligation of every society to recognize pluralism and diversity and the desire for every culture—whether majority, minority, or indigenous—to protect its values and ensure conformity must be ultimately resolved. The proper role of the state is to

[45] Buchheit (1978).

mediate between competing forces and set parameters within which the resulting conflict will be creative rather than destructive.

Outside the context of decolonization, secession claims have long been frowned upon in international law, and jurists have been extremely skeptical of the issue. This is still the case, but there are tendencies to change this, and a barometer for this is the diplomatic response to secessionism, especially in relation to the increasing commitment of the international community to mediation and to finding ways to overcome conflicts.

The rejection of secession; the limitation of the self-determination only in the context of colonialism, and its impossibility to expand are unrealistic. One of the options is to identify groups that could legitimately secede. This would inevitably involve an inquiry into the nature of the group, its condition within the state, the likelihood of its survival, and the effect of separation on the rest of the population and on the world community as a whole.

The question is, which principles should guide states in their response to secession movements? It can be said the democratic principles because, still, although they are not the only nor the best option for solving these requirements, the development of legal doctrine and state practice made them both legally and practically relevant. International law does not contain a rule guaranteeing sociocultural groups to secede to become a separate international entity, nor does it prohibit secession. Its influence in this field is limited, and it is difficult to deal with the complex relations arising from the phenomenon. At this stage of the development of international law, one cannot expect from international standards more than what they can actually offer, which is a set of general guidelines that stakeholders should pragmatically apply.

Secession and self-determination are two different concepts. Self- determination is a right, and secession is a political phenomenon that exists in world practice. Secession can involve quests for self-determination in the sense of a desire for self-government, but this may not always be the case and self-determination is not always the basis for secession. The demands for secession, regardless of the distinct "self," can grow due to various political or other interests. Secession should not be avoided in discussions within international law and its principles since international law can provide a basic framework for dealing with the phenomenon of secession. Still, secession should not be regarded as right and formulated as such, but it should remain as it is—a phenomenon that occasionally occurs worldwide. Additionally, nonviolent claims for secession cannot be considered illegal; on the contrary, they should be given a political space where they can be articulated and the demands addressed.

It is difficult to suppress secession demands in total. If they are put in place, the legitimacy of the secession demand within the democratic state can be assessed by the entire population of the state. The citizens are sharing the same destiny, and if there is a huge division inside the population, the answer is clear—the request for secession is not legitimate. Additionally, the legitimacy of an act of secession, assess or verifies it, the international community. Recognition is a factor that confirms the existence of a new entity as a state, and this means its acceptance within the international community. Through recognition, states present their standards of legitimacy as equally important and valuable.

When it comes to the situations that are accompanied when gross violation of human rights; when the system is not functional in total and is unable to secure the basic protection of the individual and the group rights; when there are civil wars or ethnic cleansing at stake—in that case, there is no point for maintaining of the mutual community by any price. Considering these situations, the legality of secession should be accessed by the international community through other already established standards of international law that are protecting human rights and community well-being. In those cases, secession can be an option, but secession should be taken into account not only as a last resort or a remedy but also as a cure for the prevention of extreme human suffering.

Apart from it, it is difficult to imagine a unified or preset position about secession in general. An international legal framework for dealing with secession cases is preferable, but expectancy toward formulating a generally acceptable firm rule on the legality of secession claims is currently inconceivable. Foremost, international law functions and operates by logic other than through national and municipal laws. The lack of a common legislator, among other features, makes international law less rigid, more dynamic, and more flexible. Arguably, the best step is to assess each case according to the same preset criteria, but it should be clear that such criteria are currently nonexistent, and additionally, it should not be forgotten that each case is a case by itself—separate and unique. It is extremely difficult to aggregate a unique, clear and objective standing about single case of secession, and it is even more ambiguous formulating a general point of view. Nevertheless, secession demands are not always within the frame of rationality, but many times they are overwhelmed with emotions. That is why it is even more difficult to place them within the legal frame that is in essence based on rationality.

Other "standards" than those described will not bring many benefits. Even if they are formed, their operationality, functionality, and even more their capacity to provide a ground for a certain independent arbiter (if that can exist) to "objectively" assess the legitimacy of the particular acts of secession would be questionable as well. The cases of secession are contextually dependable, and practice has shown that despite the lack of any international regulation in this sphere, the secessionist entity is viable and further recognized as a state when major political forces are backing it. So far, that is the only secession "standard" that proved to be coherent and consistent. Although that may not, in essence, be just, bargaining in general protects the balance of powers. The international system, for good or bad, stands on that balance, and international law protects it. It is without a doubt that any secession standard, if ever formulated, will work in that direction. However, although it is difficult to reach a consensus on this issue within international law, those questions should not be viewed with great condemnation nor be avoided nor be simply abandoned. International law has achieved a significant level of compliance in numerous areas (such as in the area of commercial law), and although secession and state creation are not one of them, dialogs and deliberations in those regards should not be suppressed. Nonetheless, since secession cases exist, they cannot be overseen as such. The best scenario is if all these complex issues are addressed within the UN system and if the UN provides and supports these endeavors. The UN system, although imperfect, still represents a general framework and is still the most appropriate place for this debate. Additionally, any effort in crystalizing the standards for the assessment of the legality of secession claims needs to be accompanied by a fundamental assessment of the capabilities of international institutions, which have to be truly effectively (re)organized to meet these challenges, i.e., to apply them.

It seems best if secession demands or tendencies are prevented from escalating, and the debates are pointed in that direction. That can be done by variety of methods that modern state has at its disposal, and political and legal arrangements further explained under the section on internal self-determination. The arrangements can be introduced gradually, and if there is a society consensus can involve creating a federation or confederation. Although this may be a step toward secession, it can balance the power and diminish hostilities. However, the promotion of the benefits of staying together can also set the course toward preserving the community instead of breaking it apart. In a globalized world, separation rarely increases living standards or does not bring any real changes. Traditional state sovereignty is largely transforming, and for the systems to be functional, they need to be interconnected. In that sense, placing the demands in regional frameworks or encouraging networking—if that is an option—can as well lower separation quests.

Following the above, secession could be considered if the various tools for the accommodation of social conflicts through the internal form of self-determination are exhausted. The continuous clash of global and local political-economic interest in certain territories has own implications, that from a humanistic point of view need to be analyzed in detail as a complex historical story of a certain collective(s), because it is precisely the cultural and political stratigraphy of a society that penetrate through the layers of each secession experience taken as a special case, and thus help in the most necessary—to perceive the key difference between—the need to establish the right of secession, and the open polemical processes of argumentation in favor of secession as an ultimate act.

References

Andrews J (2020) The world in conflict. The Economist

Brilmayer L (1991) Secession and self-determination: a territorial interpretation. Yale J Int'l Law 16:177–202

Buchheit LC (1978) Secession, the legitimacy of self-determination. Yale University Press, New Haven

Castellino J (2000) International Law and self-determination. Kluwer Law International

Chand D (1995) South Sudan claims for right of self-determination. University of Pennsylvania - African Studies Center

Cobban A (1969) The national state and national self- determination. Thomas Y. Crowell Rev

Crawford J (2006) The creation of states in international law. Oxford University Press
Declaration on the 'Guidelines on the Recognition of New States in Eastern Europe and in the Soviet Union' (16 December 1991). https://www.dipublico.org/100636/declaration-on-the-guidelines-on-the-recognition-of-new-states-in-eastern-europe-and-in-the-soviet-union-16-december-1991/. Accessed 12 Sept 2022
Deng FM (2002) Self- determination and national identity crisis: the case of Sudan. In: Danspeckgruber W (ed) Self – determination of peoples, community, nation and state in inter-dependent world. Lynne Rienner Publishers, pp 253–287
Dugard J (2003) A legal basis for secession - relevantly principles and rules. In: Dahliz J (ed) Conflict avoidance and - regional appraisals. Asser Press, pp 89–97
Galenkamp M (1995) De grenzen van de nationale zelfbeschikking (The limits of national self – determination). In: Van Bellingen J, Sybesma-Knol N (eds) Naar een nieuwe interpretatie van het recht op zelfbeschikking? (Towards a new interpretation of the right to self-determination?). V.U.B. Press, pp 89–108
Global Perspective Human Stories. https://news.un.org/en/story/2011/07/381552. Accessed 11 Jan 2023
Henrard K (2000) Devising an adequate system of minority protection. Kluwer Law International, Hague
Heraclides A (1991) The self - determination of the minorities in the international politics. Frank Cass and Company Limited
Horowitz DL (2003) A Right to Secede? Secession and self-determination. In: Macedo S, Buchanan A (eds) Secession and self-determination. New York University Press, pp 84–132
Kymlicka W (1996) Multicultural citizenship: a liberal theory of minority rights. Clarendon Press
Marzatico F (2011) Southern Sudan referendum on self-determination, legal challenges and procedural solutions. J Afr Elect 10(1):1–32
McNamee T (2012) The first crack in Africa's map? Secession and self-determination after South Sudan. The Brenthurst Foundation, Discussion Paper 01
Nanda VP (1972) A critique of the United Nations inaction in the Bangladesh crisis. Denver Law Rev 49(1):53–67
Orentlicher FD (2003) International responses to separatist claims: are democratic principles relevant? In: Macedo S, Buchanan A (eds) . New York University Press, Secession and self-determination, pp 19–49
Redslob R (1931) Le principe des nationalités. (Volume 37). In: Collected Courses of the Hague Academy of International Law. https://doi.org/10.1163/1875-8096_pplrdc_A9789028607422_01. First published online: 1931. Accessed 12 Sept 2022
Shehadi KS (1993) Ethnic self-determination and the break-up of states. The Adelphi Papers
Situation in the India-Pakistan Subcontinent (1970). https://www.un.org/securitycouncil/sites/www.un.org.securitycouncil/files/en/sc/repertoire/69-71/Chapter%208/69-71_08-13-Situation%20in%20the%20India-Pakistan%20subcontinent.pdf. Accessed 11 Jan 2023
South Sudan, UNHCR (Internet Source). https://www.unhcr.org/south-sudan.html. Accessed 11 Jan 2023
Summers J (2007) Peoples and international law, how nationalism and self-determination shape a contemporary law of nations. Leiden, Boston
The Addis Ababa Agreement on the problem of South Sudan (1972). https://peacemaker.un.org/sites/peacemaker.un.org/files/SD_720312_Addis%20Ababa%20Agreement%20on%20the%20Problem%20of%20South%20Sudan.pdf. Accessed 11 Jan 2023
UN welcomes South Sudan as 193rd Member State (2011). UN News.
United Nations General Assembly Resolution, GA Res. 2793 (XXVI) 7 December 1971. https://documents-dds-ny.un.org/doc/RESOLUTION/GEN/NR0/328/09/IMG/NR032809.pdf?OpenElement. Accessed 23 Mar 2023
United Nations General Assembly Resolution Uniting for Peace 377 A(V) (1950). https://documents-dds-ny.un.org/doc/RESOLUTION/GEN/NR0/059/75/PDF/NR005975.pdf?OpenElement. Accessed 11 Jan 2023

United Nations High Commission for Refugees, Refugees and asylum-seekers from South Sudan, May 31, 2020. https://data2.unhcr.org/en/situations/southsudan. Accessed 12 Sep 2022

United Nations Security Council Resolution 303 (1971) file:///C:/Users/Dell/Downloads/S_RES_303(1971)-EN.pdf. Accessed 11 Jan 2023

Van Der Vyver JD (2000) Self- determination of the peoples of Quebec under international law. J Transnatl Law Policy 10:1–27

With strong independence vote turnout in South Sudan, UN sees no need for extension (2011) UN News, Global perspective, Human stories. https://news.un.org/en/story/2011/01/363992-strong-independence-vote-turnout-south-sudan-un-sees-no-need-extension. Accessed 11 Jan 2023

Ylönen A (2017) Confronting the 'Arab North': interpretations of slavery and religion in Southern Sudanese Separatist Resistance. In: Taylor I, João Ramos M, Kaarsholm P (eds) Fluid networks and hegemonic powers in the Western Indian Ocean. ISCTE-IUL, pp 104–129

Part III
Internal Self-Determination

Chapter 10
The Internal Aspect of the Right to Self-Determination

10.1 Introduction

The internal aspect of the right to self-determination has generated a great deal of debate in scientific circles. Opinions prevail that the right to self-determination is the right to have a democratic, representative government, and this is often in line with attempts to address minority needs and quests for acquiring greater rights and their protection. The idea of internal self-determination has become widely accepted since the 1980s, and the starting point is the wording used in international documents concerning the right to self-determination. Namely, the "free determination of political status" in Resolution 2625 (1970) [1] does not include compulsory secession and the declaration of independence. Thus, the right to self-determination can be realized through free associations, the local government in the unitary system, or any other form that reflects the wishes of the people. The expression "any other form that reflects the wishes of the people" makes the enumeration open, allowing different ways of implementing the right to self-determination. Therefore, the full exercise of self-determination through its internal aspect can lead to numerous outcomes that can range from the protection of minority rights to representative rights to cultural and political autonomy and the like. In that respect, the principle of self-determination can best be seen as empowering people to choose their political affiliation, influence the political order in which they live, and protect their cultural, ethnic, historical, or territorial identity, and those goals can often (though not always) be achieved without gaining complete independence. [2] Concerning the division among the "internal" and "external" self-determination, internal self-determination represents a right of authentic self-government; hence, it is the right of peoples to freely and realistically choose the political and economic regime

[1] UNGA Res. 2625, (1970).

[2] Halperin et al. (1992), p. 47.

N. Shikova, *Self-Determination and Secession*,
https://doi.org/10.1007/978-3-031-34322-3_10

under which they live. Internal self-determination is a process that is neither destroyed nor interrupted when it is once begun to be practiced, unlike external self-determination, which ends when it is fulfilled. [3]

Despite the general understanding of the importance of internal self-determination, there is still not much clarity about the concept and its application. Some authors find internal self-determination narrower in scope. They consider that its practice is not absolute, it has clear limits, and it is not unconditionally available to every group. [4] Some authors consider that it is only linked to the right of states and their peoples to gain independence from foreign domination, [5] while others believe that internal self-determination effectively impedes the emergence of external self-determination. [6] There are scholars who have not found adequate terminology for the division between "external" and "internal" self-determination, and instead of that, they propose introducing descriptive terms that they found more appropriate for current times. According to them, the division between "internal" and "external" aspects of self-determination is opening doors for speculation. The problem arises when a segment of the state that wants to break away from an existing state falls into the narrow gap between internal and external self-determination. [7]

Nevertheless, many scholars relate internal self-determination to democracy. According to them, Wilson, in his 14 points, considered the idea of self-determination as a pseudonym for the "right to democracy." In that respect, the idea of giving people the means to govern themselves represents a spirit of internal self-determination. Consequently, the right to self-determination is the right to a democratic form of government or an attempt to expand, defend, or consolidate democracy. [8] For the authors in opposite camps, though the enhancement and consolidation of democracy can often respond to the demands of self-determination by creating a system capable of protecting and accommodating groups that would otherwise require change and political rearrangement of borders, in many cases, electoral democracy may not be enough. Democracy has little to do with certain groups of peoples or with indigenous peoples whose political culture and traditions are different from the rest of the population in a given state or with a group that in historical continuity needs greater protection, demands greater political power, or requests own country. For those scholars, although democracy and self-determination are interconnected and are often compatible concepts, establishing a democratic system will not always solve the demands of self-determination, nor does the full practice of self-determination always result in democracy. [9] Despite the variety of opinions, most authors do agree that international institutions have improved in ensuring

[3] Cassese (1995).

[4] Cardenas and Canas (2002).

[5] Hannum (1993).

[6] Shelton (2003).

[7] Summers (2007), Buchheit (1978) and Halperin et al. (1992).

[8] Castellino (2000).

[9] Halperin et al. (1992), p. 65.

internal self-determination. Although there are no completely satisfying solutions, in certain proportions, the struggles for external self-determination can be avoided by the timely establishment of a regime for the protection of group rights. In other situations, the conflict can be avoided through a process that grants autonomy, self-government and self-administration, or even independence. Thus, in many cases, the most constructive ways envisage tolerant dialogue and diplomacy, avoidance of violence on both sides, neutral offices, and effective human rights protection. [10]

If we consider international practice, which is visible primarily in the UN and is manifested in statements, taken positions, and resolutions, internal self-determination relates to the entire people of a sovereign state and unites the right to have a representative government, the rights of racial or religious groups living in a discriminatory state, the rights of indigenous peoples, the rights of ethnic groups, the rights of linguistic minorities, and the rights of peoples living in a federation. [11]

10.1.1 The Case of Iraqi Kurdistan: An Attempt to Accommodate Conflict by Applying Internal Self-Determination

The vast geographic region called Kurdistan spans five states—Turkey, Syria, Iran, Iraq, and Russia—and for more than 3000 years, it has been populated with Kurds. There is a rough estimation that the Kurds number from 25 to 30 million people, but despite impressive historical, demographic, and geographical they did not manage to establish a sovereign statehood. A possible prospect for it was raised and suggested, for the first time, on August 10, 1920, with the signing of the Treaty of Sèvres (France), a peace treaty between the Allies of World War I and the Ottoman Empire. The Treaty established a postwar territorial division, which through autonomy gradually increased the ideas of creating an independent state of Kurdistan. [12] The attempt for statehood collapsed already in the summer of 1923, when a new territorial revision—in favor of Turkey—was made in Lausanne (Switzerland) under a new peace treaty (Treaty of Lausanne) [13] following the Greco-Turkish War (1919–1922), whereas the idea of Kurds' autonomy was abandoned. However, the core of the Kurdish National Movement for Independence did not stand still and gravitated toward the southern parts of Kurdistan. Between January and December 1946, it was relocated and concentrated in the Kurdish provinces of northeast Iraq. Concentrated in a hard-to-reach and oil-rich mountain range—far from Baghdad (Iraq's political center)—the Kurdish people started a war for secession from Iraq,

---

[10] Falk (2002).

[11] Cassese (1995).

[12] Treaty of Sèvres (1920).

[13] Treaty of Lausanne (1923).

which lasted from 1961 to 1970 when a peace deal was finally reached. [14] The agreement concluded between the Military Administration and the Kurdish tribes had 15 articles and was known as the Autonomy Agreement. [15] It included a dynamic four-year implementation plan envisaging the recognition of Iraqi Kurds as a nation, their participation in the government, their proportionate representation, the election of a Kurd as a deputy prime minister, the establishment of Kurdish police and Kurdish administration in the Kurdish provinces, bestowing a status of official language on Kurdish in areas they are inhabiting, providing conditions for economic development, and the establishment of a Kurdish assembly. [16] The dynamics of the implementation plan were supposed to show a seemingly rapid realization of the so-called political circumstances of the treaty, but in reality, it was only a formal framework for implementing agreed political changes, without substantially altering the decisive political influence of the official Baghdad over Kurdish autonomy. Hence, political conditions were easily fulfilled, but the Agreement was not implemented or was implemented according to Iraq's version. Although the Assembly was formed, it was made up of Kurds who were appointed by Iraq without any criteria, and over time, Iraq become unwilling to share the power. This, in 1974–1975, resulted in another armed activity, and a new military conflict reopened a political situation that marked the Cold War era. The national Kurdish movement in Iraq became a pawn in the game of conflicting interests between the US and the USSR (and the UN's neutral position toward the Kurdish question). As a result, Iraq began a new tactic against the vulnerable autonomy of the Kurds. Namely, in the northeast region (the richest in oil), the Arab population significantly grew, and the territory became an open military hotspot. [17] Kurds suffered years of oppression under the Saddam Hussein regime when they had no possibility of exercising meaningful internal self-determination. [18] After overthrowing Saddam Hussein's regime in 1991, Iraq's rule was dismantled. Following the political elections, in 1992, the Government of the Autonomous Region of Kurdistan and the National Assembly of Iraqi Kurdistan (Kurdistan Parliament) were established. Kurdish referendum for independence was held in Iraqi Kurdistan in 2017, on which an overwhelming majority expressed their wish to separate from Iraq and form an independent state of Kurdistan. [19] Central governments of Iraq opposed the referenda and rejected the Kurds' claims for independence. [20]

---

[14] Adams Schmidt (1970).

[15] Manaz (2017).

[16] Research Study RNAS–10 (1972); Kurdistan 24 (2022); Sever (2021); McDowall (2004), p. 327; McDowall (1996).

[17] Heraclides (1991).

[18] Sterio (2018).

[19] Iraqi Kurds decisively back independence in referendum (2017).

[20] Morris (2017).

10.2 Attempts to Extend the Right to Self-Determination/a Legal Basis for Internal Self-Determination

The internal aspect of self-determination includes the right of all population segments to influence the constitutional and political structure of the system under which they live. Concerning international documents that empower it, the Special Report of the UN Commission for Indonesia from 1949 is one of the first documents that has cautiously made a distinction between "internal" and "external" self-determination. [21] The report summarizes the results of the UN Round Table Conference with the representatives of Indonesia and the Netherlands concerning the transfer of sovereignty from the Dutch colonies to the Republic of Indonesia. During the negotiations, it was emphasized that Indonesia's Constitution referred to the internal right of self-determination as a right of peoples to democratically determine the future status of their territories within the federal structure of the United States of Indonesia. [22]

Furthermore, the documents from the process of drafting the International Covenants on Human Rights (International Covenant on Civil and Political Rights (ICCPR), International Covenant on Economic, Social and Cultural Rights (ICESCR)) also sought delegates' attempts to distinguish between the internal and external aspects of self-determination, using the terms "domestic" and "international aspect" of self-determination. Within those reflections, "domestic" self-determination takes the form of self-government, or the right of peoples to create representative institutions and freely choose the form of government. The "international" aspect is connected with independence. Irrespectively of the terminology used, most of the expressed opinions were that the idea of self-determination is a complexity of ideas and not a single concept. Therefore, internal self-determination, or self-determination at the national level, should be separated from external self-determination, or self-determination at the international level. The internal aspect envisages the right of a nation—already constituted as a state—to choose the form of government and determine the policy that it intends to implement, and the external aspect envisages the right of a group—a nation—to form its own state. This in effect demonstrates the complexity of self-determination. Therefore, it can be said that during the drafting of the International Covenant on Civil and Political Rights, there was support for the idea that the right to self-determination also includes the right to a democratic, representative government in relation to Article 23 (1) of the Universal Declaration of Human Rights (1948). [23]

Article 25 of the International Covenant on Civil and Political Rights (1966) contains the rights of every citizen to take part in the conduct of public affairs, to vote, and to be elected at genuine periodic elections. These rights have been

[21] Special report to the Security Council on the Round Table Conference/United Nations Commission for Indonesia, UN SCOR, S/1417 (1949) para 52.

[22] Buchheit (1978).

[23] Buchheit (1978).

recognized in General Comment No. 25 (57) as related but different from the right of peoples to self-determination covered by Article 1 of the ICCPR, upon which the peoples have the right to freely determine their political status and to enjoy the right to choose the form of their constitution or government. [24] Though the Human Rights Committee did not precisely clarify the relations between self-determination and other human rights, neither made a distinction between internal and external aspects of the right; still, it gave wide support to the right to self-determination exercised as a right to democratic government. Moreover, in principle, states also accepted that constitutional arrangements should reflect the wishes of the people. [25]

Despite attempts for the legal clarification of the internal aspect of the right to self-determination, it can be said that the internal and external division of self-determination is still a challenging concept. However, undoubtedly, this concept is gaining more and more support in recent years—thus, it can be pointed out that the right to internal self-determination is in *statu nascendi* (in the process of formation). In that direction, the UN adopted numerous resolutions and declarations (such as the UN Declaration on the Rights of Indigenous Peoples from 2007). [26] Those instruments have limitations as they are often at odds with the behavior of states. Thus, it can be said that, apart from a large segment of the international community willing to crystallize the general rule of internal self-determination, there is a segment against it. According to Antonio Cassese, it will most likely take some time before customary law takes shape. If that happens, the right to internal self-determination will be a permanent right—a right in progress, not a right that can be exercised only once. [27]

The eventual birth of such a right will undoubtedly mean great progress for the international community. This process presupposes some form of international mechanism (general or specific) that will monitor the effectiveness of its implementation and its *erga omnes* status (meaning, in effect, it will be a right for all). Since currently such a mechanism does not exist, the exercise of the right to self-determination in its internal aspect can only rely on available international instruments.

10.2.1 Internal Self-Determination for Indigenous Peoples: The Example of Sámi Parliaments

The Sámi are indigenous peoples living in four states: Finland, Norway, Sweden, and Russia. The Sámi population is a numerical minority within those states, numbering between 70,000 and 100,000, with about 40,000 to 60,000 in Norway; 15,000

[24] CCPR General Comment No. 25 (1996).

[25] Buchheit (1978).

[26] UN RES. UN Declaration on the rights of indigenous peoples (2007).

[27] Cassese (1995), p. 312.

to 20,000 in Sweden; 9000 in Finland; and about 2000 in the Russian Federation. The Sámi people traditionally inhabit a territory known as Sápmi, which spreads in the northern parts of Norway, Sweden, Finland, and the Russian Kola peninsula. The Sámi people are divided by the formal boundaries of the respected states, but they continue to exist as one people united by cultural and linguistic bonds and a common identity. The Sámi people's culture and traditions rely on a close connection to nature and their land. Traditionally, the Sámi depend on hunting, fishing, gathering, and trapping, whereas reindeer herding is of particular importance for them. [28]

The Sámi Parliaments (Saamediggi in Northern Sámi) exist in the three Scandinavian countries: Norway, Sweden, and Finland. The Sámi Parliaments consist of elected Sámi representatives. The political participation of the Sámi is grounded upon objective criteria (to be registered as a voter for electing representatives of the Sámi Parliament, the person needs to speak the Sámi language or should have Sámi ancestors). The Sámi Parliaments are institutions without legislative power. They have a certain degree of political influence and autonomy that varies among the countries in which they are established. In respect of their position within the system, the Sámi Parliaments are representative bodies with administrative authorities. The misbalance between these two functions (representation and administration) exists undoubtedly and additionally differs among the countries they reside in. Each of the respective countries has different policies in respect of the institutional design, status, authority, and mandate of the Sámi Parliaments (i.e., the Sámi Parliament in Sweden is only an advisory body that monitors the issues related to the Sámi culture in Sweden, the Norwegian Sámi Parliament has a firmer position within the system of governance since the decisions brought within its competencies cannot be formally overruled by the Norwegian government, and the competences of the Sámi Parliament in Finland are not clearly defined). [29]

Sámi rights are recognized in the constitutions of Norway and Finland. [30] Sámi Parliaments are the institutional model, and though they do not have sufficient authority to realize the internal self-determination of the Sámi and provide them with a genuine autonomy, they have a representative role. [31] They govern Sámi non-territorial autonomy in the areas of culture, education, language, and indigenous status, and they are primary advisory bodies without legislative authority and with low powers in the field of policy in the three Nordic states, meaning they have a limited ability and various political constraints to act independently and make autonomous decisions. [32] Often, they are criticized for not being able to secure the indigenous self-determination in its substance. For example, the Human Rights

[28] Eriksson (1997) and Report of the Special Rapporteur (2016).

[29] Josefsen (2011), Josefsen et al. (2014) and Kuokkanen (2019).

[30] The Constitution of The Kingdom of Norway (1814) (subsequently amended, most recently by Resolution of 1 June 2022), art 108; The Constitution of Finland (1999) (731/1999, amendments up to 817/2018), sec 17.

[31] Shikova (2020).

[32] Anaya (1996) and Stepien et al. (2015).

Committee[33], in 2019, raised a concern about Finland's violation of Sámi political rights related to Sámi Parliament representation. The UNHCR pointed out that the country (Finland) improperly extended Parliament's pool of eligible candidates, and that affected the effective enjoyment of the right to internal self-determination reflected in the capacity of the Indigenous peoples to define their own group membership without excessive intervention from a state. [34]

10.3 Relevant International Instruments

International organizations, such as the UN, and regional ones, such as the Organization for Security and Co-operation in Europe (OSCE), undoubtedly show a willingness to channel the internal aspect of the right to self-determination and often act as a filter for the pacification of extreme demands. When we speak about relevant international instruments that in some way envisage the internal aspect of the right to self-determination, we need to direct the debate toward regional instruments such as the Helsinki Final Act from 1975 (adopted by the 35 member countries of the Conference on Security and Co-operation in Europe (CSCE)—today's OSCE member states) and the Declaration adopted in 1976 in Algeria by a private group of politicians, leaders of trade associations, representatives of freedom movements, and intellectuals from different countries. The two texts differ radically from one to another in terms of origin, formal status, and content. The former has much greater political power and moral weight because it was accepted by 35 state governments. The latter reflects the ideals of individuals, who do not represent a state, but their moral and intellectual standing gives an important dimension to the document. The Helsinki Final Act is significant since it formulates a new general norm of self-determination, while the Algerian Declaration is an expression of the sentiment of the public opinion segment. Both texts are a breakthrough in existing international legislation since they show a way for the world community to accommodate the aspirations of people and nations. [35] Both documents, according to Antonio Cassese, [36] contribute to the expansion of the right to self-determination, i.e. they do not limit it to cases of colonial administration and foreign domination, but their intention is for this right to become universal and to encompass the right to peaceful assembly, freedom of association, participation in public affairs directly or through freely elected representatives, the right to elect and to be elected at periodical elections, freedom of thought and conscience, freedom of information, freedom of

[33] The findings are published by the Office of the High Commissioner for Human Rights, but it is brought by the Human Rights Committee as a body of independent experts that monitors States parties' adherence to the International Covenant on Civil and Political Rights.

[34] UN human rights experts find Finland violated Sámi political rights to Sámi Parliament representation (2019).

[35] Cassese (1995).

[36] Cassese (1995).

movement, freedom to participate in cultural life, and freedom and security of person. These are the basic premises of democracy, meaning the right to self-determination includes pluralistic representative democracy and standards grounded on political pluralism, representative institutions, power sharing, the rule of law, and respect for fundamental human rights, including the rights of minorities.

10.3.1 CSCE/OSCE Documents

Colonialism and foreign occupation—the two situations that, through UN documents, triggered the emergence of external self-determination—are almost completely absent from Europe. [37] In Europe, there are no racist regimes, no foreign occupation like in Africa or in Arab countries, so it is logical to say that the principle of external self-determination has already been realized in Europe, in the USA, or in Canada. But both Europe and North America are filled with cases related to the broader concept of self-determination, such as, historically, the two Germanies and their unification; the Irish question in the UK; Catalonia in Spain; Quebec in Canada; etc. Although there were numerous disagreements over the content of the Helsinki Final Act (hereinafter referred to as the Helsinki Document), [38] the states eventually agreed that it applied to national minorities but to the entire population of the state, i.e., its citizens. Under Principle VIII, *Equal rights and self-determination of peoples,* the accepted text regarding self-determination is as follows:

- The participating States (*n.b.at the Conference*) will respect the equal rights of peoples and their right to self-determination, acting at all times in conformity with the purposes and principles of the Charter of the United Nations and with the relevant norms of international law, including those relating to territorial integrity of States;
- By virtue of the principle of equal rights and self-determination of peoples, all peoples always have the right, in full freedom, to determine, when and as they wish, their internal and external political status, without external interference, and to pursue as they wish their political, economic, social and cultural development;
- The participating States reaffirm the universal significance of respect for and effective exercise of equal rights and self-determination of peoples for the development of friendly relations among themselves as among all States; they also recall the importance of the elimination of any form of violation of this principle. [39]

---

[37] n.b. The exception of that is Gibraltar and its colonial status.

[38] Declaration on Principles Guiding Relation between Participating States, Final Act, Conference on Security and Cooperation in Europe, (1975).

[39] Principle VIII, Equal rights and self-determination of peoples.

This can be interpreted equally in favor of internal and external self-determination. [40] The principle applies to "all peoples" living in sovereign European states, and that is considered progress in comparison to the Declaration on Principles of International Law concerning Friendly Relations and Co-operation among States from 1970 (which, in narrow interpretation, refers only to colonial states, racist regimes, or states with discriminatory policies). [41] The use of the word "always" in the Helsinki Document means that the right to self-determination is regarded as a right in continuity, a right that exists even after the people have chosen a form of government or established a certain international status. Therefore, the Helsinki Document gives a wide scope of the principle of self-determination, interlinking it with other human rights. The document emphasizes that the internal and external status will be determined without external intervention, "in full freedom," which reflects the notion that self-determination cannot be implemented unless fundamental human rights and fundamental freedoms (in particular freedom of expression and association) are not granted and provided to all members of the people concerned. In fact, the people cannot choose their political status or establish economic, social, or cultural development if they live under an authoritarian government. Hence, the expression "in full freedom" means freedom from internal influence, and the expression "without external intervention" means freedom from a possible invasion by a third state. While the Helsinki Document provides a definition of self-determination that opens a new field in international relations, it primarily refers to internal self-determination, which means the permanent ability of the people to choose a social and political regime and to adapt social and political structures—meaning it gives to the principle anti-authoritarian and democratic dimension.[42]

Another important feature of the Helsinki Document is that although it considers the application of the right of self-determination to all states, and to all people living in the state, such right is not guaranteed to minorities or ethnic groups. Therefore, the right to external self-determination means the right of the people of the state to decide whether the state will change its international status—such as merging with another state, incorporating into another state, splitting it into two sovereign entities, or any similar changes—whereas the final word on the matter lies within the people, who should decide freely through referenda, plebiscites, or any other democratic procedure. [43]

Thus, it can be said that despite its extensivity, Principle VIII of the Helsinki Document is traditional since it protects the territorial integrity of states, and it

---

[40] Cassese (1995).

[41] UN RES 2625, Declaration on Principles of International Law concerning Friendly Relations and Co-operation among States (1970).

[42] Cassese A (1995) Self- determination of the peoples, a legal reappraisal. Cambridge University Press

[43] For Cassese, this means that territorial or other change can be brought about by the central government, but only with the will of the people of that state, Cassese (1995).

excludes minorities from the practice of the principle (although states should guarantee civil rights and fundamental freedoms to individual members of minority groups). Still, the Helsinki Document confirms and extends the UN principles. Although it is not a legally binding document for all members of the international community, in a very practical way, it symbolizes a code of conduct. The Document was a powerful factor in promoting legal changes, and its Principle VIII was almost literally transposed into the Final Report of the CSCE Vienna Meeting (1989). [44] However, in the process of the drafting of the latter document, the section on the development of friendly relations among nations and states was omitted, and the principle of territorial integrity was reinforced—most probably because of the fear of disintegrations of states and due to the events that were happening that time in Central and Eastern Europe (related to the fall of the Berlin Wall, the fall of the *Iron Curtain,* dissolutions of the socialist federations, etc.). A restrictive view was also expressed in the Paris Charter for a New Europe (1990), [45] which states: "(…) We reaffirm the equal rights of peoples and their right to self-determination in conformity with the Charter of the United Nations and with the relevant norms of international law, including those relating to territorial integrity of States." [46] That cast doubts on whether the CSCE had abandoned its earlier positions on self-determination and directed it toward the less liberal UN doctrine. Fearing the events that followed—due to apparent secessions and the possibility of opening Pandora's box, future CSCE (now OSCE) actions focused more on minority rights and less on self-determination. But the essence of the Helsinki Final Act was not abandoned. Interestingly, with the breakup of the Eastern Bloc, the concept did not lose its ground but showed exceptional vitality. Although post-Helsinki processes have focused more on democracy and minority rights, by advocating for the internal dimension of self-determination, the OSCE contributed to defining specific criteria that mark a pluralistic democratic society as the essence for practicing internal self-determination. Some of the mechanisms that supported those ideas were the appointment of a High Commissioner on National Minorities, establishment of the Office for Free Elections, etc. At the same time, much more advanced forms and methods for the protection of minorities than traditional ones were proposed, which were aligned with the sovereign states' interests and without violating their territorial integrity. [47]

---

[44] Concluding Document of the Vienna Meeting 1986 of Representatives of the Participating States of the Conference on Security and Cooperation in Europe, held on the basis of the provisions of the Final Act relating to the follow-up to the Conference, Vienna (1989).

[45] Charter of Paris for a New Europe, Paris (1990).

[46] Charter of Paris for a New Europe, Paris (1990).

[47] For these questions see more at Cassese (1995).

10.3.2 *Algerian Declaration (Universal Declaration of the Rights of Peoples)*

The Universal Declaration of the Rights of Peoples (hereinafter referred to as the Algerian Declaration) [48] was adopted in 1976 in Algiers, and although it is not a document signed by governments, it obtained a particular status since it tends to clarify the right to self-determination on a much more concrete way in comparison to existing international documents. Article 7 of the Algerian Declaration proclaims that the political repression of the peoples is a denial of their right to self-determination. [49] The Declaration extends the principle of internal self-determination and clarifies the weak standards set by the UN stipulated in the International Covenants on Human Rights of 1966 as well as in the Declaration on Principles of International Law concerning Friendly Relations and Co-operation among States (1970), which speak about a representative government that does not discriminate on the basis of race, color, or belief. The Algerian Declaration clearly proclaims that the government must be democratic, must not be authoritarian, and must effectively guarantee the free exercise of human rights.

Internal political self-determination is a synthesis and sum of human rights, and this does not simply mean self-government, but much more, it signifies freedom to choose a government and to exercise all the freedoms that make this choice possible. Another important feature of the Algerian Declaration is that it speaks about the people, not about the governments, and in its text, there is no provision for the preservation of territorial integrity at any cost (which would be an expected government gesture). The Algerian Declaration secures territorial integrity through banning secession for minorities, meaning minority rights must be enforced with full respect for the legitimate interests of the community as a whole and within a state that acts under the proposed principles. [50]

The Algerian Declaration also changes the image of self-determination, which is seen no longer as an instrument for friendly relations among nations and a tool for overcoming international tensions but more as a cause for tension, disharmony, and even a reason for a serious international crisis. According to the document, when the state restricts people from achieving self-determination, then two sets of rights are violated—the rights of the repressed people and the rights of all members of the international community, which irrespective of being states, national liberation movements, or other bodies, have an obligation to intervene through political, economic, and military means as an act of international solidarity. Nevertheless, the Algerian Declaration does not go far beyond what is enshrined in international norms but only clarifies the right to self-determination. Its main idea is to serve as a

[48] Universal Declaration of the Rights of People, Algerian Chart, (1976).

[49] Universal Declaration of the Rights of People, Algerian Chart, (1976), article 7.

[50] Universal Declaration of the Rights of People, Algerian Chart, (1976).

catalyst and encourage governments and international organizations to clarify the concept of self-determination and establish rules for its implementation. [51]

References

Adams Schmidt D (1970) Iraq recognizes Kurdish autonomy (Internet source). https://www.nytimes.com/1970/03/12/archives/iraq-recognizes-kurdish-autonomy.html. Accessed 12 Jan 2023

Anaya J (1996) Indigenous peoples in international law. Oxford University Press, New York

Buchheit LC (1978) Secession, the legitimacy of self-determination. Yale University Press, New Haven

Cardenas EJ, Canas MF (2002) The limits of self-determination at self-determination of peoples. In: Danspeckgruber W (ed) Self-determination of peoples, community, nation and state in interdependent world. Lynne Rienner Publishers, pp 101–119

Cassese A (1995) Self-determination of the peoples, a legal reappraisal. Cambridge University Press

Castellino J (2000) International law and self-determination. Kluwer Law International

CCPR General Comment No. 25, 1996. https://www.refworld.org/docid/453883fc22.html. Accessed 21 Sept 2022

Charter of Paris for a New Europe, Paris 1990. https://www.osce.org/files/f/documents/0/6/39516.pdf. Accessed 21 Sept 2022

Concluding Document of the Vienna Meeting 1986 of Representatives of the Participating States of the Conference on Security and Cooperation in Europe, held on the basis of the provisions of the Final Act relating to the follow-up to the Conference, Vienna (1989)

Declaration on Principles Guiding Relation between Participating States, Final Act, Conference on Security and Cooperation in Europe, Helsinki (1975). https://www.osce.org/files/f/documents/5/c/39501.pdf. Accessed 21 Sept 2022

Eriksson J (1997) Partition and redemption. A Machiavellian analysis of Sámi and Basque Patriotism. Umea University

Falk R (2002) Self-determination under international law: the coherence of doctrine versus the incoherence of experience. In: Danspeckgruber W (ed) Self-determination of peoples, community, nation and state in interdependent world. Lynne Rienner Publishers, pp 31–67

Halperin MH et al (1992) Self-determination in the new world order. Carnegie Endowment for International Peace, Washington DC

Hannum H (1993) Documents on autonomy and minority rights. Brill

Heraclides A (1991) The self-determination of the minorities in the international politics. Frank Cass and Company Limited

Iraqi Kurds decisively back independence in referendum (2017) (Internet source). https://www.bbc.com/news/world-middle-east-41419633. Accessed 12 Jan 2023

Josefsen E (2011) The Norwegian Saami parliament and Saami political empowerment. In: Minnerup G, Solberg P (eds) First world, first nations: internal colonialism and indigenous self-determination in Northern Europe and Australia. Sussex Academic Press, pp 31–44

Josefsen E et al (2014) Different institutions within similar states: the Norwegian and Swedish Sámediggis. Ethnopolit Formerly Glob Rev Ethnopolit 14(1):32–51

Kuokkanen R (2019) Restructuring relations, restructuring relations: indigenous self-determination, governance, and gender. Oxford University Press

Kurdistan 24. The March 11 Agreement of 1970 was a message that Kurds believe in peaceful resolution of conflicts: Kurdistan Region PM Barzani 2022/03/11 (Internet source). https://www.

[51] Cassese (1995).

kurdistan24.net/en/story/27571-The-March-11-Agreement-of-1970-was-a-message-that-Kurds-believe-in-peaceful-resolution-of-conflicts:-Kurdistan-Region-PM-Barzani. Accessed 25 Mar 2023

Manaz A (2017) Iraqi Kurdish referendum and international law. Cag Univ J Soc Sci 14(2):116–131

McDowall D (1996) The Kurds. Minority Rights Group. https://minorityrights.org/publications/the-kurds-december-1996/. Accessed 25 Mar 2023

McDowall D (2004) A modern history of the Kurds. I.B. Tauris

Morris L (2017) How the Kurdish independence referendum backfired spectacularly. Washington Post, 20 October 2017. https://www.washingtonpost.com/world/how-the-kurdish-independence-referendum-backfired-/2017/10/20/3010c820-b371-11e7-9b93-b97043e57a22_story.html?utm_term=.62ab5882d1b9. Accessed 12 Jan 2023

Report of the Special Rapporteur on the rights of indigenous peoples on the human rights situation of the Sámi people in the Sápmi region of Norway, Sweden and Finland, UN A/HRC/33/42/Add.3, 2016. https://digitallibrary.un.org/record/847081. Accessed 4 Oct 2022

Research Study RNAS–10 (1972) Prepared in the Bureau of Intelligence and Research. The Kurds of Iraq: renewed insurgency? Foreign relations of the United States, 1969–1976, Volume E–4, Documents on Iran and Iraq, 1969–1972. https://history.state.gov/historicaldocuments/frus1969-76ve04/d310. Accessed 25 Mar 2023

Sever A (2021) Beyond vulnerability? Turkey and the 1970 Kurdish autonomy deal in Iraq. Int Hist Rev 43(4):870–886

Shelton D (2003) Self-determination and secession: the jurisprudence of the international human rights tribunals. In: Dahliz J (ed) Conflict avoidance and - regional appraisals. Asser Press, pp 47–75

Shikova N (2020) The possibilities and limits of non-territorial autonomy in securing indigenous self-determination. Philos Soc 31(3):277–444

Special report to the Security Council on the Round Table Conference/United Nations Commission for Indonesia, UN SCOR, S/1417 (1949) para 52. file:///C:/Users/Dell/Downloads/S_1417-EN.pdf. Accessed 21 Sept 2022

Stepien A et al (2015) Sámi parliaments in Finland, Norway, and Sweden. In: Malloy TH et al (eds) Managing diversity through non-territorial autonomy: assessing advantages, deficiencies and risks. Oxford University Press, pp 117–141

Sterio M (2018) Self-determination and secession under international law: the cases of Kurdistan and Catalonia, Vol 2 (1). https://www.asil.org/insights/volume/22/issue/1/self-determination-and-secession-under-international-law-cases-kurdistan. Accessed 12 Jan 2023

Summers J (2007) Peoples and international law, how nationalism and self-determination shape a contemporary law of nations. Leiden, Boston

The Constitution of Finland (1999) (731/1999, amendments up to 817/2018 included). https://finlex.fi/en/laki/kaannokset/1999/en19990731.pdf. Accessed 12 Jan 2023

The Constitution of the Kingdom of Norway (1814) Subsequently amended, most recently by Resolution of 1 June 2022. https://lovdata.no/dokument/NLE/lov/1814-05-17. Accessed 12 Jan 2023

Treaty of Lausanne (1923) The Treaties of Peace 1919–1923, Vol. II (New York: Carnegie Endowment for International Peace, 1924). https://wwi.lib.byu.edu/index.php/Treaty_of_Lausanne. Accessed 12 Jan 2023

Treaty of Sèvres (1920) The Treaties of Peace 1919–1923, Vol. II (Carnegie Endowment for International Peace, New York, 1924). https://wwi.lib.byu.edu/index.php/Section_I,_Articles_1_-_260. Accessed 12 Jan 2023

UN human rights experts find Finland violated Sámi political rights to Sámi Parliament representation. United Nations Human Rights Office of the High Commissioner (2019) Internet source. https://www.ohchr.org/en/press-releases/2019/02/un-human-rights-experts-find-finland-violated-sami-political-rights-sami. Accessed 12 Jan 2023

UN RES 2625, Declaration on Principles of International Law concerning Friendly Relations and Co-operation among States (1970). https://digitallibrary.un.org/record/202170?ln=en. Accessed 21 Sept 2022

UN RES. UN Declaration on the rights of indigenous peoples (2007). https://www.un.org/development/desa/indigenouspeoples/wp-content/uploads/sites/19/2018/11/UNDRIP_E_web.pdf. Accessed 21 Sept 2022

Universal Declaration of the Rights of People, Algerian Chart, Algeria (1976)

Chapter 11
The Social Basis for the Realization of Internal Self-Determination

11.1 Introduction: Identity as a Basis for Special Rights

The interplay of ideas about collective and individual identity underlines the notion that identity is at the same time an image that an individual has for himself/herself and an image that others have for him/her. Different theorists find a variety of grounds upon which identity is based. In that sense, identity can derive from race, language, ethnicity, culture, religion, traditions, history, shared memory, etc. For some scholars, the basis for identity is subjective elements that form an identity, but for many others, identity represents a combination of objective elements. In any case, identity is a multidimensional, multilayered construct. Which identity line will prevail in a person depends on his/her moral code and the environment in which he/she realizes himself/herself. Some systems are more open and accept expressions of different identities, while others are more restrictive and tend to suppress certain identity features.

According to political theorist Crawford Young, identity is a subjective, individual phenomenon, shaped by the repeated ego question "Who am I?" and similar to "Who is he/she?" Generalized to the point of collectivity, that question becomes "Who are we?" and "Who are they?" But that subjective identity is also affected by the labels that others apply to it, and although identity is a multidimensional and situational fluid concept, it is not infinitely elastic. Some individual characteristics limit the choice from a possible range of social identities. [1] Physical appearance is the most visible attribute; for example, skin pigmentation is often the basis for segmentation, and not all individuals can afford race-based identity selection. [2]

In the predominantly liberal model, liberal and democratic institutions are seen as a way of realizing universal principles of rights, justice, and freedom. The model

[1] Young (1979), p. 20.

[2] Deng (2002).

N. Shikova, *Self-Determination and Secession*,
https://doi.org/10.1007/978-3-031-34322-3_11

relies on unfounded optimism that *a reason* can clear ethnic dilemmas and conflicts among different lifestyles, religions, and cultural narratives. However, the theory of liberal justice is fragile as it relies on a hidden premise for a dominant culture and also on a need for cultural consensus in society in general. Therefore, when two or more concepts of the "good way of life" collide in a set political model, the concept of liberal justice becomes breakable. [3] As a result, a liberal concept of rights has been criticized for not being able to fully absorb the ideas of equality and ignoring some essential aspects of human nature. It appears to neglect the particularities that come from different lifestyles and does not take into account the very important role of community membership over individual character, its moral reasoning, and its actions. [4]

Most authors interpret ethnic renaissance as a response to contemporary society dysfunctions. [5] More than any other informal groupings (local communities, clubs, etc.), it is perceived that ethnic groups can be a cure for tensions arising from disagreements among persons and roles or a cure for the depersonalization and dehumanization of social relationships. [6] On the other hand, globalization emphasizes the uniqueness, local diversity, ethnic identity, and return to community values. This is also evident in the parallel processes of globalization and localization. Jointly with interdependence and global action, and seemingly contradictory, new regional, national, and local identities emerge. It appears that territorial localism is a favorite among culturally oppressed nations that are now demanding the right to self-determination within their ancestral territories. [7] Jean Baudrillard summarizes this parallelism of global and local processes, and he finds discrimination and exclusion as logical consequences of globalization. Baudrillard considers that in this broken mirror of universalization reappear fragments of all kinds of singularities. [8]

Liberal nationalism, as an aspect of liberalism, and liberal nationalists (Will Kymlicka, Yael Tamir, and David Miller) do not perceive identity as a fixed category but believe that individuals need to have a right to choose. Liberal nationalists appraise the development of a personal sense of identity, founded on the value of cultural belonging (which is crucial for self-esteem) [9] or in the respect that a particular national culture enjoys within a wider social context. [10] A political model is equally important to enable an individual to assess how his or her own identity fits into the larger social picture and also to eliminate potential legal obstacles or

[3] Frckoski Lj (2012).

[4] Santiago Nino (1998).

[5] Giordano (2001).

[6] Cohen (1978).

[7] De Soza Santos (2003).

[8] Baudrillard (1991).

[9] Kymlicka (2000).

[10] Avishai and Raz (1990).

discouragements of permanent identity redefinition. Identities are resilient; thus, it is best to recognize and, to some extent, legally confirm them. [11]

According to Charles Taylor, the productivity paradox is that identity is partly shaped by its recognition and also by an absence of recognition. [12] Nonrecognition or misrepresentation can cause great harm and can be labeled as a form of repression since nonrecognition directly affects fundamental human nature. The demand for equal recognition, in turn, means recognizing the equal value of human potential. According to the "principle of equal treatment," there should be a political model that neglects differences and focuses on what is the same for all people, while the other possible approach emphasizes the need for the recognition and encouragement of uniqueness. According to Taylor, society is discriminatory if it relies on the first model. [13]

In the liberal context, the disclosure of identity should not be in isolation but should be through negotiations, i.e., through a partially open or partially closed dialogue with others, and that communication form affects identity. In fact, the possibilities of a social dialogue not only have the potential to form and define individual identity but can also play a key role in shaping the identity of a particular culture in the broader sense. Taylor places emphasis on the danger of not recognizing the cultural identity of a particular minority or a disadvantaged group, primarily because that creates a marginalized community. The most obvious disadvantage of nonrecognition is the annulment of a particular culture, which in turn causes defeatist feelings among its members and extinguishes their basis for social self-esteem. Hence, it is of exceptional importance to recognize and protect cultural traditions and achievements. [14]

Individual rights, such as the right to liberty, the right to freedom of association, and the prohibition of discrimination, do not guarantee the survival of cultures. The theory of rights that is individually constructed cannot adequately deal with recognition struggles and the establishment of collective identities. Still, the monochromatic, selective perception disappears when individual rights holders are assigned with an intersubjectively conceived identity. [15] However, if the identity conflicts with the demands of national unity, there are not many options—either the national identity to be redefined in order to be inclusive of all, or to allow groups with different identities to set their own paths. [16] Additionally, recognition *per se* is not enough, and Jurgen Habermas and Michael Walzer argue in support of that thesis. [17] The

[11] Waterbury (2002).

[12] Taylor (1994).

[13] According to Michael Walzer, the reason for the distinction between different types of liberalism is that the choices made are not made once and for all, and policies, as well as conditions, can be adapted and modified, Walzer (1994).

[14] Wolf (1994).

[15] Habermas (1994), p. 113.

[16] Deng (2002).

[17] Habermas (1994).

need for group integration into society should be based on different techniques and strategies for group accommodation that arise from group specificity. [18]

One way of expressing an identity is to practice it within a particular group. Thus, identity as a set of individual characteristics, or as a sum of elements (subjective and objective), is transformed into a group (collective) identity, which denotes individual belonging. The stereotypes and prejudices that shape group identity are closely linked to the psychological mechanism of differentiation of the *other*. Daniel Rothbart and Karina V. Korostelina argue that within societies that have economic and political inequalities, minorities and lower-status groups experience a stronger sense of collective "I" and greater internal homogeneity. Traditional practices, as well as marriages, keep the group stable and sustainable in the large system of identities. The group's identity is often projected against the "dangerous" *others* and relies on myths as a powerful tool for self-perception and guardianship. [19] From a historical perspective, group leaders benefit from the division of *us* and *them* because it reinforces their image. In fact, "parochial" sentiments are deeply ingrained in human psychology and formally influence attitudes, judgments, and preferences, so a mother tongue, even a dialect, sounds more sympathetic; customs seem much more decorative; home cuisine is better; and racial features are more complete, and all that complexity provides the basis for xenophobia. [20]

But policies that promote different identities are often at odds with the so-called processes of "nation building." Individual and group identities revolve around institutions such as family, clan, tribe, or ethnicity, but the need for national unity requires a broader framework. The crisis of national identity may arise because of the conflict between subjective and objective elements of identity or because of the tendency of the dominant hegemonic group (whether the majority or the ruling minority) to impose its identity as a framework for the nation. This can adversely affect the subjective self-esteem of disadvantaged minorities and politically weaker groups. Constitutional provisions and other legal documents may prohibit discrimination, but as long as the framework is defined in terms that exclude, subordinate, or marginalize those who do not fit in the nation, discrimination becomes inherent. [21]

One of the important questions is—which cultural identities are relevant to be prioritized in the process of accommodation? Many theorists of multiculturalism look for the answer in social identities that are solid, rooted in historical communities, and transcend all other identities. [22]

---

[18] Rothbart and Korostelina (2006).

[19] Rothbart and Korostelina (2006).

[20] Buchheit (1978).

[21] Deng (2002).

[22] Frckoski Lj (2012).

11.2 National Identity and the Content of Ethnicity

National identity is an abstract and multidimensional construct that touches a range of life spheres. Omnipresent and complex, national identity and nationalism are powerful and explosive global forces. [23] From the beginning of the twentieth century, when it first appeared, up to this day, the term *ethnicity* is often confused with other closely related terms such as *people*, *race*, or *nation*, but its narrowest political sense is constructed in the North American milieu, in which *ethnicity* relates to demands for the recognition of specific rights within the public arena. For the individual, national identity is perhaps not only the most important and comprehensive but also the most persistent identity among all that he/she possesses. Other types of collective identities—such as class, gender, race, and religion—can overlap or combine with national identity, but they rarely suppress it.

Anthony Smith considers national identity as a strong "historical and fateful community" that can serve as salvation from forgetfulness. Generations bond through collective dignity with a constant reference to the "golden age"; the realization of brotherhood through symbols, rituals, and ceremonies that link them with the sacrifice of the dead and fallen is the fiction on which national identity rests and upon them is establishing its endurance. [24] For Benedict Anderson, a national identity enables the individual to overcome his mortality by simultaneously connecting it with something that exists from time immemorial and something that extends into the future. [25] Charles Taylor also argues that there is a so-called prepolitical aspect of national identity that is based on linguistic, cultural, or ethnic similarities. [26] National identity, and in that sense—ethnicity, usually implies that the ethnic group is biologically self-sufficient, shares fundamental values reflected in cultural practices. It has a pattern for communication and interaction, and membership that identifies itself as such, but it is also identified by others as a different category than other categories of the same order. [27]

For Max Weber, ethnic groups are groups of individuals that, by virtue of their similarity in appearance or customs or both or by the memory of colonization or migration, cultivate faith in a common origin so that faith becomes an important part of community formation. [28] Ernest Renan places the ethnic element in the

---

[23] Smith (1998).

[24] Smith (1998).

[25] Anderson (1998).

[26] Taylor (1994).

[27] Barth (1998), pp. 10–11.

[28] The term—ethnicities—was introduced into the French language to describe particular group solidarity, different from that produced by a political organization, and different from the anthropological similarity. For Max Weber, racial difference differs from ethnicity because is "really" based on a common origin, while ethnicity is based on a subjective belief in a common origin, Weber (1995).

sphere of the objective and in fate. Ethnicity is a combination of biological and cultural features, and it represents a community of blood, culture, and language. [29]

Opposite those perspectives, Fredrik Barth argues that there is no link between culture and ethnicity. For him, the rooting of ethnic identities in a prior cultural reality is highly variable since every ethnic culture is a patchwork of everything. [30] Ethnicity does not drive from the cultural content, and it is not even a mere expression of an existing culture. Ethnicity creation assumes a process of selection of cultural traits in which individual characteristics are placed in particular ethnic groups, or they serve as a ground for ethnic identification. [31] Similarly, Philippe Poutignat and Jocelyne Streiff-Fenart believe that ethnic groups are educated and are sustained through the process of historical sedimentation. Continuity with the past is continually established through creative processes. To add to that, numerous groups, which are today considered to be ethnic, even 100 years ago, lacked awareness of their shared identity. [32]

Despite the economic, environmental, and strategic opening of states, it seems that national identity is best nurtured in a small, relatively closed, and homogeneous framework in which there is not a desire nor a need to cross the circle. [33] Experience has shown that as state borders become more open, communities begin to set their boundaries to preserve their uniqueness. [34] The growing social and political forms of resistance against the *global* can take collective, ethnic, religious, and linguistic forms such as nostalgic and simple expressions of negation. [35] While the post-Cold War period is characterized by the explosion of identities, it is also characterized by the fact that virtually all self-determination requirements are joined with demands for secessions. Nations-states make it clear that minorities have no right to secession since secession means a violation of territorial integrity—guaranteed by the UN Charter—and also a violation of the doctrine of *uti possidetis juris*. [36]

11.3 Clash of Identities and Accommodation of Diversity

Cultural identities—lifestyles, attitudes, and behaviors—cannot be reduced through uniformity. It is more difficult to reconcile the elements that shape an individual as a social being and to identify the diverse features that create it. Above all, history,

---

[29] Renan (1882).

[30] Barth (1998).

[31] For Bart, neither the fact that the same language is spoken nor the unity of the territory nor the similarity of customs is in itself an ethnic attribute. They become such when those who refer to common descent use them as markers of affiliation, Barth (1998).

[32] Poutignat and Streiff-Fenart (2009).

[33] Tamir (2002).

[34] Walzer (1984).

[35] Baudrillard (1991).

[36] Cohen (1978).

tradition, memory, and culture are also contributing. Our era, in comparison to the preceding ones, has clearly emphasized the right of distinction: individual, national, cultural, linguistic, ethnic, or sexual. [37] The end of the twentieth century also brought changes to the general understanding of conflicts. Ethnic and religious conflicts are now regarded as conflicts of identity. They are usually longer, more complicated, and more difficult to resolve than conflicts over resources as most of them occur in close-knit communities that share a history of violence, hostility, and casualties. [38] In times of conflict, leaders legitimize their discourse by mobilizing the symbolic order established in their cultural traditions [39] Clearly, in the process of mobilization, religious norms, myths, and legends of the cultural group are often manipulated to dehumanize the opponent and justify aggression. [40] To resolve the conflicts, there is a need to identify values that promote peace and coexistence and include them in the model for conflict resolution. Additionally, it is necessary to strengthen local institutions that are committed to justice. [41] Challenges can come out from disagreements on the established mission and vision of the state and its ability to bridge those disagreements. This creates an opportunity for political actors to propose alternatives to the preestablished construct of the dominant identity. Therefore, through such a process of destabilization, a new political identity can emerge and become dominant, radically influencing previously elaborated understandings of the *other* and helping to remove the essence of the past conflict situation. [42]

Apart from finding ways to accommodate and integrate different groups into society in order to avoid the possibilities of secession and state disintegration, it is important to find new ways of dealing with the past, which is a necessary (but not sufficient) condition for building a constructive future. This is not an insignificant task, given that the identities of the parties involved in the conflict are also based on historical memories and victimization. Thus, the undertaken measures should relieve trauma and redefine the notion of the other, involving it within a collaborative, common system. [43]

Problems of identity and individuality are usually associated with the right of individuals and communities, as well as the duty of citizens and society. Understanding the differences and particularities is directly proportional to cultural achievements and the stages of this development. [44] Therefore, it is clear that diversity is an important issue of our time: nationalism; religious sectarianism; increased awareness of gender, race, and ethnicity; increased self-confidence in sexual

[37] Matvejević (2014).

[38] Kadayifci-Orellana (2006).

[39] Foucault (1972).

[40] For Weber the legitimacy based on tradition is the oldest and the most universal type of legitimacy, see more at Weber (1995).

[41] Kadayifci-Orellana (2006).

[42] Tan (2006).

[43] Sandole (2006).

[44] Matvejević (2014).

orientation; and the reemergence of religious language in the public sphere, are just a few of the forms of specialty that we face daily, under the general rubric of diversity. [45]

The process of globalization, *inter alia,* increased the spread of ideas about democracy and human rights, as well as the rights of minorities, which most often foster demands for secession in multiethnic states. The sought rights can generally be divided into rights for full and equal opportunities in society and rights to a special means to protect cultural identity. [46] In that respect, the states can respond timely and adequate through the means of society democratization and liberalization, such as introducing language rights, autonomy, federalism, and the like. In addition to this, the methods for maintaining the system include decentralization, financial subsidies to regions showing signs of discontent, and, finally, a carefully managed referendum that could divert the wind to a different direction, apart from that of the secessionists. [47] Contrary to this, historically, the most common response to secessionist movements is suppression, although with the development of the mass media, it is almost impossible to suppress a separatist movement without an external reaction. However, until three decades ago, it was normal for a state to become homogeneous by force, even at the cost of ethnic cleansing and assimilation. Although this was a trend before the Cold War, unfortunately, the trend remains in some parts of the World today.

Apart from suppression, there are several ways of integrating different groups into a nation-state. This can be individual "crossing" into the other group, joining groups, developing a positive definition, or reinforcing the positions of the group as a whole. The first two options are a form of assimilation and have proved to be inadequate solutions to ethnic problems. The third way, by emphasizing cultural superiority and refinement, enables groups to develop pride and reinforce ethnocentrism. The fourth way involves mobilization and politicization as a two-way process that can protect the group's identity and uniqueness. This includes proportional representation, disproportionate representation as a consensual model, role changing, nonterritorial autonomy, territorial autonomy, multinational or binational federation, confederation, and various forms of semi-independence or independence politics. [48]

---

[45] Macedo (2000).

[46] Regarding the size of the group claiming the rights, it is interesting to consider the different opinions in respect of the size of the group. For Kymlicka, as the group grows bigger it is becoming less vulnerable to possible loss of its culture and that makes it more difficult to justify the requirements for special state protection, see more at Kymlicka (1996); For Tamir, some of the collective rights are very difficult or almost impossible to be exercised by very small groups, hence the application of special measures, unjustified if the group is small, becomes justified when the group becomes larger, Tamir (2002).

[47] The people are afraid of uncertainty, and the demand for 40% or 50% of the entire electorate to support a change could strike a balance in favor of the *status quo*, Birch (1989).

[48] Heraclides (1991).

Hence, the policy chosen by the center is particularly important for conflict resolution. Still, the processes are not risk-free since for some minorities, it can mean a step closer to separation. On the other hand, denying such claims is no less risky since it holds the possibility of sacrificing democracy and human rights. It can contribute toward preserving state integrity but certainly not for long. For Will Kymlicka, when the demands for autonomy and self-government are already in place, the state has no choice but to try to accommodate them since their rejection on behalf of common citizenship will only promote alienation and intensify secessionist movements. Generally speaking, multiethnic states need to accept the risk, and the international community should encourage them to do so while at the same time discouraging secession attempts. In certain situations, where there is no other way out, both the international community and the multiethnic state in which the secessionist movement occurred need to accept secession as something that would have inevitably happened. [49]

Rein Mullerson observes that integration, the devolution of power, and the transfer of powers to supranational bodies such as the European Union, without much tension, contribute to resolving minority demands. Within decentralized states, minority issues related to culture, language, and religion can be addressed with lower state intervention. [50] The state should sustain a neutral legal framework all the way with decreasing its role of a direct growth facilitator, and increasing the one as partner and catalyst. [51] Therefore, as a result of the growing interdependence and frustrations, many groups demand greater government decentralization and focus more on local problems. [52] This localization can encompass various self-sustaining initiatives, such as small-scale initiatives in agriculture and local trade, participatory forms of local self-government, and the like, underpinned by cooperative and participatory logic. Since most of these initiatives can be based on the notion that culture, community, and the economy have their roots in specific geographic locations, in the long run, this can create emancipatory multiculturalism, i.e., a democratic form of rules for mutual recognition. This can also result in multiple community forms and, consequently, double, hybrid, as well as trans-identities. [53] Along the same line, the internal aspect of the right to self-determination can greatly enhance the protection of minority rights, improving chances for their integration without assimilation. [54] Cultural diversity creates a more interesting world, but at the same time, it offers us a chance to see and apply an alternative model for social

---

[49] Kymlicka (1996).

[50] Mullerson (2003), p. 158.

[51] World Development Report, The state in a changing world (1997).

[52] Alger (1982).

[53] De Soza Santos (2003).

[54] An adequate system of minority protection is a conglomeration of rules and mechanisms that enable the effective integration of relevant population groups while allowing them to maintain their separate characteristics. In other words, it is a system that allows integration without forced assimilation, i.e., it allows formal equality to be accompanied by true equality; see more at Henrard (2000).

organization. Although, the biggest benefit from minorities rights protection, have the minorities themselves. [55]

11.4 Multiculturalism

Multiculturalism tends to establish a change in human rights understanding, focusing on excluded, socially stigmatized, and marginalized groups striving for equality and a better social place in the exclusively set hierarchical structures. [56] Although the concept of human rights and liberal-democratic constitutionalism establish a reasonable framework for the abovementioned struggles, at some point in the theoretical development, liberalism moved opposite from multiculturalism. [57] For long, it has been considered that human rights can be realized through aspects of citizenship since it imposes a single, unified model of protection and belonging, but the ideas and policies of multiculturalism that emerged in the 1960s stem from the assumption that complex history inevitably generates group-differentiated and ethnopolitical demands, which cannot be addressed solely by citizenship aspects. The main idea of multiculturalism is not to suppress various demands but to filter and frame them within the language of human rights, civil liberties, and democratic accountability. Multiculturalism helps in developing new models of democratic citizenship, based on human rights ideals, to replace the undemocratic links of hierarchy and exclusion. Thus, within this political model, different minorities struggle for new forms of multicultural citizenship, combined with antidiscrimination measures and positive forms of recognition and accommodation. Precisely, multiculturalism is about constructing new civil and political relations to overcome deep-seated injustices that have existed since the abolition of formal discrimination. [58]

It is evident that people feel the best in their societal culture, that is, the one they belong to and whose practices and institutions create significant opportunities in a range of human activities, including public and private lives. This culture tends to be territorially concentrated and, in essence, is based on a common language. Some cosmopolites easily adapt from one culture to another; hence, abandoning one's own culture is quite possible, though most people are not prone to do so. [59] Cultural belonging is a core of identity and fitting and through it the individual forms his/her values. Culture provides options as well as the criteria by which those options can be assessed. [60] One of the most prominent theoretics of multiculturalism, Will Kymlicka, considers that the syntagma "one culture" is a synonym for "one nation"

---

[55] Kymlicka (1996).

[56] Kymlica (2012).

[57] Kymlicka (1996).

[58] Kymlica (2012).

[59] Rawls (2005).

[60] Tamir (2002), p. 22; Kymlicka (1996).

and symbolizes an integration community that is more or less institutionally complete, occupies territory, and has distinct language and history. Therefore, a state that has more than one nation is not a "nation-state" but a multinational state, while the smaller cultures within constitute national minorities. [61] Multicultural policies include cultural recognition, economic redistribution, and political participation. In that sense, multiculturalism is a deeply transformative project for minorities and majorities. It requires both the dominant groups and the historically subordinated ones to engage in new practices, enter into new relationships, and embrace new concepts and discourses of identity transformation. [62]

11.4.1 Democracy and Multiculturalism

Despite the undoubted benefits of democracy, especially in terms of promoting and protecting human rights, many authors find that in certain circumstances, democracy fosters demands and aspirations for independent statehood required by different subgroups. That is happening mostly in developing countries, or young democracies, where the stimulative environment for expressing different attitudes and opinions can cause conflicts and increase divisions among classes, interest groups, ethnic groups, or regions. In that respect, unlike class or economic groups, it is likely that at some stage of the conflict, ethnic and regional groups will seek a right to self-determination. Ethnic and regional groups perceive themselves more as whole societies, as social groups with a sufficiently complex division of labor, and that is raising greater ambitions for territorial sovereignty. Additionally, their shared cultural heritage further encourages such imagination. If more such groups exist within society, possibly more self-determination movements will emerge. [63]

Almost every modern democracy uses one or more mechanisms to respond to the demand of cultural groups for group-differentiated rights. A model for minority protection has been developed within the League of Nations. The model was not extremely successful in its implementation, but it offered universal individual rights and certain group-specific rights, such as the right to education, the right to local autonomy, and the right to use a mother tongue. The main idea was based on the following: a state may give the impression of "neutrality" toward different national groups, but it can (and often does) in certain ways systematically privilege the majority nation by setting internal boundaries; the use of the official language in schools, courts, and government institutions; the choice of public holidays; and the division of power between central and local governments. All of these decisions significantly reduce the political power and cultural representation of national minorities. Unlike the League of Nations, the issue of minority rights was left out of

---

[61] Kymlicka (1996).

[62] Kymlica (2012).

[63] Crawford (2006) and Mullerson (2003).

the UN agenda and was not included in the Charter because postwar statesmen were concerned about international peace and considered that the rights of national minorities were incompatible with the political unity that took precedence over them. According to the predominant liberal practice, minority rights were unjust and divisive. The majority had an interest in making the nation-state a secure place with stable institutions, even at the cost of destroying minority cultures by enforcing the homogenization of the population. [64]

In the current days, ethnic resurgence is a matter of self-identity and self-expression. People want to identify themselves as belonging to a particular ethnic group, while they desire others to see them as meaningful and respectful (for example, in politics, in the media, and in textbooks), that is, they seek increased recognition and visibility within the wider society. In liberal democracies, one of the key mechanisms for accepting cultural differences is the protection of individual civil and political rights. However, many countries accept modes through which certain forms of cultural differences ought to be protected beyond common citizenship rights through special legal or constitutional measures. These measures can be *group-specific rights, group-differentiated rights,* as well as *external safeguards.* [65]

Within democratic society exists also nonliberal cultures and practices or groups that reject liberal values and challenge liberal democracies. However, liberal values should not be imposed upon them. It is believed that genuine and continuous intercultural dialogues will influence nonliberal cultures through liberal values or the tendency for liberal expectations. [66] Thus, the relations between the majority and the minority must be determined through peaceful negotiations, at least for the basic social principles. [67] In that line, the question arises as to whether democracy, especially democracy in developing multicultural societies, can accommodate ethnic nationalism and level the differences. Though it looks ironic, the immediate effect of democracy and democratization over developing countries is encouraging national minority demands that can lead to nationalism. A well-institutionalized state has limits for such requirements that can help avoid major political problems. But if minority demands are not accommodated, then the feeling of exclusion and injustice can push the groups into more radical actions. Thus, though democracy in developing countries encourages ethnic conflicts, it also provides a framework for dealing with them. [68]

---

[64] Kymlicka (1996).

[65] *Group-specific rights* to education, local autonomy, and the use of language help to overcome the unfavoured position of minorities in respect of decision-making and allow the minority to maintain its own way of life. *Group-differentiated rig*hts or rights for special status for minority cultures should be a part of the theory of justice in a multicultural state. *External safeguards* include responses to the group's demands toward a wider society while protecting a particular ethnic or national group from the destabilizing influence of exclusive social decisions. These measures can be special parliamentary rights or territorial or linguistic rights, Kymlicka (1996).

[66] Kymlica (2009).

[67] Chupeska (2013).

[68] Kohli (2002), p. 314.

The obstacles to a successful functioning of democracy in multicultural societies can be real or anticipated and often come as security threats, weak state institutions, lack of liberal and democratic traditions in society, weak economies, traditions of discriminatory practice, isolation of the state, and the like. All of these obstacles are more pronounced in societies in transition, or emerging democracies, due to the complex circumstances, inexperience, or greed of the political elites to whom nationalism is a curtail tool for gaining and maintaining political power. [69] Therefore, it is certainly possible that democracy in multicultural societies can contribute to the survival of large and heterogeneous communities, but we must not oversee that institutional arrangements can produce different levels of satisfaction due to various historical, cultural, and psychological factors. [70] In any case, to deal with the reality of politics, political arrangements should address the needs of different citizens through various forms of cooperation, protection, power sharing, and control. [71]

11.4.2 Building Multicultural Society

From all incorporated cultures within a society, national minorities often tend to remain separate societies within the majority culture and seek different forms of autonomy or self-management to ensure their distinctiveness. Unlike them, ethnic groups are looser groups that have emerged as a result of individual or family migration and have easily integrated into the wider society as its full members. They do not strive to become a separate and autonomous nation (as is the case with national minorities) but force institutions and laws to be more responsive to existing cultural differences. [72] Ethnic groups are more segregated and mixed. [73] National minorities are much more opposed to integration and look for ways to protect their authentic existence and strengthen their societal cultures. Ethnic groups lack the institutional cement needed to create and maintain an authentic social culture, and that is why national minorities, unlike ethnic groups, often have group-differentiated rights in the territory, in language, and in representation. [74] The challenge of multiculturalism is to embrace national and ethnic differences. [75] Examples from recent history suggest that national identities should, to some extent, be understood as given. Although the character of identity may change, identity itself, the feeling of being a separate national culture, is very stable. [76]

---

[69] Frckoski Lj (2012).

[70] Cronin (1989).

[71] Santiago Nino (1998).

[72] Kymlicka (1996).

[73] Glazer (1983).

[74] Kymlicka (1996).

[75] Gutmann (1993).

[76] Kymlicka (1996).

However, the multinational state should not deny its citizens the opportunity to perceive themselves as one nation. Multinational states cannot survive unless the different national groups are attached to the larger political community to which they belong. [77] Therefore, there is a great need to perceive connective elements that will give stability to the multinational state. It is not possible in general to determine exactly what they are, but the assumption is that they may be some shared values, such as faith in equality and fairness, consultation and dialogue, support for diversity, tolerance, compassion, generosity, commitment to freedom, peace and nonviolent changes, etc. [78] The idea of shared identity can be constructed through the acceptance of existing national identities. [79] According to Jürgen Habermas, except the respect for differences, multiculturalism requires a shared culture. [80] To achieve this, the majority culture must come out of fusion with the general political culture. But the bonding force of the common political culture must remain strong enough to protect the state from collapse. Besides, members of all cultural groups must find a common political language and common codes of conduct to be able to participate effectively in the mutual political arena. [81] Different subgroups need to have a stake in resource utilization. The lack of local investment and economic projects can lead to isolation and a sense of irrelevance for those living in local areas. Besides, a well-established market-oriented economy is essential to enable free and fair trade, protect property rights, and promote market values. [82]

The networking of multicultural societies in a wider security and economic integration is particularly important for the success of the multicultural policies. That can contribute to mitigating cultural conflicts. One way of networking is establishing *pan-nationalism*. *Pan-nationalism* can be defined as a movement for the unification of several states, usually adjacent, into a cultural and political community based on shared cultural characteristics or on families of cultures. The significance of pan-nationalisms is that they can be counterbalanced or can be suggested as an alternative to the divisive tendencies of everlasting ethnic nationalisms. The reappearance of *lingua franca*, recognizing common regional problems, especially in the environmental field, and the frequent closeness of social and political customs and institutions—including basic political values—are some of the processes that can create a context for the amortization of cultural differences in a broader context. [83]

Nevertheless, despite the initial success and due to the complexity of multicultural projects, certain attempts to adopt new models of multicultural citizenship within certain communities failed to take root. In the last 20 years, we have been

[77] Taylor (1994).

[78] Citizen's Forum on Canada Future (1991).

[79] Taylor (1994).

[80] Habermas (1998).

[81] Miller (1989).

[82] Frckoski Lj (2012).

[83] Smith (1998).

witnessing a regressive trend in multiculturalism. Though it is early for judgments and recommendations, Kymlikca considers that there are a few factors contributing to this trend. One of them is states' fear of their survival in geopolitical terms (though maybe unjustified, especially with the establishment of the North Atlantic Treaty Organization (NATO) or the EU), and the second one is the individual fear of being subjected to minority self-governing institutions or the emergence of islands of local tyranny within a wider democratic state. [84] Also, multinational, multilingual democracies have a set of issues that are difficult to be articulated through the language of democracy. Many of these questions stem from the fact that in those countries, there is more than one self that requires greater self-esteem and self-control. While in some countries it is possible to weave one identity from different identities, such as in the United States or Australia (most often from the identities of immigrants), it is only a dream for states that have historically based ethnocultural groups. [85]

11.4.2.1 Multicultural Policies

With all the shortcomings, the ideal of multiculturalism should remain an important option that is worth the consideration of policymakers. [86] Some grounds help root the multicultural policies, and one of them is the policy of inclusiveness. Following this, the policy making process should include, on equal basis all citizens whose interests are conflicted may be affected in the decision-making process. Besides providing greater control over the government, inclusive policies allow hearing the voices of those who are often ignored in the decision-making process. The policies of inclusion only work if the democratic process is the product of rules that, to the maximum possible extent, ensure participation in the discussion of those directly affected by the discussion. They can secure participants' freedom to express themselves, the equality of conditions under which the obligations are implemented, the justification of the proposals, moral debates instead of a pure presentation of interests, the opportunity to change decisions, and the like. The stakeholder's involvement in the decision-making process is one of the most problematic issues. [87] In that respect, decentralization helps in enabling direct democracy (as an aspect of deliberative democracy) and ensures the involvement in the political process of those whose interests are at stake.

Another important factor for building a multicultural society is maintaining a legal order or designing a constitutional framework and safeguards. If there are one or more communities in a multinational state, the constitution must reflect and recognize national pluralism while providing concrete measures for self-government.

---

[84] Kymlica (2012).

[85] Norman (2003).

[86] Kymlica (2012).

[87] Santiago Nino (1998).

The principles of partnership (of groups or communities, not just of equal citizens), territorial autonomy, recognition, and special representation should be taken into account. All of this must be translated into institutional mechanisms that will contribute to confidence building, as well as through the establishment of a neutral administration. [88]

A particular interest is the political promotion of the identities. National culture is not the product of (one) nation alone. [89] If people's links to their languages and cultures are strong enough, then attempts to suppress cultural identity and demands for self-management can only increase the level of alienation and division. Since there is no way to establish complete separation between the state and ethnicity (authorities' decisions on languages, internal borders, public holidays, and state symbols inevitably involve recognizing, accepting, and supporting the identities of certain specific ethnic and national groups), it is important to secure the safeguards for all groups. Protecting one's cultural background has consequences for groups of people and their different interests. The equality argument supports introducing special rights for national minorities to cure the assumed disadvantage, though the legitimate scope of those rights varies according to the circumstances. Thus, every society should provide an opportunity for all national groups to sustain themselves as separate cultures. Additionally, the viability of minority societal cultures may be shaken by the economic and political decisions taken by the majority, resource-related, or actual policy issues. Therefore, accepting differences is the essence of true equality. [90]

References

Alger CF (1982) Participation of local communities in building future worlds. In: Strassoldo R, Delli Zotti G (eds) Cooperation and conflict in border areas. Franco Angeli Editore, pp 273–308

Anderson B (1998) Замислени заедници (Imagined communities). Kultura, Skopje

Avishai M, Raz J (1990) National self-determination. J Philos (87):439–461

Barth F (1998) Ethnic groups and boundaries: the social organization of culture difference. Waveland Press

Baudrillard J (1991) Nasilje globalnog (The violence of the global). https://journals.uvic.ca/index.php/ctheory/article/view/14558/5403. Accessed 16 Aug 2022

Birch HA (1989) Nationalism and national integration. Unwin Hyman Ltd.

Buchheit LC (1978) Secession, the legitimacy of self-determination. Yale University Press, New Haven

Chupeska A (2013) The cultural identities in the politics: multicultural aspects (Културните идентитети во политиката: аспекти на мултикултурализмот). Foundation Conrad Adenauer

Citizen's Forum on Canada Future, Report to People and Government of Canada, Ottawa: Supply and Services (1991). https://caid.ca/SpicerCom1991.pdf. Accessed 26 Sept 2022

Cohen R (1978) Ethnicity: problem and focus in anthropology. Annu Rev Anthropol 7:379–403

[88] Santiago Nino (1998).

[89] Matvejević (2014).

[90] Kymlicka (1996).

Crawford J (2006) The creation of states in international law. Oxford University Press
Cronin TE (1989) Direct democracy: the politics of initiative, referendum and recall. Cambridge University Press
De Soza Santos B (2003) The processes of the globalization. Revista Crítica De Ciências Sociais. https://www.eurozine.com/the-processes-of-globalisation/
Deng FM (2002) Self-determination and national identity crisis: the case of Sudan. In: Danspeckgruber W (ed) Self-determination of peoples, community, nation and state in interdependent world. Lynne Rienner Publishers, pp 253–287
Foucault M (1972) Archaeology of knowledge and discourse on language. Pantheon Books
Frckoski Lj D (2012) Negotiations in conflict of identities, Magor
Giordano C (2001) Ogledi o interkulturnoj komunikacii (Reviews about intercultural communication). Biblioteka XX vek, Beograd
Glazer N (1983) Ethnic dilemmas. Harvard University Press, Cambridge
Gutmann A (1993) The challenge of multiculturalism to political affairs. Philos Public Aff 22(3):171–206
Habermas J (1994) Struggles for recognition in the democratic constitutional state. In: Gutmann A (ed) Multiculturalism, examining the politics of recognition. Princeton University Press, pp 107–149
Habermas J (1998) The inclusion of the other. Cambridge
Henrard K (2000) Devising an adequate system of minority protection. Kluwer Law International, Hague
Heraclides A (1991) The self-determination of the minorities in the international politics. Frank Cass and Company Limited
Kadayifci-Orellana SA (2006) Islamic tradition of nonviolence: a hermeneutical approach. In: Rothbart D, Korostelina KV (eds) Identity, morality and threat: studies in violent conflict. Lexington Books, pp 211–241
Kohli A (2002) Can democracies accommodate ethnic nationalism? The rise and decline of self-determination movements in India. In: Danspeckgruber W (ed) Self-determination of peoples, community, nation and state in interdependent world. Lynne Rienner Publishers, pp 287–315
Kymlica W (2012) Multiculturalism, success, failure and the future. Queen's University, Transatlantic Council of Migration
Kymlicka W (1996) Multicultural citizenship: a liberal theory of minority rights. Clarendon Press
Kymlicka W (2000) From enlightenment cosmopolitanism to liberal nationalism. In: Kymlicka W (ed) Politics in the vernacular: nationalism, multiculturalism, and citizenship. Oxford University Press, pp 203–220
Macedo S (2000) Diversity and distrust: civic education in a multicultural democracy. Harvard University Press, Cambridge
Matvejević P (2014) Nacionalnost postaje važnijom od humanosti (Nationality becomes more important than humanity). Autograf. hr. https://www.autograf.hr/predrag-matvejevic-nacionalnost-postaje-vaznijom-od-humanosti/. Accessed 26 Sept 2022
Miller D (1989) In what sense must socialism be communitarian? Soc Philos Policy 6(2):51
Mullerson R (2003) Sovereignty and secession: then and now, here and there. In: Dahliz J (ed) Conflict avoidance and - regional appraisals. Asser Press, pp 125–167
Norman W (2003) Domesticating secession. In: Macedo S, Buchanan A (eds) Secession and self-determination. New York University Press, pp 193–237
Poutignat P, Streiff-Fenart J (2009) Teorije o etnicitetu (Theories of ethnicity) Biblioteka XX vek, Beograd
Rawls J (2005) Political liberalism. Columbia University Press
Renan E (1882) Qu'est –ce qu'une nation? Conférence en Sorbonne. http://www.iheal.univ-paris3.fr/sites/www.iheal.univ-paris3.fr/files/Renan_-_Qu_est-ce_qu_une_Nation.pdf. Accessed 07 Aug 2022
Rothbart D, Korostelina KV (2006) Moral denigration of the other. In: Rothbart D, Korostelina KV (eds) Identity, morality and threat: studies in violent conflict. Lexington Books, pp 29–59

Sandole DJ (2006) Identity under siege. In: Rothbart D, Korostelina KV (eds) Identity, morality and threat, studies in violent conflict. Lexington Books, pp 59–101
Santiago Nino C (1998) The constitution of deliberative democracy. Yale University Press
Smith AD (1998) Nationalni identitet (National identity). Biblioteka XX vek, Beograd
Tamir Y (2002) Liberalni nacionalizam (Liberal nationalism). Filip Visnjic, Beograd
Tan L (2006) From incorporation to disengagement: East Timor and Indonesian identities, 1975–1999. In: Rothbart D, Korostelina KV (eds) Identity, morality and threat, studies in violent conflict. Lexington Books, pp 177–211
Taylor C (1994) The politics of recognition. In: Gutmann A (ed) Multiculturalism, examining the politics of recognition. Princeton University Press, pp 25–75
Walzer M (1984) Spheres of justice: a defense of pluralism and equality. Basic Books
Walzer M (1994) Comment. In: Gutmann A (ed) Multiculturalism, examining the politics of recognition. Princeton University Press, pp 99–105
Waterbury J (2002) Avoiding the iron cage of legislated communal identity. In: Danspeckgruber W (ed) Self-determination of peoples, community, nation and state in interdependent world. Lynne Rienner Publishers, pp 119–165
Weber M (1995) Economie et societe, vol 1. les categories de la sociologie. Pocket
Wolf S (1994) Comment. In: Gutmann A (ed) Multiculturalism, examining the politics of recognition. Princeton University Press, pp 75–87
World Development Report 1997: The state in a changing world. The World Bank, Oxford University Press. https://openknowledge.worldbank.org/handle/10986/5980. Accessed 27 Sept 2022
Young C (1979) The politics of cultural pluralism. University of Wisconsin Press
Kymlica W (2009) Multicultural odysseys: navigation the internal politics of diversity. Oxford University Press

Chapter 12
Tools and Forms for the Realization of Internal Self-Determination: Systems of Power Sharing

12.1 Introduction

When the parties in complicated conflicts, especially in societies divided by deep ethnic, racial, or religious differences, find themselves incapable of coming out of the conflict or if they could not find a compromise, they can invoke the power-sharing system as a potential solution. The power-sharing system is a system of government in which all major segments of society are provided with a permanent distribution of power, and this system often stands against the system—the government *vs* the opposition—in which the ruling coalitions composed of different social groups, from time to time, rotate on the political scene. Most often, power-sharing systems are realized through large government coalitions in which almost all political parties participate, the protection of minority rights, the decentralization of power, and the establishment of a consensus as a model for decision-making. [1] For a long time, there was a misconception that there is a single formula for the division of power, called *consociationalism*. The elements of this power-sharing approach are well known: large coalitions, proportionality, partial autonomy or federalism, and a mutual veto. Yet this prototype of power sharing is nothing but a form of a very wide range of political options that can help in dealing with internal conflicts. The essence of political options can be extremely different, in terms of the goals, structures, and effects they produce in promoting mediation and compromise between groups, and the goal is to make the political participation of different minority groups/segments in national policy decisions most optimal. Hence, some of the common power-sharing options are autonomy, group building block approach, and group building integration approach. [2]

[1] Sisk (2003).

[2] Sisk (2003).

N. Shikova, *Self-Determination and Secession*,
https://doi.org/10.1007/978-3-031-34322-3_12

Group Building Block Approach

This approach is based on the accommodation of ethnic group leaders in the political center and the autonomy and minority rights of the group. In essence, this approach is consensual because it encourages collaborative decision-making by the parties involved in the conflict. Its key elements are federalism, the devolution of power to the ethnic groups, a minority veto on topics that are of particular importance to the ethnic groups in question, large coalition cabinets within the parliamentary framework, and proportionality in all spheres of public life.

Group Building Integration Approach

In contrast, the integration approach represents ethnic groups as part of a common society. This approach includes options that aim to establish society integration across dividing lines. It can be called "centripetalism" because it tries to create a central direction of political dynamics. The elements of an integrative approach include an electoral system that encourages preelection pacts across ethnic lines, nonethnic federalism, and public policies that promote political alliances that transcend the groups. [3]

Some suggest that the integrative division of power is superior in theory because it seeks to strengthen ethnic adjustment by promoting mutual interests. Others argue that the use of incentives to promote reconciliation will not work in practice, at the very moment when it faces deeper hostilities fueled by larger ethnic differences, which become even stronger during brutal civil wars. [4] However, it is important to stress that power-sharing options can complement each other in countless ways. Power-sharing solutions always create temporary solutions, but in the long run, the best that can emerge is a more fluid form of democracy that allows the creation of flexible coalitions to bridge ethnic divisions. [5] The set of principles that are part of power-sharing can be summarized as the necessity of participation of all groups, the establishment of a high level of autonomy for all significant groups, proportionality in management between the groups, and the right to veto, which minorities must have concerning matters they consider are important for them. [6]

These principles can be functional as long as they suggest solutions within a democratic framework and within existing units. But is it always possible for this to happen in political practice? First of all, who defines or who decides which are the important groups, and will they be named and legally accepted once they are defined? Specific groups are guaranteed autonomy because, at a given political moment, they are judged to be significant and able to prolong and maintain that moment as much as possible. Thus, sometimes it appears that the call for a flexible identity is analytically comforting, but in practice, it is unrealistic until the "significant groups" are first legally defined as such, and sometimes this can lead to

[3] Sisk (2003).

[4] The creator of this political model is Arend Lijphart. See more in Lijphart (1980, 1999).

[5] Sisk (2003).

[6] Lijphart (1980, 1999).

complete paralysis of the state apparatus. [7] Hence, if possible, the categorization of things should be avoided. The legal frame should be flexible enough to allow groups to organize themselves across ethnic or sectoral lines. The system should not provide rewards or incentives for organizing political participation along ethnic or sectoral lines; just the opposite broad inter-ethnic and cross-linguistic coalitions must be constructed. [8]

12.2 Consociationalism

Consociational democracy seeks to maximize the participation of various factors in the sharing and exercise of political power. The consociational model is characterized by inclusion, negotiation, and compromise, and according to many authors and practitioners, it contributes to the stability of multicultural societies. This is very important for societies deeply divided on cultural grounds, where a strict majority rule is inappropriate for society as a whole, so the majority norm can very easily turn into a tyranny of the majority. The system of consociational democracy, established by political scientist Arend Lijphart and further developed by Professor Eric Nordlinger, seems static, elitist, and based on unequal representation, but it is the most realistic way to deal with problems in culturally divided societies and supposes that states can be stable if they provide a basis for the cooperation of elites coming from different cultural and social segments. To explain the benefits of consociational democracy, Lijphart starts from the basic definition of democracy as the government of the people, or in a representative democracy, the elected government is composed of the representatives of the people. At the heart of this question is the dilemma—who will govern, and to whose interests the government should be responsive when people are different and have different preferences? One answer is that the interests of the majority should come first, and this is a typical form of a majoritarian model of democracy. An alternative answer would be that the government should be responsive to the interests of as many people as possible, and that is the essence of the consensus model. This model of consociational democracy accepts only the majority rule as the minimum needed. Its rules and institutions aim at broad government participation and broad agreement about the policies that the government should pursue. The model of consociational democracy supposes the following:

- The division of executive power between broad multiparty coalitions
- Executive-legislative balance of power
- A multiparty system
- Proportional representation

[7] Waterbury (2002).

[8] Waterbury (2002).

- Corporate systems of interest groups (whereas corporatism means the ideology of social partnership and consultation in the decision-making process with the leaders of different interest groups and with different organizations);
- A federal and decentralized government
- Strong bicameralism (power is divided equally between two differently constituted chambers)
- Constitutional rigidity;
- Judicial review and assessment (to protect the rigid constitution)
- Independence of the central bank. [9]

Although consociational democracy is a model that contributes to national integration, many note that it does not promote a single and effective leadership, coherent policies, and quick decision-making. However, according to its proponents, quick and sharp decisions are not always wise. On the contrary, they consider that policies supported by a broad consensus are much easier to be successfully implemented in comparison to the policies imposed by influential leaders and contrary to the wishes of society.

There is no doubt that consociational democracy produces good results, but in the long run, not only in terms of accommodating differences but also in terms of the general progress of society. Consociational democracy makes plural societies even more plural, and the main idea of this approach is not to abolish or weaken the divisions but to explicitly recognize and turn them into constructive elements of stable democracies. [10] Often, consociational democracy is considered to be the best solution for ethnically mixed societies. However, the elements of this type of democracy can be applied, such as mutual veto, autonomy, accommodation by the elite of ethnic groups in the political center, etc. (all of them or a combination of them). The choice depends on political circumstances. Nonetheless, for the integration of plural societies, a certain level of autonomy and division of power is needed, as well as other democratic means that need to be in place, together with the forms of recognition and forms of accepting the existing differences. [11] It is important how the constitutional arrangements that establish and ensure consociational democracy are implemented in practice since there can be obstacles in reaching the goal, such as institutional and cultural traditions. In that sense, consociational democracies may not be able to take root if they are not supported by a consociational political culture. [12] Hence, the model of consociational democracy can have benefits, although it is often criticized for lacking a democratic opposition (namely, if everyone is at the center, then there is no opposition) and for its inability to be applied in countries where divisions are sharp. Ultimately, it is a system that is appealing to the minority but not to the majority, and although many countries adopt it, they are very few that can fully practice it, especially concerning the creation of large coalitions and the

[9] Lijphart (1971, 1999).

[10] Lijphart (1999), p. 42.

[11] Mullerson (2003).

[12] Lijphart (1971, 1999).

use of minority vetoes. [13] There are many reasons why governments dislike consociational democracy, and among other things, it is because power-sharing engagements are expensive, time-consuming, and energy-intensive, but for a modern democratic state faced with ethnic differences and tensions, there are fewer alternatives. [14]

12.3 Autonomy

The need to protect individual and group interests in relation to a much more powerful society can grow into a problem (due to many different factors), but the solution usually is introducing greater political autonomy for a certain segment of society. Group-differentiated rights to autonomy are compensation for the unequal conditions that place members of minority cultures in a position of systematic discrimination, regardless of their personal choices in life. It is one of the many areas in which true equality requires not an identical treatment but differential treatment in order to address differential needs. [15] As a model for internal self-determination, autonomy supports the identities of population groups, and its essential element guarantees certain rights to specific segments of a country's population based on their characteristics, by which they differ from the majority population. [16] Autonomy underlines the right of the community to determine the conditions of its existence, to establish its own government in accordance with its principles and ideas for certain purposes, and to decide about its legislation without any outside intervention. [17] Autonomous regions are regions of a state in which a population that lives usually possesses some ethnic or cultural differences and an internal administration to which (to some extent) a separate power is guaranteed. Autonomy does not only comprise rights that protect from formal discrimination but also implies the preservation of cultural, linguistic, and other values, whereas a significant level of power is transferred from the center to geographically, linguistically, or ethnically based regions. [18]

Demands for autonomy are based on the need to enact certain rights to a group, which sees those rights as fundamental to its survival. In a situation of existing confrontation among the separate groups and the ethno-nation-state, one of the solutions can be imposing cultural assimilation. That is (at least from the point of view of the minority concerned) contradictory to the core values of self-determination. Another option is the adoption of forms of autonomy and the recognition of the national and cultural identity of the minority, but this cannot be satisfactory for the

[13] Horowitz (2003).

[14] Mullerson (2003).

[15] Kymlicka (1996).

[16] Henrard (2000), pp. 297–314.

[17] Nincic (1970) and Osterland (1993).

[18] Hannum (1990).

realization of the full potential of self-determination, especially for those members of the minority who are scattered throughout the country. Still, in most multinational states, groups that require some form of political autonomy ask for territorial jurisdiction in order to ensure the full and free development of their own cultures. Thus, autonomy usually takes the form of a transfer of political power to the political unit that is largely controlled by members of a national minority. Although each situation is unique, demands for autonomy often involve initiatives to address key issues related to language; education; access to government public service, including the police and security forces; social service requirements; requirements for natural resources; establishment of representative local government structures; and the like. [19] Consequently, autonomy is not considered a temporary measure nor a cure for repression, which can and should be eliminated, but the mentioned initiatives are related to rights that are considered "inherent," i.e., permanent. [20]

In the saying of Immanuel Kant, autonomy is an ethical imperative for the individual, a principle of his being, not just a political ideal to be invoked in dangerous times. For Fichte, Schlegel, and other German Romantics, the ideal of autonomy should be connected with the groups, not with the individuals; hence, the roots of the political philosophy of national self-determination should probably be sought there. According to this line of thinking, autonomy allows the nation and its members to achieve authentic self-realization. [21] Hence, the right to national self-determination can be fully realized only if the national group is an autonomous source of human activity and creativity, recognized by both members and nonmembers of the group, but also if this recognition is accompanied by political engagements that allow members to develop their national life with as little external interference as possible. [22] Autonomy is a way to reconcile self-determination with territorial integrity because the right to autonomy includes the right of minorities and indigenous communities to exercise significant internal self-determination and control over their own affairs in a way that is not inconsistent with state sovereignty. [23] Limited autonomy, on the other hand, without secession for groups that are territorially defined or determined by common ethnic, religious, and linguistic ties, within the autonomous areas of confederations, is one of the special forms of the right to self-determination. [24]

Therefore, at least from a theoretical standing, autonomy is a model capable of satisfying the aspirations of a particular ethnic group while at the same time protecting the territorial integrity and sovereignty of the state, but one of the key questions is whether every group can claim such a "right." [25] Some authors link the possible

[19] Cassese (1995), p. 364.

[20] Kymlicka (1996).

[21] Smith (1998).

[22] Tamir (2002).

[23] Kiss (1986) and Cassese (1995).

[24] Henrard (2000).

[25] Musgrave (2000).

"right to autonomy" with the size of the group, meaning the larger is the group that should benefit from a particular policy, the greater can be the burden that can justifiably be imposed on others. [26] As an opposite opinion, there are authors who believe that size does not play a role because all nations should eventually have an equal right to autonomy. [27] This is important to mention since the basic premise on which groups claim their rights to autonomy is not simply that they are disadvantaged in the political community but that there is more than one political community, so the authority of the wider community cannot be assumed. In other words, the groups (national minorities) claim that there is more than one nation, with its own right to rule on its own. [28]

Following the above, it can be noted that equating internal self-determination with autonomy has a theoretical appeal, opposite to the much more problematic external application of the right to self-determination. [29] However, in practice, autonomy is not always the best middle ground between self-determination and territorial integrity. More specifically, states are prone to preserving political unity and do not show a general willingness to support internal division. [30] Therefore, although there is no theoretical barrier to the interpretation of autonomy as part of the right to self-determination, the real, practical support for it is thin and finds no basis in positive international law. [31] Autonomy can lead to a kind of dual citizenship. Demands for autonomy reflect a desire to weaken ties with the wider community, and they question its authority and stability. Additionally, many consider that there seems to be no natural point in stopping the increased demands for autonomy, so if limited autonomy is allowed, it is unlikely that it will spur the ambitions of nationalist leaders who would be content with nothing but their own nation-state. Hence, nation-states that recognize the right to autonomy appear to be inherently unstable. [32] On today's world map, there are several autonomous arrangements that secure minority rights and regional devolution (such as Basque Country, Catalonia, South Tyrol, Nunavut, and Tatarstan), which are followed by a guarantee from the central government, but still, they are revocable. Autonomy has been recommended in cases such as the Aaland Islands; it was also included in the 1995 Dayton Accords on Bosnia and Herzegovina, and this option was offered in the cases of Sudan, [33] North

[26] Raz (1988).

[27] Tamir (2002).

[28] Kymlicka (1996).

[29] Summers (2007).

[30] Steiner (1991) and Henrard (2000).

[31] The most important international instrument in relation to this issue is the non-binding OSCE document from Copenhagen from 1990, which noted that autonomy is one of the ways to ensure the rights of minorities, but at thc same time stressed that such a statement does not create obligations for states, i.e., the document has more political rather than legal force, Document of the Copenhagen meeting of the Conference on the human dimension of CSCE/OSCE, 1990.

[32] Kymlicka (1996).

[33] See more at Security Council support for the Comprehensive Peace Agreement between the Government of Sudan and the Sudan People's Liberation Movement/Army in SC Res. 1590 (2005).

Macedonia, [34] Abkhazia, and Georgia; it was also part of the request for an autonomous UN administration in Kosovo. However, all these recommendations are seen not as authorization of the right to autonomy arising from self-determination but as recommendations and good practices for accommodating differences between groups within the existing countries. [35] However, the authors consider that although it may appear as a Gordian knot, still it is pragmatic to guarantee these forms of internal self-determination in the hope that such a guarantor will thwart demands for secession. [36]

12.3.1 *Autonomy as a Political Tool*

The right to internal self-determination is usually guaranteed through forms of territorial autonomy. Autonomy is a political tool that provides adequate addressing of the needs and rights of groups. The form of autonomy needs to be directly linked to specific goals, though achieving "autonomy" alone does not guarantee the development or protection of an endangered culture since conflicts and tensions are inherent in any society. One of the documents that guarantee autonomy is the 1990 OSCE Copenhagen Document, which in Article 35 stipulates:

> The participating States will respect the right of persons belonging to national minorities to effective participation in public affairs, including participation in the affairs relating to the protection and promotion of the identity of such minorities. The participating States note the efforts undertaken to protect and create conditions for the promotion of the ethnic, cultural, linguistic and religious identity of certain national minorities by establishing, as one of the possible means to achieve these aims, appropriate local or autonomous administrations corresponding to the specific historical and territorial circumstances of such minorities and in accordance with the policies of the State concerned. [37]

In the quoted paragraph of this legally nonbinding document, autonomy is not set as a right, but still, it is proposed as a way for the accommodation of national minorities. Stronger encouragement for territorial autonomy contains the Recommendation 1201 of the Parliamentary Assembly of the Council of Europe, whereas in Article 11 the right to territorial autonomy is recognized, stipulating that in the regions where the persons belonging to national minorities are in a majority, they shall have the right to have at their disposal appropriate local or autonomous authorities or to have a special status, that matches the specific historical and territorial situation and by the domestic legislation of the state. [38] Although this is a recommendation, not a

---

[34] See more at Council Endorsement of the Framework Agreement at Skopje, 13 August 2001 in SC Res. 1371 (2001).

[35] Summers (2007).

[36] Kymlicka (1996).

[37] Document of the Copenhagen meeting of the Conference on the human dimension of CSCE, 1990.

[38] Recommendation 1201, on an additional protocol on the rights of national minorities to the European Convention on Human Rights Council of Europe Parliamentary Assembly, 1993,

legally binding document, still, it is important since it indicates that these European organizations give great support to territorial autonomy. However, the Framework Convention for the Protection of National Minorities, adopted within the Council of Europe several years later (in 1994), avoids any reference to territorial autonomy. Not only is territorial autonomy not set as a right, but it is not even mentioned as a principle. [39]

According to international human rights norms, the fundamental obligation of the state is to eliminate discrimination, not to destroy differences. The success of autonomy depends largely on the awareness of the groups since legal or procedural techniques do not guarantee the outcome. [40] Issues of language, education, access to public services, territory, natural resources, and local government can also be resolved on an *ad hoc* basis. Additionally, various forms of administrative decentralization may offer solutions to grievances concerning geographical or economic marginalization. However, the government must consider any demands for autonomy [41] and must try to separate ethno-cultural peculiarities from the state as a political entity. [42]

12.3.2 Territorial Autonomy

Territorial basis and linguistic rights are essential for the protection of the culture of the groups. The size of the territory that is directly related to the expansion of the population, or the exploitation of national resources, is perhaps the most common desire of groups. However, there is no specific land law mentioned in any major human rights instrument, perhaps precisely because it reflects the desire of states to maintain absolute control over their territory. The territory is a literal and figurative basis for the state as well as for any community with aspirations for political autonomy. The broad spectrum of autonomous power presupposes a sufficiently large minority population, concentrated in and/or isolated from the dominant society, in such a way that autonomous territory would be viable. Territorial control is also essential for the creation of normal bodies of local or regional government and can be important in terms of economic development. But the symbolic aspect of control over one's own "homeland" is the primary motivation underlying the claim over the autonomous territory. [43]

Equating territorial integrity with a unitary or centralized form of government is likely to be a government camouflage to hide the unwillingness to share political

---

article 11.

[39] Framework Convention for the Protection of National Minorities, Strasbourg, 1995.

[40] Fisher (1978).

[41] Hannum (1990).

[42] Cassese (1995).

[43] Hannum (1990).

power. The demands for secession and geographical disintegration are a much more powerful symbol around which the group's support is organized than the "threat" of administrative decentralization, the local control of power, and even the regional transfer of power. Territory can be seen as the primary guarantor of two fundamental human needs—identity and security. Territory or country as identifying forces are very complex concepts, so it is difficult to distinguish between the sociopolitical organization that controls the territory on the one hand and the territory itself on the other. It can also be noted that the psychological connection between the people and their ancestors' land is often underestimated, especially by those who are the product of modern, cosmopolitan, and essentially landless cultures. [44] Apart from the territorial basis, the creation of *representative government structures* is fundamental to the demands for autonomy, although, especially in small states, effective representation at the state or national level may be a more important goal. International law has no restrictions on the internal constitutional arrangements of any state. However, it does not necessarily mean that greater autonomy will be necessary and better, and this is relevant both from the perspective of the entity and from the perspective of the state. However, a "fully autonomous" territory can be expected to have the following political powers:

(a) A locally elected legislature with some independent legislative authority, limited by a constitutional document—local competencies generally include control and influence over primary and secondary education, the use of language, the structure of local government, and land use and planning.
(b) A locally elected head of the executive—but he or she may be subject to approval by the central government and may be responsible for enforcing local and national laws.
(c) An independent judiciary with full responsibility for interpreting local laws.
(d) Areas of mutual concern may be subject to power-sharing arrangements between autonomous and central governments so that local flexibility will be allowed through the broad political parameters established by the central government. Joint authority is often exercised over issues related to ports and communication opportunities, the police and the exploitation of national resources, etc. [45]

12.3.2.1 Basque Country Internal Division: Autonomy or Independence

With a total population of just under three million, the first thing most people associate with the Spanish Basque region is the Euskadi Ta Askatasuna (ETA) [46] and its violent resistance against Spain. This area—the Autonomous Community of the

[44] Hannum (1990).

[45] Hannum (1990).

[46] ETA (Euskadi Ta Askatasuna—"Basque Country and Freedom") started as an idea that evolved into a violent movement and, ultimately, into a political party.

Basque Country and Navarra Community [47]—enjoys the highest level of self-government compared to any other entity that is part of a state in the EU; nevertheless, political confrontations regarding the region's scope of autonomy are still part of everyday life. Throughout the centuries, the Basque Country has succeeded in protecting features of its special identity, and today, a large part of the population shares a collective consciousness and wishes for self-government, emulating past forms of Spanish political framework, such as absolute monarchy, the first and second Spanish Republic, and today's parliamentary monarchy. The Basque Country has succeeded in having separate fiscal systems and its own provincial parliaments. Tensions concerning the exact form of the relationship between the Basque Country and Spain have existed since Spain's founding. [48] In the contemporary period, the introduction of regional autonomy contributed to the democratization of Spain. Spain is a parliamentary monarchy, and the Spanish Constitution of 1978 (the Constitution) [49] guarantees regional autonomy. [50]

The Constitution reflects the unitary character of Spain as an indivisible country for all Spanish people. According to the Constitution, Castilian is the official language of Spain, along with the other Spanish languages that are also official in the autonomous communities. The Constitution also provides for an economic balance between different areas of the Spanish territory. According to the Constitution, the autonomous regions are established by autonomy statutes, approved by the Spanish Parliament. The autonomy statutes also regulate the jurisdiction of the autonomous regions, although, in cases of conflict, the law of the Spanish state prevails. In all other cases, Spanish state law is supplementary to the law of the autonomous regions. The constitutionality of the autonomous unit is controlled by the state Constitutional Tribunal. [51]

The Constitution established a system of divided power and determined areas where the central government retains exclusive jurisdiction, such as immigration,

---

[47] Although the term Basque Country is traditionally used to refer to the geographical area from both sides of the Pyrenees, which extends between the frontier between the territories of Spain and France, the Basque Country is referred to in government documents as the Basque provinces in Spain, the Basque Autonomy region. Currently, the historical and cultural area of the Basque Country is divided into three political structures: two in Spain, the Autonomous Community of the Basque Country, composed of three Basque provinces (Alava, Guipúzcoa, and Vizcaya), and the Community of Navarra, which have their own administrative structures, while the third province, which is significantly smaller and composed of three municipalities, is in France and does not have its own structure.

[48] Espiau Idoiaga (2006).

[49] The Spanish Constitution was formally approved by a national referendum, and Spain became a democratic state that guaranteed the protection of the nationalities and regions within their borders and historic rights. But despite these safeguards, the Constitution did not fully satisfy the Basque nationalists, given that they did not sufficiently participate in political decision-making. As a result, 55.4% of the Basque Country electorate abstained from voting, Espiau Idoiaga (2006).

[50] See more at Constitution of Spain, 1978, articles 1, 2, 3, 137–139, 143–158, Additional Provision 1.

[51] Constitution of Spain (1978).

foreign affairs, national defense and army, execution of justice, customs and labor penal legislation, international trade, monetary regulations, coordination of the general economic planning, intellectual property, and the basic conditions that guarantee the realization of rights of all Spaniards and the fulfillment of their constitutional obligations. Everything else is in the jurisdiction of the local government and is governed by the Statute of Autonomy. [52] The Basque Autonomy Statute (the Statute),[53] also referred to as the Statute of Autonomy of Guernica, established the autonomy of Basque community in the Basque Country. The Statute was adopted in 1979 by the Basque people through a referendum. [54] It established the basic institutional arrangements and is a part of the Spanish legal system. The Autonomous Community geographically covers Basque's historical territories, which extend into four Spanish provinces. According to the principle of autonomy guaranteed by the Constitution and by the Statute, the Autonomous Community of the Basque Country (the Autonomous Community) has its own flag, which is officially recognized. The language of the Basque people, Euskara, [55] alongside Spanish, is considered an official language and is promoted and protected. Discrimination based on language is prohibited. [56]

According to the Statute, the Autonomous Community enjoys broad autonomy and, in many areas, has an exclusive jurisdiction and its own public sector. In addition to the areas where the Autonomous Community has exclusive jurisdiction, the Basque Country has the authority to develop legislation within a basic state legislation framework. In certain areas, however, the legislation of the Spanish state applies, particularly in the area of labor relationships, airports, and other areas that are of special interest to the Spanish Country. Except for the rules on the establishment, organization, and function of institutions (such as the Parliament of the Basque Country (the Basque Parliament), the government, and the President of the Basque Country), the Statute ensures a functional division of power and requires common bodies able to determine the competencies of institutional mediators in a dispute between competitive institutions. The relationship between the Autonomous Community and the state is regulated by economic agreements that determine how large a percentage of tax revenue collected within the Autonomous Community's jurisdiction, and other incomes, need to be passed on to Spain in the form of quotas based on the principle of solidarity. [57] The autonomous Basque region enjoys a wide

[52] Constitution of Spain (1978).

[53] Statute of Autonomy of the Basque Country, Organic Law (Ley Orgánica) 3/1979, 18.12.1979.

[54] 53% of the population of the Basque Community voted on the referendum for acceptance of the Autonomous Statute, while 41% abstained, Espiau Idoiaga (2006).

[55] The Basques are a very old culture, and they believe that they are one of the original European cultures. The Basque language is one of the few languages in Europe that does not have Indo-European roots. It is incredibly complicated, and its concentration in the Basque Country makes it a basic identity symbol for the Basque people. See more in Spencer and Croucher (2008).

[56] See more in the Constitution of Spain (1978).

[57] Statute of Autonomy of the Basque Country, Organic Law (Ley Orgánica) 3/1979.

autonomy; still, the state of Spain retains a large portion of the power. [58] For example, in the case of a dispute between national and local laws, national law prevails, even though national law is technically intended to supplement the law of the autonomous regions. In the same way, if an autonomous region fails to meet its obligations under the Constitution and relevant laws or acts in a manner that violates the general interests of Spain, an absolute majority of the Senate—in which the provinces and autonomous regions are represented—may take the necessary measures to ensure compliance. If necessary, Parliament also has the power—with an absolute majority in each house—to harmonize regional legislation with the general interest, even in areas that are part of exclusive regional competence. [59]

Despite its autonomy arrangements, the Basque people have been divided as to the region's degree of autonomy since the founding of the Spanish state. Some citizens are satisfied with the scope of autonomy, and some advocate for its increase, but a large part of the population aims to achieve independence for the Basque Country. The support for autonomy varies during different time periods and with differing intensity and radicalism. Due to the diversity and division of the political environment in the Basque Country, there are no uniqueness connections even among similar movements. [60] Some political parties have advocated for the territorial integrity of the Spanish state and a federal autonomous status for the Basque Country, while others—primarily the ETA—advocate for secession, independence, and the uniting of the Basque Country with the three Basque provinces in France. [61] In order to achieve a change in the Statute by legal and political means and methods, as opposed to radicalism, the Basque Parliament, in 2004, supported a proposal—known as Plan Ibarretxe—for a new statute based on "free association" and "shared sovereignty" with Spain. [62] This plan sought to expand the autonomy of the region and also determine the possibility of eventual independence. The Spanish Parliament challenged the proposal as an act that was outside of the constitutional limits for regional autonomy and overwhelmingly refused it. [63]

[58] Hannum (1990).

[59] See more in the Constitution of Spain (1978).

[60] See more in Ruiz Vieytez (2013), pp. 79–105.

[61] Basque nationalism in France is supported by a very small group. Only a few rural municipalities are led by Basque nationalists, and the movement has no significant political representation at the regional level. The Basque language does not have the status of an official language. Basque separate identity is reflected through the recognition of Basque culture and language within the institutional framework of France. It is interesting to note that in the French Basque Country where the political framework provides relatively few opportunities for the political expression of a separate identity, most of the people do not see the Basque identity as active and potentially innovative, in contrast to the much more dynamic environment in Spain. See Bray (2012).

[62] The plan carries the name of the President of the Basque Government, who submitted it to the Basque Parliament in 2002 and defended it in front of the Spanish Parliament in 2005 as a new political pact for coexistence; see Fundación para la Libertad, Internet source.

[63] Shikova (2016), pp. 237–264.

12.3.3 Nonterritorial Autonomy

Nonterritorial autonomy (NTA) is considered to be a statecraft tool or policy instrument applied in ethno-culturally diverse states. [64] The literature about NTA does not point toward many common features of all applied NTAs, but a thoughtful analysis of the seminal works clarifies that NTA can be used for the representation of non-dominant groups. NTA can enhance the group's ability to self-governance over matters that are relevant for the group members. Developed by Otto Bauer and Karl Renner at the beginning of the nineteenth century and meant to address the issues related to the (at that time) eventual dissolution of the Austro-Hungarian Empire, NTA assumes national-cultural nonterritorial autonomy that resides in the "personality principle." [65] Contextual information about NTA arrangements is related to the description of the institutions, their functionality, and the legal frame that is protecting them (i.e., according to scholars, personal cultural autonomy does not exist without self-regulating institutions). The initial Renner approach envisages that self-rule is the preferred option in the sphere of cultural and educational affairs, where the consociational institutions should manage the central affairs, such as security and foreign policy. [66] In that sense, traditionally, NTA includes a mixture of different arrangements, such as consociationalism and national-cultural autonomy (NCA), and also forms of representation that deterritorialize self-determination. [67]

NTA arrangements serve the best in cases when minorities or beneficiaries are dispersed among the majority population, and there is no possibility for applying territorial autonomy. In that sense, the implementation of NTA models can be a practical solution, i.e., NTA can be extended if territorial autonomy arrangements are not applicable. [68] But that can stand even if territorial autonomy cannot be applicable due to various political factors and power balances and not only because of demographic and territorial reasons. However, in most cases, the concentrated groups will favor territorial autonomy in comparison to NTA because territorial autonomy will give a territorial basis for the management of their affairs. On the other side, territorial autonomy is often perceived as a step toward secession and the interruption of state territorial integrity and, as such, is not a much-preferred approach. [69] From that aspect, NTA has certain advantages in comparison to territorial autonomy since it enforces the personality principle and sets the rights upon it, not over the territorial principle as the territorial autonomy does. [70] NTA's applicability relies on a subjective definition of nationhood (the criteria for nationhood is the feeling toward, belonging to, or an attachment to one's particular national

[64] Salat (2015).

[65] Nimni (2000).

[66] Nimni (2005).

[67] Nimni (2015).

[68] Lapidoth (1997).

[69] Kymlicka (1996).

[70] Lapidoth (1997).

community). In that sense, national cultural autonomy is understood as a form of autonomy where the nonmajority population can establish a representative body without a territorial limitation and can carry out cultural or other activities relevant to minority groups either on a national or on a local level. [71] In some cases, those models serve to prevent territorial claims [72] that are considered to be more radical or to somehow neutralize them. [73]

Scholars distinguish between a voice, quasi-voice, and nonvoice of NTA institutions concerning their ability to ensure the participation of ethno-cultural groups in the decision-making process. [74] Concerning the reaching of desired outcomes—ensuring participation and self-rule—it cannot be overlooked that, in many cases, NTA institutions inherently lack competences, capacity, and financial stability. In many cases, the institutions are providing only symbolic representation, and when it comes to decision-making, they only secure participation in the decision-making or decision-making in mainly administrative issues (for example, election and the appointment of management boards). In that line, it is obvious that NTA institutions, in many cases, carry solely consultative functions (not independent decision-making), or at the utmost possibility, they secure codecision powers. In that regard, NTA arrangements are considered to carry weaker powers than territorial autonomy arrangements. Although NTA institutions can act as policymakers, in most cases, they failed to gain a position of serious partners to central governments. Consequently, from the public law viewpoint and in comparison to territorial autonomy arrangements, NTA has a limited range of functions. [75]

Nonetheless, irrespective of the related benefits and the envisaged constraints, both territorial autonomy and NTA arrangements are not mutually exclusive and can be applied simultaneously. [76]

12.3.3.1 The Example of NTA: The Hungarian Model of Minority Self-Governments

The provisions for cultural autonomy are contained in the Act on the Rights of Nationalities of Hungary (2011), which recognizes NTA as a form of *cultural autonomy*. [77] National-cultural autonomy is established as a collective right embodied in the independence of the institutions and the self-governance of national communities. A *national cultural institution* is an institution whose duty is to preserve and make accessible the material, spiritual, and cultural values and assets associated

[71] Vizi (2015).

[72] Smith (2013b) and Vizi (2015).

[73] Korhecz (2015), Smith (2013a, b), and Tomaselli (2016).

[74] Malloy et al. (2015).

[75] Korhecz (2015).

[76] Lapidoth (1997).

[77] Act on the Rights of Nationalities of Hungary (2011).

with the identity of a nationality and to preserve, practice, popularize, and pass on to future generations traditions and the communal use of language. *National cultural institutions* include (a) institutions of cultural heritage (serving to preserve, maintain, develop, and introduce spiritual and cultural heritage and cultural traditions), (b) public collections fulfilling national responsibilities (libraries, archives, museums, or archives of images or sound recordings), and (c) national communal events (operated on the basis of a cultural heritage agreement to provide cultural services as regular or *ad hoc* cultural heritage activities).

According to the Hungarian Constitution, [78] Hungary is an ethnonational state in which the nationalities living with the dominant group of the population (Hungarians) form part of the political community and are recognized as constituent parts of the state. In Hungary, fundamental rights are exercised by individuals and communities. [79] On the individual level, every Hungarian citizen of any nationality has the right to freely express and preserve their identity. On the collective level, nationalities have the right to use their native languages, to be educated in them, to use individual and collective names in their languages, and to promote their own cultures. Hungary has a relatively homogeneous population where the minorities (nationalities) form 6.5% of the total population. [80] Minority populations are dispersed, which makes territorial autonomy an infeasible option. [81] However, 13 ethnic nationalities present in historical communities—established in Hungary for the past 100 years—are afforded minority status and enjoy rights based on the use of national languages under Article 22 of the Act on the Rights of Nationalities of Hungary.[82]

Nationalities have the right to establish local and national self-governments, where the election rules and procedures are regulated by separate, cardinal acts. [83] Such rights are granted in the Act on the Rights of Nationalities, which has the status of a cardinal act and aims to put into effect the principles set within the fundamental law (Hungarian Constitution). Based on Articles 2 and 3 of the Act, nationalities can enjoy national-cultural autonomy, realized as self-governance. Minority self-governments (MSGs) are established in settlements where nationalities live, and being part of a minority is an individual determination. MSGs are partners with local and central authorities and have rights to consultation and agreement in matters concerning education, the use of language, and culture. Moreover, MSGs enjoy functional and financial autonomy in the establishment, running, and management of educational and cultural institutions. [84] Local MSGs are connected at the regional and national levels. At the national level, MSGs can veto not only proposals concerning cultural, educational, or language issues but also the

[78] Hungarian Constitution, 2012.

[79] Vizi (2015).

[80] N.b. According to the official data from Census 2011, Nationality data.

[81] Dobos (2016).

[82] Act on the Rights of Nationalities of Hungary (2011), art. 22.

[83] Hungarian Const., 2011, art. 29.

[84] Advisory Committee, 2010.

appointment of leaders to minority institutions. Furthermore, they can give their opinion on draft laws concerning minority communities, monitor minority education, and participate in the development of minority primary education curricula. [85]

12.4 Decentralization and Subsidiarity

Some theorists believe that decentralization will help national minorities meet their needs. However, decentralization meets the demands of national minorities only if it increases the group's capacity for self-government, which in turn depends on many factors, including how borders are delineated and how powers are distributed. Autonomy, as a model for power sharing, does not require general decentralization but only necessitates the explicit recognition of national groups by securing language rights, territorial rights, and the asymmetric distribution of political decision-making powers and by redrawing political boundaries. [86]

Subsidiarity is a link between different levels of government. It is the decentralization, devolution, and distribution of power from the central authorities to the local and municipal authorities. Subsidiarity enables the issues to be addressed to the lowest possible level, and presupposes the executive and legislative bodies to accept the decision-making process that includes the people, i.e., those to whom the decisions refer. [87] To implement the concept of self-determination based on process (process-oriented concept), primarily as a functional, and not as an elementary, concept of state sovereignty, [88] it is necessary to apply the principle of subsidiarity. The application of that principle maximizes self-determination, regardless of whether it is individual or collective self-determination, by transferring decision-making powers to the smallest effective individual capable of dealing with social problems. Subsidiarity is linked to individual autonomy and collective government, and the application of the principle of goodwill can address many demands for autonomy and self-governance while reducing the importance of territory as a basis for governance. Subsidiarity can also help to neutralize secession requirements. [89] Although criticized by those who advocate more centralized leadership and oppose the devolution of power, subsidiarity still seems to offer a sophisticated legal mechanism that can be used to avoid nationalist tensions through devolution in areas relevant to cultural identity and through support for the central government on other political and economic issues. [90]

[85] See more Shikova (2021).

[86] Kymlicka (1996).

[87] Danspeckgruber (2002).

[88] Cassese (1995).

[89] Shelton (2003), p. 68.

[90] Kohli (2002).

References

Act on the Rights of Nationalities of Hungary (2011)

Advisory Committee on the Framework Convention for the Protection of National Minorities (2010) Third opinion on Hungary

Bray Z (2012) Basque nationalism at a political crossroads. World Politics Review. https://www.worldpoliticsreview.com/basque-nationalism-at-a-political-crossroads/. Accessed 14 Aug 2022

Cassese A (1995) Self-determination of the peoples, a legal reappraisal. Cambridge University Press

Constitution of Spain (1978)

Council Endorsement of the Framework Agreement at Skopje, 13 August 2001 in SC Res. 1371 (2001)

Danspeckgruber FW (2002) Self-determination and regionalization in contemporary Europe. In: Danspeckgruber W (ed) Self-determination of peoples, community, nation and state in interdependent world. Lynne Rienner Publishers, pp 351–352

Dobos B (2016) The minority self-governments in Hungary. Autonomy arrangements in the world. http://www.world-autonomies.info/ntas/hun/Pages/default.aspx. Accessed 3 Oct 2022

Document of the Copenhagen meeting of the Conference on the human dimension of CSCE/OSCE (1990)

Espiau Idoiaga G (2006) The Basque conflict, new ideas and prospect for peace. United States Institute for Peace. https://www.usip.org/publications/2006/04/basque-conflict-new-ideas-and-prospects-peace. Accessed 14 Aug 2022

Fisher R (1978) Points of choice. Oxford University Press, Oxford

Framework Convention for the Protection of National Minorities, Strasbourg (1995)

Hannum H (1990) Autonomy, sovereignty, and self-determination, the accommodation of conflict rights. University of Pennsylvania Press

Henrard K (2000) Devising an adequate system of minority protection. Kluwer Law International, Hague

Horowitz DL (2003) The cracked foundations of the right to secede. J Democr 14(2):5–17

Hungarian Constitution, 2012

Kiss A (1986) The peoples' right to self-determination. Hum Rights Law J 7:165–174

Kohli A (2002) Can democracies accommodate ethnic nationalism? The rise and decline of self-determination movements in India. In: Danspeckgruber W (ed) Self-determination of peoples, community, nation and state in interdependent world. Lynne Rienner Publishers, pp 287–315

Korhecz T (2015) National Minority Councils in Serbia. In: Malloy TH, Osipov A, Vizi B (eds) Managing diversity through non-territorial autonomy: assessing advantages, deficiencies and risks. Oxford University Press, pp 69–91

Kymlicka W (1996) Multicultural citizenship: a liberal theory of minority rights. Clarendon Press

Lapidoth R (1997) Autonomy: flexible solutions to ethnic conflicts. United States Institute of Peace Press, Washington

Lijphart A (1971) Consociational democracy. World Polit, xxi

Lijphart A (1980) Democracy in plural societies: a comparative exploration. Yale University Press

Lijphart A (1999) Patterns of democracy, government forms and performance in thirty-six countries. Yale University Press

Malloy TH, Osipov A, Vizi B (eds) (2015) Managing diversity through non-territorial autonomy: assessing advantages, deficiencies and risks. Oxford University Press

Mullerson R (2003) Sovereignty and secession: then and now, here and there. In: Dahliz J (ed) Conflict avoidance and - regional appraisals. Asser Press, pp 125–167

Musgrave TM (2000) Self-determination and national minorities. Oxford University Press

Nimni E (ed) (2000) The question of nationalities and social democracy: Otto Bauer. University of Minnesota Press, Minneapolis

Nimni E (ed) (2005) National cultural autonomy and its contemporary critics. Routledge, London

Nimni E (2015) Minorities and the limits of liberal democracy and non-territorial autonomy. In: Malloy TH, Palermo F (eds) Minority accommodation through territorial and non-territorial autonomy. Oxford University Press, pp 57–82

Nincic D (1970) The problem of sovereignty in the charter and in the practice of the United Nations. Martinus Nijhoff

Osterland HA (1993) National self-determination and secession: the Slovak model. Case Wes Reserve J Int Law 25(3):655–702

Raz J (1988) Morality of freedom. University of Oxford

Recommendation 1201, on an additional protocol on the rights of national minorities to the European Convention on Human Rights Council of Europe Parliamentary Assembly (1993)

Ruiz Vieytez E (2013) A new political status for the Basque country? J Ethnopolit Minority Issues Europe 12(2):79–105

Salat L (2015) Conclusion. In: Malloy TH, Palermo F (eds) Minority accommodation through territorial and non-territorial autonomy. Oxford University Press

Security Council support for the Comprehensive Peace Agreement between the Government of Sudan and the Sudan People's Liberation Movement/Army in SC Res. 1590 (2005)

Shelton D (2003) Self-determination and secession: the jurisprudence of the international human rights tribunals. In: Dahliz J (ed) Conflict avoidance and - regional appraisals. Asser Press, pp 47–75

Shikova N (2016) Practicing internal self-determination vis-a-vis vital quests for secession. German Law J 17(2):237–264

Shikova N (2021) The normative base for non-territorial autonomy – a comparative legal overview. In: Vizi B et al (eds) Non-territorial autonomy as an instrument for effective participation of minorities. Centre for Social Sciences, University American College Skopje, Budapest, pp 25–39

Sisk TD (2003) Power sharing. The beyond intractability knowledge base project. https://www.beyondintractability.org/essay/power_sharing. Accessed 3 Oct 2022

Smith AD (1998) Nationalni identitet (National Identity). Biblioteka XX vek. Beograd

Smith D (2013a) Challenges of non-territorial autonomy in contemporary Central and Eastern Europe. In: Nimni E et al (eds) The challenge of non-territorial autonomy: theory and practice. Peter Lang, Oxford, pp 117–132

Smith D (2013b) Non-territorial autonomy and political community in contemporary Central and Eastern Europe. J Ethnopolit Minority Issues Europe 12(1):27–55

Spencer AT, Croucher SM (2008) Basque nationalism and the spiral of silence: an analysis of public perceptions of ETA in Spain and France. Int Commun Gazette 70(2):137–153

Statute of Autonomy of the Basque Country, Organic Law (Ley Orgánica) 3/1979

Steiner HJ (1991) Ideals and counter-ideals in the struggle over autonomy regimes for minorities. Notre Dame Law Rev 66(5):1539–1560

Summers J (2007) Peoples and international law, how nationalism and self-determination shape a contemporary law of nations. Leiden, Boston

Tamir Y (2002) Liberalni nacionalizam (Liberal nationalism). Filip Visnjic, Beograd

Tomaselli A (2016) Indigenous people and their right to political participation. Nomos, Baden-Baden

Vizi B (2015) Minority self-governments in Hungary. In: Malloy TH, Osipov A, Vizi B (eds) Managing diversity through non-territorial autonomy: assessing advantages, deficiencies and risks. Oxford University Press, pp 31–52

Waterbury J (2002) Avoiding the iron cage of legislated communal identity. In: Danspeckgruber W (ed) Self-determination of peoples, community, nation and state in interdependent world. Lynne Rienner Publishers, pp 119–165

Chapter 13
Tools and Forms for the Realization of Internal Self-Determination: *Access and Integration*

13.1 Political Participation

The right to political participation first appeared in the multilateral instruments that followed World War II. These instruments dealt with human rights and guaranteed the right to political participation so that the states parties were primarily required to hold fair elections at regular intervals. During this period, the UN began to monitor elections and plebiscites in the colonial territories and the newly independent states. [1] The right to participate in the government of a state, as expressed in Article 21 of the Universal Declaration of Human Rights and Article 25 of the International Covenant on Civil and Political Rights (ICCPR), contains three broad guarantees relevant to this issue, namely, nondiscrimination, the right to take part in public affairs, and the right to free elections. It proclaims that every citizen shall have the right and opportunity, without any distinction and without unreasonable restrictions, to take part in the conduct of public affairs, directly or through freely chosen representatives; to vote and be elected at genuine periodic elections, which shall be done by means of universal and equal suffrage and be held through secret ballots, guaranteeing the free expression of the will of the electors; and to have access, on general terms of equality, to public service in his country. [2] In many ways, the right to participation reflects the "internal" aspect of self-determination and is a fundamental right for both political democracy and economic development. The additional standards in relation to this issue are set in the following instruments:

- *The First Protocol to the European Convention on Human Rights*: it does not contain provisions on participation rights, but Article 3 provides for the holding of free elections by secret ballot at reasonable intervals. The protocol is narrower

[1] Fox (2000).

[2] UNGA Res. 2200 A (XXI) The International Covenant on Civil and Political Rights, art. 25, (1966).

N. Shikova, *Self-Determination and Secession*,
https://doi.org/10.1007/978-3-031-34322-3_13

in its scope in comparison to Article 25 of the International Covenant on Civil and Political Rights (ICCPR) since it does not call for the holding of general elections, does not prohibit discrimination, and does not mention equal access to public service. [3]
- *The American Convention on Human Rights*: it is explicitly taken from Article 25 of the ICCPR, with only minor differences. [4]

Other regional instruments guaranteeing the right to participation are as follows:

- *The African Charter on Human and Peoples' Rights*, in its Article 13, guarantees such a right, but it lacks specific standards regarding elections, discrimination, universal suffrage, and secret ballots, so its usefulness is unclear. [5]
- The Organization for Security and Co-operation in Europe (OSCE) documents contain very detailed provisions on the right to participation, namely, the *Helsinki Final Act*; *the Copenhagen Document*, which contains a set of requirements concerning the electoral systems of states, as well as standards for the observation of election; the *Charter of Paris*, which provides for the establishment of an institutional structure for the observation of election, such as the Office for Free Elections; the *Document from Moscow*, which calls for the nonrecognition of the election result by the other member states if the government is established against the will of the people.

Concerning the regional instruments focusing on the right to participation, it is important to mention that the dissolution of the Socialist Federal Republic of Yugoslavia (SFRY) raised fears for the further undermining of peace and prosperity, especially among countries transitioning to democracy. As a follow-up to the Charter of Paris for a New Europe (1990), the Organization for Security and Co-operation in Europe (OSCE), in its Helsinki Decisions (1992), established the High Commissioner on National Minorities (HCNM), with the task to ensure the prevention of ethnic and minority conflicts at the earliest possible stage. Within its activity, the HCNM identified certain recurrent issues in a number of OECD states, such as issues on minority education, the use of minority languages, and other aspects that are relevant to the maintenance and development of minority identities. In addition to these themes, attention was drawn to proposing forms of effective participation of the national minorities in the governance of states. Following these considerations, the group of internationally recognized independent experts conceived certain recommendations and alternatives—in line with relevant international standards, commonly known as the Lund Recommendations on the Effective Participation of National Minorities in Public Life (Lund Recommendations), with

[3] Protocol 1 to the European Convention for the Protection of Human Rights and Fundamental Freedoms (1952).

[4] American Convention on Human Rights (1969).

[5] The African Charter on Human and Peoples' Rights (1979).

a view to achieving appropriate and coherent application of relevant minority rights in the OSCE area. [6]

On the UN level, the need for public participation was first discussed in the context of the need to consult those directly affected by national development plans (generally those living in rural areas). [7] However, the political aspects of public participation were later recognized, [8] and several international texts of different legal nature contain elements of public participation, and some of these texts go so far as proclaiming a global right to public participation. Among those elements of public participation, recognized internationally, are the right to self-determination, the right to education, the right to participate in cultural life, the rights of minorities, the rights of unions, family rights, the right to association and peaceful assembly, and freedom of thought, conscience, religion, expression, and information. A broader definition of public participation may include the involvement of citizens in public affairs with full respect for human rights without any discrimination. [9]

States have the right and duty to formulate appropriate national policies that aim at the continuous improvement of the well-being of the entire population and all individuals based on their active, free, and significant participation in the development and fair distribution of the resulting benefits. States should encourage public participation in all areas as an important factor for the development and full realization of human rights. Although the right to universal participation *per se* is not yet enshrined in universal human rights instruments, the essential components of the right to effective participation in the political and economic decision-making processes of government are guaranteed through related rights and freedoms. If a certain segment of society is constantly excluded from any share in economic or political life, then alternative goals may be needed to ensure participation. If there is a constant denial of the chances for participation, then the group that is denied such chances can ultimately invoke the principle of self-determination to secure significant participation in the society in which they live. [10]

13.1.1 Holding Free and Fair Elections

According to the principle of equal rights and self-determination of peoples, all nations have the right to decide their future, to choose different forms of government, to set political goals, and to construct their systems without direct or indirect

[6] The Lund Recommendations on the Effective Participation of National Minorities in Public Life (1999).

[7] United Nations, Popular participation in Decision Making for Development, UN Sales No. E 75. IV.10 (1975); id., Popular Participation as a strategy for promoting community level and national development, UN sales No. E 81.IV.2 (1981).

[8] Comm. On Human Rights Res. 1983/14, UN Doc. E/1983/13, E/CN. 4/1983/60 (1983).

[9] Hannum (1990).

[10] Hannum (1990).

or internal or external pressure. Free and fair elections must be held to achieve a truly representative government as an essence of internal self-determination. An overview of global and regional systems shows that for free, fair, and legal elections (as an element of the right to self-determination and a way to exercise the right to a representative government), four general elements need to be met: (1) universal and equal voting rights (2) secret ballots (3) elections at reasonable intervals, and (4) nondiscrimination against voters, candidates, or parties.

The instruments dealing with the issue of political participation have grown into customary law; however, additional practice by states is needed in terms of their fulfillment, where the international community secures that the state acts in the interest of all its citizens. But despite the arguments in favor of the right to political participation and the right to have a representative government, there are still theoretical and practical obstacles to the justification of this idea. If the idea is accepted that the Western form of government is the only proper form of representative government, then the decisions are made by the voice of the majority, which means that the interests of the minority are often overshadowed. In addition, states have developed various techniques for manipulating this process, such as one involving eligibility—manipulating voters or excluding the ones that the government does not want to vote or forced displacement of the population, which can take various forms, from ethnic cleansing to the assassination of potential voters—ballot fraud (i.e., allowing voters to vote more than once); destroying ballot boxes; and threatening those who plan not to vote or to vote in a certain way, despite the constant emphasis on the importance of having free and fair elections. [11]

One of the mechanisms to enforce political participation rights is the monitoring of national elections. Although this was not a common practice before the end of the Cold War, recently the UN progressed in that direction as well as in the effort to establish open and democratic governments in the world. In some cases, the elections they observed were a comprehensive effort to rebuild societies recovering from long civil wars, that is, they were part of postconflict peace building; in other cases, democracy was seen as a goal—to abandon an authoritarian regime. But despite the active role of the UN in monitoring these processes, many nations around the world are still deprived of the opportunity to participate in genuine, fair, and free elections and to elect a truly representative government. Finally, even if those nations overcome the above obstacles, it is uncertain, nor is there any guarantee, that the elected government will act according to the will of the people. [12]

[11] Fox (2000).

[12] Cristescu (1981), p. 51; Moris (1998).

13.2 Special Rights of Representation

In Western democracies, there is a growing concern that the political process is unrepresentative, that is, that it fails to express the diversity of the population. An insufficient representation of historically disadvantaged groups is a general phenomenon. One way to reform this situation is for political parties to become more inclusive and to reduce the barriers that prevent women, ethnic minorities, and the poor from becoming candidates or party leaders. Another way is to accept proportional representation, which has been proven to enable the greater involvement of the candidates. Some believe that redrawing the boundaries of constituencies will ensure that inadequate representation is overcome, but this is a very limited mechanism because it does not help groups that are territorially dispersed. [13]

Hence, the government, faced with a dissatisfied minority, has many different ways to deal with dissatisfaction to protect the stability of the political system and ensure a larger representation of the minority and a greater representation of the group. The representation can appear in many different forms, such as the following:

- Symbolic representation: when flags and anthems reflect the existence of minorities in a national society
- Functional representation: when minorities appoint representatives to government agencies or organize pressure groups to provide access to the ones that make political decisions
- Electoral representation: when the electoral system enables minority interests to be articulated in the legislature
- Microcosmic representation: when minorities are reflected in proportion to their number in public service staff [14]

On the road to a society in which the need for special representation no longer exists, the rights of special representation are often seen as a temporary measure. However, special representation sometimes occurs as a result of autonomy, and the consequence of that is the existence of guaranteed representation for anybody that has the authority to interpret or change the domains of autonomy. Since the autonomy encompasses the rights that are considered to be "inherent" i.e., permanent, such are the representation rights. [15] These rights aim to overcome the ethnic imbalance in the political and social sphere. The proposed political arrangements, though imperfect, may help in avoiding options for secession. Nevertheless, the functionality of all models depends on the satisfaction of certain conditions, and in that frame, a basic precondition is the establishment and promotion of a democratic form of government.

[13] Kymlicka (1996).

[14] Birch (1989).

[15] Kymlicka (1996).

13.2.1 Employment in the Public Service

Discrimination, implemented or tolerated by the state in the field of employment, is the most visible manifestation of one of the most divisive factors in the relations between the minority and the majority. It is best to see the state as an independent arbiter in fundamental government policies. If the minority is deliberately excluded from the decision-making process at the administrative level, then its members can conclude that the political process is also fraught with prejudice. The apparent prejudice regarding the provision of government services is a general cause of ethnic resistance, so when a highly centralized government is represented ethnically or culturally in a different region through "newcomers," local sentiment is likely to surface. In such situations, some form of privileged policy seems to be needed to encourage the employment of local people. In such a situation, the freedom of expression and association and the application of the principles of nondiscrimination may not prevent the machinery of a group-dominated state, but their violation will certainly provoke conflict. If conflict and violence escalate, then discrimination by central authorities is likely to intensify because minority members will be seen as potentially disloyal. Minorities are usually underrepresented in the police and security forces, so reducing their numbers in these structures during a crisis, from a minority point of view, only strengthens the image of the state security forces as an ethnic or sectoral army, not an independent arbitrator of law. On the other hand, as the conflict escalates, minority extremists see members of their group who continue to work for the state as traitors to the minority cause. Imbalances in the state administration, employment, and security forces complicate a situation that can be resolved with neutral police. Ethnic imbalance and mistrust are often reflected in the demand for autonomous or regional control over the local police, and sometimes with demands for some local control over the security forces in the autonomous region. [16]

13.3 Control over Natural Resources

Control over natural resources is a complex issue, often more related to the history of greed than to the preservation of culture and the acquisition of certain rights in the traditional sense of the word. But, of course, the control of natural resources is a source of frequent conflicts between local/regional communities and central authorities, even when state identity is strong. Natural resource problems are rarely deeper social antagonisms that can lead to demands for autonomy. Certain state projects on how to control natural resources can lead to isolation and a sense of irrelevance among the inhabitants of a certain area. Therefore, there is a need for local input in-state economic development projects and greater public participation

[16] Hannum (1990).

in the decision-making process. [17] When it comes to indigenous peoples, states have a responsibility to protect the rights of the indigenous people in the context of natural resources, and they need to establish a "regulatory framework that recognizes indigenous peoples' rights over lands and natural resources" since they are a *sine qua non* for their well-being and a precondition for continuing to exist as a distinct people. The states have a duty to consult and to obtain their free, prior, and informed consent for investment projects ongoing on their traditional territories. The related international standards have to be applied and the state responsibilities, except from the UN Declaration on the rights of indigenous peoples, [18] are coming as well from the International Labour Organization C169—Indigenous and Tribal Peoples Convention. [19]

13.3.1 Indigenous Peoples' Rights over Lands and Natural Resources

The indigenous peoples have spiritual, social, cultural, and economic relationships with their lands. In addition to the above-mentioned concerns, the analysis of the UN reports is pointing toward inadequate protection of the indigenous rights. Namely, the Special Rapporteur on the rights of indigenous peoples raises increased concerns, especially toward investments in the Sápmi region and the states' balancing of the interests in that context. The extraction of the natural resource in the Sápmi region creates an unstable atmosphere of social conflict and that affects Sámi communities, public authorities as well as the involved companies. According to the Special Rapporteur, the limitation of Sámi property rights can only be justified upon a valid public purpose, and that is not a mere commercial interest or revenue-raising objective. Although established as an obligation to consult, the Rapporteur is notifying insufficient consultation of the Sámi Parliaments by the respective governments. Their ability to participate in and genuinely influence decision-making in matters that affect the Sámi people needs to be strengthened to overcome concerns about the limited decision-making power of Sámi institutions. [20] Notwithstanding the importance of their creation and functions, the Sámi Parliaments can be seen as an example of advanced—but limited—political participation. [21]

---

[17] Hannum (1990).

[18] UN Declaration on the Rights of Indigenous Peoples (2007).

[19] International Labour Organization Convention 169 (1989).

[20] See more in the Report of the Special Rapporteur Victoria Tauli-Corpuz on the human rights situation of the Sámi people in the Sápmi region of Norway, Sweden, and Finland within the Human Rights Council issued in 2016, as a follow-up to the Special Rapporteur Jeames Anaya's visit in 2010.

[21] Rapport (2016), Tomaselli and Granholm (2009) and Shikova (2020).

13.4 Cultural Rights and Language Rights

Except for the introduction of a system of power sharing, there are a variety of measures and policies on the enforcement of certain rights that are at the state's disposal. The state can use them in its attempts to integrate groups into a wider society and maintain harmony. These are related to cultural, language, and educational rights. Some ethnic groups and religious minorities seek public funding for their cultural practices. This includes state funding of ethnic associations, media, and festivals. These group-specific measures are intended to assist ethnic groups and religious minorities in expressing their cultural authenticity and dignity. In that respect, cultural rights represent a positive step toward eradicating discrimination and prejudice, especially against larger minorities. Just like autonomy, the scope of measures and related rights are not to be considered temporary since they protect cultural differences, and that is something that should not be eliminated. [22] In the same line, language rights are a kind of cultural defense of minorities against assimilation, which the majority generally exercises through state institutions. The subject of protection is linguistic and cultural identity, and the goal is to achieve the maximum level of individual autonomy and self-esteem. [23] Whether a culture survives or not depends on whether its language is the language of the government—that is, the language of public education, the judiciary, the legislature, healthcare, and so on. When the government decides on the language of public education, it decides on what is the most important form of support for social culture. Therefore, the government cannot avoid the question of which social cultures will be supported by the state. [24] The state uses language to educate, enact laws, make court decisions, organize elections, and provide social services. A common language is a prerequisite for the functioning of the economy, for transactions, and also for everyday communication. [25] It is generally understood that the state has a limited capacity to accommodate ethnolinguistic groups, but there is no general view about how many or which groups should be accommodated.

Linguistic rights are of particular importance to groups as they are a vehicle through which a culture is transmitted. The recognition (or nonrecognition) of a language as "official" or "national" is of great importance to the group. Although there is no obligation for the state to recognize a language as official, it usually does so in order to avoid violent conflicts. [26] Even when the free use of the minority language is permitted, the obligation (if any in international law) of the state to support a particular language by establishing educational or other methods is still unclear. Therefore, it can be said that language rights are not explicitly protected under international human rights law; however, the two conventions that form the basis of the

[22] Kymlicka (1996).

[23] Rubio-Marin (2003).

[24] Kymlicka (1996).

[25] Rubio-Marin (2003).

[26] Hannum (1990).

international human rights corpus establish restrictions on language rights, i.e., they prohibit discrimination on the basis of language. These are the Covenant on Economic and Social Rights, in Article 2 (2), [27] and the Covenant on Civil, Political and Cultural Rights, in Article 2 (1) (rights of children to compulsory protection) and Articles 26 and 27. [28]

Language is the most distinctive feature of culture and acts as a "glue" that holds a culture together, and designating a language as "official" or "national" means recognizing that those who speak that language have an essential role as cofounders or important partners of the state. [29] A typical request of minorities is the requirement to use their language in public, in the media, in education, and during communication with public authorities and the courts. The issue of toponyms and street names and municipalities in minority languages is of great emotional value to members of minorities. There are a variety of ways in addressing linguistic diversity. However, in general, several options are used the most by multilingual societies. One is to designate one language as an official language and hope that the minority language will slowly fade away from political use. The second option is to divide the country into linguistic areas in which there will be one official language and the national government to be bilingual or trilingual. [30] The third option is for the government to apply the personal principle of bilingualism, i.e., both languages, the majority and the minority, to be official in the country so that citizens can communicate in both of them. For political leaders seeking to build a sense of belonging to a particular nation, the choice between these three policies is very difficult since any choice will upset some citizens, and linguistic rivalries are likely to continue to cause political tensions. [31]

It is a fact that linguistic diversity is a difficulty and a problem for policymakers, and this problem is especially increasing with the influx of immigration in developed countries and the need for the country to deal with numerous language groups. For some authors, granting language rights to all the groups is an unsustainable solution since the official language, apart from being a mark of someone's identity,

---

[27] UNGA Res. 2200 A (XXI) ICESCR, 1966.

[28] UNGA Res. 2200 A (XXI) ICCPR, 1966.

[29] Self-determination as a concept developed in nineteenth- and early twentieth-century Europe was primarily based on linguistic groups, rather than on religion, politics, or economics, Hannum (1990).

[30] For example, the United States has one official language, but also a *norm – and – accommodation policy*. So the government and government institutions operate in one official language, and for other languages, there is a rule of adaptation, in terms of their use in the courts (translation), education (as a second language), and the like. Unlike in the United States, in Canada, there are two languages on the same level, and all communication takes place through them. In the EU, however, there are several official languages. But in that sense, the language of minorities (those whose language is not official) is often completely ignored, and their culture is not protected. The minorities enjoy accommodation at the expense of other official languages and probably can never reach the desired formality; see more in Patten (2003).

[31] Birch (1989).

primarily is a means of communication. [32] Many theorists distinguish between indigenous and ethnocultural minorities, but they also mention immigrant groups as a basis for determining which rights should be granted to which group, although there is a general notion that the nature, or the origin, of the group should not be a determining factor for the recognition of certain language rights. [33]

However, it is of particular importance to have a *lingua franca*, i.e., an official language, primarily for the efficient functioning of the administration. In general, the demand for linguistic rights for (members of) minorities should be accompanied by the search for a balance between national unity, on the one hand, and the adjustment of ethnic diversity, on the other. Factors such as the territorial concentration of linguistic groups, the state's financial resources, and religious, sociological, and cultural characteristics should also be taken into account, without giving any preference to any of them. [34] When creating state policies related to language rights, some of the deceives factors are the group's size and its territorial concentration. If the group is territorially concentrated then its number is less important, but not insignificant. If the group is larger and more concentrated, then enabling language rights is more justified. The more criteria are met, the more justified is the claim. The numbers are important because they refer to the public resources that the state possesses, i.e., state institutions that operate in many languages are expensive and often dysfunctional. [35] In that respect, most theoreticians consider that knowledge and active speaking of the official language of the country is a necessity. The balance between the legitimate need of the state to provide some degree of linguistic uniformity and the demand of minorities for the practical and/or symbolic recognition of their language may be difficult to weigh, but such efforts, as well as the degree of goodwill in that direction, are essential.

Although there is disagreement over whether the right of minorities to use their language implies a positive obligation on the part of the state, it is certain that the use of language should not be banned. Even when the minority language is not widely spoken in the country, gaining special constitutional recognition by establishing statutory or administrative provisions for the use of that minority language, in certain circumstances, may be essential for the smooth functioning of the system. [36]

[32] Patten (2003).

[33] Rubio-Marin (2003).

[34] Henrard (2000).

[35] Rubio-Marin (2003).

[36] Hannum (1990).

13.5 Educational Rights

Education, along with language, is a major driving force for the transmission of culture and is one of the most common demands of minorities. And this right, as a specific right of minorities, is not directly guaranteed by the Covenant on Civil, Political and Cultural Rights, and in essence, modern instruments of international human rights law do speak about the right to education as a state obligation to provide education on a general basis, although there are references that the parents have the right to the education of their children in accordance with their religious or moral values. [37] The Covenant on Economic and Social Rights, on the other hand, refers to the freedom of individuals and certain bodies to establish and manage educational institutions that will meet the minimum standards set by the state, but there is no affirmative state obligation to promote or support such nonstate institutions. [38]

However, educational rights are hot topics, and disagreements between the minority group and the majority over education can arise because of access to it, educational content, or a combination of both. At the primary education level, the provision of instructions on minority languages may be a major concern for many minority communities, alongside the need to control the curriculum and the selection of staff and teachers. The state naturally takes the education system as the primary mean of transmitting and establishing its values, so it is almost unlikely that it will agree to allow or guarantee exclusive control over education by any nonstate entity. Education policies can be extremely divisive even in the majority, and minorities are not immune to similar disagreements over curriculum content. [39]

13.5.1 Access to Higher Education

Although access to higher education is often linked to the issue of language and nondiscrimination, it is also often seen as a reflection of the minority's demand for wider opportunities and participation in the dominant society, rather than as an issue in itself. Conflicts are more likely to be caused by affirmative action policies that favor a subordinate group than by discrimination. Especially in developing countries, access to education is access to the government and employment in public service and social services in general; hence, it is a fundamental issue that determines the economic, social, and political influence of members of a minority group. This is often when the government is the main employer, and privileged employment or other economic policies are administered through government intervention.

[37] Covenant on Civil and Political Rights art 18(4); Covenant on Economic, Social and Cultural Rights, Article 13 (3) and (4); Protocol No. 1 to the European Convention on Human Rights, Article 2; and the American Convention on Human Rights, Article 12 (4).

[38] Hannum (1990).

[39] Sutherland (1979).

As a result, questions often arise about nondiscrimination versus privileged policies, and this can be reflected indirectly through language proficiency requirements or appropriate education that minority group members may be unable to accomplish or reach. [40]

13.6 North Macedonia, Ohrid Framework Agreement, an Example of an Internal Self-Determination Instrument

The Republic of North Macedonia became an independent state after the collapse of SFRY in 1991. After the breakdown of the Yugoslav federation, North Macedonia as well as the other former SFRY republics were preoccupied with issues of independence and international recognition and a burning desire to join the European Union (EU). Besides "the name issue" with Greece, another barrier to North Macedonia's EU accession was the internal conflict between the majority population and ethnonational minorities. The Macedonian society is multiethnic, multinational, plural, and multicultural. It is composed of ethnic Macedonians, who are a majority in the country and to whom the term people in the Constitution (1991) refers and the citizens who live within the state borders and who are comprised of the Albanian people, the Turkish people, the Vlahos people, the Serbian people, the Roma people, the Bosnjak people, and others.[41] According to the latest census (2021), the minorities represent around 30% of the population. [42] However, the legal frame uses not the term "minorities" but "communities," as well as "citizens part of other people" living in North Macedonia. Communities (or members of communities) are terms reserved for the ethnic Albanians, Turks, Roma, Serbs, Vlachs, and Bosnians.

To resolve the interethnic tensions and be more eligible for accession, with the encouragement and support of the EU and other international assistance, a series of constitutional amendments based on the introduction of power-sharing agreements with ethnonational minorities were created following the example of the Good Friday Agreement [43] and finally resulted in the Ohrid Framework Agreement (OFA). The OFA was signed on August 13, 2001, after the short ethnic conflict between the two major groups (Macedonians and Albanians), in which the minority Albanians were seeking greater rights and political representation. The OFA relies on the concept of multiculturalism and tends to build a multicultural society as a model in a young democratic society to accommodate differences between ethnic groups living

---

[40] Hannum (1990).

[41] Constitution (1991), Preamble, Amendment IV (2001).

[42] Census on population, 2021.

[43] The Good Friday Agreement was signed on Good Friday 10th April 1998. It is a peace agreement between the British and Irish governments and the conflicting organizations in Northern Ireland.

within the state. The postulates of multiculturalism, used by states to meet the needs of groups and protect their rights, seemed to be the most appropriate. The same as with the multiculturalism notion, it seemed that the state appears to be neutral to different national groups, but it can (and often did) privilege the majority group in different ways. An illustrative example can be the drawing of internal (municipal) boundaries, the establishment and use of an official language, the transfer of power at the local level, etc., which significantly reduced the political power and cultural representation of the minority group at the expense of the majority. [44] Therefore, toward acknowledged principles, it was assumed that the rights of the minority group can be best protected by establishing a system that allows the integration of the minority group into society without forced assimilation. According to theory, except for the granted formal equality, the group should have true equality, encompassing a different treatment for different people under different conditions. [45] For the system to be functional, those ideas should be accompanied by a variety of measures that provide a socially acceptable way to nurture the group's cultural differences. Consequently, a series of government policies need to be undertaken to change people's attitudes and promote loyalty to the state by developing national institutions and finding practices for political socialization. [46] In this frame, the variety of models for the division of power range from consensual models, which encourage collaborative decision-making and the accommodation of ethnic group leaders to a political center, to models that stimulate integration by dividing lines and that encourage group adjustment by promoting common interests, [47] decentralization, major government coalitions, consensus decisions, mutual vetoes, etc. [48] All these approaches, though conceptually different, can complement each other in many different ways. To achieve meaningful results, the following principles, which are in the core of ideas for building a multicultural society, need to be followed: (1) a dialogue, as a democratic way of overcoming problems; (2) involvement, the integration of communities in the social life of the country to overcome the inferior position of the group that is the most common source of dissatisfaction; (3) the acceptance of the other, mutual tolerance between the groups that exist in the political/social space, and respect for differences; (4) the expression of diversity—activities that enable the group to emphasize their diversity in a socially acceptable way; (5) the equal distribution of social resources, as a condition for overcoming the assumed inequality; and (6) a common identity, in the direction of the construction and promotion of a firm civic identity that would extend through the ethnic lines of division. [49] It is important to mention that in these encounters, the integration of the

[44] Kymlicka (1996).

[45] Henrard (2000).

[46] Birch (1989).

[47] Sisk (1966).

[48] Lijphart (1980, 1999).

[49] Shikova (2011).

minority community is multifaceted and includes political, social, and economic integration.

Considerably, signed under EU and international community patronage, the OFA became a pillar of interethnic relations in North Macedonia. In essence, the OFA envisages greater rights for minority participation, access to public administration for minority groups, the use of minority languages for official purposes, redistribution of public resources and political power, as well as the forming of institutions that will enforce and oversee its implementation. But the most important is that OFA helped to cease violent way of resolving problems and to establish a framework in which different political, ethnic and, ultimately, civic visions for the development of a democratic society, will be articulated, in a unitary state—fully integrated into the Euro-Atlantic community. The OFA promotes the peaceful and harmonious development of civil society and provides basic guidelines for taking measures that should contribute to increasing respect among ethnic groups living in North Macedonia. Thus, it is a guarantor of the multiethnic character of Macedonian society, expressed in the overall public life. Instead of the unacceptable violent way of solving problems, the OFA promotes exclusively peaceful political solutions and encourages a participatory process. Consequently, decentralization and an appropriate funding system are particularly set as possible tools for the proper distribution of competencies, especially in the areas of local economic development, culture, education, social and health care, and public services. [50]

In order to ensure the equal treatment of all before the law, there must be no discrimination, and to reflect the social reality, the OFA establishes a framework that takes into account the equitable representation of and respect for the principle of nondiscrimination, especially in the composition of public administration, police services, and others spheres of public life and access to public funding. To the minority communities in North Macedonia, the OFA provides an opportunity to directly, through a parliamentary mechanism—based on specific requirements regarding the required majority for decision-making [51] to influence the legal arrangement in respect of the culture, use of the language, minority education, personal documents, use of minority symbols, distribution of local funding, and local elections. The Macedonian language is an official language, together with the language that speaks 20% of the population on the central government as well as on the local government level. [52]

In addition to the Constitution and OFA the minority protection is granted by the systematic laws that are regulating the aspects important for the minorities (self-government, education, public administration, etc.), as well as with the by-laws. In addition to the abovementioned legal documents, there are laws regulating the position of the other no—the majority ethnic groups including the Law on local

---

[50] Ohrid Framework Agreement (2001).

[51] Adoption of a particular law requires a majority of parliamentary votes, among which there must be a majority of votes of members of the non-majority community in North Macedonia, a community to whom that specific law applies or concerns, Ohrid Framework Agreement (2001).

[52] Ohrid Framework Agreement (2001), points 6.5 and 6.6.

self-government; [53] Law for use of the languages [54] and other sub-legal acts. On the national level, there is a Ministry of Political System and Relations with the Communities, which advances and monitors all the aspects related to the rights of the communities; a Committee for the Relations with Communities, wherein all the communities are represented and whose aim is to advance the rights of the communities and manage the distribution of public funds; [55] as well as an Agency for the realization of the rights of communities that are less than 20%. [56] Within the national legal frame, the communities can establish cultural, educational, and other institutions to express and nurture their identity and use their symbols. [57] All the communities, regardless their numerical strength, have the right to education on their mother tongue. However, apart from primary and secondary education, the high education on minority languages is financed by the state for the communities that represent more than 20% of the population. [58] As for the representation and political participation of the communities, in North Macedonia in general they are organized on a level of political parties that are participating in central and local levels of government.

According to the OFA, the development of a local government is essential to encourage citizen participation in democratic life and to promote respect for identity. [59] The competencies of local self-governments primarily refer to areas of public service, urban and rural planning, environmental protection, local economic development, culture, local finance, education, social protection, and healthcare. [60] At the same time, the Law on Financing of Local Self-Government [61] should grant an adequate funding system for the local authorities. On the national level, the communities have the right to veto in respect of the decisions tackling minority issues (in the law-stated areas), and in practice, the system functions as a consociational model without an established legal ground. [62] Being a member of a community is an individual choice; minority lists do not exist. The granted rights are exercised upon the set thresholds and obtained populations proportions under the population Census in 2001 (the second one after the independence in 1991), and confirmed on a last population Census in 2021.

---

[53] Law on local self-government (2009).

[54] Law for use of the languages, Official gazette 7/2019 available at https://dejure.mk/zakon/zakon-za-upotreba-na-jazicite-1

[55] Constitution (1991), Amendment XII; Law for the Committee for the relations between communities, Official gazette 150/2007.

[56] Law for the rights of the community that are less than 20% from the population of the Republic of North Macedonia, Official gazette 18/2020.

[57] Constitution (1991), Amendment VIII.

[58] Ohrid Framework Agreement (2001), point 6.2.

[59] Ohrid Framework Agreement (2001), point 3.1.

[60] Law on Local Self Government (2009), article 22.

[61] Law on financing of local self-government units, official gazette 61/2004, 96/04, 67/07, 156/09, 47/11, and 192/2015.

[62] Shikova (2018).

Hence, the Macedonian model for minority protection is a territorial model for minority protection (with elements of NTA at the national level) and, in practice, is a consociational system of power sharing, which can theoretically provide bigger and better protection and representation of the communities.

But how can those measures prove to be effective in practice? There is no doubt that the OFA contributed to the improvement of the position of minorities, protecting their separate identity and allowing them internal self-determination within the unitary state. However, OFA's implementation still faces many challenges. Hence, more than 20 years after its signing, the Framework Agreement is still an open subject—either its justification or its potential for maintaining a stable multiethnic society is being questioned. But one thing is certain—the Framework Agreement is a step toward a more inclusive society because it is based on a multiethnic tradition and, above all, on good interpersonal relations. It proves that binary solutions between sovereignty and the absence thereof are possible, but for their functionality, there is a need for society's devotion, personal responsibility, a vision for general prosperity, and, above all, respect for the rule of law. Consequently, there are many challenges related to the implementation of this solution. The OFA is far from being a perfect instrument, but still, and with all the existing misuses of its noble intentions, it cannot be denied that it resists the test of time, providing peace and coexistence for Macedonian society.

References

African Charter on Human and Peoples' Rights (1979)

American Convention on Human Rights, 1969

Birch HA (1989) Nationalism and national integration. Unwin Hyman Ltd.

Commission On Human Rights Res. 1983/13, UN Doc. E/1983/13, E/CN. 4/1983/60 (1983). https://uvallsc.s3.amazonaws.com/travaux/s3fs-public/E-1983-13__E-CN_4-1983-60_0.pdf?null. Accessed 4 Oct 2022

Constitution of the Republic of North Macedonia (1991) with Amendments up to 2019. https://www.sobranie.mk/the-constitution-of-the-republic-of-macedonia-ns_article-constitution-of-the-republic-of-north-macedonia.nspx. Accessed 18 Jan 2023

Cristescu A (1981) The right to self-determination, historical and current development on the basis of United Nations instruments. UN

Fox GH (2000) The right to political participation in international law. In: Fox GH, Roth BR (eds) Democratic governance and international law. Cambridge University Press, pp 48–91

Hannum H (1990) Autonomy, sovereignty, and self-determination, the accommodation of conflict rights. University of Pennsylvania Press

Henrard K (2000) Devising an adequate system of minority protection. Kluwer Law International, Hague

International Labour Organization C169 - Indigenous and Tribal Peoples Convention (1989). https://www.ilo.org/dyn/normlex/en/f?p=NORMLEXPUB:55:0::NO::P55_TYPE,P55_LANG,P55_DOCUMENT,P55_NODE:REV,en,C169,/Document. Accessed 23 Oct 2022

Kymlicka W (1996) Multicultural citizenship: a liberal theory of minority rights. Clarendon Press

Law for the Committee for the relations between communities, Official gazette 150/2007

Law for the rights of the community that are less than 20% from the population of the Republic of North Macedonia, Official gazette 18/2020

Law for use of the languages, Official gazette 7/2019

Law on financing of local self-government unties, official gazette 61/2004, 96/04, 67/07, 156/09, 47/11 and 192/2015

Law on local self-government, Official gazette 5/2009

Lijphart A (1980) Democracy in plural societies: a comparative exploration. Yale University Press

Lijphart A (1999) Patterns of democracy, government forms and performance in thirty-six countries. Yale University Press

Lund Recommendations on the Effective Participation of National Minorities in Public Life. Organization for Security and Co-operation in Europe (1999)

Moris H (1998) Self-determination: an affirmative right or mere rhetoric? J Comp Int Law 4(1):201–219

Ohrid Framework Agreement (2001). https://www.osce.org/skopje/100622. Accessed 4 Oct 2022

Patten A (2003) Can the immigrant/national minority dichotomy be defended? Comment on Ruth Rubio-Marin. In: Macedo S, Buchanan A (eds) Secession and self-determination. New York University Press, pp 304–413

Popular Participation as a strategy for promoting community level and national development, UN sales No. E 81.IV.2 (1981). https://digitallibrary.un.org/record/35985?ln=en. Accessed 4 Oct 2022

Protocol 1 to the European Convention for the Protection of Human Rights and Fundamental Freedoms, 1952. https://www.refworld.org/docid/3ae6b38317.html. Accessed 4 Oct 2022

Report of the Special Rapporteur on the rights of indigenous peoples on the human rights situation of the Sámi people in the Sápmi region of Norway, Sweden and Finland, UN A/HRC/33/42/Add.3, 2016. https://digitallibrary.un.org/record/847081. Accessed 4 Oct 2022

Rubio-Marin R (2003) Exploring the boundaries of language rights: insiders, newcomers and natives. In: Macedo S, Buchanan A (eds) Secession and self-determination. New York University Press, pp 236–304

Shikova N (2011) Multiculturalism reflected in the programs of the political parties in Macedonia, their programs and leadership. In: Klekovski S (ed) Ohrid Framework Agreement, case studies. Macedonian Institute for International Cooperation, pp 7–18

Shikova N (2018) Multi-ethnic coalition governments as precondition for maintenance of the political stability, the example of the Republic of Macedonia. J Soc Hum Sci 1(1):50–60

Shikova N (2020) The possibilities and limits of non-territorial autonomy in securing indigenous self-determination. Philos Soc 31(3):277–444

Sisk TD (1966) Power sharing and international mediation in ethnic conflicts. United States Institute of Peace

State Statistical Office, Census of Population, Households and Dwellings in the Republic of North Macedonia, 2021 - first dataset. https://www.stat.gov.mk/PrikaziSoopstenie_en.aspx?rbrtxt=146. Accessed 4 Oct 2022

Sutherland MB (1979) Comparative perspective on the education of cultural minorities. In: Alcock AE, Taylor BK, Welton JM (eds) The future of cultural minorities. Red Globe Press, London, pp 44–62

Tomaselli A, Granholm P (2009) The frustrations of the right to political participation of minorities: practical limitations in the case of the Nordic Sámi and the Roma. Eur Yearb Minority Issues 8:149–185

UN RES. UN Declaration on the rights of indigenous peoples (2007). https://www.un.org/development/desa/indigenouspeoples/wp-content/uploads/sites/19/2018/11/UNDRIP_E_web.pdf. Accessed 21 Sept 2022

UNGA Res. 2200 A (XXI) The International Covenant on Civil and Political Rights (1966)

UNGA Res. 2200 A (XXI) The International Covenant on Economic, Social and Cultural Rights (1966)

United Nations, Popular participation in Decision Making for Development, UN Sales No. E 75. IV.10 (1975)

Part IV
Conclusions

Chapter 14
Self-Determination Revisited

14.1 Afterword

The idea of self-determination—as a need to govern according to the will of the governed—is part of the most important upheavals in human history. Upgraded and advanced, the idea takes on a recognizable form after World War II and in Wilson's 14 points and is fully formed in the UN system, where the right to self-determination is recognized and guaranteed to all peoples. The right to self-determination has a complex structure and is realized in several ways, whereas the acquisition of independent statehood is only one of them. Peoples are legitimate holders of this right, and minorities can use its benefits in the form of internal self-determination. Although debates over the legal nature of the principle of self-determination are still relevant—from practice to jurisprudence to theory—it can be concluded that the right to self-determination is a collective human right set out in the most important human rights documents. However, the principle of territorial integrity is still superior to the right to self-determination. [1]

The realization of the right to self-determination does not violate the principle of territorial integrity in a colonial context (which is almost overcome) and in the case of foreign occupation or domination over people who have the right to self-determination. The possibility for the realization of external self-determination outside these circumstances implicitly arises from Resolution 2625, which opens the doors for the so-called legitimate secession if certain conditions are met, and the state behaves contrary to the principle of equal rights and self-determination of peoples. [2]

The semantic meaning of the term "secession" is clear, but there is no generally accepted definition of the corresponding political phenomenon. Simplified,

---

[1] See Sects. 1.1 and 1.5.

[2] See Sect. 7.3.

N. Shikova, *Self-Determination and Secession*,
https://doi.org/10.1007/978-3-031-34322-3_14

secession is the separation of a territorial part of an existing state to create a new, independent state. In any case, secession means the cessation of continuity. Explanatory, economic, normative, moral, and other theories try to shed light on the phenomenon from its own angle and reach its essence. The theory of "secession as a last resort" sets the conditions for the legitimacy of secession claims, which potentially can be included in the corpus of international law. In general, the reasons that can trigger the occurrence of secessionist movements are numerous: repression, discrimination, subordination to a certain group and continuous denial of its political demands, territorial claims based on historical continuity with a certain territory, primordialism, the need for protection of a special culture and special identity, etc.[3] In addition to these primary factors for secessionism, various catalysts play a role that can arise from the internal social mile of the country, from the neighborhood, as well as from global trends. Most secession movements are not simple sessions but progressive secessions that last a long time and manifest in separate ways. Violence is not crucial in achieving secessionist goals, but it can draw the world's attention to secessionist events. Although each case has a separate historical narrative, still, secessionist movements have common elements and developmental dynamics. Some theoreticians consider that if certain indicators are followed, a secessionist movement can even be predicted. Secessionists and their supporters are calculating whether to continue or break the continuity with the existing state. The process also frames the attraction of third parties to the secession movement, as well as gaining the sympathy of the international community. The state on whose territory the secession movement originated can use force against it, but although it is the most common and first used counteraction, it is neither the best nor the most desirable way to resolve the secession crisis. [4]

There are several conflicting opinions as to whether there should be a "right to secession" at all and, if so, where to look for its basis. In the modern legal doctrine, there is a large number of lawyers who believe that although there is no explicit right to secession, it is still necessary to discuss and argue about it, and if such a right is articulated in the future, then it should not be an absolute right but a right subject to numerous restrictions, and its implementation should be conditioned upon the fulfillment of criteria and standards of legitimacy. [5] For some authors, requests for secession should be considered institutionally, and secession should be enshrined in the constitution of a democratic state that advocates respect for liberal values, but the place of secession in international law is still unclear, i.e., the dilemma is whether secession should be accepted as a model for self-determination in its purest form. States strongly oppose such tendencies in defense of unity and integrity. In contrast, the international community tacitly accepts secession and gradually integrates it into the doctrine of international law. For the international community, secession is acceptable in the following two cases:

---

[3] See Sect. 5.2.

[4] See Sect. 6.2.2.

[5] See Chap. 7.

- If the people freely decide about the decision to secede, which means the decision should be brought by entire population of the country, not just by the inhabitants of the region that wants to secede
- When national borders are redrawn after an armed conflict as part of a reached peace agreement. [6]

Except in the two cases described above, secession may be doctrinairely acceptable and conditionally legitimate if the following circumstances—all of them or most of them—exist and are related to the group attempting to secede:

1. The actions of the state endanger the physical survival of the members of the group (*secession as a last resort*).
2. There is a model for the systematic discrimination or exploitation of the group (*secession as a last resort*).
3. If the government of the state is unrepresentative, the group is denied internal self-determination and is excluded from the decision-making process, systematically and ultimately.
4. Apart from political marginalization, there is also economic subordination and unequal distribution of power and economic resources, systematic and on a long-term.
5. The central government rejects compromise solutions to resolve conflicts, and there are no fewer radical measures than secession.
6. It is a matter of previously sovereign territory unjustly taken away by the state (*right to territory*).

In any case, a distinction should be made between arguments in favor of unilateral secession and arguments in favor of secession; the fulfillment of the six conditions (circumstances) can provide a basis for legitimizing unilateral secession, but apart from that, some circumstances provide a basis for secession without the existence of the above conditions, although only by themselves, they cannot legitimize or justify the act of secession. They are the following:

1. There is a different (self-defined) community in the country with a solid ethnological basis (language, history), compactly inhabited in a region that openly supports separatism, original "self," and the fervent desire for self-government (*parochialistic theory*)
2. The group has territorial claims and the right to territory based on historical continuity, and the unit that wants to secede was a self-determined unit with self-government (*historical-territorial argument*).
3. There is no irreparable damage, the disturbing factor is low, secession will not upset the balance of power in the affected area, secession will not have much impact on the environment, nor will it harm the vital interests of the state (*normative* and *democratic theories of secession*). [7]

---

[6] See Sect. 9.2.

[7] See Sect. 6.5.

For secession to be considered successful, it is not enough to just change the legal and political institutions of the secessionist entity, but it is also necessary to change its political status—or to be internationally recognized. Apart from the traditional criteria for the recognition of states, the recognition of a secessionist entity depends on the political will of states and the international community, and it can be manifested in a variety of ways—from establishing diplomatic relations with the secessionist entity to formal recognition or admission to membership in international organizations. The recognition of a secessionist entity also depends on whether it is a self-defined unit, where the principle of effectiveness is not playing a crucial role. From this we conclude that there is an international tendency to relativize the traditional criteria for statehood; an attempt in international practice to insert new, additional criteria for recognition; and also a return to the declarative theory of recognition of states. [8]

By realizing self-determination through its internal aspect (expressed through representative rights, the rights of minorities, cultural and political autonomy, etc.), the demands for secession can be avoided or mitigated, as well as the apparent consequences of potential external self-determination. There is still no established right to internal self-determination in international law, which would at least include the right to a democratic, representative government, but the customary law that addresses this issue is *in statu nascendi*. Unlike external self-determination, which is a one-time right of self-determination and ceases to exist with its realization, internal self-determination tends to envisage the right to self-determination as a "developing right," a right that happens, lasts, and is ongoing. There is an effort in international documents in this direction to expand the scope of the right to self-determination, and this is in the process of being confirmed by state practice. [9] There are many tools and forms for the realization of internal self-determination for specific sociocultural groups. Within a democratic system of government, the peculiarities of multicultural societies can be accommodated through their recognition and the respect and protection of the special identity of sociocultural groups, and especially of national minorities, by guaranteeing group-specific rights. Power-sharing systems are a form of a wide range of political options for dealing with ethnic conflicts, and the purpose of those options is to enable the most optimal political participation of different groups, which ultimately depends on the goodwill of groups and their political authorities. These options have their advantages and disadvantages, which need to be carefully weighed to achieve the desired goals. Autonomy, in addition, enables the group to protect its individual interests in relation to a much more powerful society and also fosters nationalist and separatist aspirations, but in some circumstances, it is pragmatic to guarantee autonomy to avoid deeper conflicts. Autonomy requires a territorial basis, i.e., the concentration of the group, as well as the creation of special autonomous institutions, and in that direction are decentralization and subsidiarity. Consociational democracy, maximizes the participation of various factors in the power sharing, but more at the central level, by encouraging

[8] See Sects. 8.2 and 8.4.

[9] See Sects. 10.2 and 10.3.

the cooperation of elites from different cultural segments. Although it provides a fluid form of democracy and encourages the cooperation and participation of the elites of sociocultural groups, due to the need to constantly secure broad consensus on government policies, consociational democracy is a very financially demanding as well as time-consuming model. [10] Effective participation enables the full realization of the rights and freedoms of members of different social groups. In that direction is the commitment of the international community to hold fair and free elections and to establish representative governments. Increased political representation of sociocultural groups can be ensured through special representation rights. The incentive to employ members of minority groups in public service helps to overcome ethnic imbalance in this social sphere, and the state to become an independent arbiter in the implementation of the fundamental governmental policies. The exclusion of minority groups from relevant social activities can be overcome by giving them greater control over natural resources. In addition to representative rights, multiethnic rights are appropriate for addressing the specificities of larger minorities. In addition to common citizens' rights, the cultural specifics of the group can be protected through special legal or constitutional measures. In this regard, among the more specific are language rights and the rights of education for minority groups because they are instruments for dissemination of the groups' culture, as well as access to higher education for the minority group, which, although often related to language or nondiscrimination, is a chance for greater participation in the dominant society. [11] If there is a situation of competing languages and educational policies in society, then the state, in addition to recognizing and protecting the differences, must also provide unification, which is necessary to maintain social harmony. Cultural identities can be protected, promoted, and connected, and the participation of all can be provided through regionalism, which, in order to achieve this diversity, allows connecting communities based on geographical proximity, social and cultural affinities, or traditional ethnic relations. Hence, we see a very wide and flexible range of opportunities and measures to address, protect, and promote diversity and, thus, overcome identity conflicts and ensure a balance of social power. The proposed political arrangements, although imperfect, help avoid secession options, thus ensuring the stability, harmony, and prosperity of society. [12]

Although in theory models for internal self-determination are dominant as effective instruments for problem solving, the application of certain internal self-determination tools—on some levels—can create an opposite effect and sharpen the quests for secession. Often, it is perhaps because there is no natural point where the requirements for the protection and promotion of separate nationality would stop. Moreover, there is a general thought that the states that accept rights coming from models of internal self-determination seem to be inherently unstable. Perhaps that is because the national identity is the most powerful one from all the types of collective identities that persons have. Consequently, it is obvious that globalization did

[10] See Chap. 12.

[11] See Chap. 13.

[12] See Sects. 11.1 and 11.3.

not completely ruin the concept of nationality but just stopped its monopolistic position, which it held in the first half of the twentieth century.

Obviously, no options are completely satisfactory. In certain circumstances, demands for secession can be avoided by a timely establishment of a regime for the protection of group rights (such as the case of North Macedonia), [13] but on the other side, in certain circumstances, liberal policies are the ones that enable them (the case of Scotland, for example). [14] Therefore, internal self-determination effectively accommodates demands for secession, but not everywhere and not always is it the "magic cure." Practice shows that exceptional cases are to be considered where the current conditions on the ground make the application of specific tools impractical for internal self-determination (like the power-sharing system in Bosnia and Herzegovina, which sometimes blocks institutional functioning). In some cases, due to various circumstances, internal self-determination fails to achieve the desired goal (such as in the cases of Basque Country and Catalonia), while in other cases, the requirements for the separation of groups are so strong that internal self-determination is failing in its efforts to buffer (like in the Kosovo enclaves). However, there are some positive examples, such as Canada, Switzerland, Northern Ireland., etc., and there is a need to learn from them. Generally, for this aspect of self-determination to be fully realized and with success, it is important for national and international institutions to make a commitment for its implementation and to provide conditions for its realization.

One of the ways forward can be regionalism. At the community level, regionalism reflects the intention to protect a degree of self-government, which exists independently of external national borders. If subsidiarity implies government at the lowest possible level, then regionalization means connecting communities to individuals, with relations based on geographical proximity and also on social and cultural affinities or on traditional ethnic relations. The market and infrastructure, as well as the need for internal and external security, can be active actors. Regionalization encourages decentralization and democratization by strengthening accountability and encouraging bottom-up autonomy, thus contributing to inspiring regions to develop their own appropriate characteristics that are competitive with other regions. The essence of regionalism lies in the intention to overcome solid state borders, and it encourages the desire to participate in the global market, directly but not necessarily, through the central authority, since cultural and political borders do not necessarily overlap. [15]

The interplay of nationalism and fundamentalism, leadership interests and powerful global media, and also the influence of markets and finance on culture and language further complicates dilemmas traditionally associated with self-determination, namely, sovereignty, community interests, secession, and territorial boundaries. All this, in turn, has made the future development of the concept of

[13] See Sect. 13.6.

[14] See Sect. 2.3.1.

[15] See Sect. 11.3.

self-determination even more unpredictable. Attempts to formulate general principles of international law to resolve deep social conflicts through autonomy, power sharing, or linguistic rights may be unrealistic, but the option of legally affirming minimum standards for internal self-determination as a basis for dialogue is real, can accommodate diversity, and can serve as a clear counterargument to secessionist demands.